62

sts; rep from * to last 2 sts, k 2.
These four rows form patt.

Steep diagonal rib (fig. 63)

Cast on multiples of 6 sts.
1st row: * P 3, k 3; rep from * to end.
2nd row and every alt row: K all k sts and p all p sts.
3rd row: P 2, * k 3, p 3; rep from * to last 4 sts, k 3, p 1.
5th row: P1, * k 3, p 3; rep from * to last 5 sts, k 3, p 2.
7th row: * K 3, p 3; rep from * to end.
9th row: K 2, * p 3, k 3; rep from * to last 4 sts, p 3, k 1.
11th row: K 1, * p 3, k 3; rep from * to last 5 sts, p 3, k 2.
12th row: K all k sts and p all p sts.
These twelve rows form patt.

Fancy lozenge pattern (fig. 64)

Cast on multiples of 18 sts plus 2.
1st row: [Right side] P 2, * k 4, p 4, k 2, p 2, k 4, p 2; rep from * to end.
2nd row: K 3, * p 4, k 2, p 2, k 2, p 4, k 4; rep from * ending last rep k 3, instead of k 4.
3rd row: K 2, * p 2, k 4, p 4, k 4, p 2, k 2; rep from * to end.
4th row: P 1, * k 4, [p 4, k 2] twice, p 2; rep from * to last st, k 1.
5th row: P 2, * k 2, p 2, k 8, p 2, k 2, p 2; rep from * to end.
6th row: K 1, * p 2, k 4, p 6, k 2, p 2, k 2; rep from * to last st, p 1.
7th row: K 2, * p 2, k 2, p 2, k 4, [p 2, k 2] twice; rep from * to end.

64

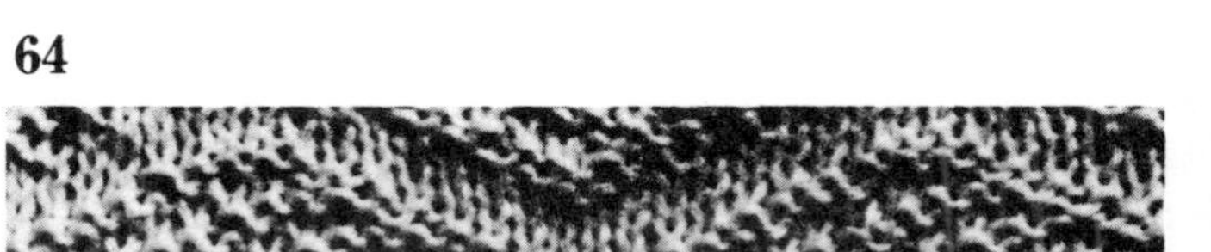

63

8th row: P 1, * k 2, p 2, k 2, p 6, k 4, p 2; rep from * to last st, k 1.
9th row: As 5th row.
10th row: K 1, * p 2, [k 2, p 4] twice, k 4; rep from * to last st, p 1.
11th row: As 3rd row.
12th row: As 2nd row.
13th row: P 2, * k 4, p 2, k 2, p 4, k 4, p 2; rep from * to end.
14th row: P 5, * [k 2, p 2] twice, k 2, p 8; rep from * ending last rep p 5.
15th row: K 4, * [p 2, k 2] twice, p 4, k 6; rep from * ending last rep, k 4.
16th row: P 3, * [k 2, p 2] 3 times, k 2, p 4; rep from * ending last rep, p 3.
17th row: K 4, * p 4, [k 2, p 2] twice, k 6; rep from * ending last rep, k 4.
18th row: As 14th row.
These 18 rows form patt.

Braid stitch (fig. 65)

Cast on multiples of 8 sts plus 4.
1st row: [Wrong side] K 4, * p 4, k 4; rep from * to end.
2nd row: P 4, *[sl 1 with yarn at back of work, k 1, y rn, pass sl-st over k st and y rn st] twice, p 4; rep from * to end.
3rd row: As 1st.
4th row: P 4, * k 1, sl 1 with yarn at back of work, k 1, y rn, pass sl–st over k st and y rn st, k 1, p 4; rep from * to end.
These four rows form patt.

65

Lace stitches

You are now ready for more exciting knitting, but obviously these stitches are more difficult than those in the previous section, so take extra care. You will already have come across most of the abbreviations used, but some of them will be new to you so refer to the abbreviations listed on page 7.

You should try these stitches using No 10 needles and 4-ply yarn as you will find these intricate stitches easier to follow at first using a thicker yarn and larger needles; once you become more competent remember that they are really beautiful when knitted in fine yarn on small needles.

Harebell stitch (fig. 66)

Cast on multiples of 8 sts plus 3.
1st row: Sl 1, k 2 tog, * y fwd, k 1, y fwd, sl 1, k 2 tog psso; rep from * to last 4 sts, y fwd, k 1, y fwd, sl 1, k 1, psso, k 1.
2nd and every alt row: Sl 1, p to last st, k 1.
3rd row: Sl 1, k 2 tog, * y fwd, k 5, y fwd, sl 1, k 2 tog, psso; rep from * to last 8 sts, y fwd, k 5, y fwd, sl 1, k 1, psso, k 1.
5th row: As 3rd.
7th row: As 3rd.
9th row: Sl 1, k 2, * y fwd, sl 1, kl, psso, k 1, k 2 tog, y fwd, k 3; rep from * to end.
10th row: As 2nd.
These 10 rows form patt.

Spider stitch (fig. 67)

Cast on multiples of 6 sts plus 1.
1st row: [Wrong side] P.
2nd row: K 1, * y fwd, sl 1, k 1, psso, k 1, k 2 tog, y fwd, k 1; rep from * to end of row.
3rd row: P.
4th row: As 2nd.
5th row: As 1st.
6th row: As 2nd.
7th row: As 1st.
8th row: K 2, * y fwd, sl 1, k 2 tog, psso, y fwd, k 3; rep from * to end, ending last rep k 2 instead of k 3.
9th row: As 1st.
10th row: K 1, * k 2 tog, y fwd, k 1, y fwd, sl 1, k 1, psso, k 1; rep from * to end.
11th row: As 1st.
12th row: K 2 tog, * y fwd, k 3, y fwd, sl 1, k 2 tog, psso; rep from * to end ending last rep y fwd, k 3, y fwd, sl 1, k 1, psso.
These 12 rows form patt.

66

67

68

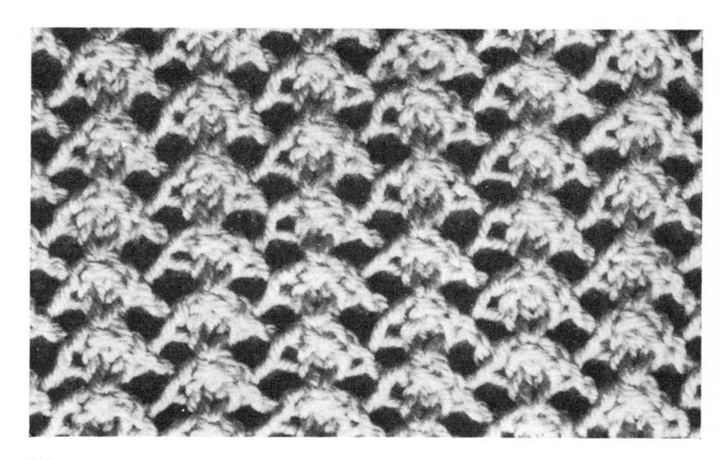

69

Shell pattern (fig. 68)
Cast on multiples of 10 plus 3.
1st row: Sl 1, * k 1, y fwd, k 2 tog tbl, k 5, k 2 tog, y fwd; rep from * to last 2 sts, k 2.
2nd and every alt row: Sl 1, p to last st, k 1.
3rd row: Sl 1, * k 1, y fwd, k 1, k 2 tog tbl, k 3, k 2 tog, k 1, y fwd; rep from * to last 2 sts, k 2.
5th row: Sl 1, * k 1, y fwd, k 2, k 2 tog tbl, k 1, k 2 tog, k 2, y fwd; rep from * to last 2 sts, k 2.
7th row: Sl 1, * k 1, y fwd, k 3, k 3 tog, k 3, y fwd; rep from * to last 2 sts, k 2.
9th row: Sl 1, * k 3, k 2 tog, y fwd, k 1, y fwd, k 2 tog tbl, k 2; rep from * to last 2 sts, k 2.
11th row: Sl 1, * k 2, k 2 tog, [k 1, y fwd] twice, k 1, k 2 tog tbl, k 1; rep from * to last 2 sts, k 2.
13th row: Sl 1, * k 1, k 2 tog, k 2, y fwd, k 1, y fwd, k 2, k 2 tog tbl; rep from * to last 2 sts, k 2.
15th row: Sl 1, k 2 tog, * k 3, y fwd, k 1, y fwd, k 3, k 3 tog; rep from * to last 10 sts, k 3, y fwd, k 1, y fwd, k 3, k 2 tog tbl, k 1.
16th row: As 2nd.
These 16 rows form patt.

Simple lace pattern (fig. 69)
Cast on multiples of 6 plus 2.
1st row: Sl 1, * k 3, y fwd, sl 1, k 2 tog, psso, y fwd; rep from * to last st, k 1.
2nd row: Sl 1, p to last st, k 1.
3rd row: Sl 1, * y fwd, sl 1, k 2 tog, psso, y fwd, k 3; rep from * to last st, k 1.
4th row: As 2nd;
These four rows form patt.

Lace rib pattern (fig. 70)
Cast on multiples of 4 plus 2.
1st row: Sl 1, * k 2, y fwd, sl 1, k 1, psso; rep from * to last st, k 1.
2nd row: Sl 1, * p 2, y rn, p 2 tog; rep from * to last st, k. 1.
These two rows form patt.

Open mock cable pattern (fig. 71)
Cast on multiples of 4 plus 2.
1st row: Sl 1, p 1, * k 1, y fwd, k 1, p 2; rep from * to last 4 sts, k 1, y fwd, k 1, p 1, k 1.
2nd row: Sl 1, k 1, * p 3, k 2,; rep from * to end of row.
3rd row: Sl 1, p 1, * y bk, sl 1, k 2, pass slipped stitch over k 2, p 2, rep from * to last 5 sts, y bk, sl 1, k 2, pass slipped st over k 2, p 1, k 1.
4th row: Sl 1, k 1, * p 2, k 2; rep from * to end of row.
These four rows form patt.

70

71

72

73

Lace stitches

Rosebud mesh (fig. 72)

Cast on multiples of 10 sts plus 1.
1st row: [Wrong side] P.
2nd row: K 2 tog, * y fwd, k 3, y fwd, k into front and back of next st, y fwd, k 3, y fwd, sl 1, k 2 tog, psso; rep from * ending last rep sl 1, k 1, psso, instead of sl 1, k 2 tog, psso.
3rd and every alt row: P.
4th row: Sl 1, k 1, psso, * y fwd, sl 2, k 1, p2sso, y fwd, k 2 tog, y fwd, sl 1, k 1, psso, [y fwd, sl 2, k 1, p2sso] twice; rep from * ending last rep k 2 tog instead of the 2nd sl 2, k 1, p2sso worked.
6th row: K 2, * k 2 tog, y fwd, k 3, y fwd, sl 1, k 1, psso, k 3; rep from * ending last rep k 2 instead of k 3.
8th row: K 1, * k 2 tog, y fwd, k 1 tbl, y fwd, sl 1, k 2 tog, psso, y fwd, k 1 tbl, y fwd, sl 1, k 1, psso, k 1; rep from * to end.
These eight rows form patt.

Pine pattern (fig. 73)

Cast on multiples of 12 sts plus 3.
1st row: Sl 1, k 2 tog, * k 4, y fwd, k 1, y fwd, k 4, k 3 tog; rep from * to last 12 sts, k 4, y fwd, k 1, y fwd, k 4, k 2 tog, k 1.
2nd row: Sl 1, p 2 tog, * [p 3, y rn] twice, p 3, p 3 tog; rep from * to last 12 sts, [p 3, y rn] twice, p 3, p 2 tog, k 1.
3rd row: Sl 1, k 2 tog, * k 2, y fwd, k 5, y fwd, k 2, k 3 tog; rep from * to last 12 sts, k 2, y fwd, k 5, y fwd, k 2 k 2 tog, k 1.
4th row: Sl 1, p 2 tog, * p 1, y rn, p 7, y rn, p 1, p 3 tog; rep from * to last 12 sts, p 1, y rn, p 7, y rn, p 1, p 2 tog, k 1.
5th row: Sl 1, k 2 tog, * y fwd, k 9, y fwd, k 3 tog; rep from * to last 12 sts, y fwd, k 9, y fwd, k 2 tog, k 1.
6th row: Sl 1, p 1, * y rn, p 4, p 3 tog, p 4, y rn, p 1; rep from * to last 13 sts, y rn, p 4, p 3 tog, p 4, y rn, p 1, k 1.
7th row: Sl 1, k 2, * y fwd, k 3, k 3 tog, k 3, y fwd, k 3; rep from * to end.
8th row: Sl 1, p 3, * y rn, p 2, p 3 tog, p 2, y rn, p 5; rep from * to last 11 sts, y rn, p 2, p 3 tog, p 2, y rn, p 3, k 1.
9th row: Sl 1, k 4 * y fwd, k 1, k 3 tog, k 1, y fwd, k 7; rep from * to last 10 sts, y fwd, k 1, k 3 tog, k 1. y fwd, k 5.
10th row: Sl 1, p 5, * y rn, p 3 tog, y rn, p 9; rep from * to last 9 sts, y rn, p 3 tog, y rn, p 5, k 1.
These 10 rows form patt.

Lacy Chevron (fig. 74)

Cast on multiples of 8 sts plus 1.
1st row: [Right side] K 1, * sl 1, k 1, psso, [k 1, y fwd] twice, k 1, k 2 tog, k 1; rep from * to end.
2nd row: P 1, * p 2 tog, [p 1, y rn] twice, p 1, p 2 tog tbl, p 1; rep from * to end.
3rd row: K 1, * y fwd, sl 1, k 1, psso, k 3, k 2 tog, y fwd, k 1; rep from * to end.
4th row: P 2, * y rn, p 2 tog, p 1, p 2 tog tbl, y rn, p 3; rep from * ending last rep p 2 instead of p 3.
5th row: K 3, * y fwd, sl 2, k 1, p2sso, y fwd, k 5; rep from * ending last rep k 3 instead of k 5.
6th row: As 2nd row.
7th row: As 1st row.
8th row: P 1, * y rn, p 2 tog, p 3, p 2 tog tbl, y rn, p 1; rep from * to end of row.
9th row: K 2, * y fwd, sl 1, k 1, psso, k 1, k 2 tog, y fwd, k 3; rep from * ending last rep k 2 instead of k 3.
10th row: P 3, * y rn, sl 2, p 1, p2sso, y rn, p 5; rep from * ending last rep p 3 instead of p 5.
These 10 rows form patt.

74

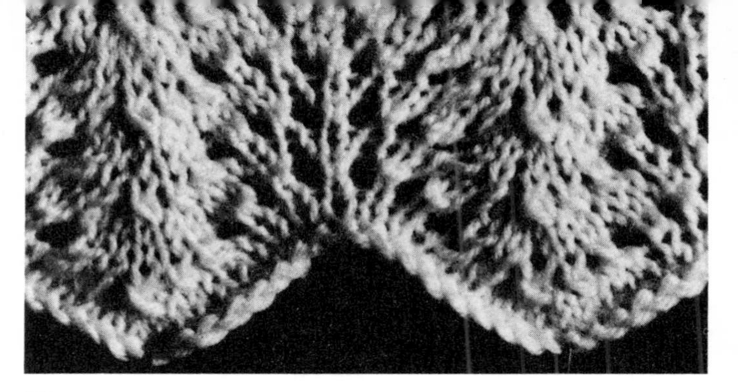

75

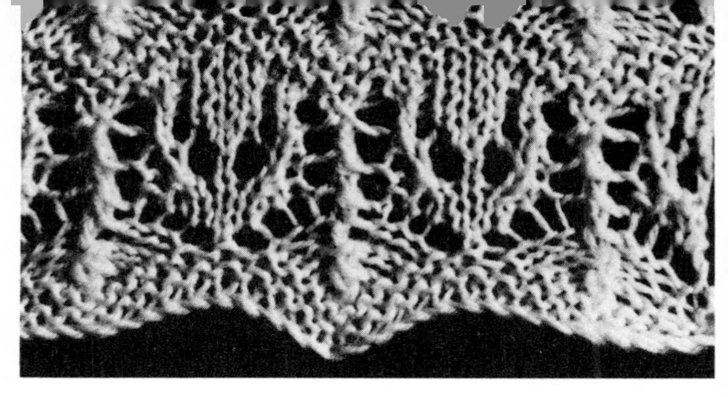

76

Ostrich plumes (fig. 75)

Cast on multiples of 16 sts plus 1.
1st row: [Wrong side and every wrong side row] P.
2nd row: K.
4th row: [K 1, y fwd] 3 times, * [sl 1, k 1, psso] twice, sl 2 k-wise, k 1, p2sso, [k 2 tog] twice, [y fwd, k 1] 5 times, y fwd; rep from * ending last rep [y fwd, k 1] 3 times instead of [y fwd, k 1] 5 times, y fwd.
6th row: As 2nd.
8th row: As 4th.
10th row: As 2nd.
12th row: As 4th.
14th row: As 2nd.
16th row: As 4th.
18th row: As 2nd.
20th row: [K 2 tog] 3 times, * [y fwd, k 1] 5 times, y fwd, [sl 1, k 1, psso] twice, sl 2 k-wise, k 1, p2sso [k 2 tog] twice; rep from * ending last rep [y fwd k 1] 5 times, y fwd, [sl 1, k 1, psso] 3 times.
22nd row: As 2nd.
24th row: As 20th.
26th row: As 2nd.
28th row: As 20th
30th row: As 2nd.
32nd row: As 20th.
These 32 rows form patt.

Lotus pattern (fig. 76)

Cast on multiples of 10 sts plus 1.
1st–5th row: K.
6th row: [Wrong side] P 1, * y rn, p 3, sl 2, p 1, p2sso, p 3, y rn, p 1; rep from * to end.
7th row: K 2, * y fwd, k 2, sl 2, k 1, p2sso, k 2, y rn, k 3; rep from * ending last rep k 2 instead of k 3.
8th row: P 3, * y rn, p 1, sl 2, p 1, p2sso, p 1, y rn, p 5; rep from * ending last rep p 3 instead of p 5.
9th row: K 4, * y fwd, sl 2, k 1, p2sso, y fwd, k 7; rep from * ending last rep k 4 instead of k 7.
10th row: P 2, * k 2, p 3; rep from * ending last rep p 2, instead of p 3.
11th row: K 1, * y rn, sl 1, k 1, psso, p 1, y rn, sl 2, k 1, p2sso, y rn, p 1, k 2 tog, y fwd, k 1; rep from * to end.
12th row: P 3, * k 1, p 3, k 1, p 5; rep from * ending last rep p 3 instead of p 5.
13th row: K 2, * y fwd, sl 1, k 1, psso, y fwd, sl 2, k 1, p2sso, y fwd, k 2 tog, y fwd, k 3; rep from * ending last rep k 2 instead of k 3.
14th row: P 2, * k 1, p 5, k 1, p 3; rep from * ending last rep p 2 instead of p 3.
15th row: K 2, * p 1, k 1, y fwd, sl 2, k 1, p2sso, y fwd, k 1, p 1, k 3; rep from * ending last rep k 2 instead of k 3.
16th row: As 14th.
These 16 rows form patt.

Lace puff (fig. 77)

Cast on multiples of 12 sts plus 2.
1st row: [Right side] K 1, * sl 1, k 1, psso, k 3, y rn, p 2, y fwd, k 3, k 2 tog; rep from * to last st, k 1.
2nd row: K 1, * p 2 tog, p 2, y fwd, k 4, y rn, p 2, p 2 tog tbl; rep from * to last st, k 1.
3rd row: K 1, * sl 1, k 1, psso, k 1, y rn, p 6, y fwd, k 1, k 2 tog; rep from * to last st, k 1.
4th row: K 1, * p 2 tog, y fwd, k 8, y rn, p 2 tog tbl; rep from * to last st, k 1.
5th row: K 1, * p 1, y fwd, k 3, k 2 tog, sl 1, k 1, psso, k 3, y rn, p 1; rep from * to last st, k 1.
6th row: K 1, * k 2, y rn, p 2, p 2 tog tbl, p 2 tog, p 2, y fwd, k 2; rep from * to last st, k 1.
7th row: K 1, * p 3, y fwd, k 1, k 2 tog, sl 1, k 1, psso, k 1, y rn, p 3; rep from * to last st, k 1.
8th row: K 1, * k 4, y rn, p 2 tog tbl, p 2 tog, y fwd, k 4; rep from * to last st, k 1.
These eight rows form patt.

77

Aran stitches

Traditional Aran stitches originated on the west coast of Ireland amongst the fishing families there. Each family had its own design and each man his own pattern. It was considered a matter of pride that a family should be known by its own variations on the traditional stitches. Many have religious associations as well as being taken from the day-to-day life of the fishermen. They have been handed down from generation to generation over the centuries and remain virtually unchanged today.

All Aran abbreviations will be given in the patterns but we give below the abbreviations used in the first two stitch patterns.

B1 Bobble 1. This is made by p 1, k 1, p 1 into the next st making 3 sts out of 1, turn and k these 3 sts, turn and p these 3 sts then sl the 2nd and 3rd st over the 1st st.

C1BB Cross 1 and Bobble 1. Sl the next st on to cable needle and hold at back of work, k 1, Bl, k 1 from left-hand needle, p 1 from cable needle.

C3FB Cross 3 and Bobble 1. Sl next 3 sts on to cable needle and hold at front of work, p 1 from left-hand needle, then k 1, Bl, k 1 on 3 sts on cable needle.

C1B Cross 1 to back. Sl next st on cable needle and hold at back of work, k 3 from left-hand needle, k 1 tbl from cable needle.

C3F Cross 3 front. Sl next 3 sts on to cable needle and hold at front of work, k 1 tbl from left-hand needle, k 3 from cable needle.

T2F Twist 2 front. K into front of 2nd st on left-hand needle then into front of 1st st and sl off needle tog.

T2B Twist 2 back. K into back of 2nd st on left-hand needle then into back of 1st st and sl off needle tog.

C2F Cross 2 front. Sl next 2 sts on to cable needle and hold at front of work, k 3 from left-hand needle, then k 2 from cable needle.

C1BP Cross 1 back and purl. Sl next st on to cable needle and hold at back of work, k 2 from left-hand needle, p 1 from cable needle.

C2FP Cross 2 front and purl. Sl next 2 sts on to cable needle and leave at front of work, p 1 from left-hand needle, k 2 from cable needle.

C1KB Cross 1 back and knit tbl. Sl next st on to cable needle and hold at back of work, k 2 from left-hand needle, k 1 tbl from cable needle.

C2FK Cross 2 front and k. Sl next 2 sts on to cable needle and hold at front of work, k 1 from left-hand needle, k 2 from cable needle.

C1BK Cross 1 back and k. Sl next st on to cable needle and hold at back of work, k 2 from left-hand needle, k 1 from cable needle.

M-st Moss-st. Either k 1, p 1 or p 1, k 1, noting that on every following row k sts are knitted and p sts purled.

Aran pattern (1) (fig. 78)

Cast on multiples of 23 plus 2.

1st row: Sl 1, * p 8, k 3, k 1 tbl, k 3, p 8; rep from * to last st, k 1.
2nd row: Sl 1, * k 8, p 3, p 1 tbl, p 3, k 8; rep from * to last st, k 1.
3rd row: Sl 1, * p 7, C1BB, k 1 tbl, C3FB, p 7; rep from * to last st, k 1.
4th row: Sl 1, * k 7, p 3, k 1, p 1 tbl, k 1, p 3, k 7; rep from * to last st, k 1.
5th row: Sl 1, * p 6, C1B, p 1, k 1 tbl, p 1, C3F, p 6; rep from * to last st, k 1.
6th row: Sl 1, * k 6, p 3, [p 1 tbl, k 1] twice, p 1 tbl, p 3, k 6; rep from * to last st, k 1.
7th row: Sl 1, * p 5, C1BB, [k 1 tbl, p 1] twice, k 1 tbl, C3FB, p 5; rep from * to last st, k 1.
8th row: Sl 1, * k 5, p 3, [k 1, p 1 tbl] 3 times, k 1, p 3, k 5; rep from * to last st, k 1.
9th row: Sl 1, * p 4, C1B, [p 1, k 1 tbl] 3 times, p 1, C3F, p 4; rep from * to last st, k 1.
10th row: Sl 1, * k 4, p 3, [p 1 tbl, k 1] 4 times, p 1 tbl, p 3, k 4; rep from * to last st, k 1.
11th row: Sl 1, * p 3, C1BB, [k 1 tbl, p 1] 4 times, k 1 tbl, C3FB, p 3; rep from * to last st, k 1.
12th row: Sl 1, * k 3, p 3, [k 1, p 1 tbl] 5 times, k 1, p 3, k 3; rep from * to last st, k 1.
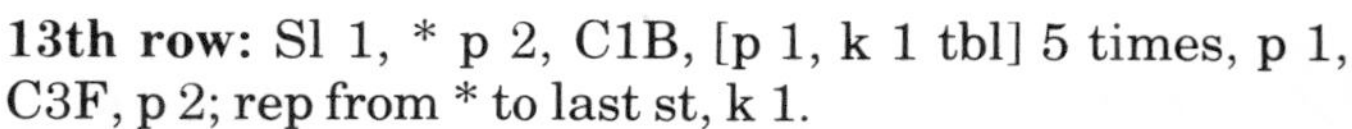
13th row: Sl 1, * p 2, C1B, [p 1, k 1 tbl] 5 times, p 1, C3F, p 2; rep from * to last st, k 1.
14th row: Sl 1, * k 2, p 3, [p 1 tbl, p 1] 6 times, p 1 tbl, p 3, k 2; rep from * to last st, k 1.
15th row: Sl 1, * p 1, C1BB, [k 1 tbl, p 1] 6 times, k 1 tbl, C3FB, p 1; rep from * to last st, k 1.
16th row: Sl 1, * k 1, p 3, [k 1, p 1 tbl] 7 times, k 1, p 3, k 1; rep from * to last st, k 1.
These 16 rows form patt.

Aran pattern (2) (fig. 79)

Cast on multiples of 31 sts plus 2.

1st row: Sl 1, * p 1, T2F, T2B, p 1, beg with k 1 m-st 6, k 7, beg with p 1 m-st 6, p 1, T2F, T2B, p 1; rep from * to last st, k 1.
2nd, 4th, 6th, 8th, 10th and 12th rows: Sl 1, * k 1, p 4, k 1, beg with k 1 m-st 6, k 1, p 5, k 1, beg with p 1 m-st 6, k 1, p 4, k 1; rep from * to last st, k 1.
3rd row: Sl 1, * p 1, T2B, T2F, p 1, m-st 6, k 1, C2F, k 1, m-st 6, p 1, T2B, T2F, p 1; rep from * to last st, k 1.
5th row: As 1st.
7th row: Sl 1, * p 1, T2B, T2F, p 1, m-st 6, k 7, m-st 6, p 1, T2B, T2F, p 1; rep from * to last st, k 1.
9th row: Sl 1, * p 1, T2F, T2B, p 1, m-st 6, k 1, C2F, k 1, m-st 6, p 1, T2F, T2B, p 1; rep from * to last st, k 1.
11th row: Sl 1, * p 1, T2B, T2F, p 1, m-st 6, k 7, m-st 6,

78

79

80

81

p 1, T2B, T2F, p 1; rep from * to last st, k 1.
13th row: Sl 1, * p 1, T2F, T2B, p 1, m-st 6, C1BP, k 1 tbl, C1FP, m-st 6, p 1, T2F, T2B, p 1; rep from * to last st, k 1.
14th row: Sl 1, * k 1, p 4, k 1, m-st 6, p 2, k 1, p 1 tbl, k 1, p 2, m-st 6, k 1, p 4, k 1; rep from * to last st, k 1.
15th row: Sl 1, * p 1, T2B, T2F, p 1, m-st 5, C1KB, p 1, k 1 tbl, p 1, C2FP, m-st 5, p 1, T2B, T2F, p 1; rep from * to last st, k 1.
16th row: Sl 1, * k 1, p 4, k 1, m-st 5, p 2, [p 1 tbl, k 1] twice, p 1 tbl, p 2, m-st 5, k 1, p 4, k 1; rep from * to last st, k 1.
17th row: Sl 1, * p 1, T2F, T2B, p 1, m-st 4, C1BP, [k 1 tbl, p 1] twice, k 1 tbl, C2FP, m-st 4, p 1, T2F, T2B, p 1; rep from * to last st, k 1.
18th row: Sl 1, * k 1, p 4, k 1, m-st 4, p 2, [k 1, p 1 tbl] 3 times, k 1, p 2, m-st 4, k 1, p 4, k 1; rep from * to last st, k 1.
19th row: Sl 1, * p 1, T2B, T2F, p 1, m-st 3, C1KB, [p 1, k 1 tbl] 3 times, p 1, C2FB, m-st 3, p 1, T2B, T2F, p 1; rep from * to last st, k 1.
20th row: Sl 1, * k 1, p 4, k 1, m-st 3, p 2, [p 1 tbl, k 1] 4 times, p 1 tbl, p 2, m-st 3, k 1, p 4, k 1; rep from * to last st, k 1.
21st row: Sl 1, * p 1, T2F, T2B, p 1, m-st 2, C1BP, [k 1 tbl, p 1] 4 times, k 1 tbl, C2FP, m-st 2, p 1, T2F, T2B, p 1; rep from * to last st, k 1.
22nd row: Sl 1, * k 1, p 4, k 1, m-st 2, p 2, [k 1, p 1 tbl] 5 times, k 1, p 2, m-st 2, k 1, p 4, k 1; rep from * to last st, k 1.
23rd row: Sl 1, * p 1, T2B, T2F, p 1, m-st 2, C2FK, [k 1 tbl, p 1] 4 times, k 1 tbl, C1BK, m-st 2, p 1, T2B, T2F, p 1; rep from * to last st, k 1.
24th row: As 20th
25th row: Sl 1, * p 1, T2F, T2B, p 1, m-st 3, C2FP, [p 1, k 1 tbl] 3 times, p 1, C1BP, m-st 3, p 1, T2F, T2B, p 1; rep from * to last st, k 1.
26th row: As 18th
27th row: Sl 1, * p 1, T2B, T2F, p 1, m-st 4, C2FK, [k 1 tbl, p 1] twice, k 1 tbl, C1BK, m-st 4, p 1, T2B, T2F, p 1; rep from * to last st, k 1.
28th row: As 16th
29th row: Sl 1, * p 1, T2F, T2B, p 1, m-st 5, C2FP, p 1, k 1 tbl, p 1, C1BP, m-st 5, p 1, T2F, T2B, p 1; rep from * to last st, k 1.
30th row: As 14th.
31st row: Sl 1, * p 1, T2B, T2F, p 1, m-st 6, C2FK, k 1 tbl, C1BK, m-st 6, p 1, T2B, T2F, p 1; rep from * to last st, k 1.
32nd row: Sl 1, * k 1, p 4, k 1, m-st 7, p 2, p 1 tbl, p 2, m-st 7, k 1, p 4, k 1; rep from * to last st, k 1.
These 32 rows form patt.

Basket stitch (fig. 80)
Cast on multiples of 6 sts.
1st row: K.
2nd row: P.
3rd row: * Sl next 3 sts on to cable needle and hold at back of work, k next 3 sts, k 3 sts from cable needle—called C6B; rep from * to end.
4th row: P.
5th row: K.
6th row: P.
7th row: K 3, * sl next 3 sts on to cable needle and hold

82

83

at front of work, k next 3 sts, k 3 sts from cable needle – called C6F; rep from * to last 3 sts, k 3.
8th row: P.
These eight rows form patt.

Honeycomb stitch (fig. 81)
Cast on multiples of 8 sts plus 2.
1st row: K 1, * sl next 2 sts on to cable needle and hold at back of work, k next 2 sts, k 2 sts from cable needle – called C4B; sl next 2 sts on to cable needle and hold at front of work, k next 2 sts, k 2 sts from cable needle – called C4F; rep from * to last st, k 1.
2nd row: P.
3rd row: K.
4th row: P.
5th row: K 1, * C4F, C4B; rep from * to last st, k 1.
6th row: P.
7th row: K.
8th row: P.
These eight rows form patt.

Lobster claw (fig. 82)
Cast on multiples of 9 sts plus 2.
1st row: P 2, * k 7, p 2; rep from * to end.
2nd row: K 2, * p 7, k 2; rep from * to end.
3rd row: P 2, * sl next 2 sts on to cable needle and hold at back of work, k next st, k sts from cable needle, k 1, sl next st on to cable needle and hold at front of work, k next 2 sts, k st from cable needle, p 2; rep from * to end.
4th row: As 2nd.
These four rows form patt.

Tree of life (fig. 83)
Cast on multiples of 17 sts plus 2.
1st row: P 2, * p 6, k 3 tbl, p 8; rep from * to end.
2nd row: K 2, * k 6, p 3 tbl, k 8; rep from * to end.
3rd row: P 2, * p 5, sl next 2 sts on to cable needle and leave at back of work, k next st tbl, p st from cable needle – called T2F – k 1 tbl, sl next st on to cable needle and hold at front of work, p next st, k st from cable needle tbl – called T2B, p 7; rep from * to end.
4th row: K 2, * k 5, p 1 tbl, k 1, p 1 tbl, k 1, p 1 tbl, k 7; rep from * to end.
5th row: P 2, * p 4, T2F, p 1, k 1 tbl, p 1, T2B, p 6; rep from * to end.
6th row: K 2, * k 4, p 1 tbl, k 2, p 1 tbl, k 2, p 1 tbl, k 6; rep from * to end.
7th row: P 2, * p 3, T2F, p 2, k 1 tbl, p 2, T2B, p 5; rep from * to end.
8th row: K 2, * k 3, p 1 tbl, k 3, p 1 tbl, k 3, p 1 tbl, k 5; rep from * to end.
9th row: P 2, * p 2, T2F, p 3, k 1 tbl, p 3, T2B, p 4; rep from * to end.
10th row: K 2, * k 2, p 1 tbl, k 4, p 1 tbl, k 4, p 1 tbl, k 4; rep from * to end.
11th row: P 2, * p 1, T2F, p 4, k 1 tbl, p 4, T2B, p 3; rep from * to end.
12th row: K 2, * k 1, p 1 tbl, k 5, p 1 tbl, k 5, p 1 tbl, k 3; rep from * to end.
13th row: P 2, * T2F, p 5, k 1 tbl, p 5, T2B, p 2; rep from * to end.
14th row: K2, * p 1 tbl, k 6, p 1 tbl, k 6, p 1 tbl, k 2; rep from * to end.
These 14 rows form patt.

Fair Isle and tubular knitting

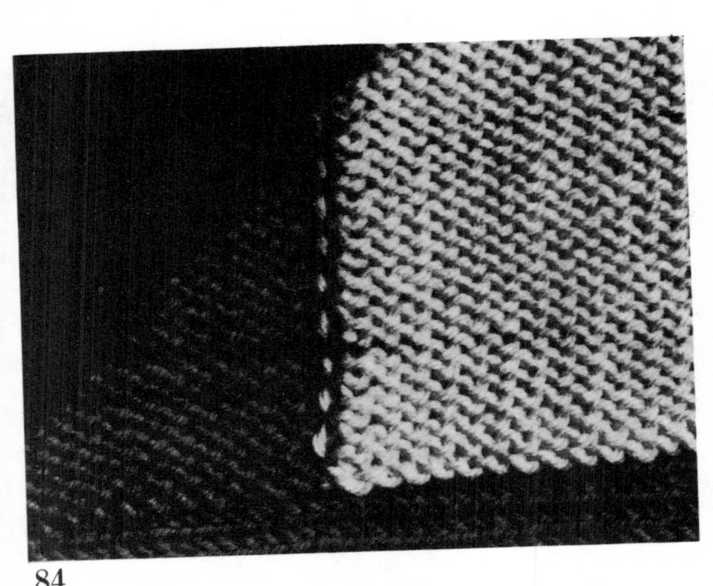

84

85

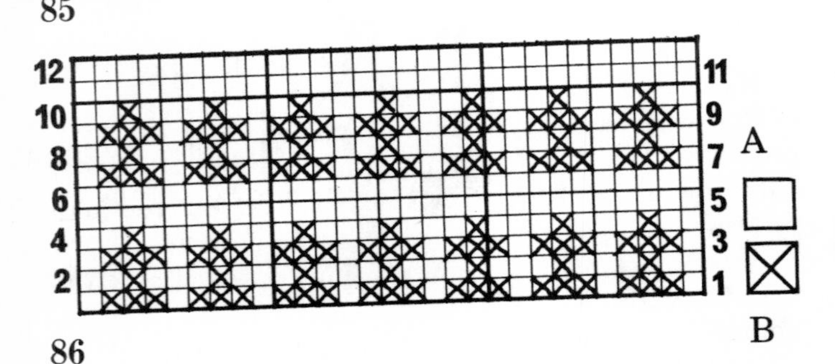

86

Two-colour knitting (fig. 84)
If a large number of stitches are to be worked in different colours, either vertically or in solid shapes in the garment, use a separate ball of yarn for each colour and twist the yarn firmly on the wrong side of the work when changing colours, to avoid making a hole.

Fair Isle or Norwegian knitting
These patterns are always worked in stocking-stitch, with groups of stitches knitted in different colours to form a pattern. The Fair Isle design is usually given in instructions as a chart, with each square representing one stitch and, unless illustrated in colour, a different symbol representing each colour. To work from a chart the odd numbered rows are the knit rows, the right side of the work, and the chart is read from RIGHT to LEFT. The purl rows are the even numbered rows, the wrong side of the work, and the chart is read from LEFT to RIGHT. See the illustration and chart of the simple Fair Isle pattern worked in two colours (figs. 85 and 86).

If you are working Fair Isle on four needles, or a circular needle, then every row on your chart will be a knit row and each row will read from Right to Left. There are two ways of working horizontal changes of colour in Fair Isle, either by stranding or by weaving the colour not in use across the back of the work.

Stranding method
When working the required number o stitches in one colour, the colour not in use i carried loosely at the back of the work unti it is required. The colour in use is ther dropped and the colour not in use taken u and used again, carrying the first colou loosely across the back of the work (fig. 87) The stranding method used over large patter repeats can produce long strands at the bac of the work between the changes of colou since these strands easily catch and ca distort the pattern, apart from causing annoy ance to the wearer, it is better to combin both the stranding and weaving method f lengths of more than two or three stitches i each colour.

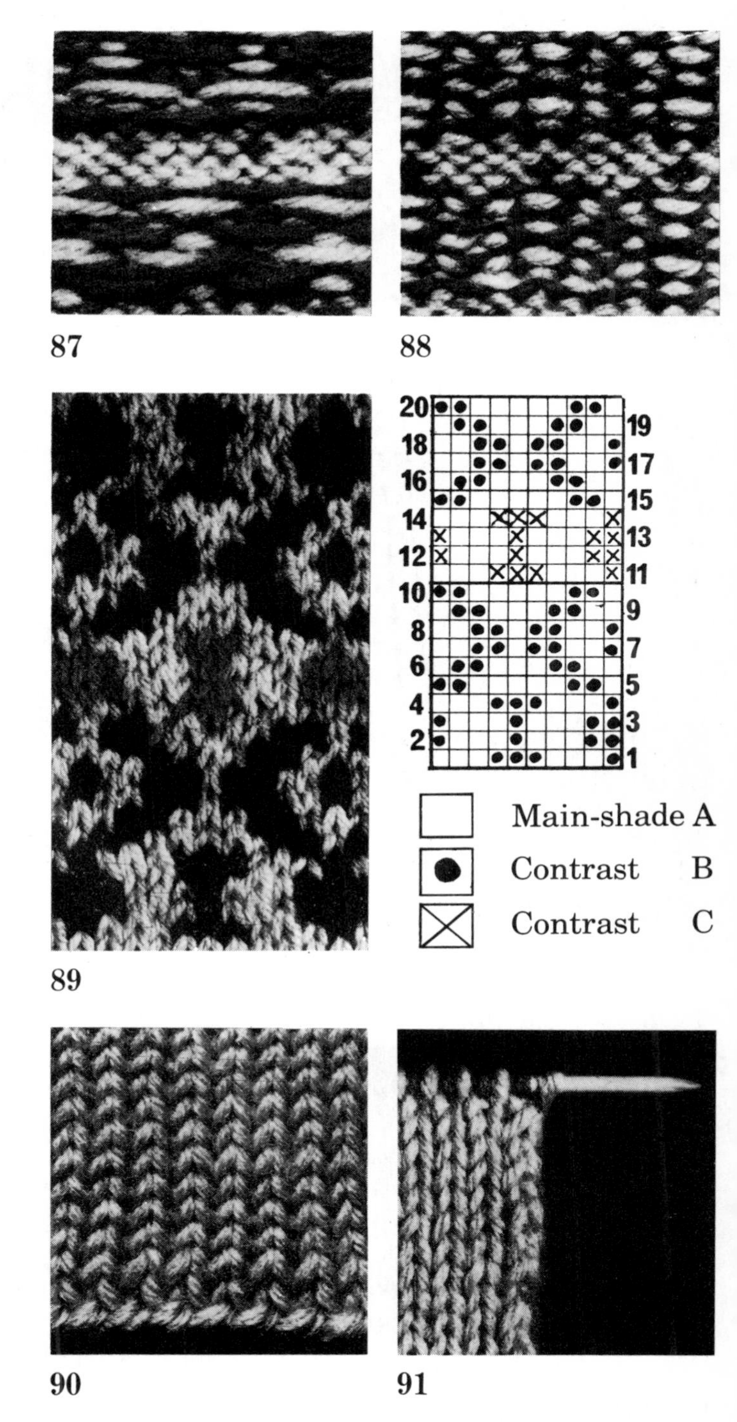

87

88

89

90

91

Weaving method

The colour in use is first taken *over* and then *under* the colour not in use on the wrong side of the work, thus:

With A only k one st, put B *over* right-hand needle at back of work and k next st with A only in usual way, k next st with A only holding B across back of work (fig. 88).

Fair Isle pattern in two colours (fig. 85)

With main shade, A cast on 29 sts.

1st row: [Right side] Working from chart from RIGHT to LEFT, * k 1 A, k 3 B; rep from * to last st, k 1 A.

2nd row: [Wrong side] Working from chart from LEFT to RIGHT, p 2 A, * p 1 B, p 3 A; rep from * to last 3 sts, p 1 B, p 2 A.

Continue working in this way from chart for the required number of rows (fig. 86).

Fair Isle pattern in three colours

With main shade, A, cast on multiples of 10 sts. Work from chart as given above from RIGHT to LEFT.

1st row: [Right side] * K 1 B, k 3 A, k 3 B, k 3 A; rep from * to end of row.

Continue working in this way from chart for the required number of rows, bringing in contrast colour C when indicated (fig. 89).

Tubular knitting

This makes a flat double fabric and is used for scarves, hems or piping (fig. 90).

Cast on an even number of sts.

1st row: * Yarn to front of work, sl 1 p-wise, yarn to back of work, k 1; rep from * to end of row. This row repeated gives a flat tube, with the knit fabric as the right side.

Double fabric can also be knitted in this way on four needles but an odd number of stitches must be cast on.

Two-colour tubular knitting

This is worked with a separate ball of each colour yarn and a pair of knitting needles pointed at both ends (fig. 91).

Cast on an even number of sts with main colour, A.

1st row: [Right side] With contrast colour, B, * k 1, y fwd, sl 1 p-wise, y bk; rep from * to end of row. DO NOT TURN WORK.

2nd row: [Right side again] With main shade, A, * sl 1 p-wise, y fwd, p 1, y bk; rep from * to end of row. TURN WORK AND TWIST COLOURS TOGETHER TO CLOSE SIDE.

3rd row: [Wrong side] With contrast colour, B, work as 2nd row. DO NOT TURN WORK.

4th row: [Wrong side again] With main shade, A, work as 1st row. TURN WORK AND TWIST COLOURS TOGETHER TO CLOSE SIDE.

These four rows form patt.

Knitting from a pattern

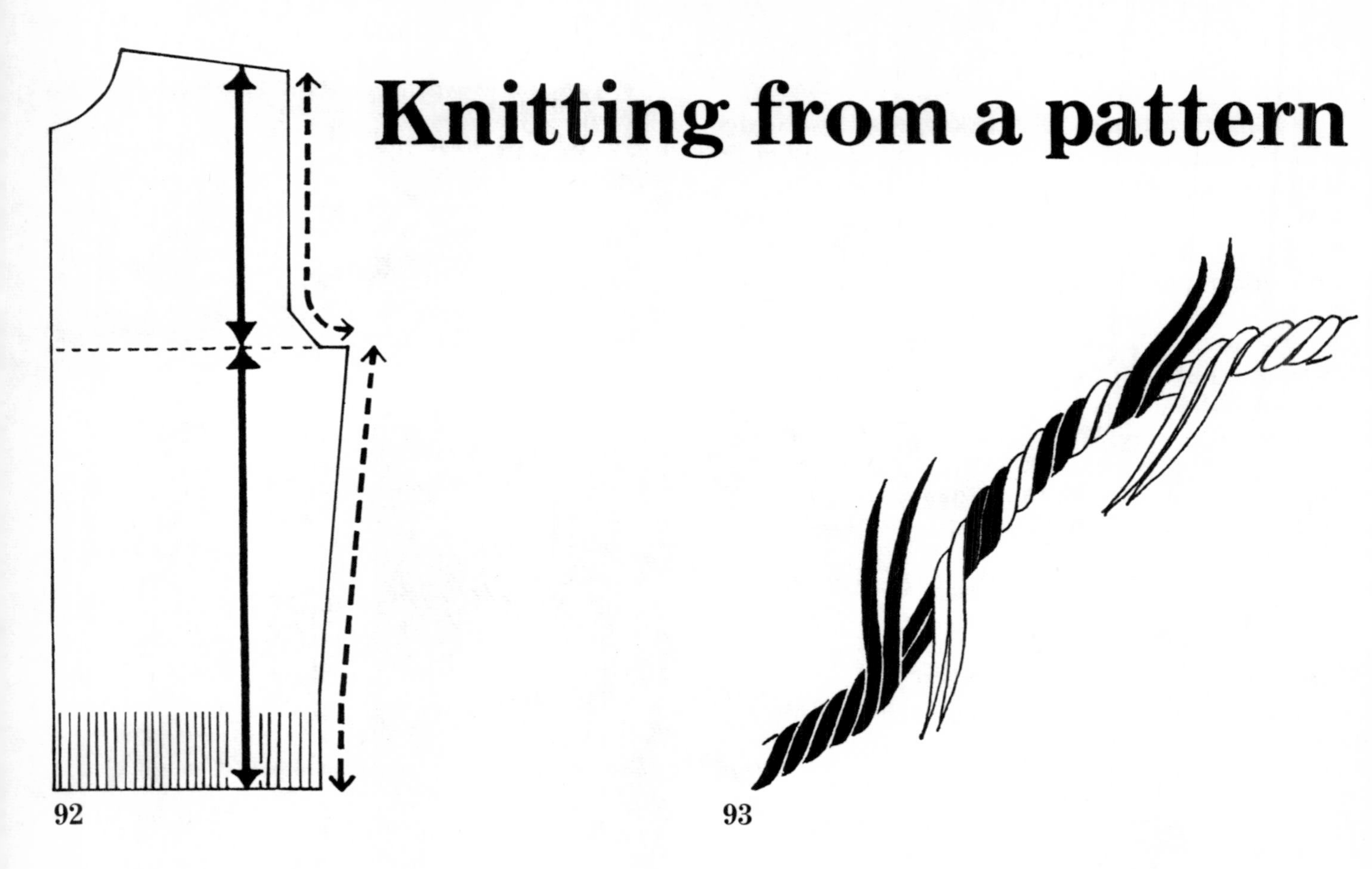

92 93

Materials

Once you have chosen the design you wish to make it is important to obtain the correct yarn as a garment which has been specially designed for a 4-ply wool cannot turn out correctly if you substitute a mohair or bouclé wool for example. If you cannot obtain the exact yarn you can substitute it for another yarn of the same type. For example a 4-ply wool for a 4-ply wool or a double knitting wool for a double knitting wool, as long as you make sure that the tension you obtain with the substitute is the same as that given in your pattern (see page 14). If you do not obtain the same tension try changing the needle size and if this does not work, please don't continue in the vain hope that it will be alright in the end. It won't be and you will only be disappointed with the results. You can write to the manufacturer of the particular yarn you require, asking them to give you the name of your nearest stockist.

It is also important to buy the given quantity of yarn at the same time so that you obtain the same dye lot for the whole garment, remembering that if you intend to add extra inches to the measurements you must allow for extra yarn. Keep one of the ball bands just in case you should need it, as this will ensure that you know the number of the original dye lot if you have to buy any more yarn.

Tension

Before beginning the pattern, CHECK YOUR TENSION as given on page 15.

Measurements

Nearly all patterns give instructions for more than one size, with the first set of figures referring to the smallest size and figures for larger sizes given in brackets, thus, 32″ (34″–36″–38″) bust. Based on these sizes, if you are making a garment in a 36″ bust size, the number of stitches and measurements for your size will be shown as the second set of figures in brackets throughout, unless only one set of figures is given, which will apply to all sizes. Before you begin knitting you may find it easier to go through the pattern and underline all the figures given for your size. Measurements for body and sleeve lengths will be given in the pattern and if you want to add to any of these measurements, always remember to allow for extra yarn.

Knitting should be placed on a flat surface and measurements should be taken in the centre of the work and not at the edges (fig. 92). Adjustments can be made to the length of the body by adding or taking away rows before the armhole shaping is reached. Where there is side shaping on the body or sleeves, adjust the length when the shaping has been completed. Be very accurate about measuring armhole depth; never measure on the side curve and never try to alter the length here if possible (see 'Making Adjustments to Patterns', page 36), as the correct fit of the sleeves depends on the correct armhole depth. Remember to work the same number of rows on pieces which have to be joined, for example, the front and back of a garment; a row counter can be very useful here.

Joining in a new ball

Always join in a new ball of yarn at the beginning of a row, if possible. You can gauge whether you have sufficient yarn for another row by spreading out your work and checking whether the yarn will cover its width four times. Any odd lengths of yarn can be saved for sewing up. If the yarn has to be joined in the middle of the work, which is necessary when working on circular needles, the ends should be spliced. Unravel the ends of yarn of the ball being used and the new ball, cut away one or two strands from each end, overlay the two ends and twist together until they hold. The twisted ends should be of the same thickness as the original yarn. Knit very carefully with the newly twisted yarn for a few stitches, then trim away the odd ends of yarn. If you cannot join the yarn at the beginning of a row, never knit a knot into your work but splice the ends as described (fig. 93).

Keeping work clean

A polythene bag pinned over the finished work and moved up as it grows will help to keep your knitting clean. Never stick the needles through the ball of yarn as this splits the yarn, and never leave your work in the middle of a row; you will find that this leaves a mark when you continue to knit.

Mistakes

Mistakes happen to the best knitters. If you notice a wrong stitch a row or two down, don't panic and pull the work off your needles. It may be possible to correct the mistake by dropping the stitch above it off the needle, letting it run down, then picking it up in the correct pattern with a crochet hook. Even if it is not as simple as this, careful unpicking by putting the needle into the row underneath and undoing the stitch above until you are back to the incorrect row may be better than ripping out. Always have a crochet hook on hand to pick up the dropped stitches.

Patterned stitches

The number of stitches cast on for each piece are calculated to fit the pattern exactly, so that for the first few rows you can follow the instructions without any alterations and get to know the pattern sequence. As soon as you start any shaping, however, the beginnings and ends of the pattern rows will change. With patterns made up from basic knitting and purling this is no problem, as you can see how you work each stitch from what has gone before. With more elaborate patterns you should analyse how the stitch works, then work in your extra stitches accordingly. With complicated lace stitches it may be best to work the increased stitches in stocking stitch or garter stitch until there are sufficient extra stitches to work another complete pattern. Keep a check on rows with a row counter so that you know exactly which pattern row you are working and when the next piece of shaping is due.

Making adjustments to patterns

Until you are fairly experienced in knitting it is advisable to find a pattern in the size you require. Most designs are worked out to standard dressmaking measurements, but once you have become adept at reading knitting instructions it is possible to alter them to suit your particular shape. The simplest way of making a garment one size smaller or larger is to use needles one size smaller or larger than those stated in the pattern; remember that a stitch sample must be worked before you begin, to make sure that the resulting fabric is not too tight or too loose. If this isn't successful then stitches have to be added to, or subtracted from, those given for the size nearest to your own measurements. For example if the sweater you would like to make only goes up to a 40″ chest, and you would like to make a 42″ chest size, first look at the TENSION paragraph and find out how many stitches are given to the inch. Secondly, if a patterned stitch is being used, check the number of stitches used for each pattern repeat. Using these two figures, extra stitches can be cast on for the Back and Front, or in the case of a Cardigan, halve the number of stitches cast on for the Back between the Left and Right Front. For example, if the number of stitches given for the TENSION is 7 to the inch, but the pattern is made up of 8 sts, it is much easier to add or subtract 8 sts, so that the pattern rows are worked out easily and exactly. When you have worked out the number of stitches to be cast on, work as given in the instructions, noting that any extra stitches must be included in any shaping you work, until the armholes are reached. At the armhole, decrease *half* the extra stitches equally at each side, then divide the remaining extra stitches into three, casting off one-third for each shoulder and one-third for the neck. The sleeves can be altered in the same way, decreasing half the extra stitches at each side at the beginning of the top shaping and the remainder on the final rows of the top shaping. If you use this method you will find it easier to mark all the alterations on the pattern first, so that you can work a complete section without having to calculate as you progress.

94

For a narrow-shouldered figure cast off extra stitches at the armhole and work more decreasings, but remember that there will be less stitches when you come to work the shoulder shaping.

For a full-busted figure cast on extra stitches on the front and work bust darts about $1\frac{1}{2}''$ before beginning the armhole shaping. The darts should be 1″ from the side seams and taper to nothing about 4″ from the edge and, once again, this is worked out from the TENSION given. For example, take a tension of 8 stitches and 10 rows to 1″. For the *length* of the dart, take the number of stitches given to the inch and multiply by four, i.e., 32 stitches, and for the *depth* of the dart, take the number of rows to 1″, i.e., 10 rows. Shaping should be worked on alternate rows, so on the 10 rows given the darts can be worked in five steps. On the 32 stitches given, this gives five steps of 6 stitches with two over, so the darts must be worked in four steps of 6 stitches and one of 8 stitches, thus:

1st row: Knit, or pattern, to the last 32 stitches, turn.
2nd row: Sl 1, purl or pattern to the last 32 stitches, turn.
3rd row: Sl 1, knit or pattern to the last 26 stitches, turn.
4th row: Sl 1, purl or pattern to the last 26 stitches, turn.
5th row: Sl 1, knit or pattern to the last 20 stitches, turn.
6th row: Sl 1, purl or pattern to the last 20 stitches, turn.
7th row: Sl 1, knit or pattern to the last 14 stitches, turn.
8th row: Sl 1, purl or pattern to the last 14 stitches, turn.
9th row: Sl 1, knit or pattern to the last 8 stitches, turn.
10th row: Sl 1, purl or pattern to the last 8 stitches, turn.
11th row: Sl 1, knit or pattern to the end of the row.
12th row: Sl 1, purl or pattern to the last stitch, k 1.

When the darts have been completed, work $1\frac{1}{2}''$ more, then cast off for the armholes (fig. 94). *Lengths* can be altered by adding to or taking away from the rows worked before, or after, the side shapings are worked. It is *never* advisable to alter the length after commencing the armhole shaping, as this can throw the whole design out of proportion. If, for any reason to suit your own individual measurements, the length of the armhole has to be adjusted, then remember that the sleeve top shaping must be altered accordingly.

Finishing touches

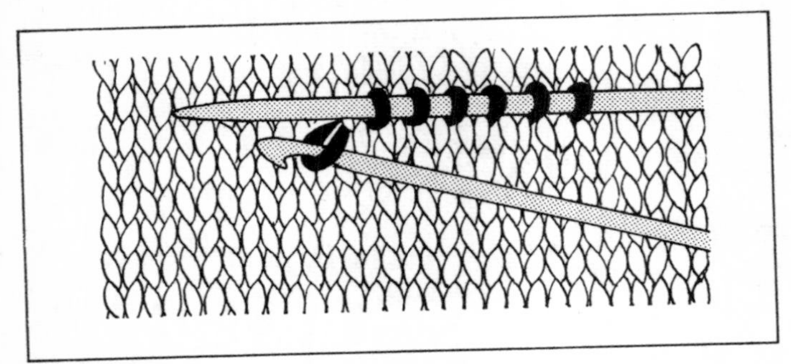

95

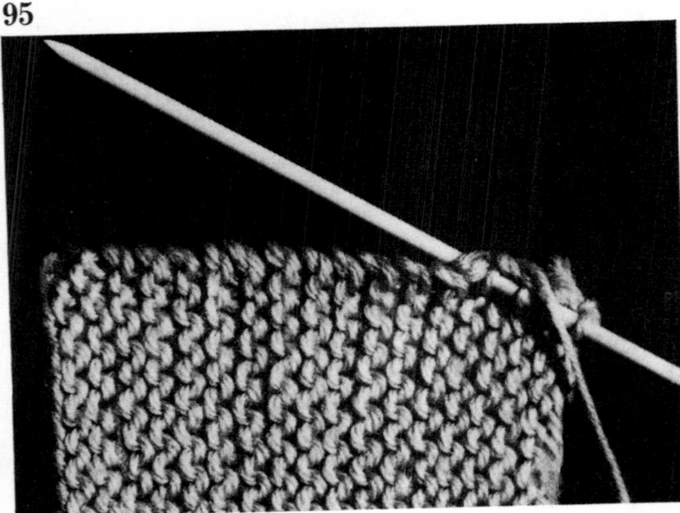

96

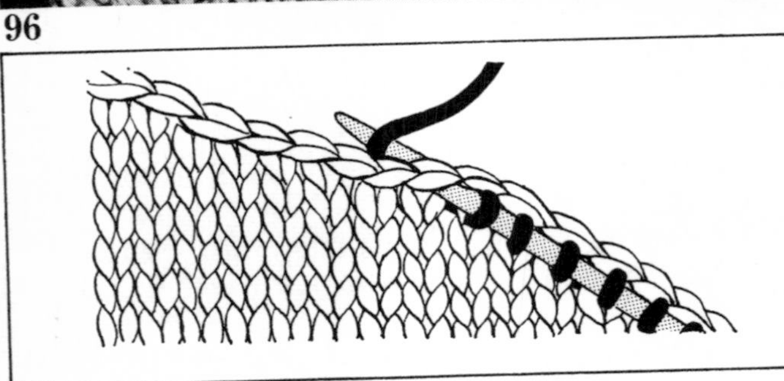

97

98

Edgings

Extra pieces, neckbands, pocket tops, etc., can be knitted on to the main work by picking up and knitting stitches. This gives a smooth and even line and when picked up with the right side of the fabric facing you the abbreviation is 'k up' and with the wrong side of the fabric facing you, 'p up'.

To knit up stitches across fabric have yarn on wrong side, * put a crochet hook through work from right side, pick up a loop of yarn, bring loop through to right side and slip the loop on to a knitting needle; repeat from * for the required number of stitches (fig. 95).

To knit up stitches along a straight garter stitch edge have yarn at back of work, * put knitting needle through from front to back, pick up a loop of yarn and bring loop through to right side and leave on needle; repeat from * for required number of stitches (fig. 96).

To knit up stitches round a curved edge, such as a neckline, have yarn at back of work, * put knitting needle through from front to back, pick up a loop of yarn and bring loop through to right side and leave on needle; repeat from * for required number of stitches taking care to knit up in a smooth curve (fig. 97).

To knit up stitches for front bands count the number of rows on the main fabric and check this against the number of stitches to be knitted up to make sure that you pick them up evenly. Work as given for straight garter-stitch edge (fig. 98).

Hems and Facings

These are usually worked in stocking-stitch and should always be a little narrower or finer than the main fabric, otherwise they may stretch the edge of the garment. Details of stitches and rows to be worked will be given in the instructions.

Plain hem

Beginning with a knit row, work in stocking-stitch on needles two sizes smaller than for the main fabric for the required hem length, ending with a knit row. On the next row, knit all the stitches through the back of the loop to mark the hemline. Change to required needles for the main fabric and either begin with a knit row for stocking-stitch or work the first row of the pattern for the main stitch. When work is completed turn the hem to the wrong side at the marked hemline and slip stitch to the wrong side (fig. 99) taking great care to stitch along the straight line of knitting (fig. 100).

Picot hem

This makes a pretty finish to any garment. Work required hem depth in stocking-stitch as given for plain hem, ending with a purl row. Next row: * knit 2 together, yarn forward between needles and over right-hand needle to make a stitch; repeat from * to end or, for an odd number of stitches, repeat from * to last stitch, knit 1. This makes a row of holes (fig. 101). Beginning with a purl row continue in stocking-stitch. When work is finished fold hem along centre of picot row to wrong side and slip stitch (fig. 102).

Knitted-up hems

This can be done for both the plain and picot hems described above and leaves virtually no mark on the right side. Cast on by the loop method given on page 8 and work the plain or picot hem as given. Work exactly the same number of rows above the hemline, ending with a purl row. If the casting on is loose enough these stitches can be picked up with a third needle pointed at both ends, taking care that you pick up the exact number of stitches, or unravel the cast on stitches and place each stitch on a third needle. Fold up the hem to the wrong side and knit together one stitch from each needle, i.e., putting the right-hand needle through the stitch on the needle nearest to you, then through the corresponding stitch on the third needle and knit both stitches together (fig. 103).

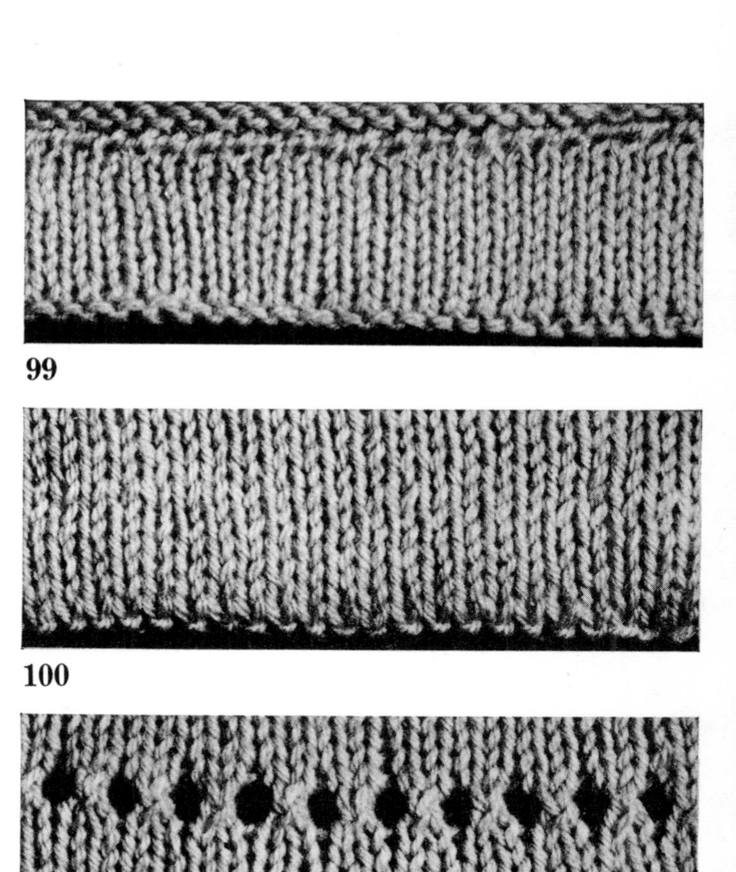

99

100

101

102

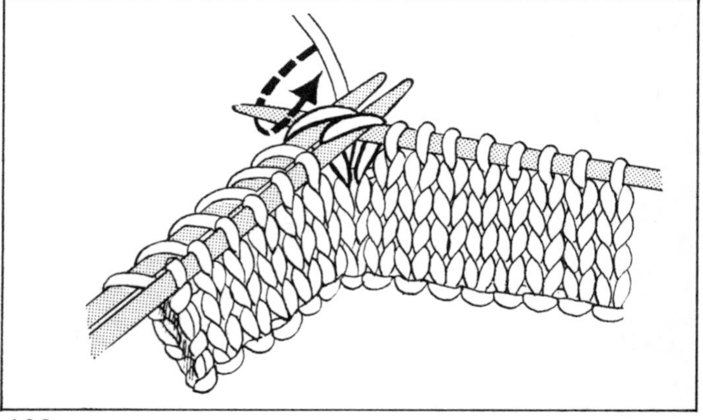

103

Finishing touches

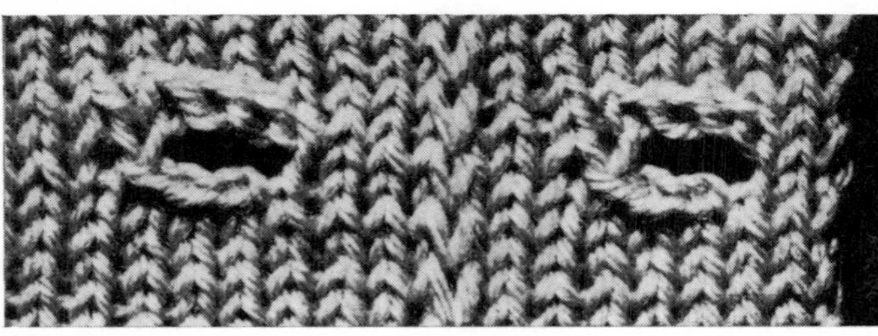
104

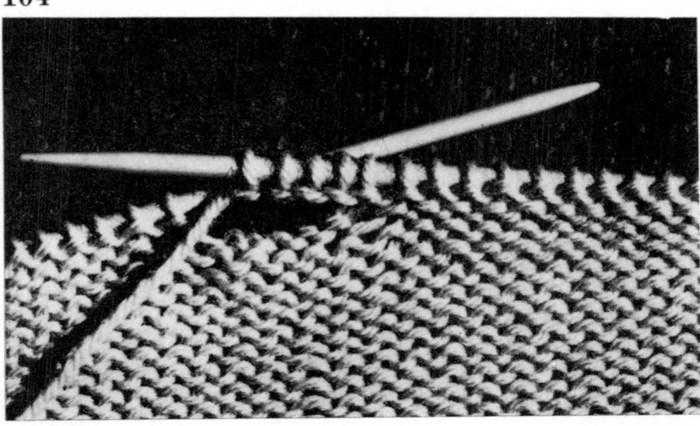
105

106

Knitted facings
Knitted facings worked in one with main fabric, such as button and buttonhole bands. If working a buttonhole band the pattern will tell you the correct number of stitches to cast on. As an example, working from the front edge to side edge, knit 4 stitches, cast off 3 stitches, knit 4 stitches including the stitch already on right-hand needle, slip next stitch purlwise, knit 4 stitches, cast off 3 stitches, knit to end of row. On the next row purl tc end including the slipped stitch, casting or two lots of 3 stitches above those cast off or the previous row (fig. 104).

Buttonholes

Your pattern will tell you how and when tc work buttonholes. If you wish to change thei size you can do so by adding or taking away stitches to be cast off on the armhole side of a horizontal buttonhole, or by changing the number of rows worked on a vertical button hole. For a very small buttonhole, make a hole in the desired position by working tw stitches together then put the yarn forwar and over, or round the needle to make a stitch before working to the end of the row.

Horizontal buttonholes
Cast off the required number of stitche rather loosely. When you have cast off thes stitches you will have one stitch left on th right-hand needle. Unless otherwise stated this stitch is counted as part of the row an not part of the buttonhole, that is to say, in row of 8 stitches with a 4 stitch buttonhole the instructions will read: knit or pattern stitches, cast off 4 stitches, knit or pattern stitches, although one of the last two stitche has already been worked. In the followin row, cast on the same number of stitche above those cast off in the previous row usin the loop method (fig. 105).

Vertical buttonholes
The number of stitches are divided on eac side of the buttonhole position, worke

separately to the desired size, then rejoined. Leave the broken end of yarn for working buttonhole stitch round the buttonhole afterwards (fig. 106).

Separate front bands

When separate bands are worked for the front of a cardigan and sewn on afterwards, save time by working both bands together using separate balls of yarn. Each time you make a buttonhole, mark the other band with coloured thread; you will then know where to sew on the buttons for a perfect match.

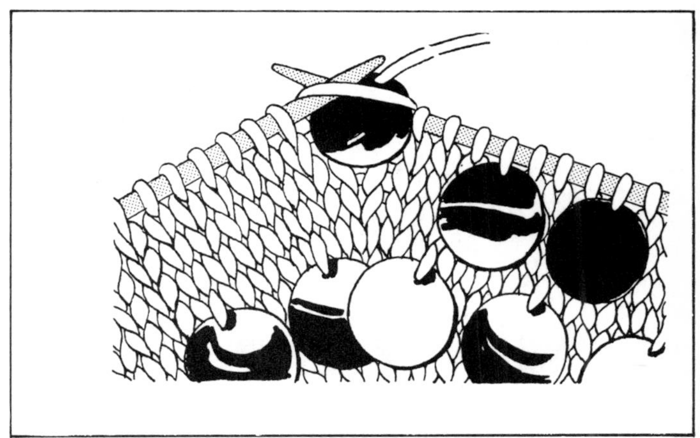

107

Knitting with beads and embroidery

Your pattern will tell you the number of beads or sequins and the size required. To thread the desired number of beads on to an ounce of yarn before beginning to knit with this, fold a 10″ strand of sewing cotton in half and thread a fine needle with *both* cut ends, leaving a loop of cotton. Pass 6″ end of yarn to be used through the loop of cotton and slide beads on to the needle, down the cotton and on to the yarn. When knitting with this beaded yarn, slip bead up close to work, knit next stitch through the back of the loop in usual way pushing bead through stitch to front of work with the loop of the stitch. This allows beads to lie flat (fig. 107). The procedure is exactly the same when knitting with sequins.

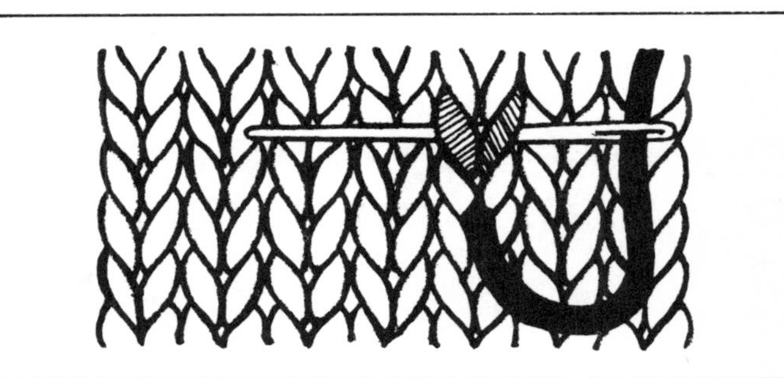

108

109

Swiss darning

This is the easiest form of embroidery for use on knitted solid fabrics, such as stocking stitch. The working method is shown in figs. 108, 109 and 110, where it can be seen that the embroidery yarn merely covers a series of knitted stitches.

The same ply yarn as the knitted fabric should be used for the embroidery to ensure that the knitted stitches are completely covered.

Begin by threading a blunt needle with the embroidery yarn, and inserting the needle from the back to the front at the centre of the

Finishing touches

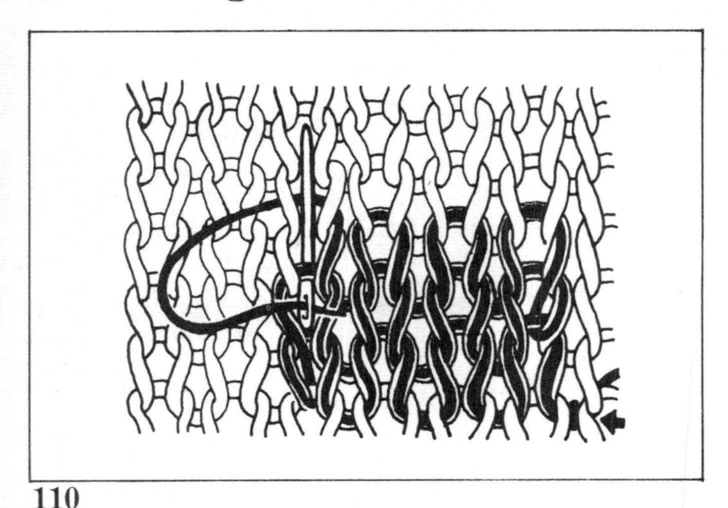
110

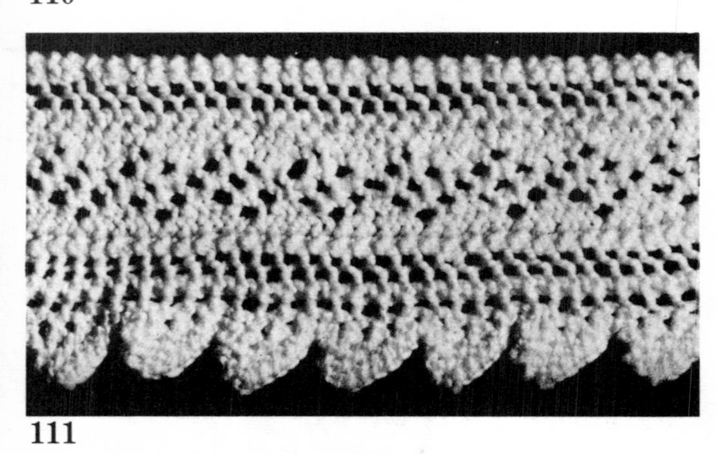
111

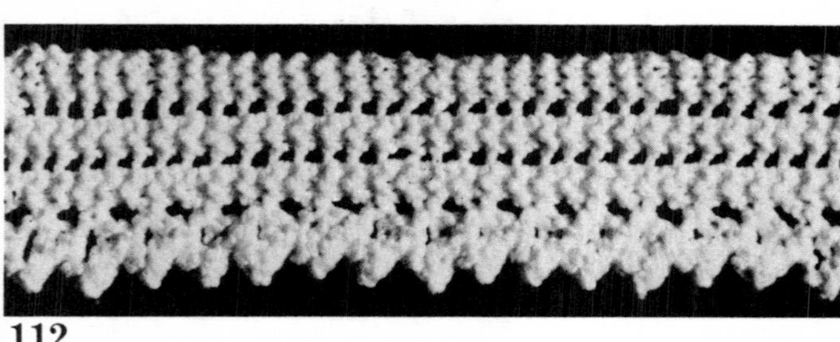
112

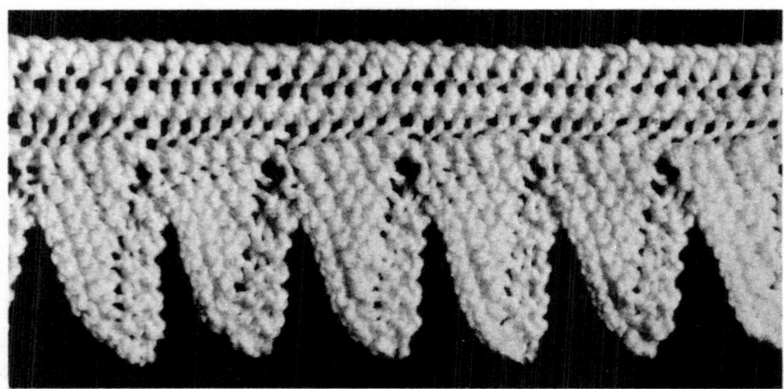
113

stitch (fig. 108), leaving an end on the wrong side which later can be sewn in. Now insert the needle as shown on figs. 108 and 109 through both strands of the stitch above. The arrow on fig. 109 shows the position for inserting the needle for the following stitch. Continue in this manner to cover a row of stitches.

Fig. 110 shows the embroidery carried over several rows of knitting. To continue on the row above, insert the needle under the head of the stitch, turn the work upside down and continue in the opposite direction over the following row.

It is important that the embroidery should be the same tension as the knitted fabric to prevent any distortion, and care should be taken that the knitted stitches are covered.

Lace edgings

To get the best results from these delicate edgings it is best to work them in either cotton or fine yarn with fine needles. They usually have a straight edge which is attached to the garment you are making, and are ideal finishes for articles such as fabric table cloths, table mats, pillow slips, and even sheets. The width of the edging is determined by the pattern rows but the length depends on the number of rows worked and can therefore be any length you wish. You will find that 'y fwd' is used frequently in these patterns. These are always treated as extra stitches, unless otherwise stated in the pattern, and will therefore be allowed for in the following rows; so be careful not to drop these extra stitches and do count your stitches carefully. You will find yourself in difficulties if you accidentally 'lose' these stitches.

Crystal Edging (fig. 111)

Cast on 18 sts.

Preparation row: [Wrong side] K 6, p 7, k 5.

1st row: Sl 1, k 2, y fwd, k 2 tog, k 2, k 2 tog, y fwd, k 5, y fwd, k 2 tog, [y fwd, k 1] twice.

2nd row: K 6, y fwd, k 2 tog, p 7, k 2, y fwd, k 2 tog, k 1.

3rd row: Sl 1, k 2, y fwd, k 2 tog, k 1, [k 2 tog, y fwd]

twice, k 4, y fwd, k 2 tog, [y fwd, k 1] twice, k 2.
4th row: K 8, y fwd, k 2 tog, p 7, k 2, y fwd, k 2 tog, k 1.
5th row: Sl 1, k 2, y fwd, k 2 tog, [k 2 tog, y fwd] 3 times k 3, y fwd, k 2 tog, [y fwd, k 1] twice, k 4.
6th row: K 10, y fwd, k 2 tog, p 7, k 2, y fwd, k 2 tog, k 1.
7th row: Sl 1, k 2, y fwd, k 2 tog, k 1, [k 2 tog, y fwd] twice, k 4, y fwd, k 2 tog, [y fwd, k 1] twice, k 6.
8th row: Cast off 8, k 3, y fwd, k 2 tog, p 7, k 2, y fwd, k 2 tog, k 1. These eight rows form patt and are rep for length required.

Loop edging (fig. 112)

Cast on 11 sts.
Preparation row: K.
1st row: K 3, [y fwd, sl 1, k 1, psso, k 1] twice, [y fwd] twice, k 1, [y fwd] twice, k 1.
2nd row: [K 2, p 1] 4 times, k 3. (On this row each double y fwd is treated as 2 sts, the first being knitted, the second purled).
3rd row: K 3, y fwd, sl 1, k 1, psso, k 1, y fwd, sl 1, k 1, psso, k 7.
4th row: Cast off 4 sts, k 3, p 1, k 2, p 1, k 3.
These four rows form patt and are rep for length required.

Shark's tooth edging (fig. 113)

Cast on 8 sts.
Preparation row: K.
1st row: Sl 1, k 1, [y fwd, k 2 tog] twice, y fwd, k 2.
2nd row: K 2, y fwd, k 2, [y fwd, k 2 tog] twice, k 1.
3rd row: Sl 1, k 1, [y fwd, k 2 tog] twice, k 2, y fwd, k 2.
4th row: K 2, y fwd, k 4, [y fwd, k 2 tog] twice, k 1.
5th row: Sl 1, k 1, [y fwd, k 2 tog] twice, k 4, y fwd, k 2.
6th row: K 2, y fwd, k 6, [y fwd, k 2 tog] twice, k 1.
7th row: Sl 1, k 1, [y fwd, k 2 tog] twice, k 6, y fwd, k 2.
8th row: K 2, y fwd, k 8, [y fwd, k 2 tog] twice, k 1.
9th row: Sl 1, k 1, [y fwd, k 2 tog] twice, k 8, y fwd, k 2.
10th row: K 2, y fwd, k 10, [y fwd, k 2 tog] twice, k 1.
11th row: Sl 1, k 1, [y fwd, k 2 tog] twice, k 10, y fwd, k 2.
12th row: Cast off 11 sts, k 2, [y fwd, k 2 tog] twice, k 1.
These 12 rows form patt and are rep for length required.

Crochet in knitting

Many knitting patterns include crochet buttons and edgings in the making-up instructions. Although this book is dealing with knitting techniques we have included instructions for working some crochet to help you with your knitting patterns. For the complete novice who is unable to understand the instructions given below we suggest that they seek the advice from a crochet guide or person who can crochet. The instructions below are very simple and will only take a short time to master. Abbreviations are shown on page 7.

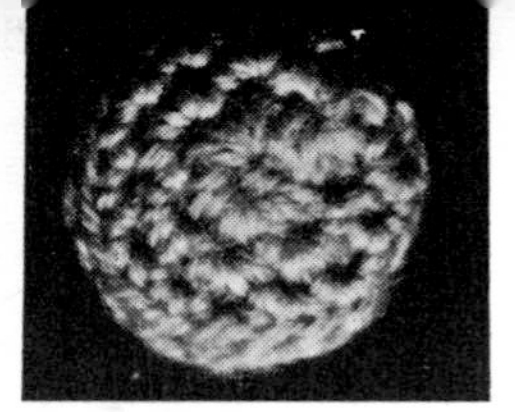

114

115

116

Round buttons (fig. 114)

Work 3 chain and join into a circle with a sl st.
1st round: Work 6 dc into circle, join with a sl st into first dc.
2nd round: Work 2 dc into each dc of previous round, joining with a sl st into first dc. Rep this round until button mould is covered.
Last round: * Miss 1 dc, 1 dc into next dc; rep from * to end, joining with a sl st into first dc. Slip crochet cover over button mould and draw together under button, leaving an end of yarn for sewing on button. An additional trim may be added by working an additional row of sl st around outer edge of button after cover has been made.

Small picot edging (fig. 115)

Make a chain of multiples of 6 plus 2, turn.
1st row: 1 dc into 2nd ch from hook, * 2 ch, miss 2 ch, 1 dc into next ch; rep from * to end, 1 ch, turn.
2nd row: * 1 dc into space, 3 ch, 1 sl st into first of these 3 ch to form a picot, 1 dc into same space, 1 dc into next dc, 2 ch, miss 2 ch, 1 dc into next dc; rep from * to end.

Scallop edging (fig. 116)

Make a chain of multiples of 6, turn.
1st row: * Miss 2 ch, work 5 tr into next ch, miss 2 ch, 1 sl st into next ch; rep from * to end.

Making up knitted garments

Most reliable patterns give detailed pressing and making up instructions and it is essential to spend plenty of time on this most important part of your work; with practise you will soon produce garments with a professional finish. Remember too, that when you have finished knitting you have made your own fabric which then has to be made up like any other piece of fabric.

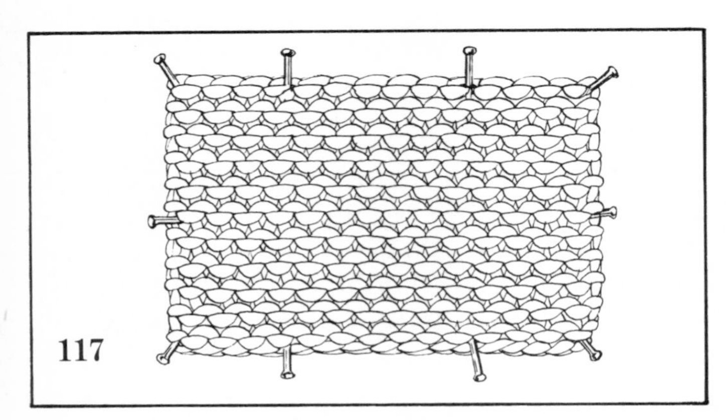

117

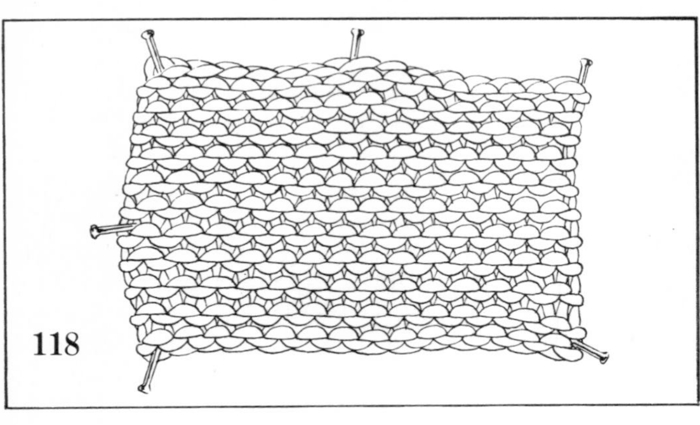

118

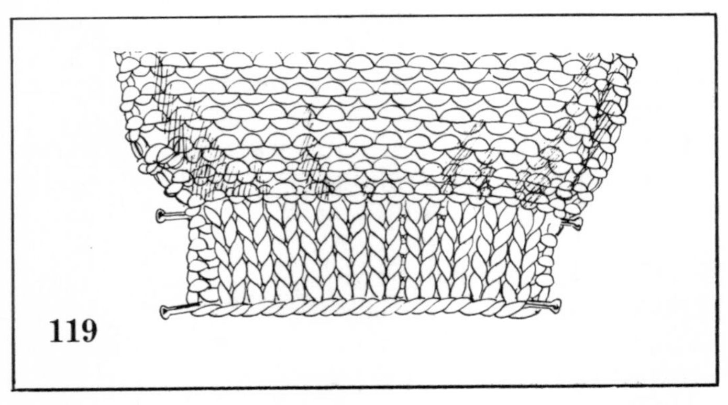

119

When pressing is directed, correctly place each *right* side down on to a well-padded surface, taking care to keep the stitches and rows running in straight lines (fig. 117). Do not stretch any part of the fabric or pin out incorrectly (fig. 118). Do not, at first, press ribbed borders but press the main part of each piece as given in the instructions. Wait until the fabric has cooled then take out the pins. If there is a ribbed border, push the ribbing together so that only the knitted stitches show and pin as illustrated, then press as given in the instructions (fig. 119). Use a blunt-ended wool needle and the original yarn for sewing together. If the yarn is not suitable for sewing, use a 3-ply yarn in the same shade. Joining seams is largely a matter of individual choice but the two methods most often used are the woven flat seam and the backstitch seam.

Woven flat seam

If you have slipped the first stitch and knitted the last stitch on every row, you will find you have a small 'pip' at the end of every two rows. With the right sides of the work facing each other, place your finger between the two pieces to be joined, insert the needle from the front through both pieces below the corresponding 'pips'; pull the yarn through and insert the needle from the back through both pieces of fabric, and pull the yarn through. The stitch should be the length of a small running stitch. Repeat this along the seam matching the 'pips' on each piece. Th seam will then be drawn together and will be flat and very neat when pressed. This method is always used for baby garments, ribbing and underclothes (fig. 120).

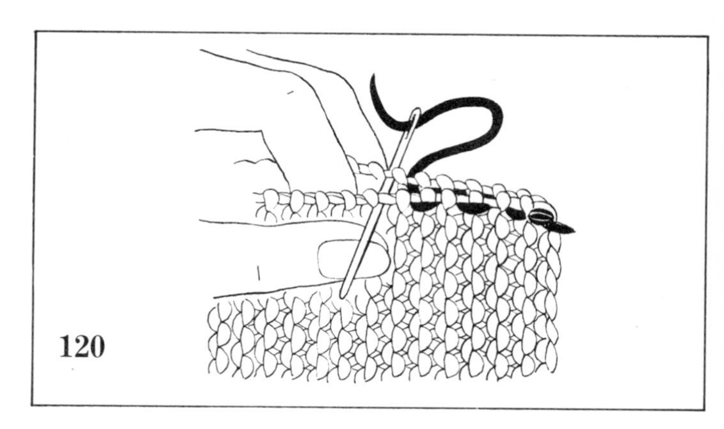

120

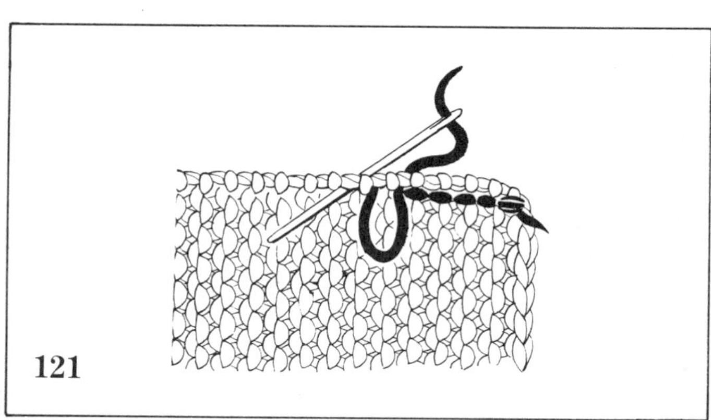

121

Backstitch seam

This method is firm, yet elastic, and it keeps the garment in shape and will not break if roughly treated. Place the two pieces to be joined right sides together, join in the sewing yarn by making three small running stitches over each other, one stitch in from the edge.

Put the needle back into the beginning of the running stitch and pull the yarn through; insert the needle from the back through the fabric and beyond the first running stitch the length of another small stitch and pull the yarn through. Repeat this along the seam, keeping stitches neat and even and one stitch in from the edge of both pieces of fabric, taking care not to split the knitted stitches (fig. 121). Your pattern will tell you which seams to sew first but they are usually worked in the following order:

Shoulder seams

Backstitch firmly one stitch from the edge, taking the stitching across the steps of shaping in a straight line. Press on the wrong side. For heavy sweaters, reinforce these seams with ribbon or tape.

Set-in sleeves

Mark centre top of sleeve and pin in position to shoulder seam, then pin cast-off stitches to cast-off underarm stitches of body. Keeping the sleeve smooth on either side of the shoulder seam, work fine backstitch round the curves as near the edge as possible.

Side and sleeve seams

Join with backstitch in one complete seam as near the edge as possible.

Sewing on collars

Place right side of collar to wrong side of neck, matching centre backs and taking care not to stretch the neckline. Join with a firm backstitch as near the edge as possible.

Making up knitted garments

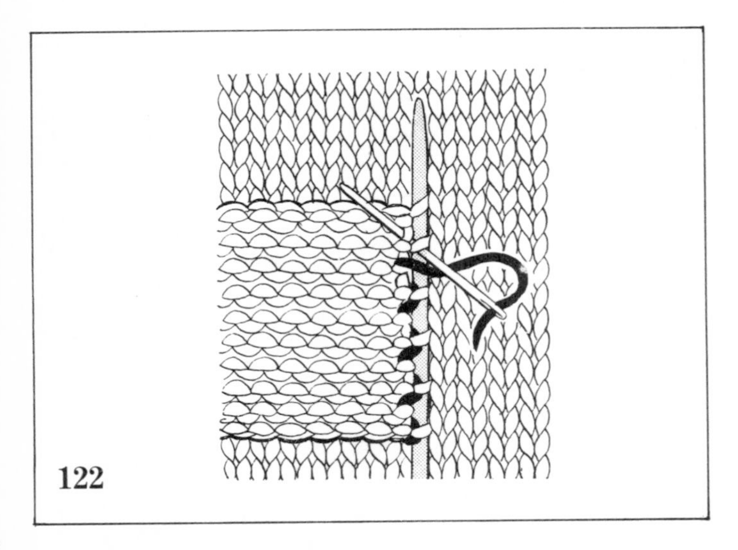
122

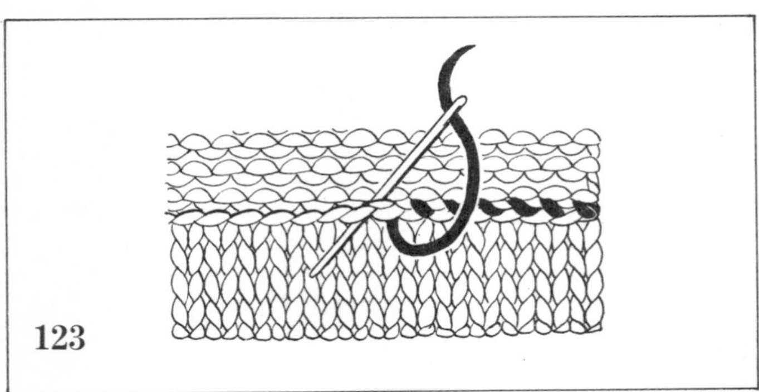
123

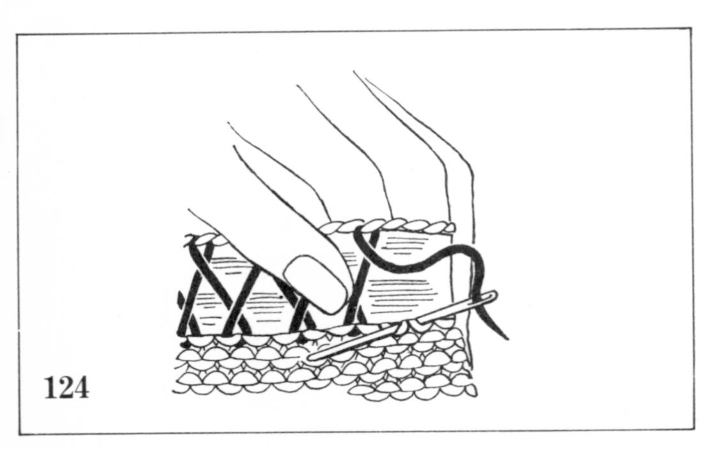
124

Helpful hints in making up

Sewn-on bands

For sewn-on bands worked separately, use a woven flat seam matching row for row.

Sewn-on pockets or any applied band or decoration

Use slip stitching, taking care to keep the line absolutely straight. A good way to ensure a straight sewing line is to thread a fine knitting needle, pointed at both ends, under every alternate stitch of the line you wish to follow and catch one stitch from the edge of the piece to be applied and one stitch from the needle alternately, using matching yarn (fig. 122).

Sewing hems

To sew hems which have not already been knitted up (as shown on page 39) use a fine slip stitch, matching stitch for stitch (fig. 123).

Skirt waist

For a skirt waist using casing, or herring-bone stitch, cut elastic to the size required and join into a circle. Mark off the waistline of the skirt and the elastic into quarters and pin the elastic into position on the wrong side, taking care to distribute the knitting evenly. Hold the knitting over the fingers of the left hand and with the elastic slightly stretched, work a herringbone stitch, catching the elastic above and below as you work (fig. 124).

Ribbon facing

Lightly press the part to be faced before sewing on the ribbon, taking care not to stretch the edge. Choose a soft ribbon, available in a wide selection of colours and widths from most stores. When facing buttonhole bands, the ribbon should be wide enough to cover the strip with $\frac{1}{4}''$ to $\frac{1}{2}''$ to spare on either side and a $\frac{1}{2}''$ hem top and bottom. Take great care not to stretch the knitting when measuring the ribbon lengths, and cut the facing for buttonhole and button bands at the same time, so that they match exactly. Fold in the turnings, pin ribbon to the wrong side, easing the knitting evenly; check that the buttonholes are evenly spaced. With matching silk, slip stitch with the smallest possible stitches along all edges. Cut buttonholes along the straight grain of the ribbon, remembering to make them wide enough for the buttons. Oversew the ribbon and knitting together to avoid fraying, then neaten by working button-hole stitch round the buttonhole with the original yarn (fig. 125).

Grosgrain ribbon can be shaped to fit a curved edge by pressing with a hot iron and gently stretching one edge until the desired curve is made.

When facing with ribbon on two edges at right angles, seam outside edge in place first, then fold ribbon into a mitred corner before seaming inside edge (fig. 126).

Net can be used for facings, as it is very light but has just enough body for the hem of a skirt. Cut the net three times the required depth and fold in three lengthwise. Pin to the wrong side of the part to be faced, turning up two rows of the knitting if it is in stocking-stitch, and slip stitch top and bottom.

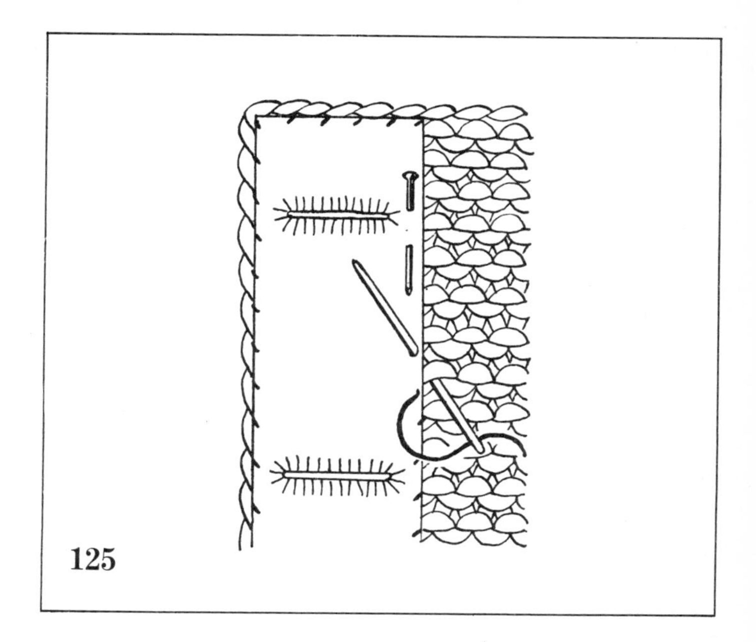

125

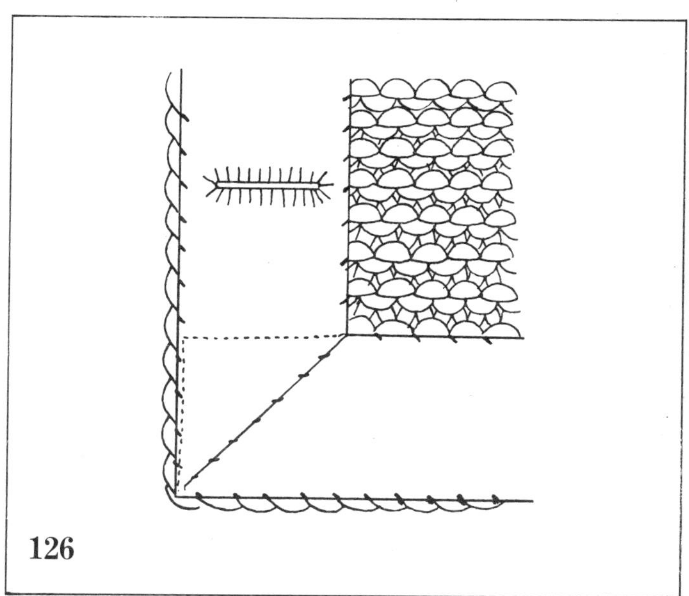

126

Decorative seam

Lapped seams can be used on yokes and square-set sleeves when a firm fabric stitch has been knitted. Place the parts to be joined right sides together, with the underneath part projecting ½″ beyond the upper part. Backstitch along edge, turn to the right side and backstitch ½″ from the first seam through both thicknesses of fabric, taking care to keep the line of stitching straight and even.

Shrinking

Provided 100% pure wool has been used, parts of garments which have stretched can be shrunk back into place. Place the part to be shrunk face down on to a well padded surface, pat and pin into shape and size required. Cover with a really wet cloth and hold a hot iron over the cloth to make plenty of steam. Alternately steam then pat into shape, taking out the pins as soon as possible, until the required shape is achieved, then leave without handling until quite dry.

Making up knitted garments

127

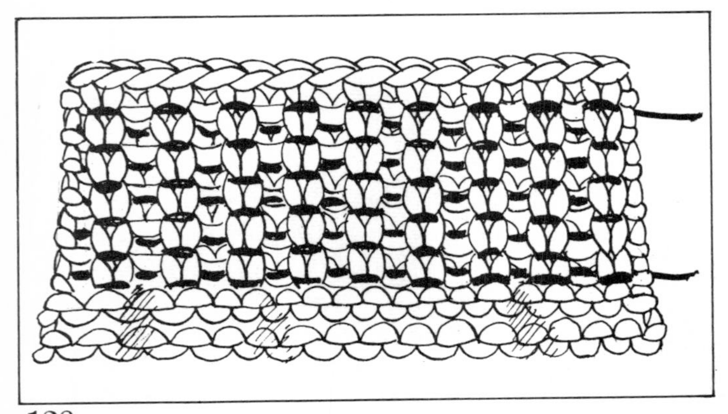

128

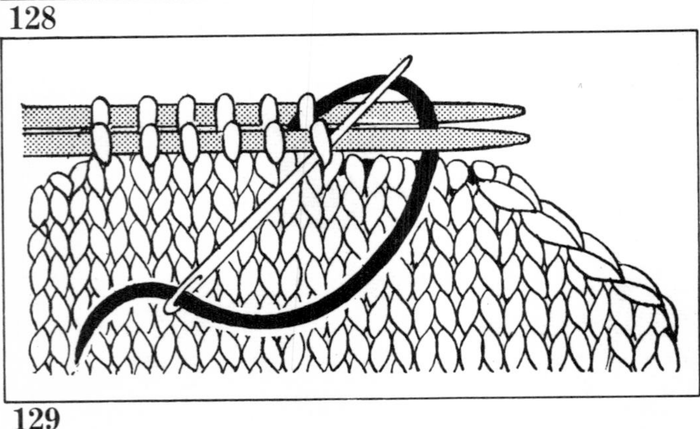

129

Sewing in zip fasteners

Pin the zip into the opening, taking great care not to stretch the knitting. Sew in zip using backstitch, keeping the grain of the knitting straight. Except on very heavy garments, it is better to use Nylon zips as they are lighter and more flexible (fig. 127).

Skirt lining

It is generally accepted that it is better not to line a knitted skirt but to wear a waist-length petticoat. If you are unable to purchase this ready-made, buy lining material the exact shade of your skirt, press the knitted pieces and cut lining pieces to match the skirt, allowing extra width for waist seams and hems. Pin waist darts in lining to fit knitting, stitch darts, sew seams and hem; turn in the seam allowance at the top and oversew to the skirt waist. Finish with a petersham waistband, hooks and eyes and sew in a zip fastener. Do not sew the lining to seams or hem of the knitted skirt.

Elasticated knitting

Better-fitting welts and sock tops can be made by weaving shirring elastic into the knitted fabric on the wrong side of the work. This method can be used for any stitch but it works particularly well in k 1, p 1 rib. If matching elastic is used it is practically invisible.

Elasticated k 1, p 1 rib

Cast on an even number of stitches. Join elastic at end of row and hold slightly stretched over index finger of left hand.

1st row: [Right side] Hold elastic at back of work, * put point of right-hand needle through front of next stitch under elastic and k 1, yarn forward, p 1 in normal way, yarn back; repeat from * to end of row.
2nd row: Hold elastic to front of work, * put point of

right-hand needle over elastic and into front of next stitch and k 1, yarn forward, put point of right-hand needle purlwise through next stitch and under elastic and p 1, yarn back; repeat from * to end. Adjust tension, twist elastic and yarn, turn. Repeat these two rows (fig. 128).

Elastic can also be added by darning in on the wrong side of the work when garment is finished.

Grafting stitches

This means the joining of two sets of stitches, horizontally and invisibly. Here we give you the method of joining two pieces of fabric worked in stocking-stitch. The pieces should each contain the same number of stitches and should be arranged on needles of the size used for the knitting of the fabric. Break off the yarn from the last piece worked leaving an end approximately one-and-a-half times the length of the row to be worked. Place *wrong* sides together with the needle points facing to the right. Using a blunt-ended wool needle threaded with the end of yarn, work as follows. * Insert sewing needle *knitwise* through the first stitch on the front needle, draw yarn through and slip stitch off knitting needle; insert sewing needle *purlwise* through next stitch on front needle, draw yarn through and leave stitch on knitting needle; insert sewing needle *purlwise* through first stitch on back needle, draw yarn through and slip stitch off knitting needle; insert sewing needle *knitwise* through next stitch on back needle, draw yarn through and leave on knitting needle; repeat from * until all stitches are worked off both needles. Before sewing in end of yarn, it may be necessary to pull the stitches with the sewing needle until they are all of an even depth and the join looks invisible. This method of joining is usually used for the toes of socks (fig. 129).

Hints on care and washing

Pure wool

Although many hand-knitting wools are now given shrink-resist finishes, the structure of hand-knitted fabrics makes elementary care in washing essential if the best results are to be obtained. If hand-knitted garments are never allowed to become badly soiled they will be easily washable, and it is important to remember that pure wool stays clean longest.

Washing should be done in warm, *not* hot, water. Detergents and soap powders should always be dissolved completely and never brought into direct contact with the garments. Rubbing should be avoided and the lather gently squeezed through the fibres. All traces of soap or detergent should be rinsed out in tepid water. A loose wringer or a spin dryer may be used to remove surplus water. Wringing by hand should be avoided. The garment should then be arranged on a clean smooth surface and gently eased into its original shape. If it is finally dried on a clothes horse the sleeves should not be allowed to hang down. When dry, the garment should be lightly pressed on the wrong side with a warm iron over a damp cloth.

Nylon

Wash often – wash soon. Nylon garments can be washed by hand or by machine. Use hot water (60°C, 140°F) for 'whites', and hand-hot (48°C, 118°F) for 'coloureds'. Use a synthetic detergent in hard water districts and dissolve thoroughly. Rinse until the water is clear. Do not wring knitwear but squeeze and dry flat. If spin drying is required, stop after the first rush of water from the outlet ceases.

Other man-made fibres

Warm wash (40°C) as soon as the garment gets soiled. Use a soapless detergent or, if your water is soft, soap flakes or powder dissolved in water pleasantly hot to the hand. Rinse thoroughly. Remove excess moisture by squeezing lightly, or rolling in a towel, or giving it a short spin dry. Finally, smooth garment and dry flat away from direct heat. Courtelle garments can be machine-washed, following instructions for delicate fabrics. When the garment is completely dry, fold neatly and store in a drawer, not on a hanger.

If absolutely necessary, synthetics may be pressed with a cool iron and a dry cloth.

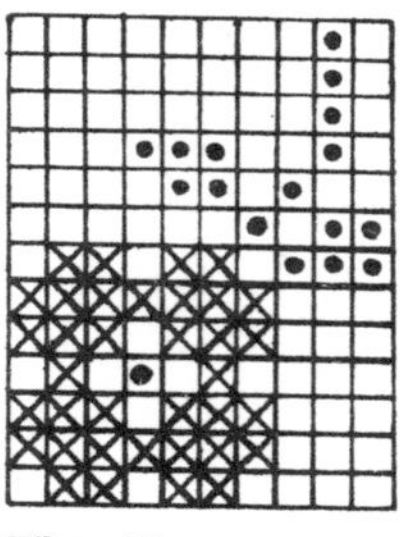

Embroidered jacket

Shown on front cover

Instructions are for a 32″ bust. Changes for 34″ and 36″ sizes are given in brackets.
MATERIALS: 5(5–6) ozs of Jaeger Celtic Spun in main shade, A; 2(2–2) ozs each in contrasting colours B and C. One pair each Nos 9 and 11 needles. Four press studs.
MEASUREMENTS: To fit a 32″(34″–36″) bust. Length at centre back: 19″(19½–20″).
TENSION: 6 sts and 8 rows to 1″ over st-st on No 9 needles.
LEFT FRONT: With No 11 needles and B cast on 95(101–107) sts. **1st row:** With B, k 2, * p 1, k 1; rep from * to last st, k 1. **2nd row:** With B, * k 1, p 1; rep from * to last st, k 1. **3rd row:** With C, as 1st row. **4th row:** With C, as 2nd row. Rep these four rows 4 times more. [Do not break wool when changing colour but carry it up the side of the work when not in use.] Change to No 9 needles and cont with A. **Next row:** K to last 18 sts, turn leaving these 18 sts on a holder. **Next row:** P. Cont on rem 77(83–89) sts. **1st row:** K to last 2 sts, k 2 tog. **2nd row:** P. Rep these 2 rows 26(28–30) times more. 50(54–58) sts. **Commence sleeve. Next row:** Cast on 6 sts, k to last 2 sts, k 2 tog. Keeping sleeve edge straight cont to dec at centre front edge on every alt row until 33(36–39) sts rem, then on every foll 4th row until 27(30–33) sts rem. Work 5(3–1) rows without shaping, ending at sleeve edge. **Shape shoulder**. Keeping neck edge straight, cast off 6(6–6) sts at beg of next row, and 5(6–7) sts at beg of foll 3 alt rows. Work 1 row. Cast off 6(6–6) rem sts.
RIGHT FRONT: With No 11 needles and B cast on 95(101–107) sts. Work 20 rows in ribbing as given for Left Front. **Next row:** Rib 18 sts and sl on to a holder. Change to No 9 needles, and with A, k to end. **Next row:** P. Cont as folls: **1st row:** K 2 tog, k to end. **2nd row:** P. Rep 1st and 2nd rows 26(28–30) times more, then 1st row once. **Commence sleeve. Next row:** Cast on 6 sts, p to end. Complete to match Left Front, working one more row before commencing shoulder shaping.
BACK: With No 11 needles and B, cast on 89(95–101) sts. Work 20 rows in ribbing as for Left Front. Change to No 9 needles and cont with A in st-st. Work until back measures same as fronts to beg of sleeves, ending with a p row. **Commence sleeves**. Cast on 6 sts at beg of next 2 rows. Work until sleeve edge measures same as fronts, ending with a p row. **Shape shoulders and back of neck. Next row:** Cast off 6(6–6) sts, k 28(31–34) sts including st on needle, cast off 33(33–33) sts, k to end. Cont on last set of sts as folls: **1st row:** Cast off 6(6–6) sts, p to last 2 sts, p 2 tog. **2nd row:** K 2 tog, k to end. **3rd row:** Cast off 5(6–7) sts, p to last 2 sts, p 2 tog. Rep 2nd and 3rd rows twice more. Work 1 row. Cast off 6(6–6) rem sts. Rejoin wool to rem sts at neck edge. **1st row:** P 2 tog, p to end. **2nd row:** Cast off 5(6–7) sts, k to last 2 sts, k 2 tog. Rep 1st and 2nd rows twice more and then 1st row once. Cast off rem 6(6–6) sts.
LEFT FRONT BORDER: Sl sts from holder on to a No 11 needle and rejoin B. **1st row:** [Right side] Cast on one st, rib to end. Cont in rib and stripes on these 19 sts until border is long enough to fit along centre-front edge, and along back edge to centre of neck. Cast off firmly in rib.
RIGHT FRONT BORDER: Work as for Left Front Border, noting that first row is wrong side.
SLEEVE BORDERS: With No 11 needles and B, cast on 19 sts. Work in striped ribbing as for Left Front. Work until border is long enough to fit along sleeve edge, ending with a stripe in C. Cast off in rib.
TO MAKE UP: Press each piece lightly with warm iron and damp cloth. Sew shoulder seams. Join cast off edges of front borders neatly. Place seam at centre back of neck and sew borders to front and neck edges. Sew borders to sleeve edge. Sew side and undersleeve seams. Press seams. Sew two press studs to Left side seam on the outside at top and bottom of welt, and two press studs to right side seam on the inside in same way. Sew other halves of press studs to edges of fron welts to match. Embroider motifs from chart as required (*see Swiss darning on page 41, which will sh**ow you how to embroider on knitted fabric*).

Butterfly vest

Instructions are for a 34″ bust. Changes for 36″ and 38″ sizes are given in brackets.

MATERIALS: 8(8–9) ozs of Lee Target Motoravia 4-ply in Main shade, A. 2 ozs of same in contrast, B; 1 oz each of same in contrasts C and D. One pair each Nos 10 and 11 needles. A No 11 (International size 3·00) crochet hook.

MEASUREMENTS: To fit a 34″(36″–38″) bust. Length from shoulder: 26″(26″–26¼″).

TENSION: 7 sts and 8½ rows to 1″ over st-st on No 10 needles.

NOTE: Use a separate ball of wool for each part of the patt and ensure that wools are twisted tog when changing colour to avoid holes. If preferred the wings can be knitted completely in the first contrasting colour and the 2nd and 3rd colours embroidered afterwards.

FRONT: With No 11 needles and A, cast on 128(134–140) sts. Beg with a k row, work 11 rows st-st. K next row to form hemline. Change to No 10 needles. Beg with a k row cont in st-st. Work 2 rows. ** **Next row:** K 9(12–15) A, * 3B, 26A, 3B, 7A; rep from * ending last rep k 9(12–15) A instead of 7A. [This is first row of chart] Cont working 3 butterflies from chart with the main part of work in A. Work 2 rows in A. ** Rep from ** to ** 4 times more. [5 rows of butterflies in all]. **Work yoke**. Cont in A only. **Next row:** K 3(6–3) sts, * p 2, k 2; rep from * to last 5(8–5) sts, p 2, k 3(6–3). **Next row:** P 3(6–3) sts, * k 2, p 2; rep from * to last 5(8–5) sts, k 2, p 3(6–3). These 2 rows form yoke patt. Work 4 more rows. **Shape armholes**. Cast off 8(10–10) sts at beg of next 2 rows. Dec 1 st at each end of every foll row until 102(104–110) sts rem, then one st at each end of every alt row until 94(94–98) sts rem. Cont without shaping until armhole measures 3¼″(3¼″–3½″) from beg, measured on straight, ending with a right side row. **Shape neck**. **Next row:** Patt 33(33–33) sts, cast off 28(28–32) sts, patt to end. Complete each side separately. Keeping armhole edge straight, dec 1 st at neck edge on every row 6 times, then 1 st on every alt row 5 times. Cont without shaping until armhole measures 6¾″(6¾″–7″) from beg, measured on straight, ending at armhole edge. **Shape shoulder**. Keeping neck edge straight, cast off at beg of next and alt rows at shoulder edge, 8(8–8) sts once and 7(7–7) sts twice. Rejoin wool to rem sts at neck edge and complete to match first side working 1 more row before commencing shoulder shaping.

BACK: Work as for Front until armhole shaping is complete. Work until armholes measure 6¼″(6¼″–6½″) from beg, ending with a right side row. **Shape neck**. **Next row:** Patt 24(24–24) sts, cast off 46(46–50) sts, patt to end. Complete each side separately. **1st row:** Patt to last 2 sts, dec 1 st. **2nd row:** Dec 1 st, patt to end. **Shape shoulder**. Keeping neck edge straight, cast off at beg of next and foll alt rows at shoulder edge, 8(8–8) sts once and 7(7–7) sts twice. Rejoin wool to rem sts at neck edge. **1st row:** Dec 1 st, patt to end. **2nd row:** Patt to last 2 sts, dec 1 st. **3rd row:** Work in patt. Shape shoulder to match first side.

TO MAKE UP: Sew in all loose ends. Press each piece lightly with a warm iron and damp cloth. Join shoulder and side seams using back st. Turn up hem and slip st. **Neck border**. Join in A to back neck edge at right shoulder. With No 11 crochet hook, work a row of dc right round neck edge, working 1 dc for each 2 rows or 3 dc for each 4 sts. Turn with 1 ch and work another row right round. Break wool and fasten off. Join edges neatly. **Armhole borders.** Join wool to underarm at side seams and work 2 rows dc round armhole edges as for neck border. Press seams and borders lightly.

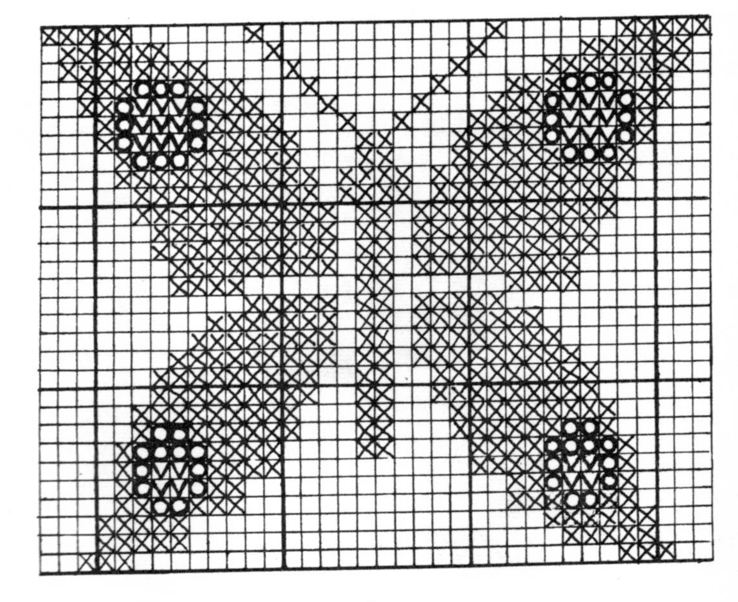

☒ B First contrasting colour

▣ C Second contrasting colour

☑ D Third contrasting colour

Sequin jacket

Instructions are for a 32″ bust. Changes for 34″, 36″, 38″ and 40″ bust are given in brackets.

MATERIALS: 5(5–6–6–7) ozs of Sirdar Fontein 4-ply Crepe in main shade, A (Aubretia); 4(4–5–5–6) ozs of same in contrast, B (Silver); contrast, C (Emerald); contrast, D (Royal); 4(4–5–5–6) strings of 8 mm sequins of each colour. 1 pair each Nos 11 and 12 needles.

MEASUREMENTS: To fit a 32″(34″–36″–38″–40″) bust. Length at centre back: $23\frac{3}{4}$″(24″–$24\frac{1}{2}$″–$24\frac{3}{4}$″–25″). Sleeve seam: $18\frac{1}{2}$″.

TENSION: 8 sts and 10 rows to 1″ over sequin patt on No 11 needles.

NOTE: Thread approx 1 string of sequins on each ounce of wool. Sequins from Ells & Farrier, 5 Princes Street, London W.1.

BACK: With No 11 needles and A, cast on 127(135–143–151–159) sts. **1st row:** * K 3, push sequin close to next st, k 1 tbl, bringing sequin through to front with st as it is knitted – called S1 tbl; rep from * to last 3 sts, k 3. **2nd and every alt row:** P. **3rd row:** * K 1, S1 tbl, k 2; rep from * to last 3 sts, k 1, S1 tbl, k 1. **4th row:** P. These four rows form patt and are rep throughout working in stripes as folls: 20 rows A, 20 rows B, 20 rows C and 20 rows D. When 3rd stripe is completed (C) inc at each end of first row of every stripe until there are 137(145–153–161–169) sts. Cont without shaping until work measures $16\frac{3}{4}$″, ending with a p row. **Shape armholes**. Cast off 6(7–8–9–10) sts at beg of next 2 rows. Dec 1 st at each end of next 6 rows, then at each end of next and every foll alt row until 101 (105–109–113–117) sts rem. Cont without shaping until armholes measure $6\frac{3}{4}$″(7″–$7\frac{1}{4}$″–$7\frac{1}{2}$″–$7\frac{3}{4}$″), ending with a p row. **Shape shoulders**. Cast off at beg of next and every row 6 sts 8 times and 6(7–8–9–10) sts twice. Cast off rem 41(43–45–47–49) sts.

LEFT FRONT: With No 11 needles and A, cast on 59 (63–67–71–75) sts. Work in patt as given for Back until 3rd(C) stripe has been completed. Inc 1 st at beg of next and every foll first row of each stripe until there are 64(68–72–76–80) sts. Cont without shaping until work measures same as back to underarm, ending with a p row. **Shape armholes**. Cast off 6(7–8–9–10) sts at beg of next row. Work 1 row. Dec 1 st at armhole edge on next 6 rows, then on next and every foll alt row until 46(48–50–52–54) sts rem. Cont without shaping until armhole measures $4\frac{3}{4}$″(5″–$5\frac{1}{4}$″–$5\frac{1}{2}$″–$5\frac{3}{4}$″) ending at front edge. **Shape neck.** Cast off at beg of next and every alt row 4(5–6–6–6) sts once, 4(4–4–5–6) sts once, 3 sts twice and 2 sts once. Cont without shaping until work measures same as Back to shoulder, ending at armhole edge. **Shape shoulder**. Cast off at beg of next and alt rows 6 sts 4 times and 6(7–8–9–10) sts once.

RIGHT FRONT: Work as for Left Front reversing shaping.

SLEEVES: With No 11 needles and D cast on 63 (63–67–67–71) sts and work $1\frac{1}{4}$″ in sequin patt, inc 1 st at each end of 5th and every foll 8th row until there are 101(105–109–113–117) sts at same time cont in sequin patt stripes [of 20 rows each beg with A], then cont straight until work measures $18\frac{1}{2}$″, ending on same patt row as back and sides. **Shape top**. Cast off 6(7–8–9–10) sts at beg of next 2 rows. Dec 1 st at each end of next 6 rows, then at each end of next and every foll alt row until 51 sts rem. Cast off 3 sts at beg of next 6 rows. Cast off rem sts.

TO MAKE UP: Join shoulder, side and sleeve seams using Back st. Set in sleeves. **Bands**. With No 12 needles and A, cast on 6 sts and work 2 rows in k 1, p 1 rib. Change to B and work 2 rows, then 2 rows C and 2 rows D [8 row patt]. Rep these eight rows, making bands long enough to fit round bottom, cuffs and neck and front edges, always beg and ending with A. Cast off each time in A. Pin bands in place and sew in given order, laying band under sequin knitting and working a flat seam. Very lightly press *bands* only.

Lace cardigan and skirt

Instructions are for a 34" bust, 36" hips. Changes for 36" bust, 38" hips are given in brackets.
MATERIALS: Cardigan. 17(18) ozs Jaeger Summer-spun. **Skirt.** 17(18) ozs of same. One pair each Nos 11 and 13 needles. Five buttons for cardigan. Waist length of 1" wide elastic for each skirt.
MEASUREMENTS: Cardigan. To fit a 34"(36") bust. Length from shoulder: 29"(29¼"). Sleeve seam: 16½" (16½"). **Skirt.** Length: 40"(40").
TENSION: 6 sts and 8½ rows to 1" on No 11 needles.

CARDIGAN

BACK: With No 11 needles cast on 125(133) sts. Beg with a k row, work 13 rows st-st. K next row on wrong side to mark hemline. **Next row:** K. **Next row:** P. Cont in patt. **1st row:** [Both sizes] K 1, * y fwd, sl 1, k 2 tog, psso, y fwd, k 1; rep from * to end. **2nd and every alt row:** P. **3rd row:** [Smaller size only] K 1, * y fwd, sl 1, k 2 tog, psso, y fwd, k 5; rep from * to last 4 sts, y fwd, sl 1, k 2 tog, psso, y fwd, k 1. **3rd row:** [Larger size only] K 5, * y fwd, sl 1, k 2 tog, psso, y fwd, k 5; rep from * to end. **5th row:** As 3rd row. **7th row:** [Smaller size only] K 1, * k 3, y fwd, sl 1, k 1, psso, k 1, k 2 tog, y fwd; rep from * to last 4 sts, k 4. **7th row:** [Larger size only] K 3, k 2 tog, y fwd, * k 3, y fwd, sl 1, k 1, psso, k 1, k 2 tog, y fwd; rep from * to last 8 sts, k 3, y fwd, sl 1, k 1, psso, k 3. **8th row:** P. These eight rows form patt. Work 8 more rows. Keeping patt correct, dec 1 st at each end of next row, then every foll 16th row until 109(117) sts rem. Cont until back measures 22"(22") from hemline, ending with a p row. **Shape armholes.** Cast off at beg of next and foll rows 6(6) sts twice and 2(2) sts twice. Dec 1 st at beg of every row until 85(93) sts rem. Cont until armholes measure 6¾"(7") measured straight, ending with a p row. **Shape shoulders.** Cast off at beg of next and foll rows 6(7) sts 6 times and 7(7) sts twice. Cast off rem 35(37) sts for back of neck.
LEFT FRONT: Pocket lining. With No 2 needles cast on 29 sts. Work 36 rows in st-st ending with a p row. Cont as folls: **1st row:** K 1, * y fwd, sl 1, k 2 tog, psso, y fwd, k 1; rep from * to end. **2nd row:** P. **3rd row:** K 5, [y fwd, sl 1, k 2 tog, psso, y fwd, k 5] 3 times. Break yarn and leave sts on holder. With No 11 needles cast on 61(65) sts. Beg with a k row work 13 rows st-st. K next row on wrong side to form hemline. **Next row:** K. **Next row:** P. Cont in patt. **1st row:** [Both sizes] K 1, * y fwd, sl 1, k 2 tog, psso, y fwd, k 1; rep from * to end. **2nd and every alt row:** P. **3rd row:** [Smaller size only] K 1, [y fwd, sl 1, k 2 tog, psso, y fwd, k 5] 3 times, y fwd, sl 1, k 2 tog, psso, y fwd, k 13, [y fwd, sl 1, k 2 tog, psso, y fwd, k 5] twice, y fwd, sl 1, k 2 tog, psso, y fwd, k 1. **3rd row:** [Larger size only] K 5, [y fwd, sl 1, k 2 tog, psso, y fwd, k 5] 3 times, y fwd, sl 1, k 2 tog, psso, y fwd, k 13, [y fwd, sl 1, k 2 tog, psso, y fwd, k 5] twice, y fwd, sl 1, k 2 tog, psso, y fwd, k 1. **5th row:** As 3rd. **7th row:** [Smaller size only] K 1, [k 3, y fwd, sl 1, k 1, psso, k 1, k 2 tog, y fwd] 3 times, k 3, y fwd, sl 1, k 1, psso, k 9, k 2 tog, y fwd, [k 3, y fwd, sl 1, k 1, psso, k 1, k 2 tog, y fwd] twice, k 4. **7th row:** [Larger size only] K 3, k 2 tog, y fwd, [k 3, y fwd, sl 1, k 1, psso, k 1, k 2 tog, y fwd] 3 times, k 3, y fwd, sl 1, k 1, psso, k 9, k 2 tog, y fwd, [k 3, y fwd, sl 1, k 1, psso, k 1, k 2 tog, y fwd] twice, k 4. **9th row:** [Smaller size only] K 1, [y fwd, sl 1, k 2 tog, psso, y fwd, k 1] 7 times, y fwd, sl 1, k 1, psso, k 7, k 2 tog, y fwd, k 1, [y fwd, sl 1, k 2 tog, psso, y fwd, k 1] 5 times. **9th row:** [Larger size only] K 1, [y fwd, sl 1, k 2 tog, psso, y fwd, k 1] 8 times, y fwd, sl 1, k 1, psso, k 7, k 2 tog, y fwd, k 1, [y fwd, sl 1, k 2 tog, psso, y fwd, k 1] 5 times. **11th row:** [Smaller size only] K 1, [y fwd, sl 1, k 2 tog, psso, y fwd, k 5] 3 times, y fwd, sl 1, k 2 tog, psso, y fwd, k 2, y fwd, sl 1, k 1, psso, k 5, k 2 tog, y fwd, k 2, [y fwd, sl 1, k 2 tog, psso, y fwd, k 5] twice, y fwd, sl 1, k 2 tog, psso, y fwd, k 1. **11th row:** [Larger size only] K 5, [y fwd, sl 1, k 2 tog, psso, y fwd, k 5] 3 times, y fwd, sl 1, k 2 tog, psso, y fwd, k 2, y fwd, sl 1, k 1, psso, k 5, k 2 tog, y fwd, k 2, [y fwd, sl 1, k 2 tog, psso, y fwd, k 5] twice y fwd, sl 1, k 2 tog, psso, y fwd, k 1. **13th row:** [Smaller size only] K 1, [y fwd, sl 1, k 2 tog, psso, y fwd, k 5] 3 times, y fwd, sl 1, k 2 tog, psso, y fwd, k 3, y fwd, sl 1, k 1, psso, k 3, k 2 tog, y fwd, k 3, [y fwd, sl 1, k 2 tog, psso, y fwd, k 5] twice, y fwd, sl 1, k 2 tog, psso, y fwd, k 1. **13th row:** [Larger size only] K 5, [y fwd, sl 1, k 2 tog, psso, y fwd, k 5) 3 times, y fwd, sl 1, k 2 tog, psso, y fwd, k 3, y fwd, sl 1, k 1, psso, k 3, k 2 tog, y fwd, k 3, [y fwd, sl 1, k 2 tog, psso, y fwd, k 5] twice, y fwd, sl 1, k 2 tog, psso, y fwd, k 1. **15th row:** [Smaller size only] K 1, [k 3, y fwd, sl 1, k 1, psso, k 1, k 2 tog, y fwd] 3 times, k 3, y fwd, sl 1, k 1, psso, k 2, y fwd, sl 1, k 1, psso, k 1, k 2 tog, y fwd, k 2, k 2 tog, y fwd, [k 3, y fwd,

Lace cardigan and skirt

sl 1, k 1, psso, k 1, k 2 tog, y fwd] twice, k 4. **15th row:** [Larger size only] K 3, k 2 tog, y fwd, [k 3, y fwd, sl 1, k 1, psso, k 1, k 2 tog, y fwd] 3 times, k 3, y fwd, sl 1, k 1, psso, k 2, y fwd, sl 1, k 1, psso, k 1, k 2 tog, y fwd, k 2, k 2 tog, y fwd, [k 3, y fwd, sl 1, k 1, psso, k 1, k 2 tog, y fwd] twice, k 4. **16th row:** P. These 16 rows form patt. Dec 1 st at beg of next row, then on foll two 16th rows. [58(62) sts] Work 1 row. **Work pocket. Next row:** Patt 17(21) sts, cast off 29 sts firmly k-wise, patt to end. **Next row:** Patt to end, working pocket lining sts in place of those cast off. Patt 12 rows. Dec 1 st at beg of next row, then every foll 16th row until 53(57) sts rem. Work until front measures 22″(22″) from hemline, ending at side edge. **Shape armhole and front. 1st row:** Cast off 6(6) sts, patt to last 2 sts, dec 1 st. **2nd row:** Work in patt. **3rd row:** Cast off 2(2) sts, patt to end. **4th row:** Work in patt. **5th row:** Dec 1 st, patt to last 2 sts, dec 1 st. **6th row:** Work in patt. **7th row:** Dec 1 st, patt to end. **8th row:** Work in patt. Rep 5th to 8th rows inclusive once more. Keeping armhole edge straight cont to dec for front on next row, then on every foll 4th row until 25(28) sts rem. Work 1 row, ending at armhole edge. **Shape shoulder.** Keeping neck edge straight, cast off at beg of next and alt rows at shoulder edge, 6(7) sts 3 times. Work 1 row. Cast off rem 7(7) sts.

RIGHT FRONT: Work pocket lining as for Left Front. With No 11 needles cast on 61(65) sts. Work hem as given for Left Front. Cont in patt. **1st row:** [Both sizes] K 1, * y fwd, sl 1, k 2 tog, psso, y fwd, k 1; rep from * to end. **2nd and every alt row:** P. **3rd row:** [Smaller size only] K 1, [y fwd, sl 1, k 2 tog, psso, y fwd, k 5] twice, y fwd, sl 1, k 2 tog, psso, y fwd, k 13, [y fwd, sl 1, k 2 tog, psso, y fwd, k 5] 3 times, y fwd, sl 1, k 2 tog, psso, y fwd, k 1. **3rd row:** [Larger size only] K 1, [y fwd, sl 1, k 2 tog, psso, y fwd, k 5] twice, y fwd, sl 1, k 2 tog, psso, y fwd, k 13, [y fwd, sl 1, k 2 tog, psso, y fwd, k 5] 4 times. This sets patt. Work 13 more rows. Dec 1 st at end of next row, then on 2 foll 16th rows. Work 1 row. **Work pocket. Next row:** Patt 12 sts, cast off 29 sts firmly k-wise, patt to end. **Next row:** Patt to end, working pocket lining sts in place of those cast off. Complete to match Left Front reversing shaping.

SLEEVES: With No 11 needles cast on 53(53) sts. Beg with a k row work 13 rows st-st. K next row to form hemline. **Next row:** K. **Next row:** P. Cont in patt. **1st row:** K 1, * y fwd, sl 1, k 2 tog, psso, y fwd, k 1; rep from * to end. **2nd and every alt row:** P. **3rd row:** K 1, [y fwd, sl 1, k 2 tog, psso, y fwd, k 5] twice, y fwd, sl 1, k 2 tog, psso, y fwd, k 13, [y fwd, sl 1, k 2 tog, psso, y fwd, k 5] twice, y fwd, sl 1, k 2 tog, psso, y fwd, k 1. This sets patt. Work 13 more rows. Inc 1 st at each end of next and every foll 8th row until there are 69(69) sts. **Smaller size only.** Inc 1 st at each end of every 12th row, and for **larger size only** cont to inc 1 st at each end of every foll 8th row until there are 77(81) sts. Cont without shaping until sleeve measures 16½″(16½″) from hemline, ending with a p row. **Shape top.** Cast off at beg of next and foll rows, 6(6) sts twice and 2(2) sts twice. Dec 1 st at beg of every row until 33 sts rem. Cast off 2 sts at beg of next 6 rows. Cast off rem 21 sts.

BORDER: With No 13 needles cast on 25 sts. **1st row:** K 12, sl 1 p-wise with yarn at back of st, to mark folding line, k 12. **2nd row:** P. Rep 1st and 2nd rows eight times more. **Next row:** K 4, cast off 4, k 4 including st already on needle, sl 1 p-wise, k 4, cast off 4, k to end. **Next row:** P to end, casting on 4 sts over those cast off on previous row. Cont until border is long enough to fit along centre front and neck edges, making four more sets of buttonholes at 2½″ intervals. Cast off.

TO MAKE UP: Pin each piece out to size and shape and press with hot iron and damp cloth. Join shoulder seams. Set in sleeves. Join side and sleeve seams using back st. Turn up hems to wrong side and sl-st. Sew neatly round pocket linings. Sew border to front and neck edges. Fold on to wrong side and sl-st. Buttonhole st round buttonholes. Press seams. Sew on buttons to correspond with buttonholes.

SKIRT

FRONT: With No 11 needles cast on 157(165) sts. Work hem as given for Cardigan Back. Cont in patt. **1st row:** K 1, * y fwd, sl 1, k 2 tog, psso, y fwd, k 1; rep from * to end. **2nd and every alt row:** P. **3rd row:** K 1, * y fwd, sl 1, k 2 tog, psso, y fwd, k 5; rep from * to last 4 sts, y fwd, sl 1, k 2 tog, psso, y fwd, k 1. **5th row:** As 3rd. **7th row:** K 1, * k 3, y fwd, sl 1, k 1, psso, k 1, k 2 tog, y fwd; rep from * to last 4 sts, k 4. **8th row:** P. These eight rows form patt. Work 24 more rows. Keeping patt correct, dec 1 st at each end of next and every foll 12th row until 117(125) sts rem. Cont without shaping until front measures 32″(32″) from hemline, ending with a p row. Dec 1 st at each end of next and every foll 8th row until 107(115) sts rem, then 1 st at each end of every foll 4th row until 95(103) sts rem. Cont without shaping until front measures 40″ (40″) from hemline, ending with a p row. Cast off.

BACK: Work as for Front.

TO MAKE UP: Pin each piece out to size and shape. Press with hot iron and damp cloth. Join side seams using back st. Turn hem to wrong side and sl st. Press seams. Join narrow edges of elastic to form a ring, then sew one edge of elastic to waist edge of skirt. Work over the elastic in casing-st to hold it in position.

Classic cable cardigan

Instructions are for a 32″/34″ bust. Changes for 34″/36″, 36″/38″ and 38″/40″ sizes are given in brackets.
MATERIALS: 14(14–15–16) ozs of Jaeger Celtic Spun. One pair each Nos 7 and 10 needles. Six buttons.
MEASUREMENTS: To fit a 32″/34″(34″/36″–36″/38″–38″/40″) bust. Length at centre back: $28\frac{1}{2}$″($28\frac{1}{2}$″–$28\frac{3}{4}$″–$28\frac{3}{4}$″). Sleeve seam: 18″($18\frac{1}{2}$″–$18\frac{1}{2}$″–$18\frac{1}{2}$″).
TENSION: 7 sts and $7\frac{1}{2}$ rows to 1″ on No 7 needles.
LEFT FRONT: With No 10 needles cast on 70(74–78–82) sts. **1st row:** * P 1, k 1; rep from * to last 2 sts, p 2. **2nd row:** K 2, * p 1, k 1; rep from * to end. Rep 1st and 2nd rows once more, then 1st row once. **Next row:** K 2, * p 5, k 2 tog, k 1; rep from * to last 4(8–4–8) sts, p 4(8–4–8). [62(66–69–73) sts] Change to No 7 needles and patt. **1st row:** K 4(8–4–8) sts, p 2, * sl 1 p-wise with wool at back of st, k 4, p 2; rep from * to end. **2nd row:** K 2, * p 4, sl 1 p-wise with wool at front of st, k 2; rep from * to last 4(8–4–8) sts, p 4(8–4–8). **3rd row:** K 4 (8–4–8), p 2, * drop sl st to front of work, k 2, pick up dropped st and k it, k 2, p 2; rep from * to end. **4th row:** K 2, * p 5, k 2; rep from * to last 4(8–4–8) sts, p 4(8–4–8). **5th row:** K 4(8–4–8) sts, p 2, * k 4, sl 1 p-wise with wool at back of st, p 2; rep from * to end. **6th row:** K 2, * sl 1 p-wise with wool at front of st, p 4, k 2; rep from * to last 4(8–4–8) sts, p 4(8–4–8). **7th row:** K 4(8–4–8) sts, p 2, * k 2, sl 2 p-wise with wool at back of sts, drop sl st to front of work, sl same 2 sts back to left-hand needle, pick up dropped st and k it, k 2, p 2; rep from * to end. **8th row:** As 4th. These eight rows form patt. Cont until front measures $19\frac{1}{2}$″ from beg, ending with a wrong side row. **Shape front. 1st row:** Work to last 2 sts, dec 1 st. **2nd and 3rd rows:** Patt. **4th row:** Dec 1 st, patt to end. **5th and 6th rows:** Patt. Rep 1st to 4th rows once more. **Shape armhole. 1st row:** Cast off 7(9–9–11) sts, patt to end. **2nd row:** Patt. **3rd row:** Dec 1 st, patt to last 2 sts, dec 1 st. **4th row:** Patt. **5th row:** Dec 1 st, patt to end. **6th and 7th rows:** As 5th row. **8th row:** Patt. Rep 3rd to 8th rows once(once–twice–twice) more. **Sizes 34″/36″ and 38″/40″ only.** Rep 3rd to 5th rows once more. Keeping armhole edge straight [for all sizes] cont to dec for front on next and every foll 3rd row until 28(28–29–29) sts rem. Patt 3(3–2–2) rows, ending at armhole edge. **Shape shoulder.** Cast off 5(5–5–5) sts at beg of next row and 6(6–6–6) sts at beg of foll 3 alt rows. Patt 1 row. Cast off 5(5–6–6) rem sts.

Classic cable cardigan

RIGHT FRONT: With No 10 needles cast on 70(74–78–82) sts. **1st row:** P 2, * k 1, p 1; rep from * to end. **2nd row:** * K 1, p 1; rep from * to last 2 sts, k 2. Rep 1st and 2nd rows once more, then 1st row once. **Next row:** P 4(8–4–8) sts, * k 2 tog, k 1, p 5; rep from * to last 2 sts, k 2. Change to No 7 needles and patt. **1st row:** * P 2, sl 1 p-wise with wool at back of st, k 4; rep from * to last 6(10–6–10) sts, p 2, k 4(8–4–8). Complete to match Left Front, reversing all shapings and working one more row before commencing to shape front.

BACK: With No 10 needles cast on 139(147–155–163) sts. **1st row:** * P 1, k 1; rep from * to last st, p 1. **2nd row:** * K 1, p 1; rep from * to last st, k 1. Rep 1st and 2nd rows once more, then 1st row once. **Next row:** P 4(8–4–8) sts, * k 2 tog, k 1, p 5; rep from * to last 7(11–7–11) sts, k 2 tog, k 1, p 4(8–4–8). [122(130–136–144) sts] Change to No 7 needles and patt. **1st row:** K 4(8–4–8) sts, p 2, * sl 1 p-wise with wool at back of st, k 4, p 2; rep from * to last 4(8–4–8) sts, k 4(8–4–8). This sets patt. Cont in patt until Back measures same as Fronts to beg of armhole shaping, ending with a wrong side row. **Shape armholes.** Cast off 7(9–9–11) sts at beg of next 2 rows. Dec 1 st at beg of every row until 96(96–100–100) sts rem. Cont without shaping until armholes measure same as front armholes, ending with a wrong side row. **Shape shoulders.** Cast off 5(5–5–5) sts at beg of next 2 rows, and 6(6–6–6) sts at beg of foll 2 rows. **Shape back of neck. Next row:** Cast off 6(6–6–6) sts, patt 14(14–15–15) sts, including st already on needle, cast off 34(34–36–36) sts, patt to end. Cont on last set of sts as folls: **1st row:** Cast off 6(6–6–6) sts, patt to last 2 sts, dec 1 st. **2nd row:** Dec 1 st, patt to end. **3rd row:** As 1st. Work 1 row. Cast off 5(5–6–6) rem sts. Rejoin wool to rem sts at neck edge. **1st row:** Dec 1 st, patt to end. **2nd row:** Cast off 6(6–6–6) sts, patt to last 2 sts, dec 1 st. **3rd row:** As 1st. Cast off 5(5–6–6) rem sts.

SLEEVES: With No 10 needles cast on 47(47–51–51) sts. Work 5 rows in ribbing as given for Back. **Next row:** P 2(2–4–4) sts, * k into front and back of next st, p 5; rep from * to last 3(3–5–5) sts, k into front and back of next st, p 2(2–4–4). [55(55–59–59) sts]. Change to No 7 needles and patt. **1st row:** K 2(2–4–4) sts, * p 2, sl 1 p-wise with wool at back of st, k 4; rep from * to last 4(4–6–6) sts, p 2, k 2(2–4–4). This sets patt. Cont in patt, work 5 more rows. Keeping patt correct, inc 1 st at each end of next row, then every foll 6th row until there are 65(73–69–85) sts, and then 1 st at each end of every foll 8th row until there are 85(89–91–95) sts. Work until sleeve measures 18″(18½″–18½″–18½″) from beg, ending with a wrong side row. **Shape top.** Cast off 7(9–9–11) sts at beg of next 2 rows. Dec 1 st at beg of every row until 45(45–45–45) sts rem. Cast off at beg of next and foll rows, 2 sts 4 times, 3 sts twice and 4 sts twice. Cast off 23 rem sts.

BORDER: With No 10 needles cast on 9 sts. **Next row:** K 1, * inc 1 st by picking up loop from between needles and p into back of it, k 1, p 1, inc 1 st by picking up loop from between needles and k into back of it, p 1, k 1; rep from * once more. [13 sts] Cont in rib. **1st row:** K 2, * p 1, k 1; rep from * to last st, k 1. **2nd row:** * K 1, p 1; rep from * to last st, k 1. These two rows form rib. Cont in rib until border measures 3″ from beg, ending with 2nd row. Make buttonhole in next 2 rows by casting off 3 centre sts in first row, and casting on 3 sts above those cast off in previous row. Work 26 rows. Make buttonhole in next 2 rows as before. Make four more buttonholes [six in all] with 26 rows between each. Work until border is long enough to fit along front and neck edges. Cast off firmly in rib.

TO MAKE UP: Join shoulder seams. Set in sleeves. Join side and sleeve seams using back st. Sew border to front and neck edges. Press seams. Sew on buttons to correspond with buttonholes.

Cardigans for beginners

Instructions are for a 34″ bust. Changes for 36″, 38″ and 40″ sizes are given in brackets.

MATERIALS: 17(18–19–20) ozs of Emu Scotch Double Knitting. One pair each Nos 9 and 11 needles. Ten buttons.

MEASUREMENTS: To fit a 34″(36″–38″–40″) bust. Length to shoulder: 22½″(23″–24″–24½″), adjustable. Sleeve seam: 18″(18″–18½″–19″), adjustable.

TENSION: 6 sts and 8 rows to 1″ over st-st on No 9 needles.

BACK: With No 11 needles cast on 109(115–121–127) sts. **Commence rib. 1st row:** K 1, * p 1, k 1; rep from * to end of row. **2nd row:** P 1, * k 1, p 1; rep from * to end of row. Rep these 2 rows 4 times more. Change to No 9 needles. Beg with a k row, cont in st-st until work measures 16″(16″–16½″–16½″) from beg, or required length to underarm ending with a p row. **Shape armholes. 1st row:** Cast off 5(5–6–6) sts, k to end. **2nd row:** Cast off 5(5–6–6) sts, p to end. **3rd row:** K 2 tog, k to last 2 sts, k 2 tog. **4th row:** P 2 tog, p to last 2 sts, p 2 tog. Rep 3rd and 4th rows twice more. **9th row:** K 2 tog, k to last 2 sts, k 2 tog. **10th row:** P to end. Rep 9th and 10th rows 1(2–2–3) times more. 83(87–91–95) sts. Work 20(22–26–28) rows without shaping on these sts. **Shape shoulders. 1st row:** Cast off 5 sts, k to end. **2nd row:** Cast off 5 sts, p to end. Rep 1st and 2nd shoulder shaping rows 4 times more. **11th row:** Cast off 4(6–7–8) sts, k to end. **12th row:** Cast off 4(6–7–8) sts, p to end. Cast off rem 25(25–27–29) sts.

LEFT FRONT: With No 11 needles cast on 55(57–61–63) sts. **Commence rib. 1st row:** K 1, * p 1, k 1; rep from * to end of row. **2nd row:** P 1, * k 1, p 1; rep from * to end of row. Rep these 2 rows 4 times more. Change to No 9 needles. Beg with a k row cont in st-st until work measures same as Back to underarm, ending with a p row. **Shape armhole. 1st row:** Cast off 5(5–6–6) sts, k to end. **2nd row:** P to end. **3rd row:** K 2 tog, k to end. **4th row:** P to last 2 sts, p 2 tog. Rep 3rd and 4th rows twice more. **9th row:** K 2 tog, k to end. **10th row:** P to end. Rep 9th and 10th rows 1(2–2–3) times more. 42(43–46–47) sts. Work 20(22–26–28) rows without shaping on these sts. **Shape shoulder. 1st row:** Cast off 5 sts, k to end. **2nd row:** P to end. Rep 1st and 2nd shoulder shaping rows once more. **5th row:** Cast off 5 sts, k to end. **Shape neck. 6th row:** Cast off 7(6–8–8) sts for neck, p to end. **7th row:** Cast off 5 sts, k to end. **8th row:** Cast off 3 sts, p to end. Rep 7th and 8th rows once more. Cast off rem 4(6–7–8) sts.

RIGHT FRONT: With No 11 needles cast on 55(57–61–63) sts. Work 10 rows rib as given for Left Front. Change to No 9 needles. Beg with a k row, cont in st-st until work measures same as Left Front to underarm, ending with a k row. **Shape armhole: 1st row:** Cast off 5(5–6–6) sts, p to end. **2nd row:** K to last 2 sts, k 2 tog. **3rd row:** P 2 tog, p to end. Rep 2nd and 3rd rows twice more. **8th row:** K to end. **9th row:** P 2 tog, p to end. Rep 8th and 9th rows 1(2–2–3) times more. 42 (43–46–47) sts. Work 21(23–27–29) rows without shaping on these sts. **Shape shoulder. 1st row:** Cast off 5 sts, p to end. **2nd row:** K to end. Rep 1st and 2nd shoulder shaping rows once more. **5th row:** Cast off 5 sts, p to end. **Shape neck. 6th row:** Cast off 7(6–8–8) sts, k to end. **7th row:** Cast off 5 sts, p to end. **8th row:**

Cast off 3 sts, k to end. Rep 7th and 8th rows once more. Cast off rem 4(6–7–8) sts.

SLEEVES: [Make two] With No 11 needles cast on 45(47–51–53) sts. Work 10 rows rib as given for Left Front. Change to No 9 needles. Cont in st-st. **1st row:** K into front then into back of first st, k to last 2 sts, k into front then into back of next st, k 1. [2 sts increased] Beg with a p row, work 7 rows without shaping. Rep the last 8 rows until there are 75(79–85–89) sts. Cont in st-st without shaping until sleeve measures 18″(18″–18½″–19″) from beg, measured on the straight, or required length to underarm, ending with a p row. **Shape sleeve top. 1st row:** Cast off 5(5–6–6) sts, k to end. **2nd row:** Cast off 5(5–6–6) sts, p to end. **3rd row:** K 2 tog, k to last 2 sts, k 2 tog. **4th row:** P

Cardigans for beginners

to end. Rep 3rd and 4th rows until 39(39–41–41) sts rem, then rep 3rd row only once more. Mark each end of last row with coloured thread. **Commence saddle shoulder.** Beg with a p row work 1(3–1–3) rows without shaping. **Next row:** K 2 tog, k to last 2 sts, k 2 tog. Beg with a p row work 3 rows without shaping. Rep last 4 rows until 23 sts rem. **Next row:** K 2 tog, k to last 2 sts, k 2 tog. **Next row:** P to end. **Shape neck edge. 1st row:** K 6 sts, turn and leave rem sts on a holder for time being. **2nd row:** P 2 tog, p to end. **3rd row:** K 2 tog, k to end. **4th row:** P 2 tog, p to end. **5th row:** K to end. Rep 4th and 5th rows once more. **Next row:** P 2 sts. Cast off. With right side of work facing rejoin wool to inner edge of rem sts on holder, cast off next 9 sts, k rem 6 sts. **2nd row:** P to last 2 sts, p 2 tog. **3rd row:** K to last 2 sts, k 2 tog. **4th row:** P to last 2 sts, p 2 tog. **5th row:** K to end. Rep 4th and 5th rows once more. **Next row:** P 2 sts. Cast off.

TO MAKE UP: Press work very lightly on wrong side under a damp cloth with a warm iron. Use back st for seams except ribbed parts, where a woven flat seam is used. Starting from coloured thread markers, join side edges of sleeve saddle shoulders to shoulder edges of Back and Fronts. Join curve of sleeve top to curve of armhole. Join side and sleeve seams. **Neckband.** With right side of work facing and No 11 needles, join wool to neck edge of Right Front and k up 12(12–13–14) sts along curve of front neck, k up 25 sts around neck edge of saddle shoulder of right sleeve, k up 25(25–27–29) sts across back neck, k up 25 sts around neck edge of saddle shoulder of left sleeve and k up 12(12–13–14) sts along curve of left front neck. 99(99–103–107) sts. **1st row:** P 1, * k 1, p 1; rep from * to end of row. **2nd row:** K 1, * p 1, k 1; rep from * to end of row. Rep these 2 rows 3 times more, then 1st row once. Cast off in rib. **Button band.** With No 11 needles cast on 11 sts. **1st row:** K 1, * p 1, k 1; rep from * to end. **2nd row:** P 1, * k 1, p 1; rep from * to end. Rep these 2 rows until Band is long enough to fit along front edge when slightly stretched. Cast off in rib. Mark positions for ten buttons, first to come ½" above cast on edge, and last to come ½" below cast off edge with eight more evenly spaced between. **Buttonhole band:** Work as given for Button band, making buttonholes (when markers on Button band are reached) as follows: **1st buttonhole row:** Rib 4 sts, cast off 3 sts, rib 4 sts. **2nd buttonhole row:** Rib 4 sts, cast on 3 sts, rib 4 sts. Sew bands to front edges, joining Buttonhole band to Right Front for woman's Cardigan or to Left Front for man's Cardigan. Sew on buttons.

His and her moss stitch sweater

Instructions are for a 36″ bust. Changes for 38″, 40″, 42″ and 44″ sizes are given in brackets.
MATERIALS: 25(26–27–28–29) ozs Lister Lavenda Double Knitting wool. One pair each Nos 10 and 11 needles.
MEASUREMENTS: To fit a 36″(38″–40″–42″–44″) bust. Length at centre back: 25½″(26″–26″–26″–26″), adjustable. Sleeve seam: 18″(18½″–19″–19½″–20″), adjustable.
TENSION: 12½ sts and 17 rows to 2″ over moss-st on No 10 needles.
NOTE: Moss-st is worked by k 1, p 1 all along the row and on next and following rows k sts are knitted and p sts are purled.
BACK: With No 12 needles cast on 119(125–131–137–143) sts. **1st row:** (Right side) P 1, * k 1, p 1; rep from * to end of row. **2nd row:** K 1, * p 1, k 1; rep from * to end of row. Rep these 2 rows 9 times more, inc 1 st at each end of last row. 121(127–133–139–145) sts. Change to No 10 needles and moss-st. Cont in moss-st until work measures 17″ from beg, or required length to underarm ending with a wrong side row. **Shape armholes**. Cast off 1 st at beg of next 2 rows. ** **1st dec row:** K 3, k 2 tog, moss-st to last 5 sts, k 2 tog tbl, k 3. **2nd dec row:** P 4, moss-st to last 4 sts, p 4. **3rd dec row:** K 4, moss-st to last 4 sts, k 4. **4th dec row:** P 4, moss-st to last 4 sts, p 4. Rep 1st to 4th dec rows 12(12–13–13–14) times more, then 1st dec row once. 91(97–101–107–111) sts. Work 7(9–9–9–9) rows in moss-st working 4 sts at each end in st-st. **Shape shoulders**. **1st row:** K 4, moss-st to last 4 sts, turn. **2nd row:** Sl 1 p-wise, p 3, moss-st to last 4 sts, turn. **3rd row:** Sl 1 k-wise, k 3, moss-st to last 8 sts, turn. **4th row:** Sl 1 p-wise, p 3, moss-st to last 8 sts, turn. Cont in this way working 4 sts less at end of every row until last 2 rows are worked as folls: Sl 1 k-wise, k 3, moss st to last 28(28–28–32–32) sts, turn. Sl 1 p-wise, p 3, moss-st to last 28(28–28–32–32) sts, turn. **Next row:** Sl 1 k-wise, k 3, moss-st to end. Work 3 more rows in moss-st across all sts. **Next row:** Cast off 27(29–30–32–33) sts, moss-st 37 (39–41–43–45) sts, cast off rem 27(29–30–32–33) sts. Leave centre sts on holder for back neck.
FRONT: Work as for Back to **. Rep 1st to 4th dec rows as given for Back 13(13–14–14–15) times, ending with a 4th row. 93(99–103–109–113) sts. **Shape neck. Next row:** K 3, k 2 tog, moss-st 34(37–38–40–41) sts, turn. Complete left shoulder first. Keeping armhole edge straight, dec 1 st at neck edge on next 8 rows, then on foll alt rows 3(4–4–4–4) times. 27(29–30–32–33) sts. Work 3 rows in moss-st after last dec row. **Next row:** K 3, k up loop lying between sts, moss-st to end. Work 3 rows in moss-st. Rep last 4 rows once more, then first of these rows once more. 30(32–33–35–36) sts. Work 1 row. Cast off. Sl centre 15(15–17–19–21) sts on to a holder. With right side of work facing and No 10 needles, rejoin wool to rem 39(42–43–45–46) sts. Moss-st to last 5 sts, k 2 tog tbl, k 3. Complete to match left shoulder reversing shaping.
SLEEVES: With No 12 needles cast on 53(55–57–59–61) sts. Work 24 rows in rib as given for back inc 1 st at each end of last row. 55(57–59–61–63) sts. Change to No 10 needles and work in moss-st, inc 1 st at each end of 7th and every foll 6th row until there are 91(93–97–99–103) sts. Cont without shaping until sleeve measures 18″(18½″–19″–19½″–20″) from beg, or required length to underarm, ending with a wrong side row. **Shape top**. Cast off 1 st at beg of next 2 rows. **1st dec row:** K 3, k 2 tog, moss-st to last 5 sts, k 2 tog tbl, k 3. **2nd dec row:** P 4, moss-st to last 4 sts, p 4. **3rd dec row:** K 3, k 3 tog, moss-st to last 6 sts, k 3 tog tbl, k 3. **4th dec row:** P 4, moss-st to last 4 sts, p 4. Rep these 4 dec rows 10 times more, then 1st and 2nd rows 1(1–2–2–3) times more. 21(23–25–27–29) sts. Cast off 6(6–6–7–7) sts at beg of next 2 rows. Cast off rem 9(11–13–13–15) sts.
NECK RIBBING: With right side of work facing, sl sts from back neck holder on to No 12 needle.*** Beg with a 2nd rib row as given for Back work 8 rows in rib. **Next row:** K. Work 8 more rows in rib. Cast off in rib. *** With right side of Front facing and No 12 needles k up 31(31–32–31–31) sts down left side of neck, k up 1(k up 1–p 1, k up 1–k 1, p 1, k up 1–k up 1), * p 1, k 1, p 1, k up 1; rep from * 4(4–4–4–6) times more, then k up 31(k up 31–p 1, k up 32–p 1, k 1, k up 31–k up 31) up right side of neck. [83(83–87–87–91) sts.] Rep from *** to *** as given for back neck.
TO MAKE UP: Press each piece under a damp cloth with a hot iron. Join shoulder, side and sleeve seams using back st. Join neckband seams. Set in sleeves, the first inc st being shoulder line for centre of sleeve top. Press seams. Turn neck ribbing in half to wrong side and sl st. Press seams.

Fair Isle pullovers

Instructions are for a 32″ bust/chest. Changes for 34″, 36″, 38″, 40″, 42″ and 44″ sizes are given in brackets.

MATERIALS: Short version. 5(6-6-6-7-7-7) ozs Lee Target Motoravia 4-ply in main shade, A; 1(1-1-2-2-2-2) ozs in contrast, B; 1(1-1-1-2-2-2) ozs each in contrasts, C, D, E; 1(1-1-1-1-1-1) ozs in contrast, F. **Long version.** 6(6-7-7-8-8-8) ozs of same in main shade A; 2(2-2-2-2-2-2) ozs each of contrasts B and C; 1(1-1-1-2-2-2) ozs in contrast, D; 2(2-2-2-2-2-2) ozs in contrast, E; 1(1-1-1-1-1-1) ozs in contrast, F. One pair each Nos 10 and 12 needles. Set of four No 12 needles, pointed at both ends.

MEASUREMENTS: To fit a 32″(34″-36″-38″-40″-42″-44″) bust/chest. Length to shoulder: **Short version.** 17½″(18″-18½″-19″-19½″-20″-20½″); **Long version.** 22½″ (23″-23½″-24″-24½″-25″-25½″).

TENSION: 8 sts to 1″ on No 10 needles over Fair Isle pattern.

BACK: With No 12 needles and A, cast on 137(145-153-161-169-177-185) sts. **1st row:** K 1, * p 1, k 1; rep from * to end. **2nd row:** P 1, * k 1, p 1; rep from * to end. Rep these 2 rows for 4″, ending with a 2nd row. Change to No 10 needles. Join in B. **Commence Fair Isle pattern. 1st row:** K 1B, * 1A, 1B; rep from * to end. **2nd row:** P 1A, * 1B, 1A; rep from * to end. **3rd row:** As 1st. **4th row:** Join in C. P 1C, * 3A, 1C; rep from * to end. **5th row:** K 2C, * 1A, 3C; rep from * to last 3 sts, 1A, 2C. **6th row:** P 1C, * 1A, 5C, 1A, 1C; rep from * to end. **7th row:** K 1A, * 3C, 1A; rep from * to end. **8th row:** As 6th. **9th row:** As 5th. **10th row:** As 4th. **11th to 13th rows:** Join in B and work as 1st to 3rd rows. **14th row:** Join in D. P 1A, * 3D, 1A; rep from * to end. **15th row:** K 1A, * 2D, 3A, 2D, 1A; rep from * to end. **16th row:** P 1A, * 1D, 1A; rep from * to end. **17th row:** K 4A, * 1D, 7A; rep from * to last 5 sts, 1D, 4A. **18th row:** As 16th. **19th row:** As 15th. **20th row:** As 14th. **21st to 23rd rows.** Join in B and work as 1st to 3rd rows. **24th row:** Join in E and F. P 2F, * 2A, 1E, 2A, 3F; rep from * to last 7 sts, 2A, 1E, 2A, 2F. **25th row:** K 1F, * 1A, 2E, 1A, 2E, 1A, 1F; rep from * to end. **26th row:** P 1A, * 2E, 3A, 2E, 1A; rep from * to end. **27th row:** K as 26th row. **28th row:** P 1A, * 2E, 1A, 1F, 1A, 2E, 1A; rep from * to end. **29th row:** K as 28th row. **30th row:** P 1A, * 1E, 2F, 1A, 2F, 1E, 1A; rep from * to end. **31st row:** As 29th. **32nd row:** As 28th. **33rd row:** As 27th. **34th row:** As 26th. **35th row:** As 25th. **36th row:** As 24th. These 36 rows form patt and are rep throughout. Cont in patt until work measures 11″ from beg for Short version, or 16″ for Long version, ending with a p row. **Shape armholes.** Keeping patt correct, cast off at beg of next and every row 6(6-7-7-7-8-8) sts 4 times and 6(7-6-7-8-7-8) sts twice. 101(107-113-119-125-131-137) sts. Cont without shaping until armholes measure 6½″(7″-7½″-8″-8½″-9″-9½″) from beg, ending with a p row. **Shape shoulders.** Cast off at beg of next and every row 6(7-7-8-8-8-9) sts 8 times and 7(5-7-5-7-9-7) sts twice. Leave rem 39(41-43-45-47-49-51) sts on holder.

FRONT: Work as given for Back until Front measures 1½″ less than Back to underarm, ending with a p row. **Divide for neck. Next row:** Patt 68(72-76-80-84-88-92) sts, turn. Complete this side first. Dec 1 st at neck edge on 2nd and every foll 3rd row until work measures same as Back to underarm, ending with a p row. **Shape armholes.** Work as given for Back, **at the same time** cont to dec 1 st at neck edge on every foll 4th row until 31(33-35-37-39-41-43) sts rem. Cont without shaping until armhole measures same as Back to shoulder, ending with a p row. **Shape shoulder.** Cast off at beg of next and every foll alt row 6(7-7-8-8-8-9) sts 4 times and 7(5-7-5-7-9-7) sts once. With right side of work facing, rejoin wool to rem sts, sl first st on to holder and patt to end. Complete to match first side, reversing shaping.

NECKBAND: Join shoulder seams using back st. With right side of work facing and using set of four No 12 needles and A, k across sts on holder for back neck, k up 60(63-66-69-72-75-78) sts down front neck, k centre front st on holder and k up 60(63-66-69-72-75-78) sts up other side of front neck. 160(168-176-184-192-200-208) sts. Arrange sts on 3 needles. **Next round.** * K 1, p 1; rep from * to 2 sts before centre front st, p 2 tog, k 1, p 2 tog, rib to end. Rep this round for ¾″, working one st less on either side on centre front st. Cast off in rib, still dec at centre front.

ARMBANDS: With right side of work facing, No 12 needles and A, k up 18(19-20-21-22-23-24) sts along cast off sts at armhole, 48(51-54-57-60-63-66) sts up side of armhole to shoulder, 47(50-53-56-59-62-65) sts down side of armhole and 18(19-20-21-22-23-24) sts along other cast off sts. 131(139-147-155-163-171-179) sts. **1st row:** P 1, * k 1, p 1; rep from * to end. **2nd row:** Rib 16(17-18-19-20-21-22) sts, work 3 tog, rib to last 19(20-21-22-23-24-25) sts, work 3 tog, rib to end. **3rd row:** As 1st. **4th row:** Rib 15(16-17-18-19-20-21) sts, work 3 tog, rib to last 18(19-20-21-22-23-24) sts, work 3 tog, rib to end. Cont in this way, dec on every alt row until Band measures ¾″. Cast off in rib.

TO MAKE UP: Press work under a damp cloth with a warm iron. Join side seams using back st. Join armbands. Press seams.

Aran sampler cardigan

Instructions are for a 34″/36″ bust. Changes for 38″/40″ size are given in brackets.

MATERIALS: 15(16) 50 grm balls of Mahony's Blarney Bainin. One pair each Nos 7, 8 and 10 needles for first size and one pair each Nos 6, 7 and 9 needles for second size. Two cable needles. Seven (eight) buttons.

MEASUREMENTS: To fit a 34″/36″(38″/40″) bust. Length: 24″(27″). Sleeve seam: 17″(19″).

TENSION: 10 sts and 13 rows to 2″ over st-st on No 7 needles. 9 sts and 11½ rows to 2″ over st-st on No 6 needles.

ABBREVIATIONS: Cable 5: Sl next 2 sts on to cable needle and leave at front, sl next st on to 2nd cable needle and leave at back, k next 2 sts, then p 1 from back cable needle and k 2 from front cable needle. **C3R:** [Cross 3 to the right] Sl next st on to cable needle and leave at back, k 2, then p 1 from cable needle. **C3L:** [Cross 3 to the left] Sl next 2 sts on to cable needle and leave at front, p 1, then k 2 from cable needle. **T2P:** [Twist 2 p-wise] Put needle behind first st on left-hand needle, p the 2nd st, then p 1st st and sl both off. **T2R:** Miss 1st st on left-hand needle, k 2nd st, then p 1st st and sl both off. **T2L:** Put needle behind 1st st on left-hand needle, p 2nd st, then k 1st st and sl both off. **C4F:** [Cable 4 front] Sl next 2 sts on to cable needle at front, k 2, then k 2 from cable needle. **C4B:** As C4F but leave 2 sts at back on cable needle. **C2B:** Sl next st on to cable needle and hold at back, k 1 tbl, then p 1 from cable needle. **C2F:** Sl next st on to cable needle and hold at front, p 1, then k 1 tbl from cable needle.

BACK: With No 7(6) needles cast on 102(102) sts. K 1 row. Work in Bramble stitch. **1st row:** [Right side] P. **2nd row:** K 1, * [k 1, p 1, k 1] into next st—called 3 in to 1, p 3 tog; rep from * to last st, k 1. **3rd row:** P. **4th row:** K 1, * p 3 tog, 3 into 1; rep from * to last st, k 1. Rep these 4 rows 3 times more. Change to No 8(7) needles and k 4 rows [g-st]. Change to No 7(6) needles, and work in Diamond patt. **1st row:** P 9, * cable 5, p 11; rep from * ending last rep, p 8 instead of p 11. **2nd and every wrong side row:** K all sts purled in previous row and p all sts knitted in previous row. **3rd row:** P 8, * C3R, k 1, C3L, p 9; rep from * ending last rep, p 7. **5th row:** P 7, * C3R, k 1, p 1, k 1, C3L, p 7; rep from * ending last rep, p 6. **7th row:** P 6, * C3R, [k 1, p 1] twice, k 1, C3L, p 5; rep from * to end. **9th row:** P 5, * C3R, [k 1, p 1] 3 times, k 1, C3L, p 3; rep from * ending last rep, p 4. **11th row:** P 5, * C3L, [p 1, k 1] 3 times, p 1, C3R, p 3; rep from * ending last rep, p 4. **13th row:** P 6, * C3L, [p 1, k 1] twice, p 1, C3R, p 5; rep from * to end. **15th row:** P 7, * C3L, p 1, k 1, p 1, C3R, p 7; rep from * ending last rep, p 6. **17th row:** P 8, * C3L, p 1, C3R, p 9; rep from * ending last rep, p 7. **19th row:** As 1st row. **20th row:** As 2nd row. Change to No 8(7) needles and g-st 4 rows, but in 3rd row inc in 34th and 68th sts. 104(104) sts. Change to No 7(6) needles and work in Trellis patt. **1st row:** P 3, * k 2, p 4; rep from *, ending last rep, p 3. **2nd row:** K 3, * T2P, k 4; rep from *, ending last rep, k 3. **3rd row:** P 2, * T2R, T2L, p 2; rep from * to end. **4th row:** K 2, * p 1, k 2; rep from * to end. **5th row:** P 1, * T2R, p 2, T2L; rep from * to last st, p 1. **6th row:** K 1, p 1, k 4, * T2P, k 4; rep from * to last 2 sts, p 1, k 1. **7th row:** P 1, * T2L, p 2, T2R; rep from *, ending last rep, p 1. **8th row:** As 4th. **9th row:** P 2, * T2L, T2R, p 2; rep from * to end. **10th row:** As 2nd. Rep 3rd to 10th rows inclusive once more. Change to No 8(7) needles and g-st 4 rows, but in 3rd row k 2 tog on 35th and 36th, 69th and 70th sts. 102(102) sts. Change to No 7(6) needles and work Crossed Diamond patt. **1st row:** P 1, k 2, p 6, [C4F, p 6] 9 times, k 2, p 1. **2nd row:** K 1, p 2, [k 6, p 4] 9 times, k 6, p 2, k 1. **3rd row:** P 1, [C3L, p 4, C3R] 10 times, p 1. **4th and every wrong side row:** K all sts purled on previous row and p all knitted sts as in 2nd row. **5th row:** P 2, [C3L, p 2, C3R, p 2] 10 times. **7th row:** P 3, C3L, C3R, [p 4, C3L, C3R] 9 times, p 3. **9th row:** P 4, C4B, [p 6, C4B] 9 times, p 4. **11th row:** P 3, C3R, C3L, [p 4, C3R, C3L] 9 times, p 3. **13th row:** P 2, [C3R, p 2, C3L, p 2] 10 times. **15th row:** P 1, C3R, [p 4, C3L, C3R] 9 times, p 4, C3L, p 1. **16th row:** As 2nd row. **17th and 18th rows:** Rep 1st and 2nd rows. Change to No 8(7) needles and g-st 4 rows, dec 1 st in centre of 3rd row. 101(101) sts. Change to No 7(6) needles and work Zig-Zag patt. **1st row:** P 7, * [p 1, k 1 tbl] 3 times, p 6; rep from * ending last rep, p 4. **2nd row:** K 4, * [p 1, k 1] 3 times, k 6; rep from * ending last rep, p 7. **3rd row:** P 7, * [C2B] 3 times, p 6; rep from * ending last rep, p 4. **4th and every wrong side row:** K all sts purled in previous row and p all k sts as in 2nd row. **5th row:** P 6, * [C2B] 3 times, p 6; rep from * ending last rep, p 5. **7th row:** P 5, * [C2B] 3 times, p 6; rep from * ending last rep, p 6. **9th row:** P 4, * [C2B] 3 times, p 6; rep from * ending last rep, p 7. **11th row:** P 4, * [C2F] 3 times, p 6; rep from * ending last rep, p 7. **13th row:** P 5, * [C2F] 3 times, p 6; rep from *

Aran sampler cardigan

to ending. **15th row:** P 6, * [C2F] 3 times, p 6; rep from * ending last rep, p 5. **17th row:** P 7, * [C2F] 3 times, p 6; rep from * ending last rep, p 4. **18th row:** As 2nd row. Change to No 8(7) needles and g-st 4 rows, inc 10 times evenly across 3rd row. 111(111) sts. Change to No 7(6) needles and work Cable and Moss st patt. **1st row:** P 2, * k 4, p 1, k 4, [p 1, k 1] twice, p 1; rep from * to last 11 sts, k 4, p 1, k 4, p 2. **2nd row:** K 2, * p 4, k 1, p 4, k 2, p 1, k 2; rep from * to last 11 sts, p 4, k 1, p 4, k 2. **3rd row:** P 2, * C4B, p 1, C4F, [p 1, k 1] twice, p 1; rep from * to last 11 sts, C4B, p 1, C4F, p 2. **4th row:** As 2nd. **5th and 6th rows:** Rep 1st and 2nd rows. **7th row:** P 2, * C4F, p 1, C4B, [p 1, k 1] twice, p 1; rep from * to last 11 sts, C4F, p 1, C4B, p 2. **8th row:** As 2nd row. These eight rows form patt. **Shape armholes.** Cont in patt, cast off 6 sts at beg of next 2 rows, dec 1 st at each end of next 5 right-side rows. Work 1 row patt. 89(89) sts. Change to No 8(7) needles. **Next row:** K 2 tog, k 6, [k 2 tog, k 10] 6 times, k 2 tog, k 5, k 2 tog. 80(80) sts. Work 3 rows g-st. Change to No 7(6) needles and work Tree of Life patt. **1st row:** P 1, * p 4, C2B, k 1 tbl, C2F, p 4; rep from * to last st, p 1. **2nd row:** K 1, * k 4, [p 1 tbl, k 1] twice, p 1 tbl, k 4; rep from * to last st, k 1. **3rd row:** P 1, * p 3, C2B, p 1, k 1 tbl, p 1, C2F, p 3; rep from * to last st, p 1. **4th row:** K 1, * k 3, p 1 tbl, [k 2, p 1 tbl] twice, k 3; rep from * to last st, k 1. **5th row:** P 1, * p 2, C2B, p 2, k 1 tbl, p 2, C2F, p 2; rep from * to last st, p 1. **6th row:** K 1, * k 2, p 1 tbl, [k 3, p 1 tbl] twice, k 2; rep from * to last st, k 1. **7th row:** P 1, * p 1, C2B, p 3, k 1 tbl, p 3, C2F, p 1; rep from * to last st, p 1. **8th row:** K 1, * k 1, p 1 tbl, [k 4, p 1 tbl] twice, k 1; rep from * to last st, k 1. Rep these eight rows once more. Change to No 8(7) needles and g-st 4 rows, inc twice in 3rd row. 82(82) sts. Change to No 7(6) needles and work in Open Cable patt. **1st row:** P 1, * p 2, k 1 tbl; rep from * to last 3 sts, p 3. **2nd row:** K 1, * k 2, p 1 tbl; rep from * to last 3 sts, k 3. **3rd row:** P 1, * p 2, C2F, C2B; rep from * to last 3 sts, p 3. **4th row:** K 4, * p 2 tbl, k 4; rep from * to end. **5th row:** P 4, * sl next st on to cable needle and hold at front, k 1 tbl, then k 1 tbl from cable needle, p 4; rep from * to end. **6th row:** As 4th. **7th row:** P 1, * p 2, C2B, C2F; rep from * to last 3 sts, p 3. **8th row:** As 2nd. **9th and 10th rows:** Rep 1st and 2nd rows. **11th to 18th rows:** Rep 1st to 8th rows inclusive. Change to No 8(7) needles and g-st 4 rows. **Shape shoulders.** Cont in g-st, cast off 6 sts at beg of next 4 rows and 7 sts at beg of foll 4 rows. Cast off rem 30 sts.

LEFT FRONT: With No 7(6) needles cast on 50(50) sts. K 1 row. Work in Bramble stitch as for Back. Change to No 8(7) needles and work 4 rows g-st. Change to No 7(6) needles and work Diamond patt as for Back but with one p st less at each end and one less between diamonds thus: **1st row:** P 8, * cable 5, p 10; rep from * ending last rep, p 7. **3rd row:** P 7, * C3R, k 1, C3L, p 8; rep from * ending last rep, p 6. Cont in patt as set until 20 rows are complete. Change to No 8(7) needles and g-st 4 rows. Change to No 7(6) needles and work Trellis patt as given for Back. Change to No 8(7) needles and g-st 2 rows. **Next row:** [K 16, k twice into next st] twice, k 16. K one more row on 52 sts. Change to No 7(6) needles and work in Crossed Diamond patt as given for Back, reading 4 times for 9 times and 5 times for 10 times. Change to No 8(7) needles and g-st 4 rows, dec 1 st in centre of 3rd row. Change to No 7(6) needles and work in Zig-Zag patt as given for Back but with one p st less at each end thus; **1st row:** P 6, * [p 1, k 1 tbl] 3 times, p 6; rep from * ending last rep, p 3. **2nd row:** K 3, * [p 1, k 1] 3 times, k 6; rep from * to end. **3rd row:** P 6, * [C2B] 3 times, p 6; rep from * ending last rep, p 3. Cont in patt as set until 18 rows are complete. Change to No 8(7) needles and g-st 4 rows, inc 4 times evenly across 3rd row. 55(55) sts. Change to No 7(6) needles and work 8 rows Cable and Moss-St patt as given for Back. **Shape armholes.** Cont in patt, cast off 6 sts at beg of next row. Dec 1 st at armhole edge on next 5 right-side rows. Work 1 more row patt on 44 sts. Change to No 8(7) needles. **Next row:** K 2 tog [last armhole dec], [k 12, k 2 tog] twice, k 14. K 3 more rows on 41 sts. Change to No 7(6) needles and work Tree of Life patt as given for Back. Change to No 8(7) needles and g-st 4 rows, dec 1 st in centre of 3rd row. Change to No 7(6) needles and work Open Cable patt as given for Back on 5 rows. **Shape neck.** Keeping patt correct, cast off 7 sts at beg of next row, then dec 1 st at same edge on next 7 rows. Work 5 rows without shaping on 26 sts to complete patt. Change to No 8(7) needles and g-st 4 rows. **Shape shoulder**. Cont in g-st cast off at beg of armhole edge rows, 6 sts twice and 7 sts twice.

RIGHT FRONT: Work as for Left Front reversing armhole by working 1 extra row in patt before casting off 6 sts and reversing last armhole dec row by reading it backwards. Work 1 extra row also before shaping neck and shoulders.

SLEEVES: With No 10(9) needles cast on 46(46) sts. Work 2½″ in k 1, p 1 rib. Change to No 7(6) needles and patt. **1st row:** P 1, * k 8, p 1; rep from * to end. **2nd row:** K 1, * p 8, k 1; rep from * to end. **3rd and 4th rows:** Rep 1st and 2nd rows. **5th row:** P. **6th row:** K. These six rows form patt. Cont in patt inc 1 st at each end of foll 3rd and every foll 10th row until there are 62(62) sts, working inc sts into patt. Cont without shaping until sleeve measures 17″(19″) from beg, ending with a wrong side row. **Shape top**. Cast off 5 sts at beg of next 2 rows. Dec 1 st at each end of every right-

side row until 30 sts rem, ending with a dec row, then each end of next 5 rows. Cast off 3 sts at beg of next 2 rows. Cast off rem 14 sts.
BORDERS AND NECK BAND: Join shoulder seams using back st. Mark front edge with pins as buttonhole guide, approx 3″($3\frac{1}{4}$″) from neck edge and 6 rows from lower edge, with 4(5) more evenly spaced between. With No 10(9) needles cast on 10 sts for Left Front border and work in p 1, k 1, rib [regarding 1st row as right side]. For Man's version only make buttonholes in this border as markers are reached thus: **Buttonhole row:** [Right side facing] Rib 3, cast off 3, rib to end. **Next row:** Cast on 3 sts above those cast off in previous row. Work in rib until border fits front edge, slightly stretched, ending with a wrong side row. * Break wool and leave sts on a holder. Work Right Front border to match, working in k 1, p 1 rib and make buttonholes for Woman's version thus: **Buttonhole row:** Rib 4, cast off 3, rib to end. **Next row:** Cast on 3 sts above those cast off in previous row. Work as for Left Front border to *. Do not break wool but keep rib sts on same needle, k up 73 sts around neck and rib 10 sts from holder. Work 9 rows in k 1, p 1 rib [beg and end first row with p 1] making final buttonhole in 4th row as before. Cast off in rib.
TO MAKE UP: Pin out and press work on wrong side with a damp cloth and hot iron. Join side and sleeve seams using back st. Set in sleeves. Sew on front borders and buttons. Press seams.

Smock

Instructions are for a 32″/34″ bust. Changes for 34″/36″ and 36″/38″ sizes are given in brackets.
MATERIALS: 23(24–25) ozs of Sirdar Double Knitting. One pair each Nos 8 and 9 needles. Five small buttons.
MEASUREMENTS: Length: 30″(30″–30″). Sleeve seam: 19″(19″–19″).
TENSION: $5\frac{1}{2}$ sts and $7\frac{1}{2}$ rows to 1″ over st-st No 9's.
ABBREVIATIONS: C2F [Cross 2 front]—Take the needle in front of the first stitch on left-hand needle and knit the 2nd stitch; now knit the first stitch, slip both stitches off the needle together; g-st: [garter stitch]—Every row k.
FRONT: ** With No 9 needles cast on 122(130–138) sts. Work 17 rows g-st. Change to No 8 needles and st-st. Work until front measures 21″ from beg, ending with a p row. ** Change to No 9 needles. **Beg yoke patt and divide for front opening. 1st row:** [P 2, take

Smock

the needle in front of the first st on left-hand needle and k the 2nd st, k the first st, sl both sts off needle tog—called C2F—] 14(15–16) times, p 2, turn and cast on 6 sts for underflap, leaving rem sts on holder. **2nd row:** K 8, * p 2, k 2; rep from * to end. **3rd row:** [P 2, C2F] 14(15–16) times, p 2, k 6. **4th row:** As 2nd. 3rd and 4th rows form patt. Work 4 more rows. **Shape armhole.** Cast off 4(6–6) sts at beg of next row and 2(2–2) sts at beg of foll alt row. Dec 1 st at beg of every alt row until 52(52–56) sts rem. Work 26(22–22) rows without shaping, ending at opening edge. **Shape neck. Next row:** Work 12(12–12) sts and sl on to holder, patt to end. Work back to neck edge. Keeping armhole edge straight, dec 1 st at neck edge on next 7 rows and on foll 4(4–5) alt rows, ending at armhole edge. **Shape shoulder.** Dec 1 st at neck edge on alt rows twice more, cast off 6(6–8) sts at beg of next row and 7(7–7) sts at beg of foll 2 alt rows. Work 1 row. Cast off 7(7–8) sts rem. Sl sts from holder back on to needle. **1st row:** K 6, * p 2, C2F; rep from * to last 2 sts, p 2. **2nd row:** * K 2, p 2; rep from * to last 8 sts, k 8. Cont in patt. Work 4 more rows. **Next row:** [Make buttonhole] K 2, k 2 tog, w fwd, patt to end. Now making a buttonhole on every 12th row in this way, cont as follows: Work 2 more rows. **Shape armhole.** Cast off 4(6–6) sts at beg of next row and 2(2–2) sts at beg of foll alt row. Dec 1 st at beg of every alt row until 52(52–56) sts rem. Work 26(22–22) rows without shaping, ending at opening edge. **Shape neck. Next row:** K 6, p 2 tog, C2F, p 2 tog, sl these 10 sts on to a holder, patt to end. Keeping armhole edge straight, dec 1 st at neck edge on next 7 rows, then on foll 4(4–5) alt rows. Work 1 row, ending at armhole edge. Shape shoulder and complete neck shaping to match first side.

BACK: Work as given for Front from ** to **. Change to No 9 needles and beg yoke patt. **1st row:** * P 2, C2F; rep from * to last 2 sts, p 2. **2nd row:** * K 2, p 2; rep from * to last 2 sts, k 2. These two rows form patt. Work 6 more rows. **Shape armholes.** Cast off 4(6–6) sts at beg of next 2 rows and 2(2–2) sts at beg of foll 2 rows. Dec 1 st at beg of every row until 98(98–106) sts rem. Cont until armholes measure same as front to beg of shoulder shaping, ending with a wrong side row. **Shape shoulders.** Cast off 6(6–8) sts at beg of next 2 rows. **Shape back of neck. Next row:** Cast off 7(7–7) sts, patt 17(17–18) sts including st already on needle, cast off 38(38–40) sts, patt to end. Cont on last set of sts as follows: **1st row:** Cast off 7(7–7) sts, patt to last 2 sts, dec 1 st. **2nd row:** Dec 1 st, patt to end. **3rd row:** As 1st. Work 1 row. Cast off 7(7–8) rem sts. Rejoin wool to rem sts at neck edge. **1st row:** Dec 1 st, patt to end. **2nd row:** Cast off 7(7–7) sts, work to last 2 sts, dec 1 st. **3rd row:** As 1st. Cast off rem 7(7–8) sts.

SLEEVES: With No 9 needles cast on 46(50–50) sts. **1st row:** * P 2, C2F; rep from * to last 2 sts, p 2. **2nd row:** * K 2, p 2; rep from * to last 2 sts, k 2. Rep 1st and 2nd rows for 3″, ending with 2nd row. Change to No 8 needles and st-st. Work 8 rows. Inc 1 st at each end of next row and then every 8th row until there are 58(62–62) sts, then 1 st at each end of every 10th row until there are 68(72–74) sts. Work until sleeve measures 19″(19″–19″) from beg, ending with a p row. **Shape top.** Cast off 4(6–6) sts at beg of next 2 rows, and 2(2–2) sts at beg of foll 2 rows. Dec 1 st at beg of every row until 32(32–32) sts rem. Cast off 2 sts at beg of next 4 rows, 3 sts at beg of foll 2 rows. Cast off rem 18 sts.

COLLAR: With No 9 needles cast on 33 sts. Work in g-st [1st row wrong side] until collar measures 14″ (14″–14½″) unstretched, ending with a right side row. Cast off k-wise.

POCKETS: [Make two] With No 9 needles cast on 33 sts. Work 17 rows g-st. Change to No 8 needles and st-st. Work until pocket measures 6″ from beg, ending with a p row. Cast off.

NECK BORDER: Press each piece lightly with warm iron and damp cloth. Join shoulder seams. Sl 10 sts on holder at right side of neck on to a No 9 needle, pick up and k 16(16–17) sts up right side of neck, 37(37–39) sts along back neck edge, [pick up 1 st only from each p rib] and 16(16–17) sts down left side of neck. Work across the 12 sts on holder as follows: P 2 tog, C2F, p 2 tog, k 6. Cont in g-st. Work 5 rows. Make buttonhole in next row as before. Work 4 rows. Cast off firmly k-wise.

TO MAKE UP: Sew sleeves into armholes. Join side and sleeve seams. Sew lower edge of underflap neatly at back of overflap. Sew pockets to front as illustrated; sew side edge of collar to cast-off edge of neck border, starting and ending ½″ from centre front edges. Press seams. Sew on buttons to correspond with buttonholes.

Ribbed hat

MATERIALS: 3 balls Patons Doublet. One pair No 5 needles. Cotton wool for stuffing.
TENSION: $4\frac{1}{2}$ sts to 1″ over st-st on No 5 needles. With No 5 needles cast on 94 sts. **1st row:** * P 2, k 2; rep from * to last 2 sts, p 2. **2nd row:** * K 2, p 2; rep from * to last 2 sts, k 2. Rep these 2 rows for $6\frac{1}{2}$″ ending with a 2nd row. Cont in st-st. Beg with a k row work 8 rows. **Next row:** K 4, * k 2 tog, k 4; rep from * to end. [79 sts] Work 5 rows st-st. **Next row:** K 1, * k 2 tog, k 3; rep from * to last 3 sts, k 2 tog, k 1. [63 sts] Work 5 rows st-st. **Next row:** K 3, * k 2 tog, k 2; rep from * to end. [48 sts] Work 3 rows st-st. **Next row:** K 2, * k 2 tog, k 1; rep from * to last 4 sts, k 2 tog, k 2. [33 sts] Work 3 rows st-st. **Next row:** K 1, * k 2 tog; rep from * to end. [17 sts] **Next row:** P 1, * p 2 tog; rep from * to end. [9 sts] Break wool leaving enough to thread through sts, draw up and fasten off.

TO MAKE UP: Join seam, reversing the seam for the ribbing. Press lightly. Form cotton wool into a roll 24″ long and about 2″ in diameter. Place roll of cotton wool round hat in centre of the ribbing. Fold ribbing over roll and oversew the cast-on edge neatly to the last row of ribbing.

Angora cardigans

Instructions are for a 32″ bust. Changes for 34″, 36″ and 38″ sizes are given in brackets.
MATERIALS: 14(15–16–17) $\frac{1}{2}$-oz balls of Patons Fuzzy-Wuzzy. One pair each Nos 10 and 12 needles. Seven buttons if required.
MEASUREMENTS: To fit a 32″(34″–36″–38″) bust. Length: $23\frac{1}{2}$″($23\frac{1}{2}$″–$24\frac{1}{2}$″–$24\frac{1}{2}$″), adjustable. Sleeve seam: $12\frac{1}{2}$″($12\frac{1}{2}$″–$12\frac{1}{2}$″–$12\frac{1}{2}$″).
TENSION: 7 sts and 9 rows to 1″ on No 10 needles.
LEFT FRONT: Pocket lining. With No 10 needles, cast on 33(33–35–35) sts. Work 37(37–39–39) rows in st-st, ending with a k row. Break yarn and leave sts on spare needle. With No 12 needles cast on 67(71–75–79) sts. Change to No 10 needles. **1st row:** [Wrong side] Sl 1, * p 1, k 1; rep from * to end. **2nd row:** K 2, * p 1, k 1; rep from * to last st, k 1. Rep 1st and 2nd rows 5 times more, then 1st row once. **Next row:** K to last 11 sts, rib 11 sts for border. [Always k border sts firmly, or use a size finer needle for the border sts only.] **Next row:** Sl 1, [p 1, k 1] 5 times, p to end. Cont in st-st with 11 sts in rib for border. Work 34(34–36–36) more rows. Work pocket in next 2 rows as folls: **Next row:** K 42(44–47–49) sts, sl last 33(33–35–35) sts just worked on to a st holder, patt to end. **Next row:** Work to end, working pocket lining sts in place of those sts on a holder. Cont until front measures $14\frac{1}{2}$″($14\frac{1}{2}$″–15″–15″) from beg, or required length to underarm, ending at side edge. **Shape armhole. Next row:** Cast off 12(15–18–20) sts, patt to end. Work until armhole measures 6″(6″–$6\frac{1}{4}$″–$6\frac{1}{4}$″), ending at centre front edge. **Shape neck. Next row:** Work 17(17–17–18) sts and sl on to a holder, patt to end. Work back to neck edge. Keeping armhole edge straight, dec 1 st at neck edge on the next 9 rows, then on the foll 6 alt rows, ending at armhole edge.

Angora cardigans

Shape shoulders. Dec at neck edge on alt rows twice more, cast off 6(5–6–6) sts at beg of next row and 5(6–6–6) sts at beg of foll 2 alt rows. Work 1 row. Cast off 5(5–5–6) rem sts. **Pocket border.** Sl sts from holder on to a No 12 needle. **Next row:** [Wrong side] [Sizes 32″ and 34″ only] * [K 1, p 1] twice, inc 1 st by picking up loop from between needles and k into back of it, p 1; rep from * to last 3 sts, k 1, p 1, k 1. **Next row:** [Wrong side] [Sizes 36″ and 38″ only] * [K 1, p 1] twice, k 1, inc 1 st by picking up loop from between needles and p into back of it; rep from * to last 5 sts, [k 1, p 1] twice, k 1. Cont in rib. **1st row:** K 2, * p 1, k 1; rep from * to last st, k 1. **2nd row:** * K 1, p 1; rep from * to last st, k 1. Rep first and 2nd rows 4 times more. Cast off in rib.

RIGHT FRONT: [Omit buttonholes if not required] Work pocket lining as for Left Front. With No 12 needles cast on 67(71–75–79) sts. Change to No 10 needles. **1st row:** [Wrong side] * K 1, p 1; rep from * to last st, k 1. **2nd row:** Sl 1, * k 1, p 1; rep from * to last 2 sts, k 2. Rep 1st and 2nd rows once more, then 1st row once. Make buttonhole in next 2 rows as folls: **Next row:** Rib 5, cast off 3, rib to end. **Next row:** Rib to end, casting on 3 sts over those cast off in preceeding row. Pin positions of 6 buttons on Left Front border, [7th will come in neck border], the bottom button level with buttonhole just worked, and the rest equally spaced. Note that as 7th buttonhole comes in neck border, the measurement between the top button and beg of neck shaping should be ½″ less than the measurement between the other buttons. Making buttonholes to correspond with marked positions, cont as folls: Work 6 more rows in rib. **Next row:** Rib 11 sts for border, k to end. **Next row:** P to last 11 sts, rib 11. Cont in st-st with 11 sts in rib for border, work 34 (34–36–36) more rows. Work pocket in next 2 rows as folls: **Next row:** Work 58(60–63–65) sts, sl last 33 (33–35–35) sts just worked on to a holder, k to end. **Next row:** Patt to end, working pocket lining sts in place of those on a holder. Cont until front measures 14½″(14½″–15″–15″) from beg, or required length to underarm, ending at side edge. [Work 1 more row than on Left Front] **Shape armhole. Next row:** Cast off 12(15–18–20) sts, patt to end. Cont until armhole measures 6″(6″–6¼″–6¼″), ending at centre front edge. **Shape neck. Next row:** Work 17(17–17–18) sts, sl these sts on to a holder, patt to end. Keeping armhole edge straight, dec 1 st at neck edge on next 9 rows and then on foll 6 alt rows. Work 1 row ending at armhole edge. Shape shoulder and complete neck shaping to match Left Front. **Pocket border.** Work as for Left Front.

BACK: With No 12 needles cast on 119(127–135–143) sts. Change to No 10 needles. **1st row:** [Wrong side] * K 1, p 1; rep from * to last st, k 1. **2nd row:** K 2, * p 1, k 1; rep from * to last st, k 1. Rep 1st and 2nd rows 5 times more, then 1st row once. Cont in st-st. Work until back measures same as Fronts to underarm, ending with a p row. **Shape armholes.** Cast off 12(15–18–20) sts at beg of next 2 rows. Work until armholes measure same as fronts to beg of shoulder shaping, ending with a p row. **Shape shoulder.** Cast off 6(5–6–6) sts at beg of next 2 rows. **Shape back of neck. Next row:** Cast off 5(6–6–6) sts, k 13(14–14–15) sts including st already on the needle, cast off 47(47–47–49) sts, k to end. Cont on last set of sts as folls: **1st row:** Cast off 5(6–6–6) sts, p to last 2 sts, p 2 tog. **2nd row:** K 2 tog, k to end. **3rd row:** As 1st. Work 1 row. Cast off 5(5–5–6) rem sts. Rejoin yarn to rem sts at neck edge. **1st row:** P 2 tog, p to end. **2nd row:** Cast off 5(6–6–6) sts, k to last 2 sts, k 2 tog. **3rd row:** As 1st row. Cast off 5(5–5–6) rem sts.

SLEEVES: With No 12 needles cast on 83(83–87–87) sts. Change to No 10 needles. Work 13 rows in ribbing as given for back. Cont in st-st. Work until sleeve measures 9½″(9½″–9½″–9½″) from beg, ending with a p row. Inc one st at each end of next row, then every alt row until there are 99(99–103–103) sts, then one st at each end of every row until there are 121(121–125–125) sts. Work 17(20–24–27) rows without shaping. Cast off.

NECK BORDER: Press each piece lightly with warm iron and damp cloth. Join both shoulder seams. Sl 17(17–17–18) sts on holder at right neck edge, on to a No 12 needle. Pick up and k 31 sts up right neck edge, 57(57–57–59) sts along back neck edge and 31 sts down left neck edge, then work across sts on holder. **1st row:** Sl 1, * p 1, k 1; rep from * to end. **2nd row:** Sl 1, * k 1, p 1; rep from * to last 2 sts, k 2. Rep 1st and 2nd rows once more, then 1st row once. Make buttonhole in next 2 rows as given for Right Front. Work 6 more rows in rib. Cast off firmly in rib.

TO MAKE UP: Join side seams using back st. Join sleeve seams, reversing the seam for 6½″ from cuff edge, and leaving the straight edges at top open. Set in sleeves, sewing the straight edges at top of sleeves to the cast-off sts at underarms. Sew neatly round pocket linings on the wrong side. Sew side edges of pocket borders to fronts. Press seams lightly. Sew on buttons if required. Roll up cuffs.

Cap-sleeved sweaters

Relief stitch sweater

Instructions are for a 32″ bust. Changes for 34″ and 36″ sizes are given in brackets.

MATERIALS: 4(5–5) balls of Patons Cameo Crepe in main shade, A; 2(2–2) balls of same in contrast, B. One pair each Nos 10 and 12 needles. Set of four No 12 needles pointed at both ends.

MEASUREMENTS: Length: 19″.

TENSION: 7 sts and 9 rows to 1″.

FRONT: ** With No 10 needles and A cast on 4 sts. **1st row:** [Wrong side] P. **2nd row:** Inc in first st, [with the right-hand needle pick up p loop in previous row at back of next st to be knitted and k into it, k st on needle—called M1R] twice, inc in last st. **3rd row:** Inc in first st, p to last st, inc in last st. **4th row:** Inc in first st, k 3, [M1R] twice, k 3, inc in last st. **5th row:** As 3rd row. **6th row:** Inc in first st, k 6, [M1R] twice, k 6, inc in last st. **7th row:** As 3rd. **8th row:** Inc in first st, k 9, [M1R] twice, k 9, inc in last st. Cont in st-st inc in this way until there are 100(112–118) sts. Working in patt of 6 rows reverse st-st [p 1 row, k 1 row] 6 rows st-st, 6 rows reverse st-st and 22 rows st-st cont thus: P 2 centre sts on wrong side throughout cont inc as before until there are 128(140–146) sts. Work 1 row. **Next row:** K2 tog, work 61(67–70) sts, [M1R] twice, work to last 2 sts, k 2 tog. **Next row:** Patt to end. Rep last 2 rows 27 times more **. **Shape armholes and neck. Next row:** K 2 tog, patt 60(66–69) sts, k 2 tog, turn leaving rem sts on spare needle. Cont on these rem sts. Dec 1 st at each end of next 4 rows, then dec 1 st at neck edge on foll 3 rows. Work 27(27–29) rows without shaping, ending at neck edge. **Shape shoulder.** Keeping armhole edge straight, cast off at beg of next and alternate rows 3 sts 4 times and 4(5–5) sts 3 times. Work 1 row. Cast off 27(30–33) rem sts. Rejoin wool to rem sts at neck edge. **Next row:** K 2 tog, patt to last 2 sts, k 2 tog. Dec 1 st at each end of next 4 rows and dec at neck edge only on 3 foll rows. Work 26(26–28) rows without shaping, ending at neck edge. Shape shoulder to match first side.

BACK: Work as for front from ** to **. **Shape armholes.** Cont to inc in centre of work, dec 1 st at each end of next 5 rows. Work 9(9–11) rows, still inc in centre of work. **Shape neck. Next row:** Work 64(70–74) sts, k 2 tog turn, leaving rem sts on holder. Cont on these sts. Keeping armhole edge straight, dec 1 st at neck edge on next 14(14–15) rows. Work 6(6–5) rows without shaping, ending at neck edge. Shape shoulder as for front. Rejoin wool to rem sts at neck edge, k 2 tog, work to end. Keeping armhole edge straight, dec 1 st at neck edge on next 14(14–15) rows. Work 5(4–4) rows without shaping, ending at neck edge. Shape shoulder to match first side.

FRONT WELT: With No 12 needles and B and with right side of work facing, k up 86(94–98) sts evenly along lower edge. Work 5 inches k 1, p 1 rib. Cast off loosely in rib.

BACK WELT: Work as for Front Welt.

NECK BORDER: Press each piece lightly with warm iron and damp cloth. Join shoulder seams. With set of four No 12 needles and B, k up 50 sts evenly along back neck edge, and 68(68–72) sts along Front neck edge. Work 10 rounds k 1, p 1 rib. Cast off loosely in rib.

ARMHOLE BORDERS: With No 12 needles and B, k up 92(92–96) sts round armhole edge. Work 5 rows k 1, p 1 rib. Cast off in rib.

TO MAKE UP: Join side seams including armhole borders. Press seams.

Striped sweater

Instructions are for a 34″ bust. Changes for 36″ and 38″ sizes are given in brackets.

MATERIALS: 2(2–2) balls of Patons Cameo Crepe in main shade, A; 3(3–4) balls of same in contrast, B; 1(1–1) ball of same in 2nd contrast, C. One pair each Nos 9 and 11 needles. Set of four No 11 double-pointed needles.

Measurements: Length: 17″.

TENSION: 6½″ sts and 8½ rows to 1″.

FRONT: ** With No 9 needles and A, cast on 4 sts. **1st row:** [Wrong side] P. **2nd row:** Inc in first st, [with the right hand needle pick up the p loop in previous row at back of next st and k into it, k next st on needle—called M1R] twice, inc in last st. **3rd row:** Inc in first st, p to last st, inc in last st. **4th row:** Inc in first st, k 3, [M1R] twice, k 3, inc in last st. **5th row:** As 3rd row. **6th row:** Inc in first st, k 6, [M1R] twice, k 6, inc in last st. **7th row:** As 3rd row. **8th row:** Inc in first st, k 9, [M1R] twice, k 9, inc in last st. Cont in st-st inc in this way until there are 100(112–118) sts. Break off A and join in B. Now working in stripes of 6 rows B, 6 rows C, 6 rows B and 18 rows A cont as follows: Cont to inc as before until there are 128(140–146) sts. Work 1 row. [4th row of last C stripe completed] **Next row:** K 2 tog, k 61(67–70) sts, [M1R] twice, k to last 2 sts, k 2 tog. **Next row:** P. Rep last 2 rows 24 times more. [6th row of A stripe should now be completed] ** **Shape armholes and neck. Next row:** Cast off 5(7–7) sts, k 57 (61–64) sts, k 2 tog, turn leaving rem sts on holder. Cont on these sts. Dec 1 st at each end of next 7 rows. Work 23 rows without shaping, ending with a k row. **Shape shoulder.** Keeping armhole edge straight, cast off at beg of next and foll alt rows 3 sts 4(3–2) times and 4 sts 3(4–5) times. Work 1 row. Cast off rem 20(23–25) sts.

Striped sweater

Rejoin wool to rem sts at neck edge. **Next row:** K 2 tog, k to last 5(7–7) sts, cast off 5(7–7) sts. Rejoin wool to rem sts at armhole edge. Dec 1 st at each end of next 7 rows. Work 22 rows without shaping, ending with a p row. Shape shoulder to match first side.
BACK: Work as given for Front from ** to **. **Shape armholes. Next row:** Cast off 5(7–7) sts, k 58(62–65) sts, including st already on needle, [M1R] twice, k to last 5(7–7) sts, cast off 5(7–7) sts. Turn and rejoin wool at armhole edge. Cont to inc in centre of work, dec 1 st at each end of next 7 rows. Work 2 rows inc in centre on first row. **Shape neck. Next row:** K 55(59–62) sts, k 2 tog, turn, leave rem sts on holder. Cont on these sts. Keeping armhole edge straight dec 1 st at neck edge on next 12 rows. Work 8 rows without shaping, ending with a k row. Shape shoulder as given for front. Rejoin wool to rem sts at neck edge, k 2 tog, k to end. Keeping armhole edge straight, dec 1 st at neck edge on next 12 rows. Work 7 rows without shaping, ending with a p row. Shape shoulder to match first side.
FRONT WELT: With No 11 needles and right side of work facing and with B, k up 86(94–98) sts along lower edge. Work 58 rows in k 1, p 1 rib. Cast off loosely in rib.
BACK WELT: Work as for Front Welt.
NECK BORDER: Press each piece lightly with warm iron and damp cloth. Join shoulder seams. With set of four No 11 double pointed needles and B k up 46 sts evenly along Back neck edge and 64 sts along Front neck edge. Work 10 rounds in k 1, p 1 rib. Cast off loosely in rib.
ARMHOLE BORDERS: With No 11 needles and B, k up 96 (100–100) sts round armhole edge. Work 5 rows k 1, p 1 rib. Cast off in rib.
TO MAKE UP: Join side seams using back st, including armhole borders. Press seams.

Cable bikini designed by Frances Easterling

Instructions are for a 34" bust.
MATERIALS: 4 ozs of Twilleys Crysette. One pair Nos 13 and 14 needles. One cable needle. Shirring elastic. Two buttons.
Measurements: To fit a 34" bust, 36" hips.
TENSION: 7 sts and 9 rows to 1" in reverse st-st No 13's.

TOP

FRONT CENTRE SECTION: With No 14 needles cast on 85 sts. Work in k 1, p 1 rib for 6 rows. Change to No 13 needles. **1st row:** [Right side] P 33, k 8, p 3, k 8, p 33. **2nd row:** K 33, p 8, k 3, p 8, k 33. Rep these 2 rows once more. **5th row:** P 33, sl next 4 sts on to cable needle and hold at back of work, k 4, then k 4 from cable needle [called C4B] p 3, C4B, p 33. **6th row:** Inc 1 st in first st, k 12, inc 1 st in next st, k 19, p 8, k 3, p 8, k 19, inc 1 st in next st, k 12, inc 1 st in last st. **7th row:** P 35, k 8, p 3, k 8, p 35. **8th row:** K 14, inc 1 st in next st, k 20, p 8, k 3, p 8, k 20, inc 1 st in next st, k 14. **9th row:** P 36, k 8, p 3, k 8, p 36. **10th row:** Inc 1 st in first st, k 13, inc 1 st in next st, k 21, p 8, k 3, p 8, k 21, inc 1 st in next st, k 13, inc 1 st in last st. **11th row:** P 38, C4B, p 3, C4B, p 38. **12th row:** K 15, inc 1 st in next st, k 22, p 8, k 3, p 8, k 22, inc 1 st in next st, k 15. **13th row:** P 39, k 8, p 3, k 8, p 39. **14th row:** Inc 1 st in first st, k 14, inc 1 st in next st, k 23, p 8, k 3, p 8, k 23, inc 1 st in next st, k 14, inc 1 st in last st. **15th row:** P 41, k 8, p 3, k 8, p 41. **16th row:** K 41, p 8, k 3, p 8, k 41. [101 sts] Rep last 2 rows twice more. **21st row:** P 41, C4B, p 3, C4B, p 41. **22nd row:** K 16, sl 1, k 1, psso, k 23, p 8, k 3, p 8, k 23, k 2 tog, k 16. **23rd row:** P 40, k 8, p 3, k 8, p 40. **24th row:** K 2 tog, k 14, sl 1, k 1, psso, k 22, p 8, k 3, p 8, k 22, k 2 tog, k 14, k 2 tog. **25th row:** P 38, k 8, p 3, k 8, p 38. **26th row:** K 15, sl 1, k 1, psso, k 21, p 8, k 3, p 8, k 21, k 2 tog, k 15. **27th row:** P 37, k 8, p 3, k 8, p 37. **28th row:** K 2 tog, k 13, sl 1, k 1, psso, k 20, p 8, k 3, p 8, k 20, k 2 tog, k 13, k 2 tog, **29th row:** P 35, k 8, p 3, k 8, p 35. [89 sts] **30th row:** K 35, p 8, k 3, p 8, k 35. **31st row:** P 35, C4B, p 3, C4B, p 35. **32nd row:** As 30th. **33rd row:** As 29th. **34th row:** As 30th. **35th row:** P 35, k 8, p 3, k 8, p 21, turn. **36th row:** K 21, p 8, k 3, p 8, k 21, turn. **37th row:** P 21, k 8, p 3, k 8, p 16, turn. **38th row:** K 16, p 8, k 3, p 8, k 16, turn. **39th row:** P 16, k 8, p 1, place rem 45 sts on holder. Cast on 6 sts, p these 6 sts, k 1, p 8, k 1, place rem 34 sts on holder. Cont on these 16 sts only for first shoulder strap. **41st row:** P 1, C4B, p 1, k 6. **42nd row:** P 6, k 1, p 8, k 1. **43rd row:** P 1, k 8, p 1, k 6. Rep these 2 rows working cable row on every 10th row. Cont until work measures 18" from divided cable. Cast off. **2nd cable.** With right side of cable facing take 11 sts at centre from holder. Leave rem 34 sts on holder. Cast on 5 sts for facing at centre [between cables], k 6, p 1, C4B, p 1. Cont working as for first

TO A BLUE PA

cable for 18″. Cast off.
LEFT SIDE: With No 14 needles cast on 63 sts and work in k 1, p 1 rib for 6 rows. Change to No 13 needles. **1st row:** K 59, p 4. **2nd row:** K 4, p 59. Rep these 2 rows 6 times more. **15th row:** Inc 1 st at beg of row. Work 3 more rows. Inc 1 st at beg of next row. Cont without shaping until work measures 2¼″ from cast-on edge, ending with a p row. **Next row:** K to last 25 sts turn patt to end. **Next row:** K to last 35 sts, turn, patt to end. **Next row:** K to last 45 sts, turn, patt to end. Cont in this way until 10 sts rem. Leave all sts on holder.
RIGHT SIDE: Work as for Left side, reversing shaping.
LEFT RIBBED EDGE: With No 14 needles and right side facing, take the left side at the top, k 4 sts, p 61 sts, then take Front section and p across sts on holder on left side. Work in k 1, p 1 rib for 6 rows. Cast off. Work right ribbed edge in same way reversing shaping.
TO MAKE UP: Press with a damp cloth and warm iron. Join side seams. Turn back facing of cable straps and st to outside edge. Make loops at end of each strap. Turn back facings on right and left sides [back overwrap] and sew on hooks and eyes.

PANTS

Beg at top of Back. With No 13 needles cast on 98 sts. Work in reverse st-st for 46 rows. Cast off 5 sts at beg of next 6 rows. Cast off 2 sts at beg of next 4 rows. Dec 1 st at each end of next and every foll alt row 20 times in all. Work 10 rows without shaping. Inc 1 st at each end of next and foll 4th row. Work 4 rows without shaping. Inc 1 st at each end of next and every foll alt row 10 times in all. Inc 1 st at each end of next 30 rows. Work 58 rows without shaping. Cast off.
CABLE INSERTIONS: [Make two] With No 13 needles cast on 21 sts. **1st row:** P 1, k 8, p 3, k 8, p 1. **2nd row:** K 1, p 8, k 3, p 8, k 1. Rep these 2 rows once more and 1st row once. **6th row:** P 1, C4B, p 3, C4B, p 1. Cont in this way working cable on every 10th row until work measures 3½″. **Divide cables.** P 1, k 8, p 2 tog, turn and work this side only until single cable measures 10½″ to make edging for legs of Bikini. K other 10 sts of cable to correspond.
TO MAKE UP: Sew inserts of double cable to back and front of st-st sides [easing slightly to fit]. Sew divided cable around legs grafting tog cables where they meet. **Top edging.** With No 14 needles k up 208 sts and work 12 rows k 1, p 1 rib. Cast off. Thread shirring elastic through top if required.

Lace stitch bikini

Instructions are for a 34″ bust, 36″ hips. Changes for 36″ bust, 38″ hips are given in brackets.
MATERIALS: 3(3) balls of Wendy Invitation Crochet Cotton in White, A; 3(3) balls of same in contrast, B. One pair No 12 needles. 2½ yards round elastic.
MEASUREMENTS: To fit a 34″(36″) bust; 36″(38″) hips.
TENSION: 8 sts and 10 rows to 1″.

TOP

With No 12 needles and A, cast on 50(54) sts. **1st row:** K. **2nd row:** P 2 tog, p to last 2 sts, p 2 tog tbl. Rep these 2 rows 3(4) times more. **Commence patt. 1st row:** K 6(7), [y fwd, sl 1, k 1, psso] 4 times, * k 3, [y fwd, sl 1, k 1, psso] 4 times; rep from * once more, k 6(7). **2nd and every even row:** P 2 tog, p to last 2 sts, p 2 tog tbl. **3rd row:** K 6(7), [y fwd, sl 1, k 1, psso] 3 times, * k 5, [y fwd, sl 1, k 1, psso] 3 times; rep from * once more, k 6(7). **5th row:** K 6(7), [y fwd, sl 1, k 1, psso] twice, * k 7, [y fwd, sl 1, k 1, psso] twice; rep from * once more, k 6(7). **7th row:** K 6(7), y fwd, sl 1, k 1, psso, * k 9, y fwd, sl 1, k 1, psso; rep from * once more, k 6(7). **9th row:** K 8(9), [y fwd, sl 1, k 1, psso] 4 times, k 3, [y fwd, sl 1, k 1, psso] 4 times, k 7(8). **11th row:** K 8(9), [y fwd, sl 1, k 1, psso] 3 times, k 5, [y fwd, sl 1, k 1, psso] 3 times, k 7(8). **13th row:** K 8(9), [y fwd, sl 1, k 1, psso] twice, k 7, [y fwd, sl 1, k 1, psso] twice, k 7(8). **15th row:** K 8(9), y fwd, sl 1, k 1, psso, k 9, y fwd, sl 1, k 1, psso, k 7(8). **17th row:** K 10(11), [y fwd, sl 1, k 1, psso] 4 times, k 8(9). **19th row:** K 10(11), [y fwd, sl 1, k 1, psso] 3 times, k 8(9). **21st row:** K 10(11), [y fwd, sl 1, k 1, psso] twice, k 8(9). **23rd row:** K 10(11), y fwd, sl 1, k 1, psso, k 8(9). **24th row:** As 2nd. Now work 16(18) more rows in st-st, dec as before on every p row. K tog 2 rem sts. Fasten off. Work another piece in exactly the same way.
STRAPS: [Make two] With No 12 needles and B, cast on 6 sts. **1st row:** K 1, inc 1 st by picking up loop from between needles and p into back of it, k 1, p 1, inc 1 st by picking up loop and k into back of it, p 1, k 1, inc 1 st by picking up loop and p into back of it, k 1. [9 sts] Cont in rib. **1st row:** K 2, * p 1, k 1; rep from * to last st, k 1. **2nd row:** * K 1, p 1; rep from * to last st, k 1. Rep these 2 rows until strap measures 40″(42″) when

slightly stretched. Cast off firmly in rib.

BORDERS: [Make two] With No 12 needles and B, cast on 6 sts and work inc row as given for straps. Work 6″(6½″) in rib. Cast off firmly in rib.

TO MAKE UP: Press each piece lightly with warm iron and damp cloth. Sew borders to cast-on edges of cup pieces. Leaving an equal amount at each end for ties, pin straps in position as illustration; the first strap to lower edge of right cup and top edge of left cup; the 2nd strap to top edge of right cup and lower edge of left cup and with 2nd strap overlapping first strap at centre. Sew on by backstitching. Press seams lightly.

PANTS

BACK: ** With No 12 needles and A, cast on 137(146) sts. **1st row:** K. **2nd row:** P. Cont in patt. **1st row:** K 4(3), [y fwd, sl 1, k 1, psso] 4 times, * k 3, [y fwd, sl 1, k 1, psso] 4 times; rep from * to last 4(3) sts, k 4(3). **2nd and every alt row:** P. **3rd row:** K 5(4), [y fwd, sl 1, k 1, psso] 3 times, k 1, * k 4, [y fwd, sl 1, k 1, psso] 3 times, k 1; rep from * to last 4(3) sts, k 4(3). **5th row:** K 6(5), [y fwd, sl 1, k 1, psso] twice, k 2, * k 5, [y fwd, sl 1, k 1, psso] twice, k 2; rep from * to last 4(3) sts, k 4(3). **7th row:** K 7(6), y fwd, sl 1, k 1, psso, k 3, * k 6, y fwd, sl 1, k 1, psso, k 3; rep from * to last 4(3) sts, k 4(3). **9th row:** K 10(9), * [y fwd, sl 1, k 1, psso] 4 times, k 3; rep from * to last 6(5) sts, k 6(5). **11th row:** K 10(9), * k 1, [y fwd, sl 1, k 1, psso] 3 times, k 4; rep from * to last 6(5) sts, k 6(5). **13th row:** K 10(9), * k 2, [y fwd, sl 1, k 1, psso] twice, k 5; rep from * to last 6(5) sts, k 6(5). **15th row:** K 10(9), * k 3, y fwd, sl 1, k 1, psso, k 6; rep from * to last 6(5) sts, k 6(5). **16th row:** P. Cont in st-st. Work 4 rows. **. **Shape legs.** Cast off 3 sts at beg of next 18(20) rows and 2 sts at beg of foll 16 rows. Dec 1 st at beg of every row until 23(24) sts rem. Work 2 rows. Cast off.

FRONT: Work as for Back from ** to **. **Shape legs.** Cast off 36 sts at beg of first 2 rows, 3 sts at beg of next 6(8) rows and 2 sts at beg of foll 6(6) rows. Dec 1 st at beg of every row until 23(24) sts rem. Work 2 rows. Cast off.

WAIST BORDER: With No 12 needles and B cast on 6 sts and work inc row as given for straps of top. Cont in rib until border measures 32″(34″) when slightly stretched. Cast off firmly in rib.

LEG BORDERS: [Make two] Work 18″(19″) as for waist border.

TO MAKE UP: Press each piece lightly with warm iron and damp cloth. Sew side and crutch seams. Join narrow edge of borders. Pin borders in position, sew on by backstitching. Press seams lightly. Thread elastic through knitting at waist and legs and fasten ends securely.

Shawl and handbag

MATERIALS: 14 50-grm balls of Patons Doublet. One pair No 2 needles. One crochet hook, International size 5·00.
TENSION: 3 sts and $4\frac{1}{2}$ rows to 1" over patt on No 2 needles.
With No 2 needles cast on 259 sts. **1st row:** K 1, sl 1, k 1, psso, k to last 3 sts, k 2 tog, k 1. **2nd row:** K 1, p 2 tog, p to last 3 sts, p 2 tog tbl, k 1. Cont in st-st dec 1 st at each end of every row in this way until 5 sts rem. **Next row:** K 1, sl 2 p-wise, k 1, p 2sso, k 1. **Next row:** K 3 tog. Fasten off.
BORDER: Join wool to right shaped edge at cast on edge, and, with crochet hook, work a row of dc along the 2 shaped edges, and then along the cast on edge, working 1 dc for each row along the shaped edges, 1 dc into st at point, and 2 dc for each 3 sts along cast on edge. Join with a sl st. Do not turn. **Next row:** * 7 ch, miss 3 sts, 1 dc into next st; rep from * along shaped edges only, and missing 2 sts instead of 3 at each side of point. Turn with 7 ch. **Next row:** * 1 dc into centre ch of 7 ch loop, 7 ch; rep from * ending with 1 dc into sl st. Turn with 7 ch. Rep last row twice more, but working twice into loop at point and working last dc into centre ch of turning ch loop. Fasten off.
TO MAKE UP: Pin out shawl in the form of a triangle, stretching the shaped edges as necessary. Press. **Fringe.** Using four strands of wool 15" long for each tassel work a fringe along the shaped edges, working a tassel into each 7 ch loop. Trim ends.

Handbag

MATERIALS: 4 ozs Robin Crepe Double Knitting in main shade, A; 4 ozs in contrast, B; 3 ozs in contrast, C. One pair each Nos 5 and 8 needles. One No 9 crochet hook, International size 3·50. Three 1" diameter rings.
MEASUREMENTS: Bag measures approx $11\frac{1}{2}'' \times 11\frac{1}{2}''$.
TENSION: $4\frac{1}{2}$ sts to 1".
NOTE: **(A)** Sl all sts p-wise carrying yarn loosely at back of sts on right-side rows. Sl all sts p-wise carrying yarn loosely in front of sts on wrong side rows. **(B)** Do not break off wool when changing colour but carry it up side of work when not in use.
USE DOUBLE WOOL THROUGHOUT.
With No 8 needles and A, cast on 43 sts. **1st row:** * K 1, p 1; rep from * to last st, k 1. Rep this row 7 times more. Break off A. Change to No 5 needles. **Commence patt. 1st row:** With B, k. **2nd row:** As 1st. **3rd row:** With C, k 3, * [sl 1, k 1] twice, sl 1, k 3; rep from * to end. **4th row:** With C, p 3, * [sl 1, k 1] twice, sl 1, p 3; rep from * to end. **5th row:** With B, k 1, sl 2, * k 5, sl 3; rep from * ending k 5, sl 2, k 1. **6th row:** With B, k 1, sl 2, * k 5, sl 3; rep from * ending k 5, sl 2, k 1. **7th row:** With C, as 3rd. **8th row:** With C, as 4th. **9th row:** With B, as 1st. **10th row:** With B, as 2nd. **11th row:** With C, [k 1, sl 1] twice, * k 3, [sl 1, k 1] twice, sl 1; rep from * ending k 3, [sl 1, k 1] twice. **12th row:** With C, [k 1, sl 1] twice, * p 3, [sl 1, k 1] twice, sl 1; rep from * ending p 3, [sl 1, k 1] twice. **13th row:** With B, k 4, * sl 3, k 5; rep from * ending k 4 instead of k 5. **14th row:** With B, k 4, * sl 3, k 5; rep from * ending k 4 instead of k 5. **15th row:** With C, as 11th. **16th row:** With C, as 12th. These 16 rows form patt. Rep patt rows 6 times more, then 1st and 2nd rows once. Break off B and C, join in A. Cont with No 8 needles. **Next row:** K. **Next row:** * K 1, p 1; rep from * to last st, k 1. Rep last row 7 times more. Cast off in patt.
WORK BORDER: With No 8 needles and right side of work facing and A, pick up and k 67 sts along one side edge, working 1 st for each 2 rows and 1 st for cast off row. **Next row:** * K 1, p 1; rep from * to last st, k 1. Rep this row 7 times more. Cast off in patt. Work border along other side edge in same way. Make another piece the same, but rep 16 patt rows 4 times instead of 6 and pick up 51 sts along side edges.
TO MAKE UP: Press each piece lightly with warm iron and damp cloth. Place two pieces tog with wrong sides of work towards each other, and cast-on edges matching. With A, saddle st through both thicknesses along side and cast-on edges. Make buttonloop in centre of cast off edge of flap as follows: Join wool A with a dc into edge, work 8 ch, leave space, work 1 dc into edge; fasten off.
BUTTON: Using crochet hook and double wool in A, work a row of dc firmly all round one ring. Break wool, leaving two ends. Thread these ends on to a needle, thread through each st right round ring. Draw up tightly to centre of ring and fasten with several sts. Sew button to bag to match loop.
STRAP RINGS: With double wool, work a row of dc firmly round 2 rem rings, leaving ends for sewing. Sew a ring to each side of bag at opening edge.
STRAP: With No 8 needles and A, cast on 5 sts. **1st row:** [K 1, p 1] twice, k 1. Rep this row until strap measures 36", when slightly stretched lengthwise. Cast off in patt. Sew ends of straps to rings.

Gloves and socks

Gloves

MATERIALS: 1 oz each of contrasting colours A, B, C, D and E in Robin Vogue 4-ply. One pair No 11 needles.
RIGHT HAND: ** With No 11 needles and A, cast on 54 sts. **1st row:** * P 2, k 2; rep from * to last 2 sts, p 2. **2nd row:** * K 2, p 2; rep from * to last 2 sts, k 2. These two rows form patt. Work 4 more rows. Break off A and join in E. **Next row:** K. **Next row:** As 2nd patt row. Break off E and join in A. **Next row:** K. **Next row:** As 2nd patt row. Work 10 more rows in patt. Break off A and join in E. **Next row:** K. **Next row:** As 2nd patt row. Break off E. Join in A. **Next row:** K. **Next row:** As 2nd patt row. Work 4 more rows in patt. Break off A and join in B and cont in st-st. Work 10 rows. ** **Shape thumb. 1st row:** K 29 sts, inc 1 st by picking up loop between needles and k into back of it, k 2, inc 1, k to end. **2nd row:** P. Break off B and join in C. **3rd row:** K. **4th row:** P 23 sts, inc 1 st by picking up loop from between needles and p into back of it, p 4, inc 1, p to end. Break off C and join in B. **5th row:** K. **6th row:** P. **7th row:** K 29 sts, inc 1 st as before, k 6, inc 1, k to end. **8th row:** P. **9th row:** K. **10th row:** P 23, inc 1 st as before, p 8, inc 1, p to end. Break off B and join in D. Cont to inc in this way on every 3rd row, working 6 rows D, 6 rows B and 2 rows C. [70 sts] Break off C and join in B. **Commence thumb. 1st row:** K 47 sts, turn and cast on 2 sts. **2nd row:** P 20, turn and cast on 2 sts. Cont on these 22 sts. Work 4 more rows in B, 2 rows C, 6 rows B, 6 rows E and 2 rows D. **Shape top. 1st row:** * K 2 tog; rep from * to end. **2nd row:** P. **3rd row:** * K 2 tog; rep from * to last st, k 1. Break off wool leaving enough to thread through sts, draw up and fasten off. Sew seam to base of thumb. With right side of work facing and B, using right-hand needle pick up and k 3 sts at base of thumb, k to end. Cont on these 55 sts. Work 5 more rows B, 6 rows E and 6 rows D. Break off D and join in B. **First finger. Next row:** K 35, turn and cast on 2 sts. **Next row:** P 17, turn and cast on 2 sts. Cont on these 19 sts. Work 4 more rows B, 2 rows C, 6 rows B, 6 rows E and 6 rows D. Break off D and join in B. **Shape top. 1st row:** * K 2 tog; rep from * to last st, k 1. **2nd row:** P. **3rd row:** * K 2 tog; rep from * to end. Break off wool and complete as for thumb. **2nd finger.** With right side of work facing and B, using right hand needle pick up and k 3 sts at base of 1st finger, k 7, turn, cast on 2 sts. **Next row:** P 19, turn, cast on 2 sts. Cont on these 21 sts. Work 4 more rows B, 2 rows C, 6 rows B, 6 rows E, 6 rows D and 2 rows B. **Shape top. 1st row:** * K 2 tog; rep from * to last st, k 1. **2nd row:** P. **3rd row:** As 1st. Break wool and complete to match thumb. **3rd finger.** With right side of work facing and B, using right-hand needle, pick up and k 3 sts at base of 2nd finger, k 6, turn, cast on 2 sts. **Next row:** P 17 sts, turn, cast on 2 sts. Complete to match first finger. **4th finger.** With right side of work facing and B, using right-hand needle, pick up and k 3 sts at base of 3rd finger, k to end. **Next row:** P 17. Cont on these 17 sts. Work 4 more rows in B, 2 rows C, 6 rows B, 6 rows E and 2 rows D. **Shape top. 1st row:** * K 2 tog; rep from * to last st, k 1. **2nd row:** P. **3rd row:** As 1st. Break wool and complete as for thumb, sewing along side of glove to the cast-on edge. Press lightly with warm iron and damp cloth.
LEFT HAND: Follow instructions for Right Hand from ** to **. **Shape thumb. 1st row:** K 23, inc 1 st, k 2, inc 1, k to end. **2nd row:** P. Break off B and join in C. **3rd row:** K. **4th row:** P 29, inc 1 st, p 4, inc 1 st, p to end. Cont to inc on every 3rd row, working in stripes as for Right-hand to beg of thumb. **Next row:** K 41 sts, turn, cast on 2 sts. **Next row:** P 20 sts, turn, cast on 2 sts. Complete thumb and fingers as for Right hand. Press lightly with warm iron and damp cloth.

Long socks

MATERIALS: 1 oz of Robin Vogue 4-ply in main shade, A; 3 ozs in contrast, B; 1 oz each of contrasts C and D; 2 ozs in contrast, E. One pair each Nos 10 and 11 needles. $\frac{3}{4}$ yd round elastic.
With No 10 needles and A, cast on 78 sts. **1st row:** * P 2, k 2; rep from * to last 2 sts, p 2. **2nd row:** * K 2, p 2; rep from * to last 2 sts, k 2. These two rows form patt. Work 10 more rows. Break off A and join in B. **Next row:** K. **Next row:** As 2nd patt row. Work 10 more rows in patt. Break off B and join in C. Now k the first row on each change of colour, cont in stripes as folls; 2 rows C, 12 rows B, 2 rows C, 6 rows B, 6 rows D, 6 rows B, 12 rows A, 6 rows B, 2 rows C, 6 rows B, 6 rows

D, 6 rows B, 2 rows C, 6 rows B, 6 rows E, 16 rows A and 6 rows E. Change to No 11 needles and cont in stripes of 12 rows B, 2 rows C, 6 rows B, 16 rows E, 6 rows B and 5 rows D. **Next row:** With D, k 2 tog, patt to last 2 sts, k 2 tog. Break off D. With right side of work facing, sl first 19 sts on to a holder, join in B and k over centre 38 sts, sl rem 19 sts on to a holder. **Work instep.** Work 5 more rows in B. Cont in stripes of 2 rows C, 6 rows B, 6 rows D, 6 rows B, 6 rows D, 6 rows B, 2 rows C and 8 rows B. [Adjust length of foot here] Break off B and join in E. **Next row:** K 3, * k 2 tog, k 4; rep from * to last 5 sts, k 2 tog, k 3. [32 sts] **Next row:** P. **Shape toe. 1st row:** K 1, sl 1, k 1, psso, k to last 3 sts, k 2 tog, k 1. **2nd row:** P. Rep last 2 rows 8 times more. Break off wool and leave rem 14 sts on a holder. Return to heel sts and slip 2 sets of sts on to one No 11 needle with outside edges to centre. [38 sts] Join in E. **Shape heel. 1st row:** [Right side] Sl 1, k 36 sts, turn. **2nd row:** Sl 1, p 35 sts, turn. **3rd row:** Sl 1, k 34 sts, turn. **4th row:** Sl 1, p 33 sts, turn. Cont working 1 st less on each row until 11 sts rem unworked on each side. [Last row will be sl 1, p 15] Turn and cont as folls: **1st row:** Sl 1, k 15, pick up strand of wool from between needles on to left-hand needle and k this loop tog with next st, [thus preventing a hole], turn. **2nd row:** Sl 1, p 16, pick up strand between needles and p tog with next st, turn. Cont in this way working one more st on each row until 38 sts are on one row. Break off E and join in D. **Next row:** K 3, * k 2 tog, k 4; rep from * to last 5 sts, k 2 tog, k 3. [32 sts] **Next row:** P. Cont in st-st until work measures same as instep to beg of toe shaping, ending with a p row. Break off D and join in E. Work 2 rows. Shape toe as for instep. Graft or cast off 2 sets of sts tog.

TO MAKE UP: Pin out and press each sock. Join foot and leg seams. Cut two lengths of elastic and thread through knitting at cast on edges. Join ends firmly. Press seams lightly.

Short socks

MATERIALS: 1 oz of Robin Vogue 4-ply in main shade. A; 2 ozs of same in contrast, B; 1 oz each of same in contrasts C and D. One pair No 11 needles. ½ yd round elastic.
With No 11 needles and A cast on 78 sts. **1st row:** * P 2, k 2; rep from * to last 2 sts, p 2. **2nd row:** * K 2, p 2; rep from * to last 2 sts, k 2. These two rows form patt. Work 10 more rows. Break off A and join in B. **Next row:** K. **Next row:** As 2nd patt row. Cont in patt. Work until sock measures 5½″ from cast on edge, ending with 1st patt row. **Next row:** K 2 tog, patt to last 2 sts, k 2 tog. Break off wool. With right side of work facing, sl first 19 sts on to a holder, rejoin wool and work in patt over centre 38 sts, sl rem 19 sts on to a holder. Cont in patt for instep on centre 38 sts for 5″, ending with 2nd patt row. [Adjust length here if required] Break off B and join in C. **Next row:** K 3, * k 2 tog, k 4; rep from * to last 5 sts, k 2 tog, k 3. [32 sts] **Next row:** P. **Shape toe. 1st row:** K 1, sl 1, k 1, psso, k to last 3 sts, k 2 tog, k 1. **2nd row:** P. Rep last 2 rows 8 times more. Break off wool and leave rem 14 sts on a holder. Return to heel sts, sl 2 sets of sts on to 1 needle with outside edges to the centre. [38 sts] Join in D. **Shape heel. 1st row:** [Right side] Sl 1, k 36 sts, turn. **2nd row:** Sl 1, p 35 sts, turn. **3rd row:** Sl 1, k 34 sts, turn. **4th row:** Sl 1, p 33 sts, turn. Cont working 1 st less on each row in this way until 11 sts rem unworked at each side. [Last row will be sl 1, p 15] Turn and cont as folls: **1st row:** Sl 1, k 15, pick up strand of wool between needles on to left-hand needle and k this loop tog with next st [thus preventing a hole], turn. **2nd row:** Sl 1, p 16, pick up strand between needles and p tog with next st, turn. Cont in this way working 1 st more on each row until 38 sts are again on 1 row. Break off D and join in B. **Next row:** K 3, * k 2 tog, k 4; rep from * to last 5 sts, k 2 tog, k 3. [32 sts] **Next row:** P. Cont in st-st until work measures same as instep to beg of toe, ending with a p row. Break off B and join in C. Work 2 rows. Shape toe as for instep. Graft or cast off 2 sets of sts tog.
TO MAKE UP: Pin out and press each sock. Join foot and leg seams. Cut two lengths of elastic and thread through knitting at cast-on edges. Join ends firmly. Press seams lightly.

Child's cable sweater

Instructions are for a 24″ chest. Changes for 26″ and 28″ sizes are given in brackets.
MATERIALS: 6(7–8) ozs of Jaeger Celtic Spun. One pair each Nos 7 and 10 needles.
MEASUREMENTS: To fit a 24″(26″–28″) chest. Length at centre back: 14½″(15½″–16½″), adjustable. Sleeve seam: 11″(12″–13″), adjustable.
TENSION: 7 sts and 7½ rows to 1″ over patt on No 7 needles.

FRONT: ** With No 10 needles cast on 73(79–85) sts. **1st row:** K 2, * p 1, k 1; rep from * to last st, k 1. **2nd row:** * K 1, p 1; rep from * to last st, k 1. Rep 1st and 2nd rows once more, then 1st row once. **Next row:** K into front and back of first st, * p 5, k into front and back of next st; rep from * to end. [86(93–100) sts] Change to No 7 needles. **Commence patt. 1st row:** P 2, * sl 1 p-wise with wool at back of st, k 4, p 2; rep from * to end. **2nd row:** K 2, * p 4, sl 1 p-wise with wool at front of st, k 2; rep from * to end. **3rd row:** P 2, * drop sl-st to front of work, k 2, pick up dropped st and k it, k 2, p 2; rep from * to end. **4th row:** K 2, * p 5, k 2; rep from * to end. **5th row:** P 2, * k 4, sl 1 p-wise with wool at back of st, p 2; rep from * to end. **6th row:** K 2, * sl 1 p-wise with wool at front of st, p 4, k 2; rep from * to end. **7th row:** P 2, * k 2, sl 2 p-wise with wool at back of sts, drop sl-st to front of work, sl same 2 sts back to left-hand needle, pick up dropped st and k it, k 2, p 2; rep from * to end. **8th row:** As 4th. These eight rows form patt. Work until front measures 9½″(10″–10½″) from beg, or required length to underarm, ending with a wrong side row. **Shape armholes.** Cast off 5(6–7) sts at beg of next 2 rows. Dec 1 st at beg of every row until 68(71–74) sts rem. ** Cont without shaping until armholes measure 3½″(4″–4½″) from beg, ending with a right side row. **Shape neck. Next row:** Patt 26(27–28) sts, cast off 16(17–18) sts, patt to end. Cont on last set of sts as folls: Keeping armhole edge straight, dec 1 st at neck edge on next 6 rows, then on foll 3 alt rows, ending at armhole edge. **Shape shoulder.** Keeping neck edge straight, cast off 5(6–7) sts at beg of next row, and 6 sts at beg of foll alt row. Work 1 row. Cast off rem 6(6–6) sts. Rejoin wool to rem sts at neck edge. Keeping armhole edge straight dec 1 st at neck edge on next 6 rows. Then on foll 3 alt rows. Work 1 row ending at armhole edge. Shape shoulder to match first side.

BACK: Work as given for Front from ** to **. Work until armholes measure same as Front to beg of shoulder shaping, ending with a wrong side row. **Shape shoulders and back neck. Next row:** Cast off 5(6–7) sts, patt 15(15–15) sts, cast off 28(29–30) sts, patt to end. Cont on last set of sts. **1st row:** Cast off 5(6–7) sts, patt to last 2 sts, dec 1 st. **2nd row:** Dec 1 st, patt to end. **3rd row:** Cast off 6(6–6) sts, patt to last 2 sts, dec 1 st. **4th row:** Work in patt. Cast off rem 6(6–6) sts. Rejoin wool to rem sts at neck edge. **1st row:** Dec 1 st, patt to end. **2nd row:** Cast off 6(6–6) sts, patt to last 2 sts, dec 1 st. **3rd row:** As 1st. Cast off rem 6(6–6) sts.

SLEEVES: With No 10 needles cast on 43(45–49) sts. Work 5 rows in ribbing as given for Front. **Next row:** [Sizes 24″ and 28″ only] K into front and back of first st, * p 5, k into front and back of next st; rep from * to end. **Next row:** [26″ size only] P into front and back of first st, p 3, * k into front and back of next st, p 5; rep from * ending last rep, p into front and back of last st. [51(54–58) sts] Change to No 7 needles. **Commence patt. 1st row:** [Sizes 24″ and 28″ only] P 2, * sl 1 p-wise with wool at back of st, k 4, p 2; rep from * to end. **1st row:** [26″ size only] * Sl 1 p-wise with wool at back of st, k 4, p 2; rep from * to last 5 sts, sl 1 p-wise, k 4. This sets patt. Work 7 more rows. Keeping patt correct, inc 1 st at each end of next and every foll 6th row until there are 71(76–82) sts. Cont without shaping until sleeve measures 11″(12″–13″) from beg, or required length to underarm, ending with a wrong side row. **Shape top.** Cast off 5(6–7) sts at beg of next 2 rows and 2(2–2) sts at beg of foll 4 rows. Dec 1 st at beg of every row until 43(44–44) sts rem. Cast off at beg of next and foll rows, 2 sts 4 times, 3 sts twice and 4 sts twice. Cast off rem 21(22–22) sts.

NECK BORDER: Press each piece lightly with a warm iron and damp cloth. Join left shoulder seam. With No 10 needles k up 37(38–39) sts along back neck edge, 17(17–17) sts down left side of neck to cast off sts, 16(17–18) sts from cast off sts at centre front and 17 (17–17) sts up right side of neck. **1st row:** * K 1, p 1; rep from * to last st, k 1. **2nd row:** K 2, * p 1, k 1; rep from * to last st, k 1. Rep 1st and 2nd rows 3 times more, then 1st row once. Cast off loosely in rib.

TO MAKE UP: Join right shoulder seam and neck border seam. Sew sleeves into armholes. Join side and sleeve seams. Press seams lightly.

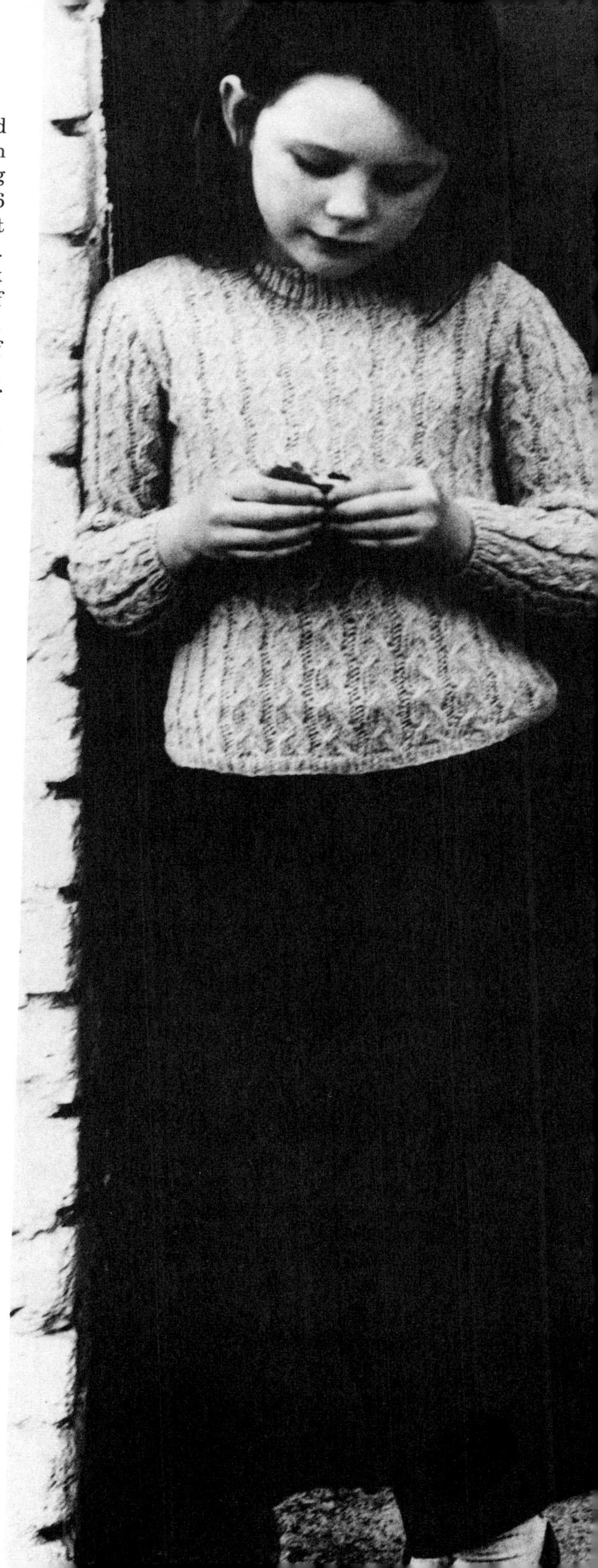

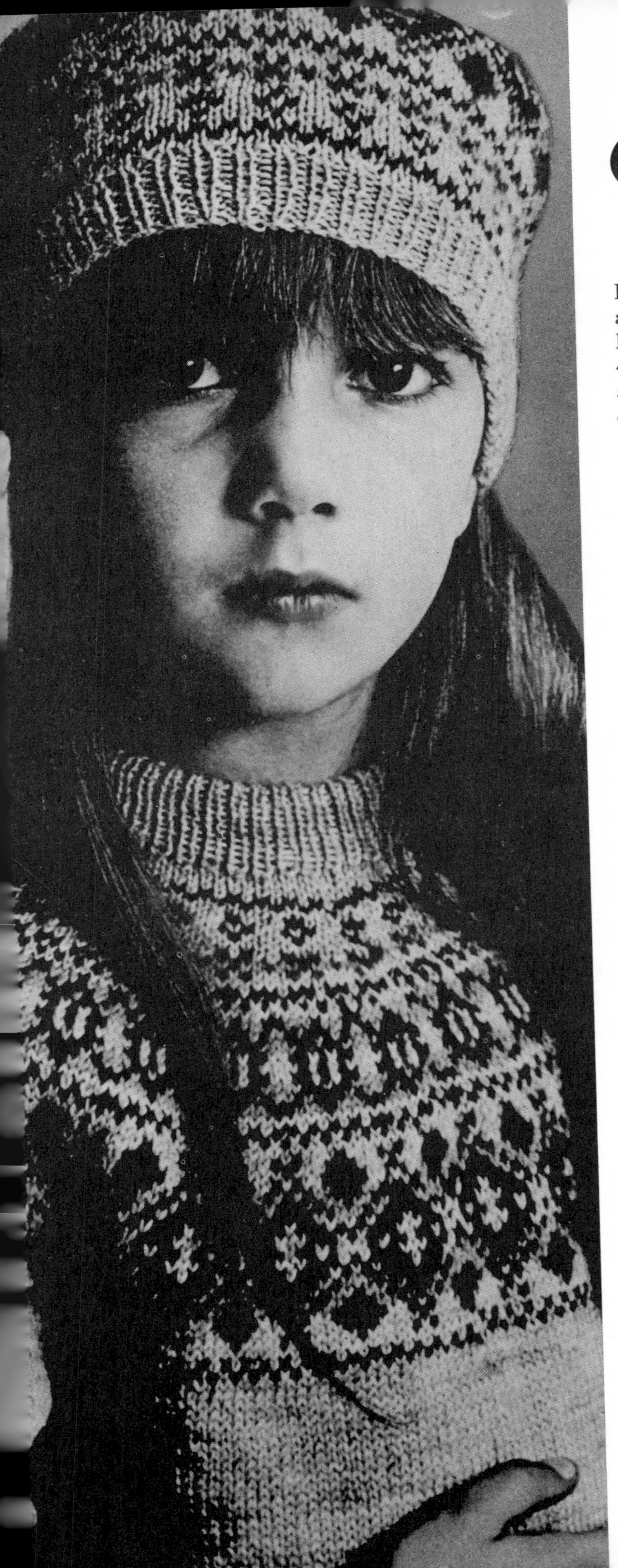

Child's Fair Isle

Instructions are for a 26″ chest. Changes for 28″, 30″ and 32″ sizes are given in brackets.
MATERIALS: 8(9–9–10) ozs of Lee Target Motoravia 4-ply in main shade, A; 1 oz each of contrasts B, C, D, E and F. One pair each Nos 10 and 12 needles. One set of four Nos 10 and 12 needles, pointed at both ends.
MEASUREMENTS: To fit a 26″(28″–30″–32″) chest. Length to shoulder: 16½″(18″–19½″–21″), adjustable. Sleeve seam: 13″(14″–15″–16″), adjustable.
TENSION: 7 sts to 1″ over st-st on No 10 needles.

SWEATER

BACK: With No 12 needles and A, cast on 99(107–113–121) sts. Work 1″ k 1, p 1 rib. Change to No 10 needles. **Commence Fair Isle patt. 1st row:** [Wrong side] With A, p to end. Beg with a k row, work rows 1 to 23 as given on chart, noting that 1st size will beg and end at point marked C, 2nd size will beg and end at point marked A, 3rd size will beg and end at point marked D and 4th size will beg and end at point marked B. **Next row:** Break off contrast colours, with A only p to end, inc 1 st in centre of row on 1st and 3rd sizes only. 100(107–114–121) sts. Beg with a k row cont in st-st until work measures 11″(12″–13″–14″) from beg, or required length to underarm, ending with a p row. **Shape armholes.** Cast off 6 sts at beg of next 2 rows. ** **Next row:** K 1, sl 1, k 1, psso, k to last 3 sts, k 2 tog, k 1. **Next row:** P. Rep last 2 rows 2(3–4–5) times more. ** 82(87–92–97) sts. Leave sts on holder for yoke.
FRONT: Work as given for Back.
SLEEVES: With No 12 needles and A, cast on 47(49–51–53) sts. Work 1″ k 1, p 1 rib. Change to No 10 needles. **Commence Fair Isle patt. 1st row:** [Wrong side] With A, p to end. Beg with a k row work rows 1 to 23 as given on chart, noting that 1st size will beg and end at point marked A, 2nd size will beg and end at point marked B, 3rd size will beg and end at point marked C and 4th size will beg and end at point marked D, **at the same time**, inc 1 st at each end of 7th and every foll 6th row. **Next row:** Break off contrast colours. With A only, p to end. Beg with a k row, cont in st-st inc 1 st at each end of every 6th row as before until there are 75(79–83–87) sts. Cont without shaping until sleeve measures 13″(14″–15″–16″) from beg, or required length to underarm, ending with a p row. **Shape top.** Cast off 6 sts at beg of next 2 rows. Work from ** to ** as given for Back. 57(59–61–63) sts. Leave sts on holder

sweater and beret

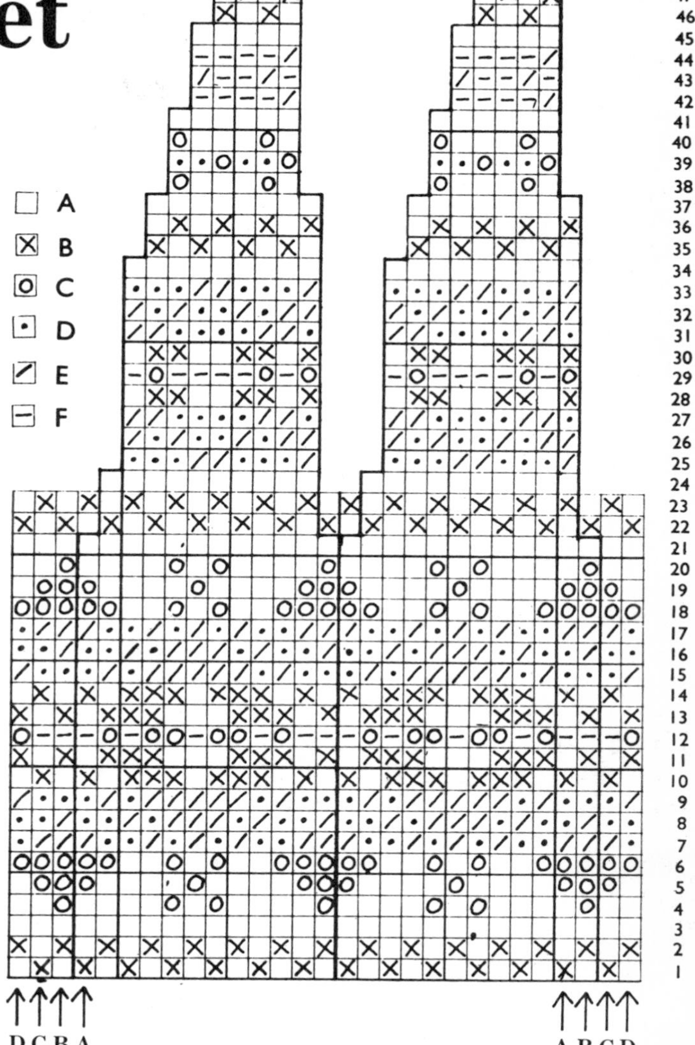

A 2nd size body; 1st size sleeves.
B 4th size body; 2nd size sleeves.
C 1st size body; 3rd size sleeves; yoke and beret.
D 3rd size body; 4th size sleeves.

YOKE: Join raglan seams using back st. With set of four No 10 needles and A, k across all sts on holders, k 2 tog at each raglan seam and, on **1st size only**, inc 1 st at centre back and front; on **3rd size only**, dec 1 st at centre back and front; on **4th size only** dec 1 st at centre back and front and at centre of each sleeve. [276 (288–300–312) sts] Arrange sts on three needles so that round commences at centre back. **Commence Fair Isle patt.** Beg with a k row, work rounds 1 to 20 as given on chart noting that yoke on all sizes will beg at point marked B. **21st round:** [Dec round] K 2 in patt, * k 2 tog, k 4; rep from * to last 4 sts, k 2 tog, k 2. [230(240–250–260) sts] **22nd round.** Work as given on chart. **23rd round:** Work as given on chart. **24th round:** [Dec round] K 5, * k 2 tog, k 8; rep from * to last 5 sts, k 2 tog, k 3. [207(216–225–234) sts] Work rounds 25–33 as given on chart. **34th round:** [Dec round] K 6, * k 2 tog, k 7; rep from * to last 3 sts, k 2 tog, k 1. [184(192–200–208) sts] **35th round:** Work as given on chart. **36th round:** Work as given on chart. **37th round:** [Dec round] K 1, * k 2 tog, k 2; rep from * to last 3 sts, k 2 tog, k 1. [138(144–150–156) sts] Work rounds 38 to 40 as given on chart. **41st round:** [Dec round] K 2, * k 2 tog, k 4; rep from * to last 4 sts, k 2 tog, k 2. [115(120–125–130) sts] Work rounds 42 to 44 as given on chart. **45th round:** [Dec round] K 1, * k 2 tog, k 3; rep from * to last 4 sts, k 2 tog, k 2. [92(96–100–104) sts] **46th round:** Work as given on chart. **47th round:** Work as given on chart. Break off contrast colours. With A only k 1(1–3–5) rounds. Change to set of four No 12 needles. Work 2″ k 1, p 1 rib. Cast off loosely in rib.

TO MAKE UP: Press pieces under a damp cloth with a hot iron. Join side and sleeve seams using back st. Fold neckband in half to wrong side and sl-st. Press seams.

BERET

With set of four No 12 needles and A, cast on 104(112) sts. Work in rounds of k 1, p 1 rib for 1″. Change to set of four No 10 needles. **Next round:** * K 3, k into front and back of next st; rep from * to end. [130(140) sts] Cont in rounds of st-st, working rounds 1 to 3 as given on chart, noting that both sizes for Beret will beg at point marked B on chart. Work rounds 42 to 44 as given on chart. **Next round:** * K 4, k into front and back of next st; rep from * to end. [156(168) sts] Work rounds 38 to 41 as given on chart omitting dec on 41st round. Work rounds 1 to 33 as given on chart, shaping on rounds as given for Yoke. [117(126) sts] **Next round:** * K 3, k 2 tog, k 2, k 2 tog; rep from * 12(14) times, k 2, k 3 tog, k 2, k 2 tog(k 0). 90(98) sts. Work rounds 35 and 36 as given on chart. **Next round:** * K 1, k 2 tog; rep from * to last 0(2) sts, k 0(2). [60(66) sts] Cont working rounds 38 to 47 as given on chart, working shaping on rounds as given for Yoke. [40(44) sts] **Next round:** Break off contrast colours, with A only, * k 2 tog; rep from * to end. 20(22) sts. Break off A. Thread through sts and fasten off. Press under a damp cloth with a hot iron.

Child's military coat with beret

Instructions are for a 21″ chest. Changes for 22″, 23″, 24″ and 25″ sizes are given in brackets.

MATERIALS: Coat. 11(12–13–14–15) ozs Hayfield Beaulon Double Knitting in main shade, A; 1(1–1–2–2) ozs of same in contrast, B. **Beret.** 2 ozs of A and 1 oz of B. One pair each Nos 7, 8 and 9 needles. Ten buttons.

NOTE: For 23″ size. If making coat only, 14 ozs of A and 2 ozs of B are required. This does *not* apply if making beret too.

MEASUREMENTS: Coat. To fit a 21″(22″–23″–24″–25″) chest. Length to shoulder: 16″(18″–20″–22″–24″), adjustable. Sleeve seam: 8½″(10″–11½″–12½″–13½″), adjustable. **Beret.** To fit an average head (two sizes given).

TENSION: 11 sts to 2″ over patt on No 7 needles.

NOTE: Make Left Front first for a girl and Right Front first for a boy.

BACK: With No 8 needles and A, cast on 85(91–97–103–109) sts. Beg with a k row work 7 rows st-st. Change to No 7 needles. **Commence patt. 1st row:** [Wrong side] K 1, * y fwd, sl 1 p-wise, pass y back over sl-st, k 1; rep from * to end. **2nd row:** K 1, * k sl st and y on tog tbl, k 1; rep from * to end. These two rows form patt and are rep throughout. Cont in patt, dec 1 st at each end of 18th (20th–22nd–24th–26th) row and every foll 12th row until 69(75–81–87–93) sts rem. Cont without shaping until work measures 11″(12½″–14″–15½″–17″) from beg of patt, or required length to underarm, ending with a wrong side row. **Shape raglan.** Cast off 2 sts at beg of next 2 rows. Keeping patt correct, dec 1 st at each end of next and every foll alt row until 23(25–27–29–31) sts rem. Work 1 row. Cast off.

POCKET LININGS: [Make two] With No 7 needles and A, cast on 19 sts. Work in patt as given for Back for 24(26–28–30–32) rows. Break off yarn. Leave sts on holder.

RIGHT FRONT: Note: Buttonholes are made on Right Front for girl and Left Front for boy, working from centre front edge as follows: **Buttonhole row.** Patt 3 sts, cast off 2 sts, patt 14(16–18–20–22) sts, cast off 2 sts, patt to end. **Next row:** Patt to end, casting on 2 sts above those cast off in previous row. With No 8 needles and A, cast on 55(59–63–67–71) sts. Beg with a k row work 7 rows st-st. Change to No 7 needles. Cont in patt as given for Back, dec 1 st at end of 18th(20th–22nd–24th–26th) row and every foll 12th row, **at the same time**, when work measures 6½″ from beg of patt, make 1st set of buttonholes for girl. Cont in patt, inc as before, until work measures 7½″(8″–8½″–9″–9½″) from beg of patt, ending at front edge. ** **Insert pocket lining. Next row:** Patt 22(24–26–28–30) sts, cast off 19 sts, patt to end. **Next row:** Work in patt to cast off sts, then work in patt across 19 pocket lining sts on holder, patt to end. Cont in patt dec as before and making 2 more sets of buttonholes as markers are reached for a girl, until 8 decs in all have been worked. [47(51–55–59–63) sts] Cont without shaping until work measures same as Back to underarm, ending with a right side row. **Shape raglan.** Cast off 2 sts at beg of next row. Keeping patt correct, dec 1 st at raglan edge on next and every alt row until 30(32–34–36–38) sts rem, ending at front edge. **Shape neck. Next row:** Cast off 17(19–21–23–25) sts, patt to last 2 sts, work 2 tog. **Next row:** Patt to end. Cont in patt, dec 1 st at each end of next and every alt row until 2 sts rem. Work 1 row. K 2 tog and fasten off. Mark position for 3 sets of buttonholes on this side for a boy, first to come 6½″ from beg of patt and 2 more sets evenly spaced between, allowing for 4th set to be made in neck border.

LEFT FRONT: Work as given for Right Front, reversing shaping and making 1st set of buttonholes for a boy when work measures 6½″ from beg of patt, to **, ending with a wrong side row. **Insert pocket lining. Next row:** Patt to last 41(43–45–47–49) sts, cast off 19 sts, patt to end. **Next row:** Patt to end working across pocket lining sts on holder in place of those cast off in previous row. Complete as given for Right Front making 2 more sets of buttonholes as markers are reached for a boy and reversing all shaping. Mark position for 3 sets of buttonholes on this side for a girl, as given on Right Front.

SLEEVES: With No 9 needles and B, cast on 35(39–43–47–51) sts. Work 17 rows k 1, p 1 rib. **Next row:** K. Break off B and join in A. Change to No 7 needles. Cont in patt as given for Back, inc 1 st at each end of 12th and every foll 6th row until there are 51(55–59–65–69) sts. Cont without shaping until sleeve measures 8½″(10″–11½″–12½″–13½″) from beg, when ribbed cuff is folded in half, ending with a wrong side row. **Shape raglan.** Cast off 2 sts at beg of next 2 rows. Dec 1 st at each end of next 2 rows. Dec 1 st at each end of next and every alt row until 5(5–5–7–7) sts rem. Work 1 row. Cast off.

POCKET BORDERS: [Make two] With right side of work facing, No 9 needles and B, k up 21 sts evenly along cast off edge of pocket. Work 8 rows k 1, p 1 rib. Cast off in rib.

FRONT EDGES: With right side of work facing, No 8 needles and A, k up 71(77–83–89–95) sts evenly along Right Front edge. K 1 row. Cast off. Work Left Front edge in same way.

COLLAR: Join raglan seams using back st. With right side of work facing, No 9 needles and B, k up 25(27–29–31–33) sts up Right Front neck, 5(5–5–7–7) sts along top of sleeve, 23(25–27–29–31) sts along back neck, 5(5–5–7–7) sts along 2nd sleeve and 25(27–29–31–33) sts down Left Front neck. Work 3 rows k 1, p 1, rib making buttonholes on next 2 rows as before. Work 6 more rows k 1, p 1 rib, then work 2 buttonhole rows as before. Work 3 rows k 1, p 1 rib. Cast off in rib.

BELT: With No 9 needles and A, cast on 25 sts. Work in k 1, p 1 rib for 46(50–54–58–62) rows. Cast off in rib.

TO MAKE UP: Press work lightly on wrong side under a dry cloth with a warm iron. Join side and sleeve seams using back st. Turn hem to wrong side and sl st. Fold cuff in half to wrong side and sl st to last row of B. Fold pocket tops in half to wrong side and sl st. Neaten short ends. Fold Collar in half to wrong side and sl st. With right sides facing, fold Belt in half and join short ends turn to right side and join seam. Work buttonhole st round buttonholes. Press seams and edges. Sew on buttons and attach Belt to back with a button at each end.

BERET

With No 9 needles and B, cast on 91 (105) sts. Work 17 rows k 1, p 1 rib. **1st size only. Next row:** * Inc 1 st in first st, k 1, inc 1 st in next st, k 1, inc 1 st in next st, k 2; rep from * to last 4 sts, k 4. [129 sts] **2nd size only. Next row:** * Inc 1 st in first st, k 2, inc 1 st in next st, k 2, inc 1 st in next st, k 1; rep from * to end, inc 1 st in last st. [145 sts] **Both sizes.** Break off B and join in A. Change to No 7 needles and work in patt as given for Coat for 31(37) rows. **Shape top.** Work as given for Cap until 17(19) sts rem. Break yarn, draw through sts and fasten off.

TO MAKE UP: Press as given for Coat. Join seam. Fold rib in half to wrong side and sl st.

Baby's shawl

MATERIALS: 7 ozs of Hayfield Beaulon 3-ply fingering. One pair each Nos 7, 8 and 9 needles.
MEASUREMENTS: Approx 42″ across.
TENSION: Approx 8 sts and 9 rows to 1″ over lace patt worked on No 9 needles.
Begin at centre. With No 9 needles cast on 8 sts. **1st row:** Inc once in each st [16 sts] **2nd row:** As 1st. [32 sts]. **3rd row:** * P 2, y 2rn, p 2; rep from * to end. **4th row:** Counting y 2rn on previous row as 2 sts, * p 1, p 2 tog, y 2rn, p 2 tog, p 1; rep from * to end. **5th row:** As 4th. **6th row:** As 4th. [48 sts] **7th row:** * P 1, p up thread before next st [called p up 1], p 2 tog, y 2rn, p 2 tog, p up 1, p 1; rep from * to end. [64 sts] **8th row:** * P 2, p 2 tog, y 2rn, p 2 tog, p 2; rep from * to end. **9th row:** As 8th. **10th row:** As 8th. **11th row:** * P 1, p up 1, p 1, p 2 tog, y 2rn, p 2 tog, p 1, p up 1, p 1; rep from * to end. [80 sts] **12th row:** * P 3, p 2 tog, y 2rn, p 2 tog, p 3; rep from * to end. **13th row:** As 12th. **14th row:** As

12th. **15th row:** * P 1, p up 1, p 2, p 2 tog, y 2rn, p 2 tog, p 2, p up 1, p 1; rep from * to end. **16th row:** * P 4, p 2 tog, y 2rn, p 2 tog, p 4; rep from * to end. **17th row:** As 16th. **18th row:** As 16th. **19th row:** * P 1, p up 1, p 3, p 2 tog, y 2rn, p 2 tog, p 3, p up 1, p 1; rep from * to end. **20th row:** * P 5, p 2 tog, y 2rn, p 2 tog, p 5; rep from * to end. **21st row:** As 20th. **22nd row:** As 20th. Cont in this way inc on every 4th row until the foll row has been worked: * P 1, p up 1, p 17, p 2 tog, y 2rn, p 2 tog, p 17, p up 1, p 1; rep from * to end. [336 sts] **Shape sections and begin lace patt. 1st row:** * P 19, p 2 tog, y rn, p 2 tog, p 19; rep from * to end. **2nd row:** * P 18, p 2 tog, m 1, p 1, m 1, p 2 tog, p 18; rep from * to end. **3rd row:** * P 17, p 2 tog, m 1, p 3, m 1, p 2 tog, p 17; rep from * to end. **4th row:** * P 16, p 2 tog, m 1, p 1, m 1, p 3 tog, m 1, p 1, m 1, p 2 tog, p 16; rep from * to end. **5th row:** * P 15, p 2 tog, m 1, p 3, m 1, p 1, m 1, p 3, m 1, p 2 tog, p 15; rep from * to end. **6th row:** * P 14, p 2 tog, m 1, p 1, m 1, p 3 tog, m 1, p 3, m 1, p 3 tog, m 1, p 1, m 1, p 2 tog, p 14; rep from * to end. **7th row:** * P 13, p 2 tog, m 1, p 3, m 1, p 1, m 1, p 2 tog, p 1, p 2 tog, m 1, p 1, m 1, p 3, m 1, p 2 tog, p 13; rep from * to end. **8th row:** * P 12, p 2 tog, m 1, p 1, m 1, p 3 tog, m 1, [p 3, m 1, p 3 tog, m 1] twice, p 1, m 1, p 2 tog, p 12; rep from * to end. **9th row:** * P 11, p 2 tog, m 1, p 3, m 1, p 1, m 1, [p 2 tog, p 1, p 2 tog, m 1, p 1, m 1] twice, p 3, m 1, p 2 tog, p 11; rep from * to end. **10th row:** * P 10, p 2 tog, m 1, p 1, [m 1, p 3 tog, m 1, p 3] 3 times, m 1, p 3 tog, m 1, p 1, m 1, p 2 tog, p 10; rep from * to end. **11th row:** * P 9, p 2 tog, m 1, p 3, [m 1, p 1, m 1, p 2 tog, p 1, p 2 tog] 3 times, m 1, p 1, m 1, p 3, m 1, p 2 tog, p 9; rep from * to end. **12th row:** * P 8, p 2 tog, m 1, p 1, [m 1, p 3 tog, m 1, p 3] 4 times, m 1, p 3 tog, m 1, p 1, m 1, p 2 tog, p 8; rep from * to end. **13th row:** * P 7, p 2 tog, m 1, p 3, m 1, p 1, [m 1, p 2 tog, p 1, p 2 tog, m 1, p 1] 4 times, m 1, p 3, m 1, p 2 tog, p 7; rep from * to end. **14th row:** * P 6, p 2 tog, m 1, p 1, [m 1, p 3 tog, m 1, p 3] 5 times, m 1, p 3 tog, m 1, p 1, m 1, p 2 tog, p 6; rep from * to end. **15th row:** * P 5, p 2 tog, m 1, p 3, [m 1, p 1, m 1, p 2 tog, p 1, p 2 tog] 5 times, m 1, p 1, m 1, p 3, m 1, p 2 tog, p 5; rep from * to end. **16th row:** * P 4, p 2 tog, m 1, p 1 [m 1, p 3 tog, m 1, p 3] 6 times, m 1, p 3 tog, m 1, p 1, m 1, p 2 tog, p 4; rep from * to end. **17th row:** * P 3, p 2 tog, m 1, p 3, [m 1, p 1, m 1, p 2 tog, p 1, p 2 tog] 6 times, m 1, p 1, m 1, p 3, m 1, p 2 tog, p 3; rep from * to end.

18th row: * P 2, p 2 tog, m 1, p 1, [m 1, p 3 tog, m 1, p 3] 7 times, m 1, p 3 tog, m 1, p 1, m 1, p 2 tog, p 2; rep from * to end. **19th row:** * P 1, p 2 tog, m 1, p 3, [m 1, p 1, m 1, p 2 tog, p 1, p 2 tog] 7 times, m 1, p 1, m 1, p 3, m 1, p 2 tog, p 1; rep from * to end. **20th row:** * P 2 tog, m 1, p 1, [m 1, p 3 tog, m 1, p 3] 8 times, m 1, p 3 tog, m 1, p 1, m 1, p 2 tog; rep from * to end. **21st row:** P 1, * m 1, p 3, [m 1, p 1, m 1, p 2 tog, p 1, p 2 tog] 8 times, m 1, p 1, m 1, p 3, m 1, p 2 tog; rep from * ending last rep p 1. **22nd row:** * P 2, m 1, p 3 tog, m 1, p 1; rep from * to last st, p 1. **23rd row:** * P 1, p 2 tog, m 1, p 1, m 1, p 2 tog; rep from * to last st, p 1. **24th row:** P 2 tog, * m 1, p 3, m 1, p 3 tog; rep from * to last 5 sts, m 1, p 3, m 1, p 2 tog. **25th row:** * P 1, m 1, p 2 tog, p 1, p 2 tog, m 1; rep from * to last st, p 1. Change to No 8 needles and cont rep last 4 rows until work measures 16″ from centre. Change to No 7 needles and rep last 4 rows for a further 2″. **To work lace edging.** Cast on 11 sts at end of last row. Edging is worked on these sts gradually working off all sts until 11 only rem. **1st row:** Y rn, p 3 tog, [y rn, p 2 tog] 4 times, m 1, p 1, p 2 tog. **2nd row:** P 2 tog, [y rn, p 2 tog] 4 times, y rn, p 1, p 2 tog. **3rd row:** [Y rn, p 2 tog] 5 times, y rn, p 1, p 2 tog. **4th row:** P 2 tog, p 1, [y rn, p 2 tog] 4 times, y rn, p 2. **5th row:** [Y rn, p 2 tog] 5 times, y rn, p 2, p 2 tog. **6th row:** P 2 tog, p 2, [y rn, p 2 tog] 4 times, y rn, p 2. **7th row:** [Y rn, p 2 tog] 5 times, y rn, p 3, p 2 tog. **8th row:** P 2 tog, p 3, [y rn, p 2 tog] 4 times, y rn, p 2. **9th row:** [Y rn, p 2 tog] 5 times, y rn, p 4, p 2 tog. **10th row:** P 2 tog, p 4, [y rn, p 2 tog] 4 times, y rn, p 2. **11th row:** [Y rn, p 2 tog] 5 times, y rn, p 5, p 2 tog] **12th row:** P 2 tog, p 5, [y rn, p 2 tog] 4 times, y rn, p 2. **13th row:** Y rn, p 3 tog, [y rn, p 2 tog] 4 times, y rn, p 5, p 2 tog. **14th row:** P 2 tog, p 4, [y rn, p 2 tog] 5 times, p 1. **15th row:** Y rn, p 3 tog, [y rn, p 2 tog] 4 times, y rn, p 4, p 2 tog. **16th row:** P 2 tog, p 3, [y rn, p 2 tog] 5 times, p 1. **17th row:** Y rn, p 3 tog, [y rn, p 2 tog] 4 times, y rn, p 3, p 2 tog. **18th row:** P 2 tog, p 2, [y rn, p 2 tog] 5 times, p 1. **19th row:** Y rn, p 3 tog, [y rn, p 2 tog] 4 times, y rn, p 2, p 2 tog. **20th row:** P 2 tog, p 1, [y rn, p 2 tog] 5 times, p 1. These 20 rows form edging rep and are cont until only 11 sts rem. Cast off.

TO MAKE UP: Seam from centre to lace edge. Pin out to shape and press lightly with a cool iron over a dry cloth.

Bedspread

Shown on back cover

MATERIALS: Three 50-gm balls of Mahony's Blarney Bainin for each square. 59 balls will make 20 squares for a bedspread 64″ × 90″. Seven extra balls to fringe three sides of bedspread. One pair No 7 needles. Large crochet hook.

MEASUREMENTS: Each square measures 16″ × 16″ when pinned out for pressing.

TENSION: 19 sts and 30 rows measure 4″ square over background patt.

THE SQUARE: Cast on 2 sts. **1st row:** K 1, y fwd, k 1. **2nd row:** K 3. **3rd row:** K 1, y fwd, k 1, y fwd, k 1. **4th row:** K 5. **5th row:** K 1, y fwd, k 3, y fwd, k 1. **6th row:** K 7. **7th row:** K 1, y fwd, k 5, y fwd, k 1. **8th row:** K 9. Cont in background patt of 4 rows st-st, 4 rows g-st with bobbles on 3rd row of st-st bands and inc as before thus: **1st row:** K 1, y fwd, k to last st, y fwd, k 1. **2nd row:** K 1, p to last st, k 1. [11 sts] **3rd row:** K 1, y fwd, k 4, k into front, back, front, back, front of next st, turn, p 5, turn, k 5, turn, p 5, turn, sl 2nd, 3rd, 4th and 5th sts over 1st st and k into back of bobble st [called B 1], k 4, y fwd, k 1. **4th row:** As 2nd. **5th row:** As 1st. **6th row:** K. **7th row:** As 5th. **8th row:** As 6th. Rep these 8 rows working 1 more bobble on 3rd patt row each time thus: **2nd bobble row:** [19 sts on needle] K 1, y fwd, k 5, [B 1, k 5] twice, y fwd, k 1. **3rd bobble row:** [27 sts on needle] K 1, y fwd, k 6, [B 1, k 5] twice, B 1, k 6, y fwd, k 1. **4th bobble row:** [35 sts on needle] K 1, y fwd, k 7, [B 1, k 5] 3 times, B 1, k 7, y fwd, k 1. **5th bobble row:** [43 sts on needle] K 1, y fwd, k 8, [B 1, k 5] 4 times, B 1, k 8, y fwd, k 1. After 5th bobble row, cont in patt omitting bobbles for a further 19 rows [2 rows of g-st band worked and 63 sts on needle] **63rd row:** K 1, y fwd, k 1, * y fwd, k 2 tog; rep from * to last st, y fwd, k 1. **64th row:** K. Work 6 more rows in background patt. [71 sts] **71st row:** As 63rd row. **72nd row:** As 64th row. Work 18 more rows in background patt [2 rows of st-st band worked and 91 sts on needle] **91st row:** K 1, y fwd, [k 5, B 1] 14 times, k 5, y fwd, k 1. **92nd row:** K 1, p to last st, k 1. Work 6 more rows in background patt [2 rows of st-st band worked and 99 sts on needle] Beg dec thus: **1st row:** K 1, y fwd, k 3 tog, k to last 4 sts, k 3 tog, y fwd, k 1. **2nd row:** K 1, p to last st, k 1. **3rd row:** As 1st row. **4th row:** K. **5th row:** As 3rd row. **6th row:** As 4th row. **7th row:** As 1st row. **8th row:** As 2nd row. [91 sts] **9th row:** K 1, y fwd, k 3 tog, k 2, [B 1, k 5] 13 times, B 1, k 2, k 3 tog, y fwd, k 1. **10th row:** K 1, p to last st, k 1 Work 18 more rows in background patt dec as before. [71 sts] **29th row:** K 1, y fwd, k 3 tog, k 1, * y fwd, k 2 tog rep from * to last 4 sts, k 3 tog, y fwd, k 1. **30th row:** K Cont to match first half, working holes on 37th row a 29th row and dec as before until 43 sts rem, then beg bobble 'Triangle' thus: **1st bobble row:** [57th row K 1, y fwd, k 3 tog, k 5, [B 1, k 5] 5 times, k 3 tog, y fwd k 1. **2nd bobble row:** [35 sts on needle] K 1, y fwd, k tog, k 4, [B 1, k 5] 3 times, B 1, k 4, k 3 tog, y fwd, k 1 **3rd bobble row:** [27 sts on needle] K 1, y fwd, k 3 tog k 3, [B 1, k 5] twice, B 1, k 3, k 3 tog, y fwd, k 1. **4t bobble row:** [19 sts on needle] K 1, y fwd, k 3 tog, k B 1, k 5, B 1, k 2, k 3 tog, y fwd, k 1. **5th bobble row** [11 sts on needle] K 1, y fwd, k 3 tog, k 1, B 1, k 1, k tog, y fwd, k 1. After 5th bobble row cont thus: **Ne row:** K 1, p 7, k 1, now cont in g-st. **Next row:** K 1, k tog, k 3, k 2 tog, k 1. **Next row:** K 7. **Next row:** K k 2 tog, k 1, k 2 tog, k 1. **Next row:** K 5. **Next row:** K k 3 tog, k 1. **Next row:** K 3. **Next row:** Sl 1, k 2 to psso. Fasten off. Make 19 more squares in same wa Note that the piece will appear slightly diamon shaped but this is rectified in pressing and joining.

TO MAKE UP: Mark out a 16″ square with four pi and stretch square to fit, pinning at each corner, th along all sides. Press on wrong side using a wet clo and hot iron but pressing lightly to avoid flattening the bobbles. Arrange squares in four groups of four taking care to place the four cast-on corners to the centre each time. Using a finer matching yarn, backstitch just inside edges, pressing each seam as it is completed. Join the final two 'pairs' to two of the larger squares then sew main seams. For the **fringe**, cut the wool into 18″ lengths and, using three strands together, knot into alternate holes at edge; space them similarly where solid g-st occurs between squares. Finally knot together three strands from one group and three strands from the next about 1″ below the original knots.

Domino cushion

MATERIALS: Four balls of Mahony's Blarney Bainin for one side of cushion. Seven balls will make both sides. One pair No 7 needles; 1 cable needle. (Fabric for back of cushion if required).
MEASUREMENTS: Approx 16″ square when completed.
TENSION: 9½ sts to 2″ worked on g-st.
MAKE FOUR TRIANGLES ALIKE: Cast on 73 sts. K two rows. **3rd row:** K 1, sl 1, k 1, psso, k 1, * y fwd, k 2 tog; rep from * to last 3 sts, k 2 tog, k 1. **4th row:** K. **5th row:** K 1, sl 1, k 1, psso, k to last 3 sts, k 2 tog, k 1. Cont in m-st. **6th row:** K 2, * p 1, k 1; rep from * to last 3 sts, p 1, k 2. **7th row:** K 1, sl 1, k 1, psso, * k 1, p 1; rep from * to last 4 sts, k 1, k 2 tog, k 1. **8th row:** K 2, * k 1, p 1; rep from * to last 3 sts, k 3. **9th row:** K 1, sl 1, k 1, psso, * p 1, k 1; rep from * to last 4 sts, p 1, k 2 tog, k 1. **10th to 13th rows:** Rep 6th to 9th rows. **14th row:** As 6th row. This completes m-st. Work bobble band. **15th row:** K 1, sl 1, k 1, psso, k to last 3 sts, k 2 tog, k 1. **16th row:** K 2, p to last 2 sts, k 2. **17th row:** K 1, sl 1, k 1, psso, k 1, [make bobble on next st thus: k into front, back, front, back, front of next st, turn, p 5, turn, k 5, turn, p 5, turn, sl 2nd, 3rd, 4th and 5th sts over first st, k into back of bobble st—called B 1, k 4] 10 times, B 1, k 1, k 2 tog, k 1. **18th row:** As 16th. **19th row:** As 15th. Beg diamond on g-st background. **20th row:** K 25, p 2, k 1, p 2, k 25. **21st row:** K 1, sl 1, k 1, psso, k 21, sl next st on cable needle and hold at back of work, k 2, then k 1 from cable needle—called C3R, k 1, sl next 2 sts on to cable needle and hold at front of work, k 1, then k 2 from cable needle—called C3L, k 21, k 2 tog, k 1. **22nd row:** K 23, p 2, k 3, p 2, k 23. **23rd row:** K 1, sl 1, k 1, psso, k 19, C3R, k 3, C3L, k 19, k 2 tog, k 1. **24th row:** K 21, p 2, k 5, p 2, k 21. **25th row:** K 1, sl 1, k 1, psso, k 17, C3R, k 5, C3L, k 17, k 2 tog, k 1. **26th row:** K 19, p 2, k 7, p 2, k 19. Cont thus dec at each end of every right side row with 2 more sts in centre of diamond each time until the 32nd row. [43 sts]. **33rd row:** K 1, sl 1, k 1, psso, k 9, C3R, k 6, B 1, k 6, C3L, k 9, k 2 tog, k 1. **34th row:** K 11, p 2, k 15, p 2, k 11. Cont dec as before and with 2 more sts in diamond on every right side row for further 6 rows. 35 sts. **41st row:** K 1, sl 1, k 1, psso, k 1, C3R, k 6, B 1, k 7, B 1, k 6, C3L, k 1, k 2 tog, k 1. **42nd row:** K 3, p 2, k 23, p 2, k 3. Beg dec diamond. **43rd row:** K 1, sl 1, k 1, psso, C3L, k 21, C3R, k 2 tog, k 1. **44th row and every wrong side row:** K 3, p 2, k to last 5 sts, p 2, k 3. **45th row:** K 1, sl 1, k 1, psso, C3L, k 19, C3R, k 2 tog, k 1. **47th row:** K 1, sl 1, k 1, psso, C3L, k 17, C3R, k 2 tog, k 1. **49th row:** K 1, sl 1, k 1, psso, C3L, k 7, B 1, k 7, C3R, k 2 tog, k 1. [Last bobble]. Cont dec as before with 2 sts less in diamond each time until the 64th row. [11 sts], thus: **64th row:** K 3, p 2, k 1, p 2, k 3. **65th row:** K 1, sl 1, k 1, psso, sl next 2 sts on to cable needle and hold at front of work, k 1, k 2 tog, k 2 tog from cable needle, k 2 tog, k 1. **66th row:** With a No 10 needle, k 1, p 2 tog, p 1, p 2 tog, k 1, break wool leaving a few inches and leave these 5 sts on a holder.

TO MAKE UP: With right side down, pin out corners of cast-on edge 16″ apart then pin all along this edge. Pin sides of triangle so that centre is 8″ deep and press

with a damp cloth and hot iron, pressing outer edges firmly but bobbles lightly. Thread wool left on last piece worked through all four sets of 5 sts, draw up tight and fasten off, neatly running in the other ends. Sew the four triangles tog and press seams. Cut fabric to fit, allowing small turnings, turn in edges and hem to wrong side of knitting along first ridge above cast on edge. Leave opening on one side to insert cushion, then stitch opening.

Leaf cushion

MATERIALS: 1 square requires 5 balls of Sirdar Sportswool. 1 pair No. 7 needles.
MEASUREMENTS: 20″ × 20″.
TO MAKE A SQUARE: With No. 7 needles cast on 3 sts. **1st row:** W on, k 3. **2nd row:** W on, k 4. **3rd row:** W on, k 2, w fwd, k 1, w fwd, k 2. **4th row:** W on, k 2, p 3, k 3. **5th row:** W on, k 3, k 1, w fwd, k 1, w fwd, k 1, k 3. **6th row:** W on, k 3, p 5, k 4. **7th row:** W on, k 4, k 2, w fwd, k 1, w fwd, k 2, k 4. **8th row:** W on, k 4, p 7, k 5. **9th row:** W on, k 5, k 3, w fwd, k 1, w fwd, k 3, k 5.

10th row: W on, k 5, p 9, k 6. **11th row:** W on, k 6, k 4, w fwd, k 1, w fwd, k 4, k 6. **12th row:** W on, k 6, p 11, k 7. **13th row:** W on, k 7, k 5, w fwd, k 1, w fwd, k 5, k 7. **14th row:** W on, k 7, p 13, k 8. **15th row:** W on, k 8, sl 1, k 1, psso, k 9, k 2 tog, k 8. **16th row:** W on, k 8, p 11, k 9. **17th row:** W on, k 9, sl 1, k 1, psso, k 7, k 2 tog, k 9. **18th row:** W on, k 9, p 9, k 10. **19th row:** W on, k 10, sl 1, k 1, psso, k 5, k 2 tog, k 10. **20th row:** W on, k 10, p 7, k 11. **21st row:** W on, k 11, sl 1, k 1, psso, k 3, k 2 tog, k 11. **22nd row:** W on, k 11, p 5, k 12. **23rd row:** W on, k 12, sl 1, k 1, psso, k 1, k 2 tog, k 12. **24th row:** W on, k 12, p 3, k 13. **25th row:** W on, k 13, sl 2 sts as if to k 2 tog, k 1, p2sso, k 13. **26th row:** W on, k 1, p to end. **27th row:** W on, k to end. **28th and 29th rows:** As 27th row. Rep 26th to 29th rows 5 times more, then 26th row once. 53 sts. **51st row:** W on, * k 2 tog, w fwd; rep from * to last st, k 1. **52nd row:** As 26th row. **53rd row:** W on, k 1, * w fwd, k 2 tog; rep from * to last 2 sts, k 2. **54th row:** As 26th row. **55th row:** As 53rd row. **56th row:** As 26th row. **57th to 59th rows:** As 27th row. **60th row:** As 26th row. **61st and 62nd row:** As 27th row. **63rd row:** W on, k 1, p 1, * w on, k 1, w rn, p 9; rep from * to last 3 sts, w on, k 1, w rn, p 1, k 1. **64th row:** W on, k 2, * p 3, k 9; rep from * ending p 3, k 3. **65th row:** W on, k 1, p 2, * k 1, w fwd, k 1, w fwd, k 1, p 9; rep from * ending k 1, w fwd, k 1, w fwd, k 1, p 2, k 1. **66th row:** W on, k 3, * p 5, k 9; rep from * ending p 5, k 4. **67th row:** W on, k 1, p 3, * k 2, w fwd, k 1, w fwd, k 2, p 9; rep from * ending p 3, k 1, instead of p 9. **68th row:** W on, k 4, * p 7, k 9; rep from * ending p 7, k 5. **69th row:** W on, k 1, p 4, * k 3, w fwd, k 1, w fwd, k 3, p 9; rep from * ending p 4, k 1, instead of p 9. **70th row:** W on, k 5, * p 9, k 9; rep from * ending p 9, k 6. **71st row:** W on, k 1, p 5, * sl 1, k 1, psso, k 5, k 2 tog, p 9; rep from * ending p 5, k 1, instead of p 9. **72nd row:** W on, k 6, * p 7, k 9; rep from * ending p 7, k 7. **73rd row:** W on, k 1, p 6, * sl 1, k 1, psso, k 3, k 2 tog, p 9; rep from * ending p 6, k 1, instead of p 9. **74th row:** W on, k 7, * p 5, k 9; rep from * ending p 5, k 8. **75th row:** W on, k 1, p 7, * sl 1, k 1, psso, k 1, k 2 tog, p 9; rep from * ending p 7, k 1, instead of p 9. **76th row:** W on, k 8, * p 3, k 9; rep from * to end. **77th row:** W on, k 1, p 8, * sl 2, k 1, p2sso, p 9; rep from * ending p 8, k 1, instead of p 9. **78th row:** As 26th row. **79th row:** As 27th row. **80th row:** As 26th row. **81st row:** As 27th row. Cast off p-wise. Break wool leaving a long end for sewing. Work 3 more pieces in same way.
TO MAKE UP: Join pieces by oversewing through the corresponding loops formed by made sts. Press. A large number of these squares can be made and joined together to form a bedspread.

Doll with clothes

MATERIALS: Doll. Three balls of Wendy Invitation Cotton in pale pink. One pair No 12 needles. Stuffing. Two blue buttons for eyes. Red felt for mouth. Small pink button for nose. One ball brown Wendy Diabolo Double Double knit for hair. **Clothes.** 2 ozs Wendy 4-ply Nylonised in main shade, A. 1 oz in contrast, B. One pair No 9 needles. Two small buttons. Shirring elastic.
MEASUREMENTS: Doll. Height: approx 15″. Body: approx 10″ round. **Dress.** Length: approx 6″.
TENSION: In cotton: 8 sts to 1″ over st-st on No 12 needles. In wool: 6 sts to 1″ over g-st on No 9 needles.

DOLL

BODY AND HEAD: [Beg at base] With No 12 needles and cotton, cast on 64 sts. Work 40 rows st-st. **Shape neck. Next row:** K 2 tog across row. [32 sts] Work 7 rows st-st without shaping. **Shape head.** Inc in each st across row. [64 sts] Work 27 rows st-st without shaping. **Shape top of head.** K 2 tog across row. P 1 row. K 2 tog across row. P 1 row. Draw thread through rem 16 sts, pull tight and finish securely.
LEGS: [Make two alike] Beg at foot. Cast on 39 sts and work 8 rows st-st. **Shape instep. 1st row:** K 18, k 3 tog, k 18. **2nd row:** P 17, p 3 tog, p 17. **3rd row:** K 16, k 3 tog, k 16. **4th row:** P 15, p 3 tog, p 15. Work 50 rows without shaping. Cast off.
ARMS: [Make two alike] Beg at hand. Cast on 16 sts. Inc 1 st at each end of next and foll 3 rows. [24 sts] Work 40 rows without shaping. Cast off.
TO MAKE UP: Fold all pieces with right sides tog. Sew centre-back of head and body and turn to right-side. Stuff head and neck firmly. Tie tape round neck to keep shape while stuffing body firmly. Sew across base from side to side. Sew sole of foot and centre back of legs. Turn right side out and stuff firmly to within ¾″ of top. With seams at back, sew each leg to half of base seam of body. Sew arm seams. Turn right side out and stuff firmly to within ¾″ of top. Gather top and sew to shoulders with seams at back. Wind a few strands of matching cotton around arm about 1½″ from end to form wrist. Tie tightly. **To make hair.** Wind brown Diabolo yarn 30 times round a 10″ card or book, slip off and tie hank tightly with matching yarn. Sew to top of head, cut loops and trim off fringe. Add features.

DRESS

BACK AND FRONT ALIKE: With B and No 9 needles, cast on 60 sts. Work 7 rows g-st. Cont in st-st working 2 rows A, 2 rows B and 30 rows A. **Next row:** [Waistband] With B, k 2 tog across row. K 1 more row with B. Break off B. Join in A and work 2¼″. Cast off.
SLEEVES: With B cast on 26 sts. K 1 row. Break off B and join in A. Work 15 rows g-st. Cast off.
TO MAKE UP: With wrong sides of work tog oversew ¼″ at outside edges of shoulders. Sew cast-off row of sleeves between B waistbands of back and front. Join underarm and side seams. Sew a button on back at each side of neck and make loops on front to fasten.

PANTS

[Make two pieces alike] With A, cast on 20 sts and work 57 rows g-st. Cast off.
TO MAKE UP: Fold one piece with cast-on and cast-off edges tog and sew ¾″ from one end. Rep with other leg. Now sew the two pieces tog to form front and back seams. Thread shirring elastic around waist.

SOCKS

[Both alike] With A cast on 30 sts. K 3 rows. Cont in g-st work 2 rows B and 30 rows A. **Next row:** K 2 tog across row. Cast off.
TO MAKE UP: Sew foot and back seam on wrong side.

Yarn conversion chart

UNITED KINGDOM	UNITED STATES	CANADA	SOUTH AFRICA	AUSTRALIA
EMU Scotch Double Knitting	*Standard double knitting	Scotch double knitting	*Standard double knitting	*Standard double knitting
HAYFIELD Beaulon 3-ply	*Standard 3-ply	*Standard 3-ply	*Standard 3-ply	*Standard 3-ply
JAEGER Summer Spun	Linen yarn – no equivalent	Linen yarn – no equivalent	Linen yarn – no equivalent	Linen yarn – no equivalent
Celtic Spun	*Standard double knitting, but more yarn may be needed	*Standard double knitting, but more yarn may be needed	*Standard double knitting, but more yarn may be needed	Summer Spun
LEE TARGET Motoravia 4-ply	*Standard 4-ply	Motoravia 4-ply	Motoravia 4-ply	*Standard 4-ply
LISTER Lavenda Double Knitting	*Standard double knitting	*Standard double knitting	Lavenda Double Knitting	*Standard double knitting
MAHONY Blarney Bainin	Blarneyspun	Blarneyspun	Blarney Bainin	Blarney Bainin
PATONS Fuzzy Wuzzy	*Angora/Wool blend yarns	Fuzzy Wuzzy	Fuzzy Wuzzy	Fuzzy Wuzzy
Cameo Crepe	*Standard 4-ply	*Patons Beehive Fingering Patons Patwin 4-ply Patons Atlantic Fingering Patons Sterling Fingering	Cameo Crepe	Bluebell Crepe
Doublet	*Standard double double knitting	*Standard double double knitting	Doublet	*Standard double double knitting
ROBIN Crepe Double Knitting	Crepe Double Knitting	Crepe Double Knitting	Crepe Double Knitting	Crepe Double Knitting
Vogue 4-ply	*Standard 4-ply	*Standard 4-ply	*Standard 4-ply	*Standard 4-ply
SIRDAR Fontein Crepe 4-ply	Fontein Crepe 4-ply	Fontein Crepe 4-ply	Fontein Crepe 4-ply	Fontein Crepe 4-ply
Double Knitting	*Standard double knitting	*Standard double knitting	Double Knitting	Double Crepe
Sportswool	Nearest to Triple Knitting	Sportswool	Sportswool	Sportswool
TWILLEY Crysette	Crysette or standard 4-ply	Crysette	Crysette	Crysette
WENDY Invitation Cotton	*Standard 8's cotton	No equivalent	Invitation Cotton	*Standard 8's cotton
4-ply Nylonised	*Standard 4-ply	*Standard 4-ply	*Standard 4-ply	*Standard 4-ply
Diabolo Double Knitting	*Standard double knitting	*Standard double knitting	*Standard double knitting	*Standard double knitting

***These yarns are only equivalents and tension must be checked before starting work**

Editor: Judy Brittain
Assistant Editor: Susan Read
Editor Condé Nast Books: Alex Kroll

Acknowledgements: Drawings: Barbara Firth. Photographers: Anthony Boase – page 143. Norman Eales – pages 131, 134, 150. Patrick Hunt – pages 132, 137, 139, 140, 144, 146, 148. Tessa Traeger – page 98. John Wingrove – pages 161, 162. Still life photography: Ronald Serbin and Maurice Dunphy. Malcolm Scoular – Front cover. John Wingrove – Back cover.

Abbreviations

alt	alternate
beg	begin(ing)
ch	chain
cl(s)	cluster(s)
cont	continue(ing)
dc	double crochet
dec	decrease
d tr	double treble
foll	following
h tr	half treble
inc	increase
no(s)	number(s)
oz(s)	ounces(s)
patt	pattern
rem	remaining
rep	repeat
sl st	slip stitch
sp	space
st(s)	stitch(es)
t ch	turning chain
tog	together
tr	treble
tr tr	triple treble

Crochet Contents

Introduction

Crochet is an exceedingly old and beautiful craft whose history is difficult to trace. It has been taken from one country to another, to a great extent by nuns, who have used and taught it for many generations. The word itself is French for 'hook'. Crochet has always been more popular abroad than in Britain, but during the nineteenth century it came into its own both for household and personal use. At this time its popularity grew in Ireland, where the thriving industry of crochet spread rapidly from homestead to homestead. Many very beautiful examples of crochet are in use today on church linen and vestments.

Now crochet has reached a new and very important fashion height and is seen in most boutiques and shops throughout Europe and the United States. To illustrate this fashion interest we have given a selection of designs ranging from a simple cardigan to a really beautiful fairytale wedding dress. All of which you will be able to make yourself.

The boom in crochet has also spread to household items such as bedspreads, cushions and even curtains. Once a bedspread has been made it will last for years and in time will become an object of pride and interest for children and grandchildren. We have given several patterns for bedspreads and also for cushions. With the cushion patterns it is simple to make more and more squares so that eventually you will have enough to join together and thus make a bedspread.

Crochet may also be used for trimming sheets, pillowcases, tablecloths, etc. and by adding a fringe or lace inset you will make a mundane article into something beautiful and unusual. We have given various ideas for these finishes at the end of the book.

Once the basic principles of crochet have been mastered it becomes quick and fascinating to work. It is important not to go too fast in the beginning stages but to read each page slowly and carefully before beginning to work the crochet. At first you may find that your work is tight and unsatisfactory, that your movements are awkward, but do not worry, just let the rhythm of yarn and hook take over. Soon you will find that the motion is becoming natural to you and then you will know you can crochet.

The look of crochet and fashion. Cushions designed by Tessa Traeger with instructions on page 163.

The ingredients

Crochet will undergo a complete change of mood depending on what size hook and weight of yarn is being used. For instance, a big hook and thick yarn will give a fabric warm and chunky enough for a blanket, whilst a very small hook and fine yarn will give an extremely delicate fabric suitable for the finest tablecloth or lacy trimmings. All the various ways and weights of crochet are illustrated in designs throughout the book.

Types of yarn

'Yarn' is the collective name for the threads which have been spun for crocheting. These threads can consist of wool, cotton, nylon, silk, hair, flax, hemp, metals or numerous man-made fibres, all of which can be used alone or in various combinations. These strands are known to the spinners as 'counts' and they, in turn, make up the ply, 2, 3, 4 or more, which make up the yarn. A ply can be any number of strands or counts and does not necessarily refer to the thickness of the yarn. It is for this reason that it is not advisable to substitute one yarn for another when working from a pattern. A 2-ply can be thicker than a 3-ply, as is the case with Shetland or other homespun yarns, and it is most important to use the particular yarn recommended for a design. The character of the yarn is determined in the process known as 'doubling', which forms a workable crochet yarn. If the twist of the yarn is tight, it will crochet up into a hard-wearing garment and is suitable for men's pullovers, socks and outer garments. Looser twisted yarns are more suitable for babies' wear, undergarments and bedjackets. In the case of man-made fibres used alone or in combination with wool, the yarn can be loose and yet very hard wearing. Fancy doubling or twisting produces bouclés, knop yarns and tweed wools. The character of any yarn is always taken into account when planning a design, and if the designer has stipulated a bouclé yarn, you will not obtain satisfactory results by using, say, a 4-ply crêpe quality.

Types of hooks—see chart

Until recently leading British manufacturers of crochet hooks have made a separate range of wool and cotton hooks, but this has now changed and all crochet hooks are supplied to a British standard so that the ranges of hooks numbered from the largest size 7, to the smallest size 0.60, are now interchangeable. Before this standard applied not only were the ranges not interchangeable, but in some cases specific numbers, such as a No. 2, were available in three of these four ranges but referred, in fact, to three entirely different sizes. It is therefore essential to check any crochet instructions very carefully before commencing work to find the size and, if it is referred to, the range of hook used. The question of tension in crochet is also of vital importance in order to obtain the correct measurements of anything you intend to make.

Aero

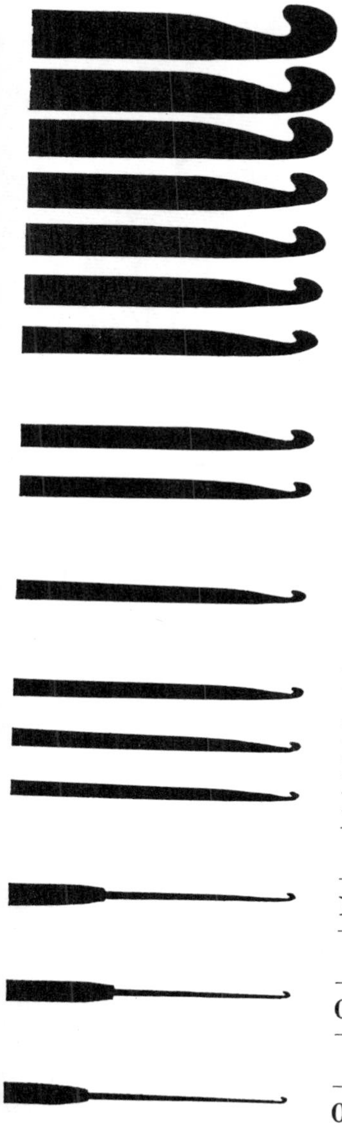

New international sizes (millimetres)	Old range cotton sizes	Old range wool sizes
7·00		2
6·00		4
5·50		5
5·00		6
4·50		7
4·00		8
3·50		9
3·00	3/0	10
2·50	0	12
2·00	1½	14
1·75	2½	15
1·50	3½	16
1·25	4½	
1·00	5½	
0·75	6½	
0·60	7	

Milwards

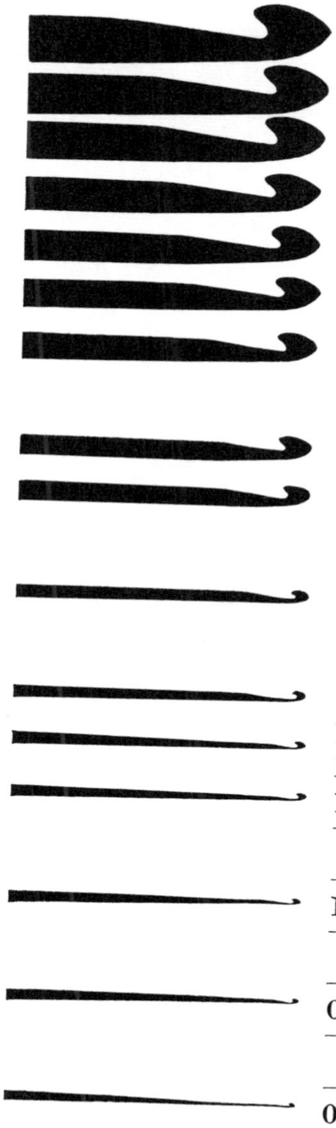

New international sizes (millimetres)	Old range cotton sizes	Old range wool sizes
7·00		2
6·00		4
5·50		5
5·00		6
4·50		7
4·00		8
3·50		9
		10
3·00	3/0	11
2·50	2/0	12
	1/0	13
2·00	1	14
	1½	
1·75	2	
1·50	2½	
1·25	3	
	3½	
1·00	4	
	4½	
0·75	5	
	5½	
0·60	6	
	6½	
	7	
	8	

How to begin

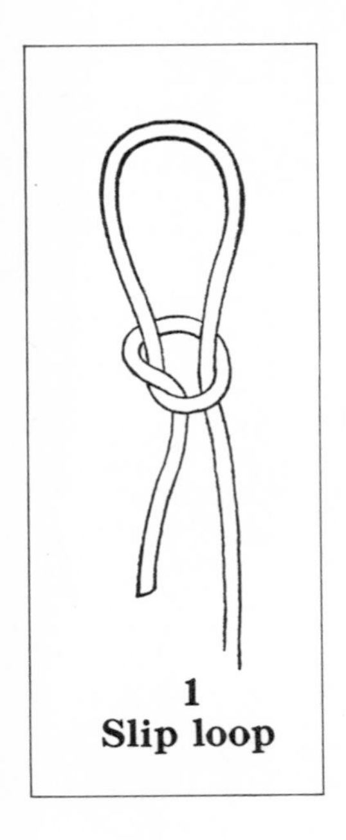

1
Slip loop

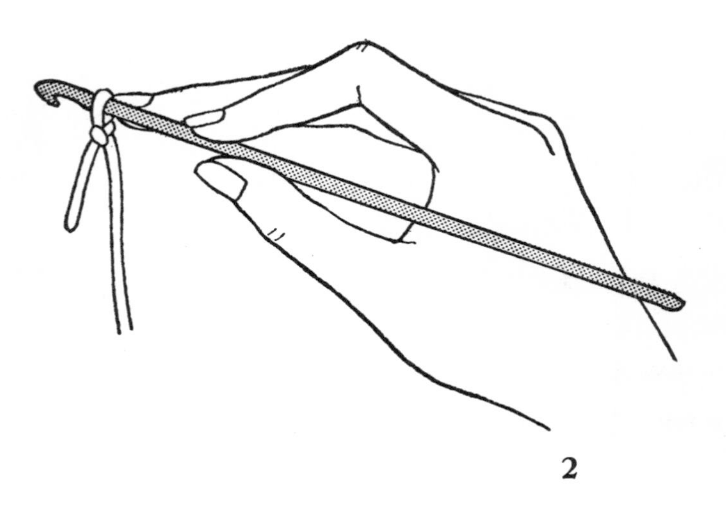

2

The majority of crochet begins with one single slip loop (fig. 1). Casting on in crochet is achieved by making the required length of chain loops, and the abbreviation for this is 'ch'. It is easier to learn to crochet by using a large hook and a double knitting yarn. The reason for this is that until you have learned to manipulate both the hook and the yarn you will find that you are inclined to work very tightly. Do not worry about your tension at this stage, but practise the first steps until you are completely relaxed. We will give a way of holding the hook and yarn as a guide, but the important thing is to develop a style which you find easy and comfortable. Do not become too discouraged with your first few efforts as a little practice and confidence will help you to achieve regular and even tension.

To work a chain

Put the slip loop first made on to the crochet hook, which should be held between the thumb and index finger of the right hand, having the middle finger resting close to the tip of the hook and the shank held in the crook of the thumb and palm of the hand (fig. 2). If you find it more comfortable, hold the crochet hook between the thumb and middle finger of the right hand, with the index finger resting close to the tip of the hook and the shank held against the palm of the hand by the 3rd and 4th fingers (fig. 3). The yarn to be used should be held over the index and middle fingers of the left hand, under the 3rd finger and over the 4th finger, then a loop pulled from between the 3rd and 4th fingers and passed over the 4th finger (fig. 4). Holding the beginning of the slip loop between the index finger and thumb of the left hand, put the hook underneath the yarn in the left hand so that the yarn passes over the top of the hook and downwards on the side of the hook facing you (fig. 5). Draw the yarn through the slip loop, thus leaving the first loop below the new loop formed (fig. 6). Continue to lengthen the chain in this way by putting the yarn over the hook and drawing a new loop through the existing loop until the chain is the required length. When you have

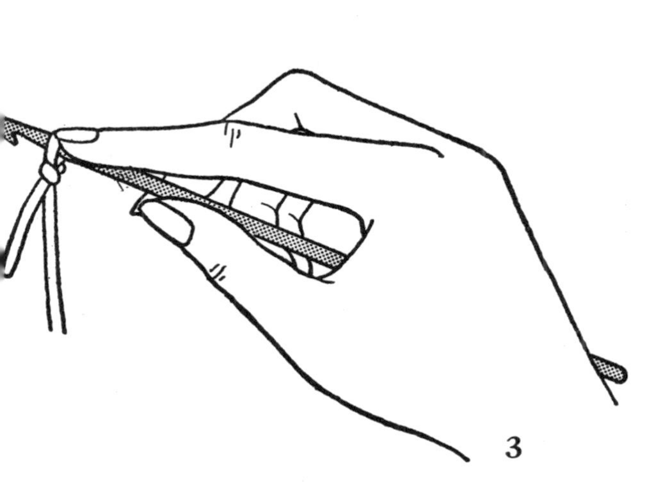

3

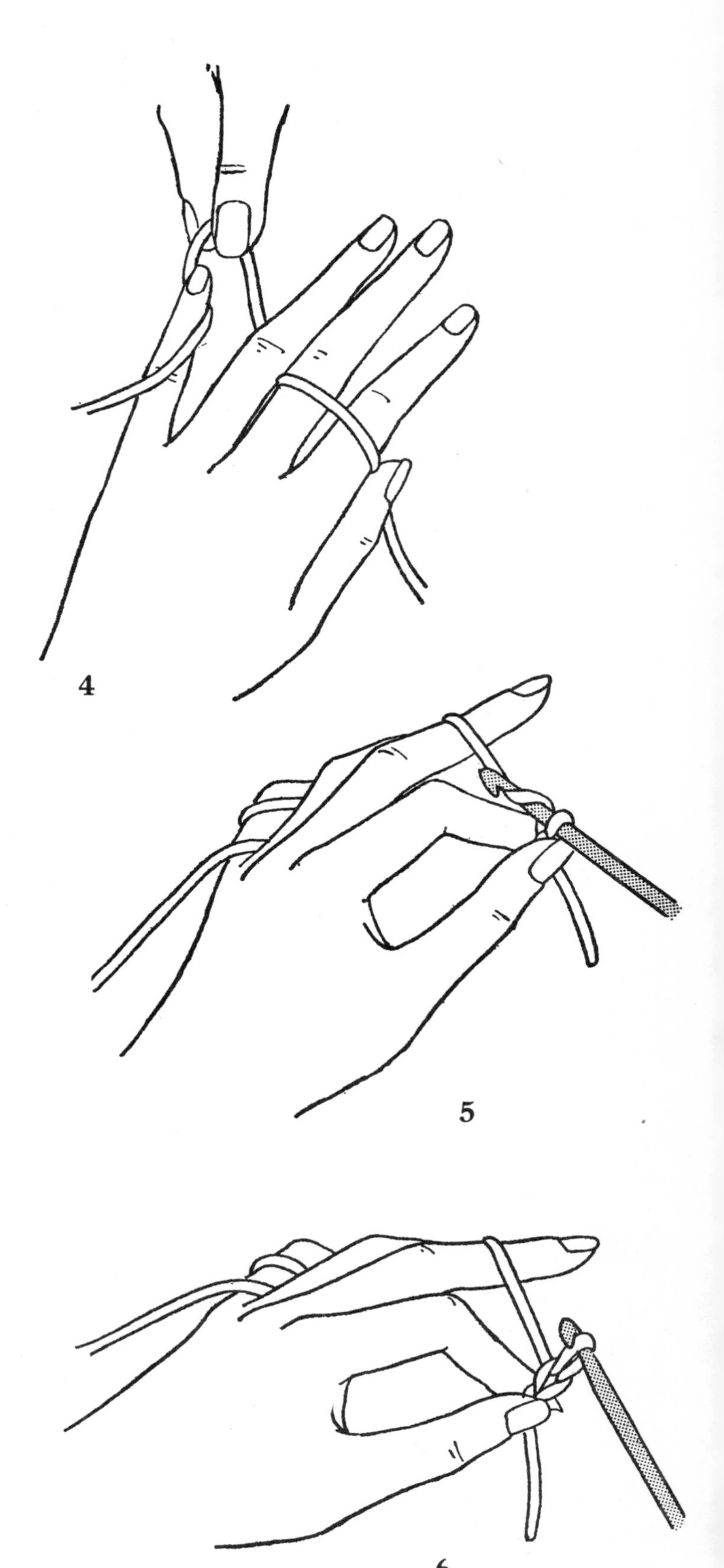

4

5

6

made the required number of chains you will have one loop left on hook which is *not* counted as a stitch. The abbreviation for this is 'ch'.

Turning chains

When working in rows in crochet, i.e. to and fro across the work and not in rounds, extra chains are added at the *end* of each row *before* turning the work to proceed with the next row. These chains form the first stitch of the next row, and the abbreviation for this is 't ch'. Where the number of stitches is given for any row for checking purposes, it will include the turning chain as the first stitch. The number of stitches required to form this turning chain depends on the stitch being used for the fabric, and the following table gives the usual number, unless otherwise stated in the pattern instructions:

Double crochet	–	1 turning chain
Half treble	–	2 turning chains
Treble	–	3 turning chains
Double treble	–	4 turning chains
Triple treble	–	5 turning chains

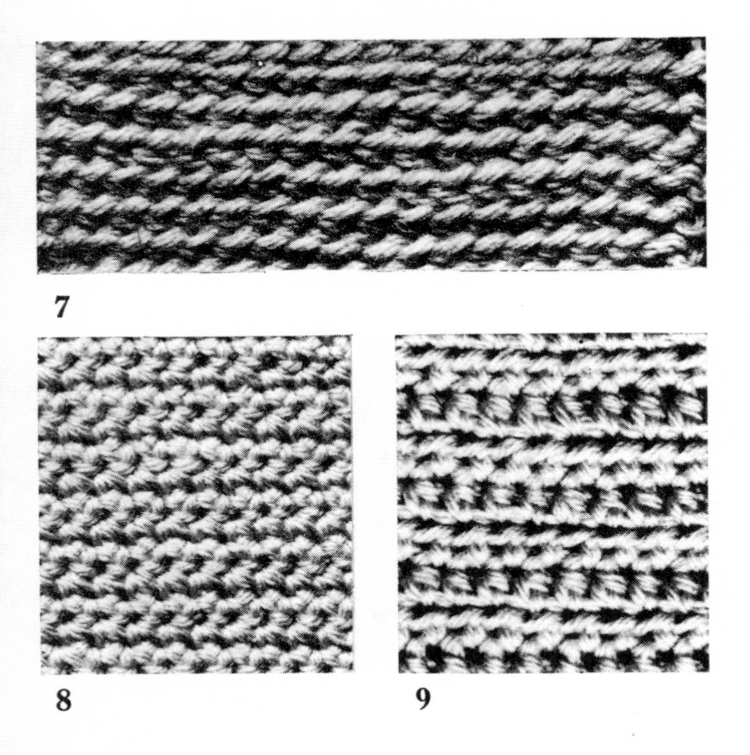

7

8

9

Basic stitches

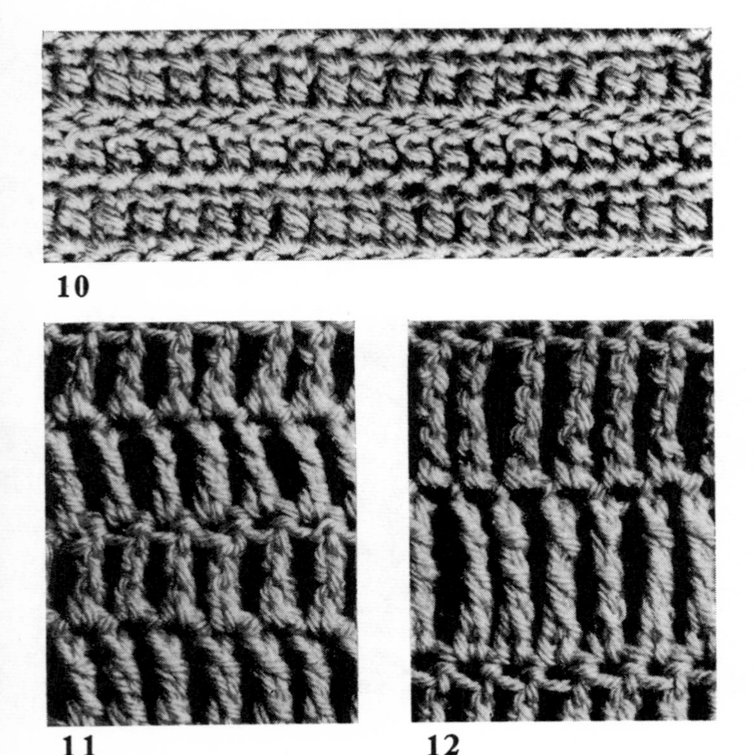

10

11

12

All crochet patterns are based on the following stitches, either worked separately stitch by stitch to give an even fabric, or in combinations and groups to give various lace effects. Each of these stitches varies in length and twist, and where combinations are used to produce, say, a 'shell' pattern, the instructions will tell you how many of each type of stitch to work to give this effect. Practise these basic stitches in rows, holding your hook and yarn as given on page **102**, until you can achieve a firm even fabric, paying particular attention to the paragraph on turning chains, see page **103**.

Slip Stitch, sometimes called Single Crochet (fig. 7) ✓
Work a chain of required length plus one turning chain, turn.
1st row: Miss the first chain from hook, * insert hook from front to back between 2 loops of next chain, yarn over hook, draw new loop of yarn through both chain and loop already on hook [1 slip stitch now formed and 1 loop on hook] repeat from * to end of chain, make one turning chain to count as first stitch of next row, turn. Work following rows in the same way as 1st row but miss the first slip stitch from hook and put the hook under the *double* loop at the top of each stitch on previous row and work last stitch into turning chain of last row. The abbreviation for this is 'sl st'. This is the shortest of all crochet stitches and is seldom used for a complete garment, although it is widely used in shaping and edgings and can be combined with other stitches to form a pattern.

Double Crochet (fig. 8) ✓
Work a chain of required length plus one turning chain, turn.
1st row: Miss the first chain from hook, * insert hook from front to back between 2 loops of next chain, yarn over hook, draw new loop of yarn through chain [2 loops remain on hook], yarn over hook, draw new loop through both loops on hook [1 double crochet now formed and 1 loop on hook]; repeat from * to end of chain, make one turning chain to count as first stitch of next

row, turn. Work following rows in same way as 1st row, but miss the first double crochet from hook and put the hook under the *double* loop at the top of each stitch on previous row and work the last stitch into the turning chain of the last row. The abbreviation for this is 'dc'.

Half Treble, sometimes called Short Treble √ (fig. 9)
Work a chain of required length plus 2 turning chains, turn.
1st row: Miss the first 2 chains from hook, * yarn over hook, insert hook from front to back between 2 loops of next chain, yarn over hook, draw new loop of yarn through chain only [3 loops remain on hook], yarn over hook, draw new loop through 3 remaining loops on hook [1 half treble now formed and 1 loop on hook]; repeat from * to end of chain, make 2 turning chains to count as first stitch on next row, turn. Work following rows in same way as 1st row, but miss the first half treble from hook and put the hook under the *double* loop at the top of each stitch on previous row and work the last stitch into the turning chain of the last row. The abbreviation for this is 'h tr'.

Treble (fig. 10)
Work a chain of required length plus 3 turning chains, turn.
1st row: Miss the first 3 chains from hook, * yarn over hook, insert hook from front to back between 2 loops of next chain, yarn over hook, draw new loop of yarn through chain only [3 loops remain on hook], yarn over hook, draw new loop of yarn through next 2 loops on hook [2 loops remain on hook], yarn over hook, draw new loop through 2 remaining loops on hook [1 treble now formed and 1 loop on hook]; repeat from * to end of chain, make 3 turning chains to count as first stitch of next row, turn. Work following rows in same way as 1st row, but miss the first treble from hook and put the hook under the *double* loop at the top of each stitch on previous row and work the last stitch into the turning chain of the last row. The abbreviation for this is 'tr'.

Double Treble, or Long Treble (fig. 11) √
Work a chain of required length plus 4 turning chains, turn.
1st row: Miss the first 4 chains from hook, * yarn over hook *twice*, insert hook from front to back between 2 loops of next chain, yarn over hook, draw new loop of yarn through chain only [4 loops remain on hook], yarn over hook, draw new loop of yarn through next 2 loops on hook [3 loops remain on hook], yarn over hook, draw new loop of yarn through next 2 loops on hook [2 loops remain on hook], yarn over hook, draw new loop of yarn through 2 remaining loops on hook [1 double treble now formed and 1 loop on hook]; repeat from * to end of chain, make 4 turning chains to count as first stitch of next row, turn. Work following rows in same way as 1st row, but miss the first double treble from hook and put the hook under the *double* loop at the top of each stitch on previous row and work the last stitch into the turning chain of the last row. The abbreviation for this is 'd tr'.

Triple Treble (fig. 12)
Work a chain of required length plus 5 turning chains, turn.
1st row: Miss the first 5 chains from hook, * yarn over hook 3 *times*, insert hook from front to back between 2 loops of next chain, yarn over hook, draw new loop of yarn through chain only [5 loops remain on hook], yarn over hook, draw new loop of yarn through next 2 loops on hook [4 loops remain on hook], yarn over hook, draw new loop of yarn through next 2 loops on hook [3 loops remain on hook], yarn over hook, draw new loop of yarn through next 2 loops on hook [2 loops remain on hook], yarn over hook, draw new loop of yarn through 2 remaining loops on hook [1 triple treble now formed and 1 loop on hook]; repeat from * to end of chain, make 5 turning chains to count as first stitch of next row, turn. Work following rows in same way as 1st row, but miss first triple treble from hook and put the hook under the *double* loop at the top of each stitch on previous row and work the last stitch into the turning chain of the last row. The abbreviation for this is 'tr tr'.

Tension

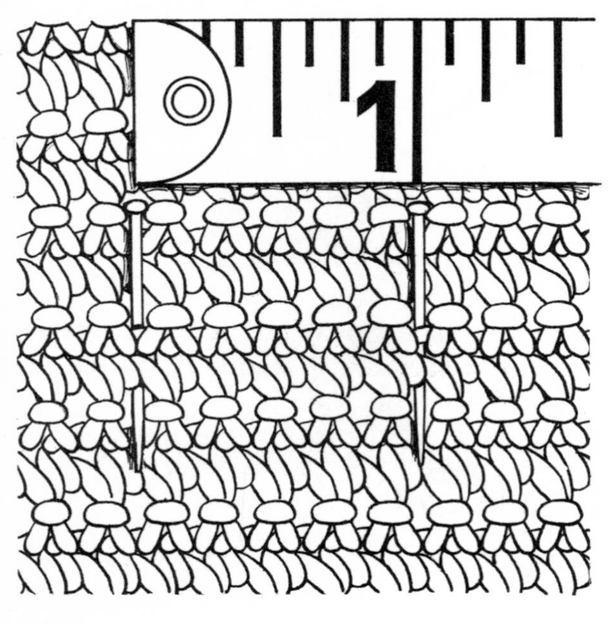

13

The vital point of achieving correct tension in crochet is possibly the most important factor in successful work and, as in knitting, the one step so often overlooked

All reliable crochet patterns will state the number of stitches and, where possible, the number of rows to a given measurement – usually one inch – and also the correct number and type of hook and yarn which the designer has used to produce the garment. Because crochet is an exceedingly 'personal' craft resulting in enormous variances between one worker and another, it is of the *utmost* importance that you obtain the same number of stitches to the given measurement, but it does not matter in the least if you have to use several sizes smaller or larger hook to achieve this measurement. Confusion has been caused in the past by some books stating that a certain size of hook is 'correct' for a certain thickness of yarn, which has led many readers to use the size stated without first checking their own tension, in the belief that the exact results would thus be obtained. It must be remembered that when a particular tension is stated in a pattern it means that this tension has been worked by a designer, and unless you work to the same tension you will not achieve the same results. Using the correct yarn and crochet hook stated, if the tension is given as, say, 4 trebles to the inch, and your tension is 4½ trebles to the inch, your fabric will be too tight, and if your tension is 3½ trebles to the inch your fabric will be too loose. Even a quarter of a stitch difference can make an overall difference in measurements of 2 inches or more.

How to check your tension

Before commencing any garment, work a small sample about 4 inches square in the main pattern and on the hook stated. Place the sample on a flat surface and mark out one inch with pins (fig. 13). Count the number of stitches and rows very carefully, and if your tension is correct then you can begin the design of your choice. If you have any doubt at all, mark out 2 or even 3 inches with pins as a further check. If you have *fewer* stitches to the inch than stated your tension is too loose and you should work another sample using a size smaller hook. If you have *more* stitches to the inch then your tension is too tight and you should work another sample using a size larger hook. Continue in this way, altering the size of your hook until you obtain the correct tension given – only then is it safe to start the pattern.

After the introduction of the New International hook sizes (see page 101) checking tension will be of even greater importance as some patterns may refer to a No. 2 hook in this new size range, and if you already have an existing No. 2 hook in either a wool or cotton range, you will be able to see from the chart shown on page 7 that the circumference of the shanks vary considerably. To illustrate this point samples of double crochet have been worked on an old Aero No. 2 wool hook, the largest in that range, and a New International No. 2 hook, which is the equivalent of a No. 14 hook in the old Aero wool range, and one inch pinned out on both samples. Double Knitting quality yarn was used for both samples, and you will see that 4 stitches to the inch have been obtained with the old No. 2 hook and 6 stitches to the inch with the new No. 2 hook.

These two samples will give you some idea of the difference in the hook sizes when used by the same worker, and if you multiply this difference by the tension variations between each individual worker, you will begin to see that this question of tension cannot be stressed too often or too strongly. You will note that in the instructions given for the crochet garments included in this book alternative hook sizes in both the old and the new ranges have been given. A few minutes spent in checking this vital point will avoid disappointment with the finished garment. Do NOT read beyond this chapter until you have mastered all the preceding stages.

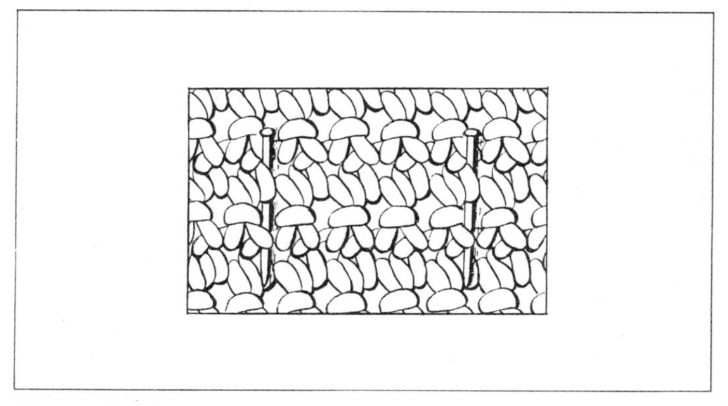

Sample 1
worked on old No. 2 hook

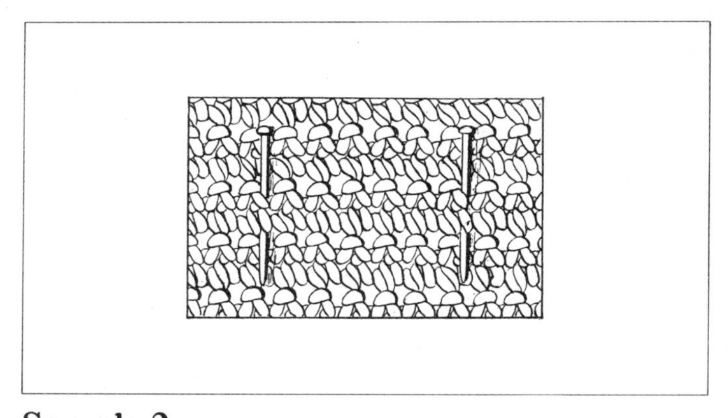

Sample 2
worked on New International No. 2 hook

Shaping

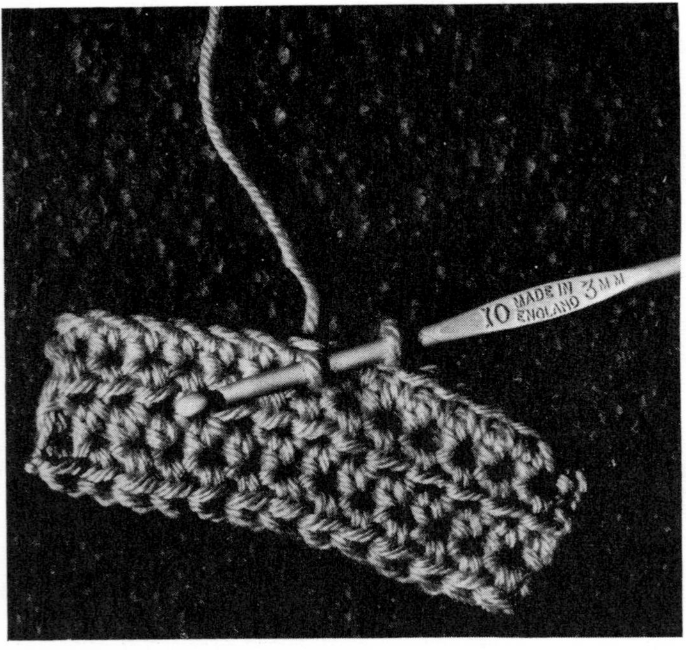

14

All shaping is worked by adding to or taking away from the number of stitches on a row. Increasing a stitch means adding a stitch, and decreasing a stitch means losing it. It must be borne in mind that the average row in crochet is much deeper than in knitting, so when shaping a garment care must be taken not to decrease or increase in such a way as to leave an uneven edge, which could cause difficulty in making up the garment. Most reliable patterns give shaping in detail, but you will find that many give instructions for decreasing by omitting the first and last stitches on a row, and increasing by working twice into the first and last stitches on a row. This, however, is liable to produce a very uneven edge which will prove awkward and untidy to seam when the garment is ready to be made up. The following methods of shaping are very neat and give a most satisfactory finish.

15

Decreasing

To cast off in crochet

Work the required number of rows, *omitting* the turning chain at the end of the last row. On the next row work in slip stitch over the number of stitches to be cast off, now work the turning chain to count as the first stitch of this row, miss the first stitch from hook then work in pattern to the end of the row. If groups of stitches are to be cast off at each end of the row, work as given above, then work in pattern to the required number of stitches from the end of the row, work the turning chain and turn. If stitches are to be cast off on the *following* row, omit the turning chain at the end of the row (fig. 14).

To decrease a stitch

Unless a pattern is being used where individual decreasing instructions are given, work the turning chain to count as the first stitch in the usual way, miss the 2nd stitch from hook, work in pattern to the last 2 stitches, miss the next stitch and work the last stitch, then work the turning chain. If a long stitch, such as double or triple treble is being worked, an alternative method of decreasing avoids a gap which tends to form where the missed stitch would have been. In this method the turning chain forms the first stitch, then work the 2nd stitch in the usual way, *omitting* the last stage [2 loops remain on hook], work 3rd stitch also omitting the last stage [3 loops remain on hook], yarn over hook, draw new loop of yarn through all loops on hook, leaving one loop on hook. In this way, the 2nd and 3rd stitches become one stitch only at the top of the stitch, thus giving the correct number of stitches for the following row, but filling what would otherwise be a space at the base of the stitches. The same method can be used at the end of a row, taking the 2nd and 3rd from last stitches together and working the last stitch in the usual way (fig. 15).

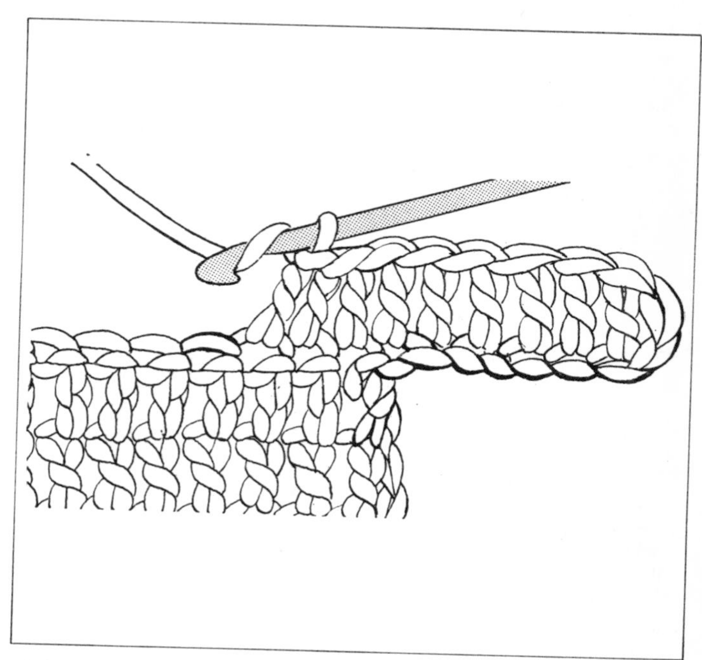

16

Increasing

To cast on in crochet

Work the required number of rows, *omitting* the turning chain at the end of the last row. Work a chain for the required number of stitches to be cast on plus the turning chain, turn. Count the turning chain as the first stitch, then work in pattern across other chain stitches and to end of row (fig. 16).

To increase a stitch

Work the turning chain to count as the first stitch, then work 2 stitches into the 2nd stitch and 2 stitches into the 2nd from last stitch, work last stitch in the usual way, work the turning chain to count as first stitch of the next row (fig. 17).

17

Crochet stitches

Ridged treble (fig. 18)
With this stitch both sides of the work are alike. Work as given for Treble, see page 105, but work into the back loop *only* of the loop at the top of each stitch.

Ridged treble (fig. 19)
With this stitch the right side of the work only is ridged.
1st row: Work as given for Treble, see page 105.
2nd row: Work as given for Treble, working into the back loop *only* of the loop at the top of each stitch.
3rd row: Work as given for Treble, working into the front loop *only* of the loop at the top of each stitch.
Repeat the 2nd and 3rd rows throughout to form pattern.

You will find it helpful to work some of these stitch samples as it will accustom you to the rhythm and terminology of crochet

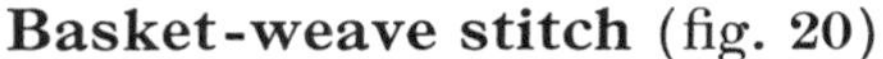

Basket-weave stitch (fig. 20)
This is a variation of treble stitch, formed by putting the hook round the stem of the treble from the back or the front, NOT using the loops at the top of the stitches.
Work a chain having multiples of 6 plus 2 turning chain.
1st row: 1 treble into 3rd chain from hook, 1 treble into each chain to end, 2 chain, turn.
2nd row: Yarn over hook, insert hook from back of work between 1st and 2nd stitches round 2nd stitch and back between 2nd and 3rd stitches, draw new loop of yarn through and work 1 treble in usual way, work 2 more trebles in this way on next 2 stitches – called 3 tr Bk – * yarn over hook, insert hook from front of work between next 2 stitches round stitch and back between next 2 stitches, draw new loop of yarn through and work 1 treble in usual way, work 2 more trebles in this way on next 2 stitches – called 3 tr Ft – work 3 tr Bk; repeat from * to last 3 stitches, work 3 tr Ft on next 3 stitches, 2 chain, turn.
3rd and 4th row: As 2nd.
5th row: * Work 3 tr Ft, 3 tr Bk; repeat from * to end, 2 chain, turn.
6th and 7th row: As 5th.
Repeat the 2nd to 7th rows throughout to form pattern.

Crazy pattern (fig. 21)
Work a chain having multiples of 4 plus 8 chain.
1st row: Miss 3 chain, work 3 treble into next chain, miss 3 chain, work 1 double crochet into next chain, * work 3 chain, work 3 treble into *same* chain as double crochet was worked, miss 3 chain, work 1 double crochet into next chain; repeat from * to end of row, 3 chain, turn.
2nd row: Work 3 treble into double crochet of previous row, * 1 double crochet into top of 3 chain loop on previous row, work 3 chain, work 3 treble into same chain loop as double crochet was worked; repeat from * to end of row, ending with 1 double crochet into last loop, 3 chain, turn.
Repeat the 2nd row throughout to form pattern.

Crochet stitches

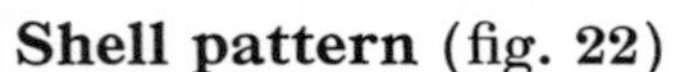

Shell pattern (fig. 22)
Work a chain having multiples of 8.
1st row: Miss 3 chain, work 5 treble into next chain, miss 3 chain, * work 1 double crochet into next chain, miss 3 chain, work 5 treble into next chain, miss 3 chain; repeat from * ending with 1 double crochet, 3 chain, turn.
2nd row: Work 3 treble into double crochet of previous row, * work 1 double crochet into 3rd treble of 5 treble shell of previous row, work 5 treble into the next double crochet of previous row; repeat from * ending with 3 treble to form half a shell, 3 chain, turn.
3rd row: Work 5 treble into double crochet between half shell and first complete shell on previous row, * work 1 double crochet into 3rd treble of next 5 treble shell of previous row, work 5 treble into next double crochet of previous row; repeat from * to end of row, ending with a complete shell and 1 double crochet, 3 chain, turn.
Repeat the 2nd and 3rd rows throughout to form pattern.

Bobble stitch (fig. 23)
Work required length of chain, turn.
1st row: Work 1 double crochet into 3rd chain from hook, 1 double crochet into each chain to end, 3 chain, turn.
2nd row: * Yarn round hook, insert hook into next stitch, draw 1 loop through loosely, [yarn round hook, insert hook into same space, draw loop through loosely] twice, [7 loops on hook], yarn round hook and draw through 7 loops, 1 double crochet into next stitch; repeat from * to end, 2 chain, turn.
3rd row: Work 1 double crochet into back loop of each stitch to end, 3 chain, turn.
Repeat the 2nd and 3rd rows throughout to form pattern.

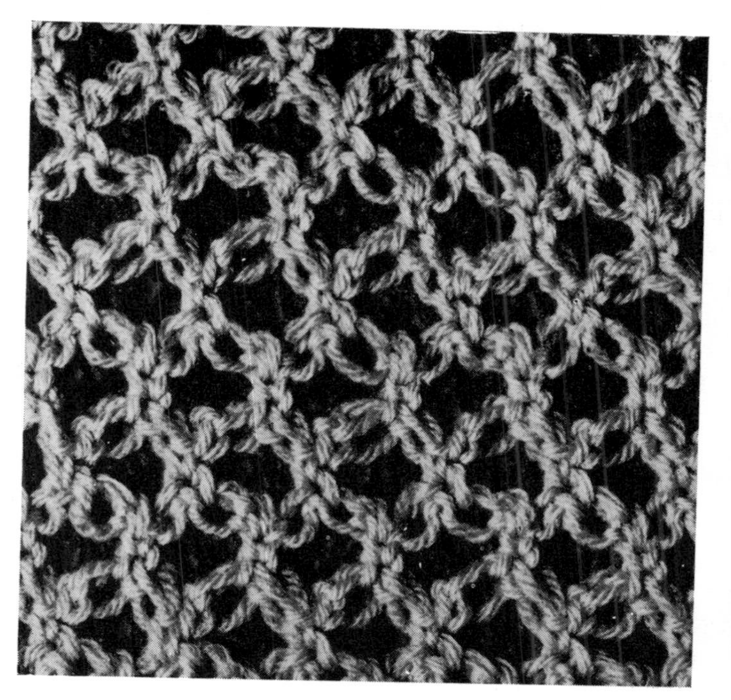

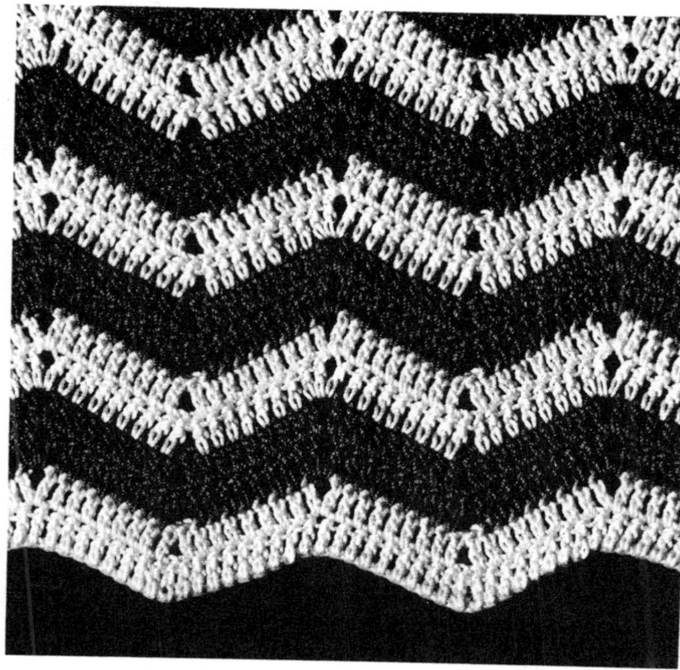

King Solomon's knot (fig. 24)

1st row: Put a slip loop on hook and make 1 chain through slip loop, * draw loop up to ½″, yarn over hook, draw new loop of yarn through forming a loose chain stitch, insert hook between double and single loop of chain stitch and draw yarn through, yarn over hook, draw new loop of yarn through both loops on hook making one knot stitch; repeat from * to required length, make one more knot stitch with ¾″ loop and one with ⅜″ loop, turn.

2nd row: Work 1 double crochet into 3rd knot stitch from hook, * work 2 knot stitches drawing loop out to ⅜″, work 1 double crochet into next knot stitch of previous row; repeat from * working 1 double crochet at end of row into first chain of commencing row, make 1 knot stitch with ¾″ loop and 1 knot stitch with ⅜″ loop, turn.

3rd row: Work 1 double crochet into 4th knot from hook, work as given for 2nd row working last double crochet into knot in centre of turning stitches.

Repeat the 3rd row throughout to form pattern. To work the last row work 1 knot stitch with ½″ loop between double crochet to correspond with 1st row.

Note: When the loop is drawn out to the required length, it should be held firmly in the left hand between thumb and fingers to prevent it slipping until the knot is completed.

Chevrons (fig. 25)

Note: Mc = main colour; cc = contrast colour.

Using Mc, commence with a length of ch having a multiple of 19 ch plus 4.

1st row: 1 tr into 4th ch from hook, 1 tr into each ch, 3 ch, turn.

2nd row: Miss first 2 tr, * 1 tr into each of next 8 tr, into next tr work 1 tr 2 ch and 1 tr [a V st made], 1 tr into each of next 8 tr, miss 2 tr; rep from * ending with miss 1 tr, leaving the last loop on hook work 1 tr into next ch, drop Mc, pick up cc and draw through rem 2 loops, 3 ch, turn. [Always change colours in this way.]

3rd row: Miss first 2 tr, * 1 tr into each of next 8 tr, a V st into sp of next V st, 1 tr into each of next 8 tr, miss 2 tr; rep from * ending with miss 1 tr, 1 tr into next ch, 3 ch, turn.

4th row: As 3rd, dropping cc and picking up Mc, 3 ch, turn.

5th row: As 3rd.

6th row: As 3rd, dropping Mc and picking up cc, 3 ch turn. Rep 3rd to 6th rows for length required, omitting t ch at end of last row. Fasten off.

Crochet stitches

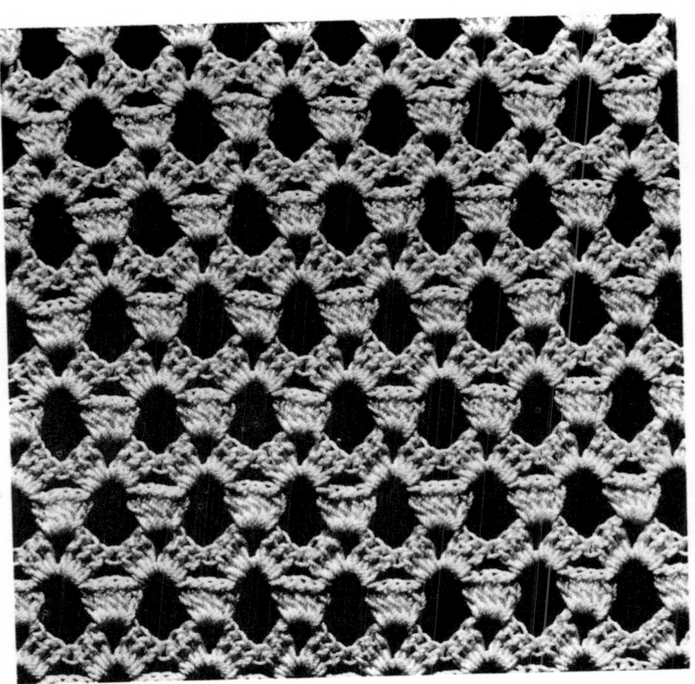

Stitch in blocks (fig. 26)
Commence with a length of ch having a multiple of 4 ch plus 3.
1st row: Into 7th ch from hook work [1 tr, 1 ch] 3 times and 1 tr [a shell made], * miss 3 ch, into next ch work [1 tr, 1 ch] 3 times and 1 tr [another shell made]; rep from * to within last 4 ch, miss 3 ch, 1 tr into next ch, 3 ch, turn.
2nd row: A shell into centre sp of first shell, * a shell into centre sp of next shell; rep from * to within last shell, a shell into centre sp of next shell, miss next sp of same shell, 1 tr into next ch, 3 ch, turn.
Rep 2nd row for length required, omitting t ch at end of last row. Fasten off.

Lace shell pattern (fig. 27)
Commence with a length of ch having a multiple of 6 ch plus 3.
1st row: 4 tr into 6th ch from hook, * 4 ch, miss 5 ch, 5 tr into next ch; rep from * to within last 9 ch, 4 ch, miss 5 ch, 4 tr into next ch, miss 2 ch, 1 tr into next ch, 3 ch, turn.
2nd row: 2 tr into first tr, * into next sp work 3 tr 3 ch and 3 tr; rep from * ending with miss 4 tr, 3 tr into next ch, 6 ch, turn.
3rd row: * 5 tr into next 3 ch sp, 4 ch; rep from * to within last sp, 5 tr into next ch sp, 3 ch, 1 tr in 3rd of 3 ch, 6 ch, turn.
4th row: 3 tr into first sp, * into next sp work 3 tr 3 ch and 3 tr; rep from * to within last sp, 3 tr into next sp, 3 ch, 1 tr into 3rd of 6 ch, 3 ch, turn.
5th row: 4 tr into first 3 ch sp, * 4 ch, 5 tr into next sp; rep from * to within last sp, 4 ch, 4 tr into next sp, 1 tr into 3rd of 6 ch, 3 ch, turn.
Rep 2nd to 5th rows for length required, omitting t ch at end of last row. Fasten off.

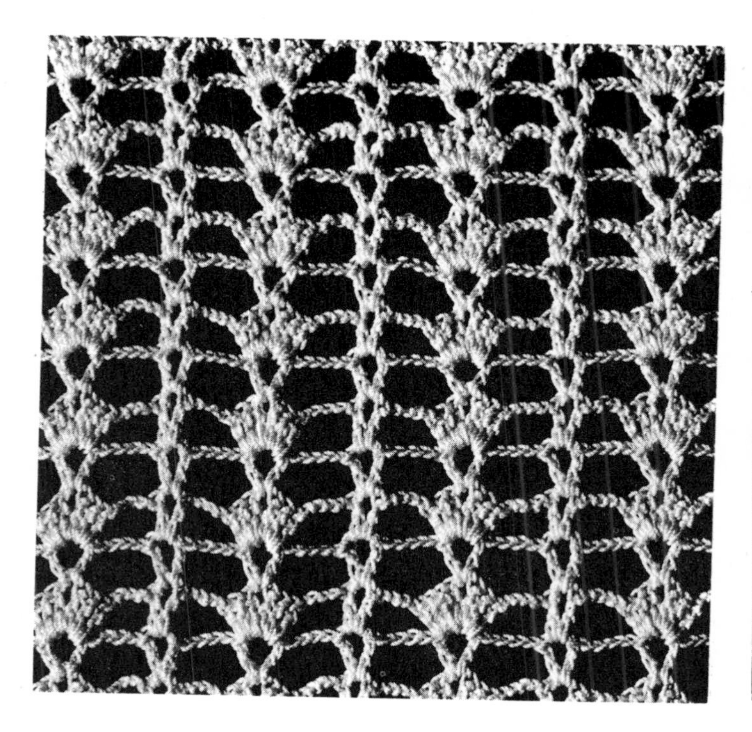

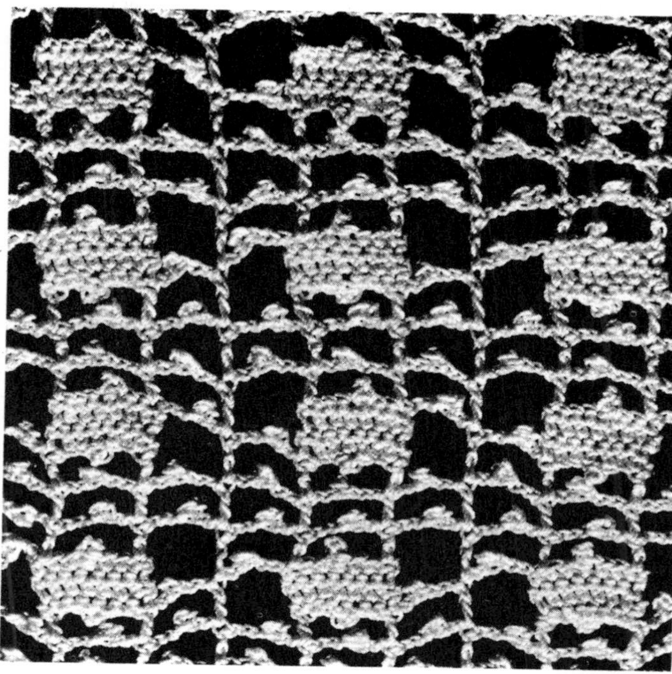

Shell and trellis pattern (fig. 28)
Commence with a length of ch having a multiple of 12 ch plus 7.
1st row: Into 5th ch from hook work 1 tr 2 ch and 1 tr [a V st made], * 4 ch, miss 5 ch, into next ch work 1 tr 2 ch and 1 tr [another V st made]; rep from * to within last 2 ch, miss 1 ch, 1 tr into next ch, 3 ch, turn.
2nd row: A V st into sp of first V st, * 4 ch, into sp of next V st work 3 tr 2 ch and 3 tr [a shell made] 4 ch, a V st into sp of next V st; rep from * ending with 1 tr into next ch, 3 ch, turn.
3rd row: A V st into sp of first V st, * 4 ch, a V st into sp of next shell, 4 ch, a V st into sp of next V st; rep from * ending with 1 tr into 3rd of 3 ch, 3 ch, turn.
Rep 2nd and 3rd rows for length required, omitting t ch at end of last row. Fasten off.

Trellis pattern (fig. 29)
Commence with a length of ch having a multiple of 15 ch plus 8.
1st row: 1 dc into 3rd ch from hook [a picot made], 2 ch, 1 tr into 10th ch from picot, * 5 ch, a picot, 2 ch, miss 4 ch, 1 tr into next ch; rep from * ending with 8 ch, turn.
2nd row: A picot, 2 ch, miss first tr, * 1 tr into next tr, 5 ch, a picot, 2 ch; rep from * ending with miss 2 ch after next picot, 1 tr into next ch, 8 ch, turn.
3rd row: A picot, 2 ch, miss first tr, 1 tr into next tr, * 5 ch, a picot, 2 ch, 1 tr into next tr, 1 ch, turn, 1 dc into each of next 7 sts working behind picot, 1 ch, turn, [1 dc into each dc, 1 ch, turn] twice, 1 dc into each of next 4 dc, 3 ch, 1 dc into last dc, 1 dc into each of next 3 dc [a block made], 5 ch, a picot, 2 ch, 1 tr into next tr, 5 ch, a picot, 2 ch, 1 tr into next tr; rep from * omitting 5 ch, a picot, 2 ch and 1 tr at end of last rep and working last tr into 3rd of 8 ch, 8 ch, turn.
4th row: * A picot, 2 ch, 1 tr into next dc, 5 ch, a picot, 2 ch, miss next 2 dc, a picot and 2 dc, 1 tr into next dc, 5 ch, a picot, 2 ch, 1 tr into next tr, 5 ch; rep from * omitting 5 ch at end of last rep and working last tr into 3rd of 8 ch, 8 ch, turn.
Rep 2nd to 4th row for length required, omitting t ch at end of last row. Fasten off.

Working from a pattern

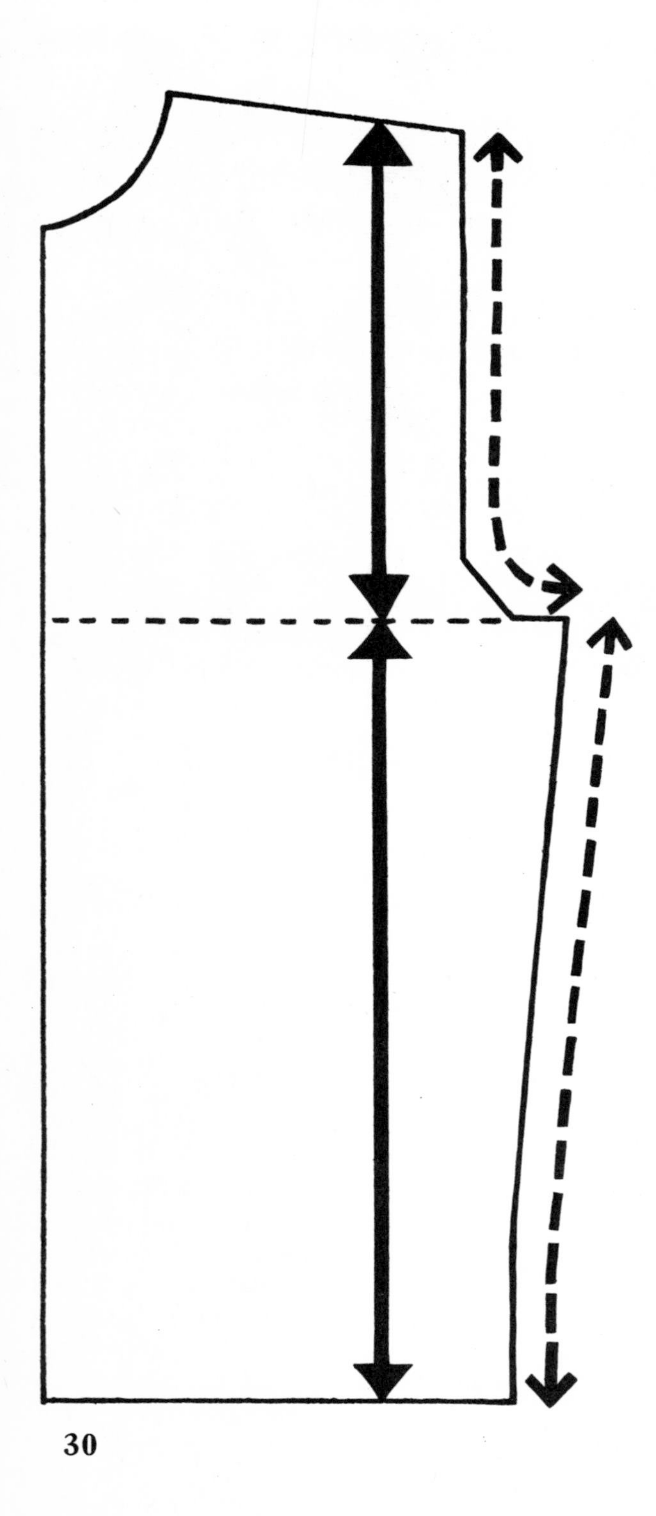

30

Choosing your pattern

Before beginning any crochet design it is advisable to make sure that you are not being too ambitious at first – it is much better to complete a simple cushion cover or baby's blanket rather than starting on a complicated dress pattern which may have you floundering after the first few rows and will eventually remain unfinished. Always read right through a pattern before starting to crochet to make sure it is not too difficult, particularly the making-up section, as a plain but tailored coat will entail as much in making up as in all the work which has gone before.

In this book the following patterns are simple to work and good ones to start on: the matinee jacket, the baby's shawl, the front cover shawl, and both the cushion designs.

Materials

Once you have chosen your design, it is essential to buy the yarn stated in the pattern. Only by using the yarns quoted in the materials paragraph can you be sure that you will obtain the correct tension and that your garment will work out to the measurements given. It is very unwise to try and substitute a different yarn, especially now-a-days when there are so many types on the market, as they will all vary slightly. The terms '3-ply', '4-ply', etc. are not standard thickness but simply refer to the number of strands twisted together to make the yarn, see 'Types of yarn', page 100. If you cannot obtain the yarn stated, write to the spinner of the yarn for the name and address of your nearest stockist. Always make sure you buy sufficient yarn to complete your garment, remembering to allow extra if you wish to add to the given measurements. Keep a ball band from one ball of yarn, which will quote the exact shade and dye lot number, in case you do need extra.

Measurements

Nearly all patterns give instructions for more than one size, with the first set of figures referring to the smallest size and figures for larger sizes in brackets, thus, 32″ (34″–36″) bust. Based on these sizes, if you are making a garment in a 36″ bust, the number of stitches and measurements for your size will be shown as the second set of figures in brackets throughout, unless only one set of figures is given, which will apply to all sizes. Before beginning your pattern you may find it easier to go through and mark the figures given for your size. Measurements for body and sleeve lengths will be given in the pattern and if you want to add to any of these always remember to allow for extra yarn.

Your work should be placed on a flat surface and measurements taken from the *centre* of the work and not at the edges (fig. 30). Adjustments can be made to the length of the body by adding or taking away rows *before* the armhole shaping is reached. Where there is side shaping on the body or sleeves, adjust the length when the shaping has been completed. Be very accurate about measuring armhole depth – never on the side curve and never try to alter the length here if possible as the correct fit of the sleeves depends on the correct armhole depth. Remember to work the same number of rows on pieces which have to be joined, for example, the front and back of a garment – a row counter can be useful here.

Tension

Do not miss this paragraph – it is vital to the success of your work. See page 106.

31

Joining in a new ball

Always join in a new ball of yarn at the beginning of a row if possible. If the yarn has to be joined in the middle of the work, which is necessary when working in rounds, the ends should be spliced. Unravel the ends of yarn of the ball being used and the new ball, cut away one or two strands from each end, overlay the two ends and twist together until they hold. The twisted ends should be of the same thickness as the original yarn. Work very carefully with the newly twisted yarn for a few stitches, then trim away the odd ends of yarn. If you cannot join in the yarn at the beginning of a row *never* crochet a knot into your work but splice the ends as described (fig. 31).

Working from a pattern

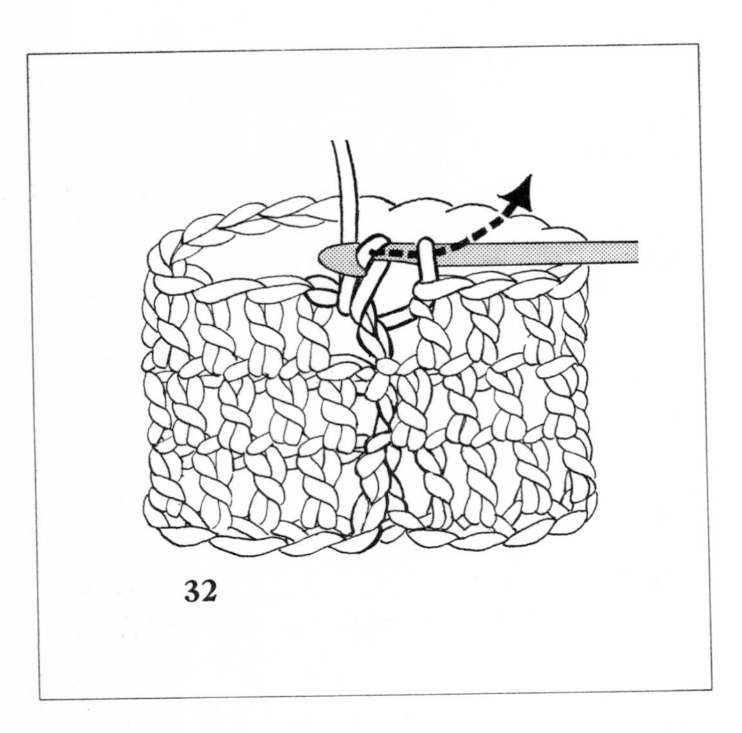

32

Mistakes

If these occur there is only one solution and that is to unpick work back to the error and correct it.

Patterned stitches

The number of stitches cast on for each piece are calculated to fit the pattern exactly, so that for the first few rows you can follow the instructions without any alteration and get to know the pattern sequence. As soon as you start any shaping, however, the beginnings and ends of th pattern rows will change. With patterns mac up from basic stitches this is no problem, as yc can see how to work each stitch from what ha gone before. With more elaborate patterns yc should analyse how the stitch works, then wo in your extra stitches accordingly. With con plicated lace stitches it may be best to work tl increased stitches in double crochet or trebl depending on the basic stitch of the pattern un there are sufficient extra stitches to work anoth complete pattern. Keep a check on rows with row counter so that you know exactly whi pattern row you are working and when the ne piece of shaping is due.

Abbreviations

See 'Abbreviations', page 3. The abbreviatio for any unusual or difficult stitches will be giv in individual instructions.

Methods of working

Working to and fro in rows

Commencing with a chain of the required leng the work is turned at the end of each row, 'Turning chains', page 103. Work continues this way, row by row, until required length achieved.

Working in rounds

Commencing with a given chain, this chain formed into a circle by joining the last ch worked to the first chain by means of a slip stitch. Further rounds are then worked into this circle, each round being completed by means of a slip stitch into the first stitch of the round, or as stated in the instructions (fig. 32).

Working motifs

Some designs are based upon a number of small units or motifs, and very attractive results can be obtained by combining different shapes. Details of the motif used and the making up will be given in the instructions, and in some cases, once the first motif is completed, the second motif is joined to this as part of the pattern on the last round. Where this is not given, the correct number of motifs must be worked, and these are then sewn or crocheted together (fig. 33).

Joining in new colours for motifs

Instructions for splicing are given on page 117. Splicing is the most professional method for joining in a new colour or new ball of yarn, however a further method is as follows: Fasten off old colour or yarn then put hook back into same place and with new colour put yarn over hook and pull it through so that you have a loop on hook. Work one chain with double yarn using both the short end and the working end then proceed with pattern. When work is complete sew in all ends.

Both these methods are used for working in rows or rounds.

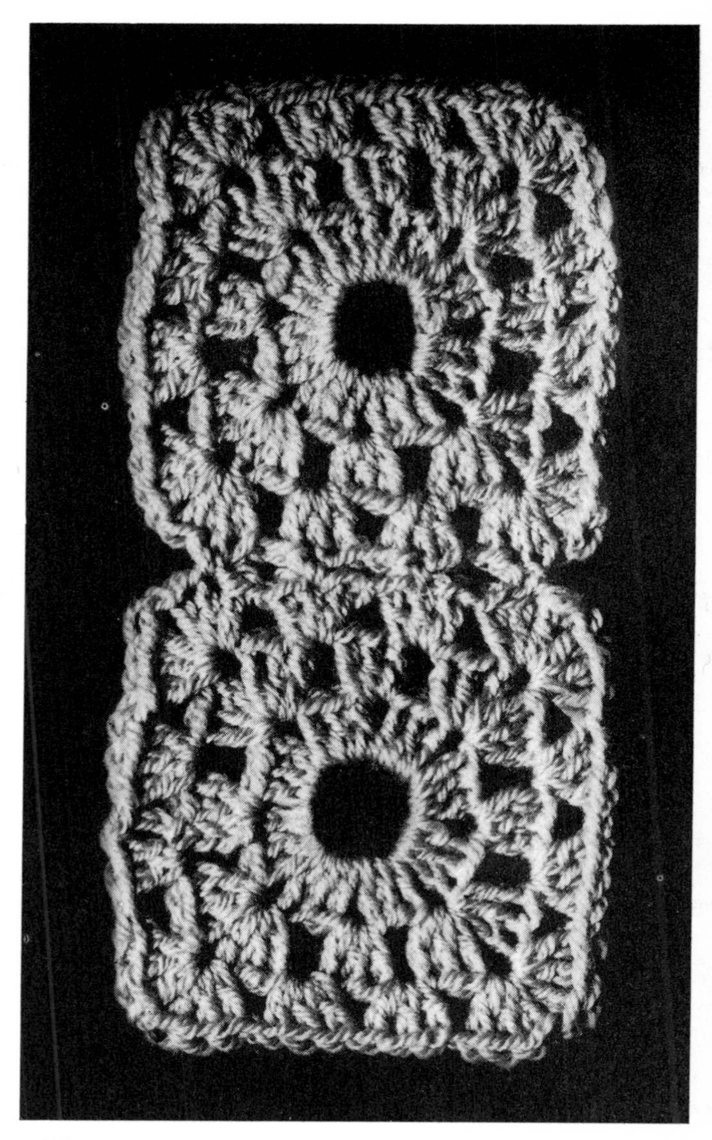

33

Finishing touches

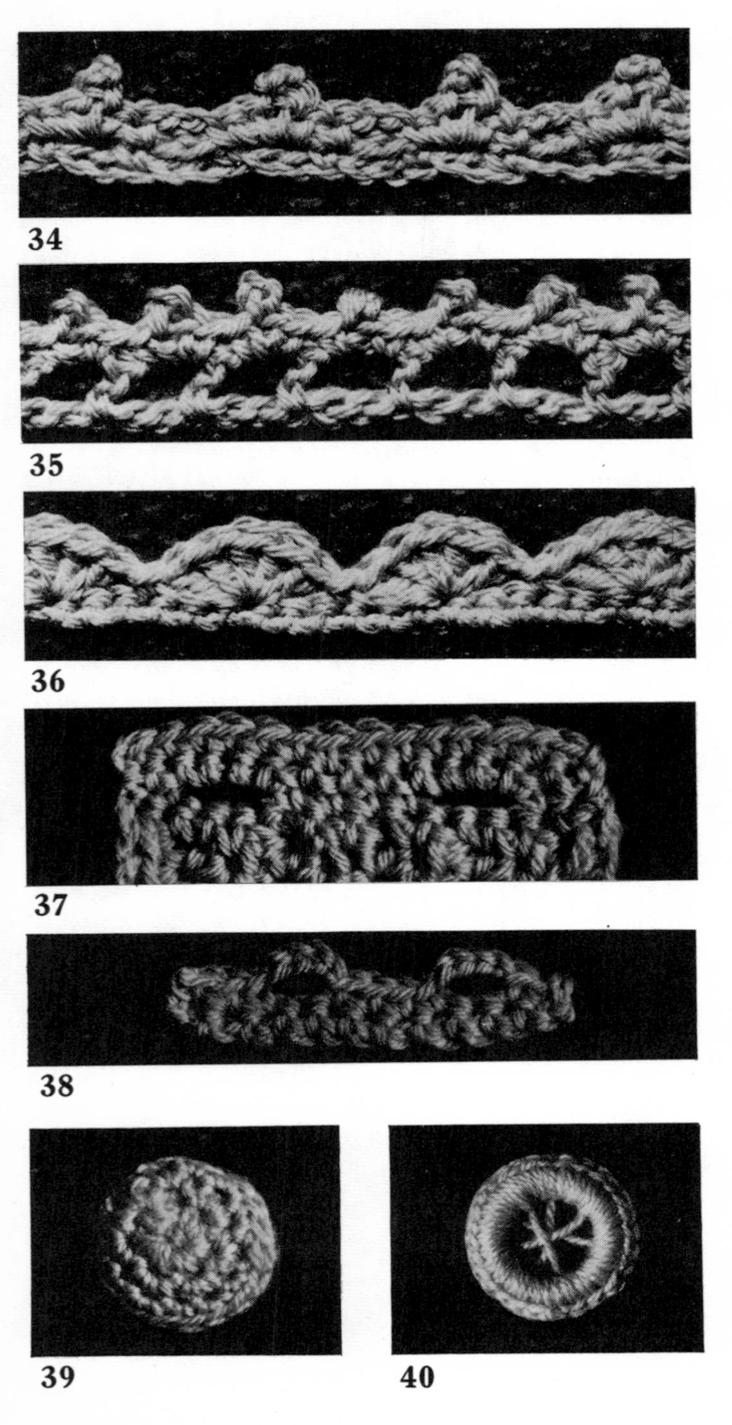
34
35
36
37
38
39
40

Because of the depth of crochet stitches and the thickness of the fabric it is not generally desirable to have a turned under hem, and most reliable patterns will give instructions for neatening hems and edges, either by means of rows of double crochet or with special stitch effects. We give below instructions for three edgings which can be used to give an attractive finish, some buttoning ideas, and fine picots for delicate crochet.

Edgings

Small picot edging (fig. 34)
Make a chain of multiples of 6 plus 2, turn.
1st row: 1 dc into 2nd ch from hook, * 2 ch, miss 2 ch, 1 dc into next ch; rep from * to end, 1 ch, turn.
2nd row: * 1 dc into space, 3 ch, 1 sl st into first of these 3 ch to form picot, 1 dc into same space, 1 dc into next dc, 2 ch, miss 2 ch, 1 dc into next dc; rep from * to end.

Picot edging (fig. 35)
Make a chain of multiples of 3 plus 5, turn.
1st row: Work 1 tr into 8th ch from hook, * 2 ch, miss 2 ch, 1 tr into next ch; rep from * to end, 3 ch, turn.
2nd row: * 1 dc into first 2 ch space, 3 ch, 1 dc into first of these 3 ch to form picot, 1 dc into same space; rep from * into each space to end.

Scallop edging (fig. 36)
Make a chain of multiples of 6, turn.
1st row: * Miss 2 ch, work 5 tr into next ch, miss 2 ch, 1 sl st into next ch; rep from * to end.

Buttonholes

Chain buttonhole
Work one row of dc along edge of work where buttonholes are required. On the 2nd row of dc, buttonholes are made by missing the number of stitches required for the width of the button and working a chain of the same number. On the

3rd row work dc into the space left by the chain, making sure that there are the same number of dc as there are ch. Work a final row of double crochet. The number of rows and position and size of the buttonholes depend on the garment design (fig. 37).

Loop buttonhole
Work one row of dc along edge of work where buttonholes are required. On the 2nd row of dc a loop of ch is made of sufficient size to slip over the button. This loop may be strengthened by being covered by a close row of dc worked into and around loop (fig. 38).

Covered buttons
Crochet covered buttons are a simple way of obtaining perfectly matching buttons. They may be round button moulds covered in crochet or a ring covered with crochet.

Round buttons (fig. 39)
Work 3 ch and join into a circle with a sl st.
1st round: Work 6 dc into circle, joining with a sl st nto first dc.
2nd round: Work 2 dc into each dc of previous round, oining with a sl st into first dc.
3rd round: Work 1 dc into each dc of previous round, oining with a sl st into first dc. Repeat 3rd round ıntil button mould is covered.
Last round: * Miss 1 dc, 1 dc into next dc; rep from * o end, joining with a sl st into first dc.
Slip crochet cover over button mould and draw together under button, leaving an end of yarn for sewing on button. An additional trim may be added by working one row of sl st around outer edge of button after over has been made.

Ring buttons (fig. 40)
Work a round of close dc all round ring, joining with a sl st into first dc. Across back of ring work strands of yarn diagonally across ring and sew to garment through centre of these threads.

41

42

43

Fine picots

Top (fig. 41)
MATERIALS: Coats Chain Mercer–Crochet No. 20. No. 3 crochet hook or New International size No. 1.25.
TENSION: Width of trimming $\frac{1}{8}$″.
* 4 ch, 1 dc into 4th ch from hook; rep from * for length required. Fasten off.

Centre (fig. 42)
MATERIALS: Coats Chain Mercer–Crochet No. 20. No. 3 crochet hook or New International size No. 1.25.
TENSION: Width of trimming $\frac{1}{4}$″.
* 5 ch, 3 tr into 4th ch from hook; rep from * for length required. Fasten off.

Bottom (fig. 43)
MATERIALS: Coats Chain Mercer–Crochet No. 20. No. 3 crochet hook or New International size No. 1.25.
TENSION: Width of trimming $\frac{3}{8}$″.
4 ch, * 3 d tr into 4th ch from hook, 1 sl st into same ch, 6 ch; rep from * for length required. Fasten off.

Making up

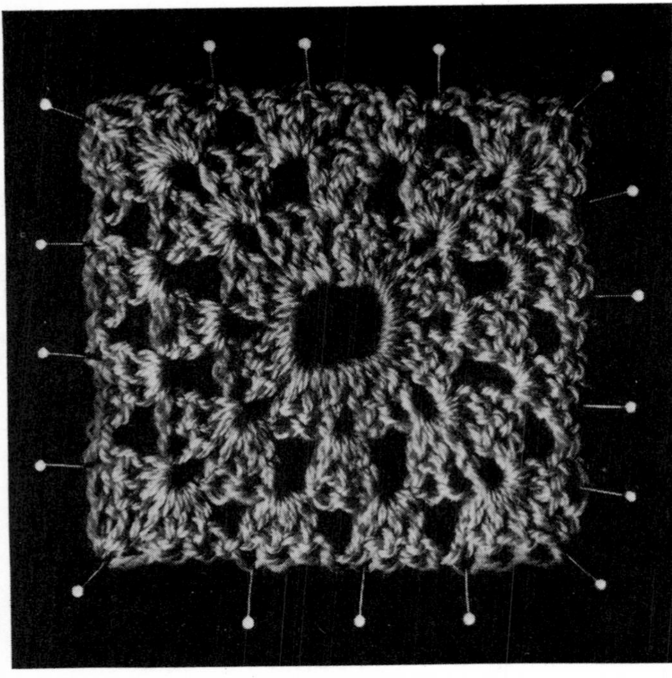

44

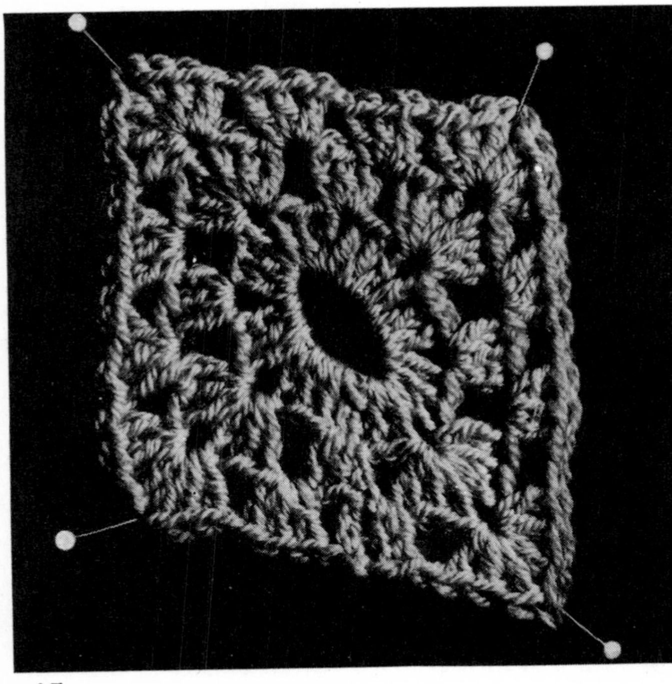

45

Pressing

Before making up instructions are given, most patterns will give pressing details, but the following points will prove very useful:

Wool
Press under a damp cloth with a warm iron.

Mixtures of wool and any man-made fibres
Press *lightly* under a damp cloth with a warm iron.

Nylon
Press under a *dry* cloth with a warm iron.

Mohair
Press *lightly* under a damp cloth with a warm iron.

Courtelle
Do not press.

Acrilan
Do not press.

Cotton
Press under a damp cloth with a fairly hot iron.

Embossed patterns
These should be *steamed* rather than pressed, using a very damp cloth and holding the iron over the surface, simply to make steam and not using any pressure. This will even up and neaten the work without flattening or spoiling the pattern.

Angora
Steam as given for embossed patterns.

When pressing is directed pin out pieces on to a flat surface using plenty of pins and taking care to keep stitches and rows in even lines (fig. 44). It is essential not to pull the work out of shape by pinning too tightly or unevenly (fig. 45). Place each piece right side down on to a well padded surface, taking care to keep the stitches and rows running in straight lines. Press the main part of each piece as given in the instructions. Wait until the fabric has cooled then take out the pins.

46

Seams

Use a blunt-ended wool needle and the original yarn for sewing together. If the yarn is not suitable for sewing use a 3-ply yarn in the same shade. On an even patterned garment such as double crochet, half treble or treble crochet seams may be joined by a single row of double crochet, great care being taken to ensure that the seam is the same length as the finished garment and that you have not stretched it or pulled it too tightly (fig. 46). Woven flat seams and backstitch seams may be used where they prove suitable. More open patterns obviously require the use of a woven flat seam to bring the two edges together without any ridge forming.

Woven flat seam

With the right sides of the work facing each other, place your finger between the two pieces to be joined, insert the needle from the front through both pieces below the corresponding pips, pull the yarn through and insert the needle from the back through both pieces the length of a small running stitch, pull the yarn through. Repeat this along the seam matching the 'pips' on each piece. The seam will then be drawn together and will be flat and very neat when pressed. This method is always used for baby garments, ribbing and underclothes (fig. 47).

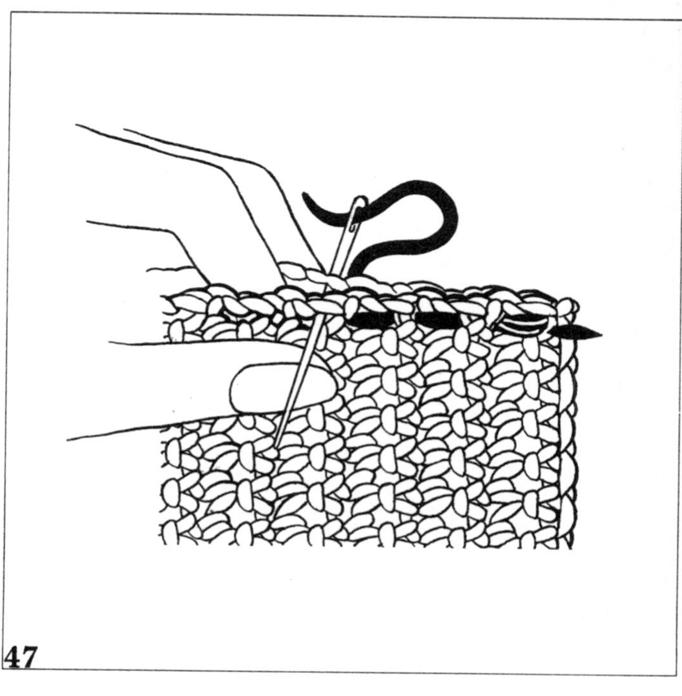

47

Backstitch seam

This method is firm, yet elastic, keeps the garment in shape and will not break if roughly treated. Place the two pieces to be joined right sides together, join in the sewing yarn by making small running stitches over each other one stitch in from the edge. Put the needle back into

Making up

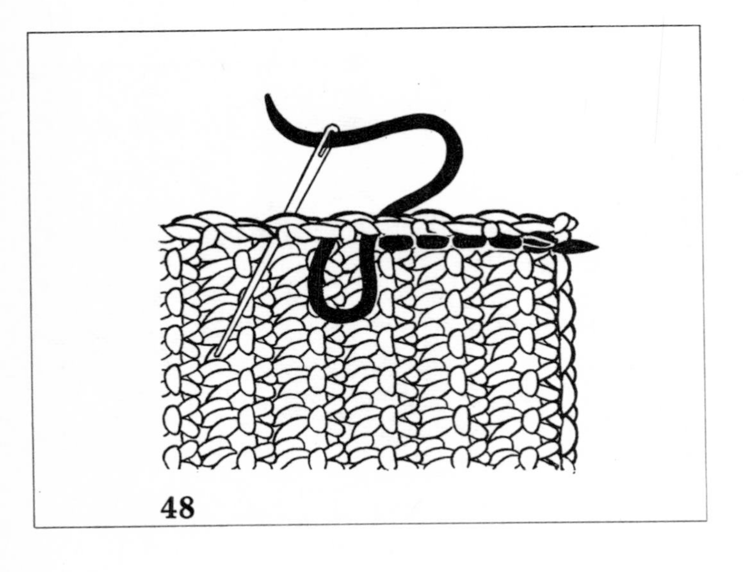

48

the beginning of the running stitch and pull the yarn through, insert the needle from the back through the fabric and beyond the first running stitch the length of another small stitch and pull the yarn through. Repeat this along the seam, keeping stitches neat and even and one stitch in from the edge of both pieces of fabric and taking great care not to split the knitted stitches (fig 48). Your pattern will tell you which seams to sew first, but they are usually worked in the following order:

Shoulder seams
Backstitch firmly one stitch from the edge taking the stitching across the steps of shaping in a straight line. Press on the wrong side. For heavy sweaters, reinforce these seams with ribbon or tape.

Set in sleeves
Mark centre top of sleeve and pin in position to shoulder seam, then pin cast off stitches to cast off underarm stitches of body. Keeping the sleeve smooth on either side of the shoulder seam, work fine backstitch round the curves as near the edge as possible.

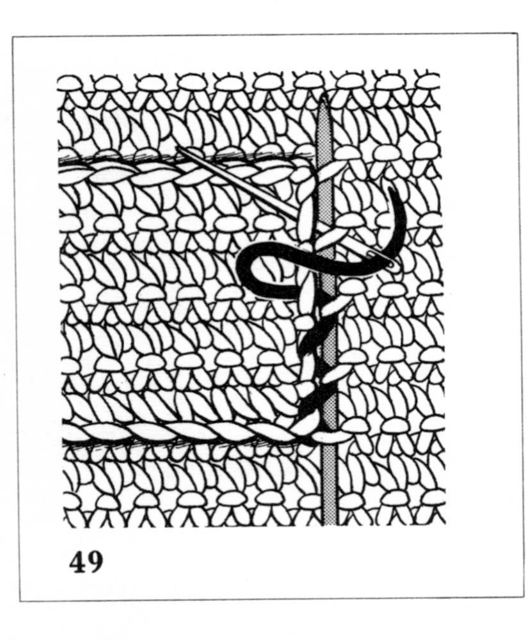

49

Side and sleeve seams
Join with backstitch in one complete seam as near the edge as possible.

Sewing on collars
Place right side of collar to wrong side of neck matching centre backs and taking care not to stretch the neckline. Join with a firm backstitch as near the edge as possible.

Sewn-on bands
Sewn-on bands worked separately. Use a woven flat seam matching row for row.

Sewn-on pockets or any applied band or decoration
Use slip stitching, taking care to keep the line

absolutely straight. A good way to ensure a straight sewing line is to thread a fine knitting needle, pointed at both ends, under every alternate stitch of the line you wish to follow and catch one stitch from the edge of the piece to be applied and one stitch from the needle alternately, using matching yarn (fig. 49).

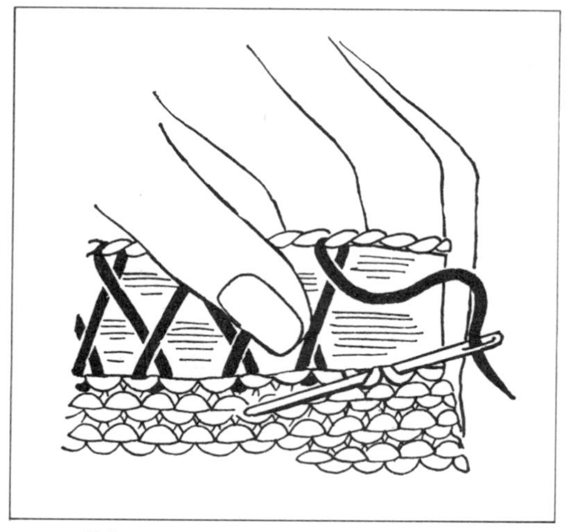

50

Skirt waist

Skirt waist using casing or herringbone stitch. Cut elastic to the size required and join into a circle. Mark off the waistline of the skirt and the elastic into quarters and pin elastic into position on the wrong side, taking care to distribute the work evenly. Hold the work over the fingers of the left hand and with the elastic slightly stretched work a herringbone stitch, catching the elastic above and below as you work (fig. 50).

Ribbon facing

Lightly press the part to be faced before sewing on the ribbon, taking care not to stretch the edge. Choose a soft ribbon, available in a wide selection of colours and widths from most stores. When facing buttonhole bands, the ribbon should be wide enough to cover the strip with ¼″ to ½″ to spare on either side and a ½″ hem top and bottom. Take great care not to stretch the crochet when measuring the ribbon lengths, and cut the facing for buttonhole and button bands at the same time, so that they match exactly. Fold in the turnings, pin ribbon to the wrong side, easing the crochet evenly and checking that the buttonholes are evenly spaced. With matching silk, slip stitch with the smallest possible stitches along all edges. Cut buttonholes along the straight grain of the ribbon, remembering to make them wide enough for the buttons. Oversew the ribbon and crochet together to avoid fraying, then neaten by working buttonhole stitch round the buttonhole with the original yarn (fig. 51).

Grosgrain ribbon can be shaped to fit a curved

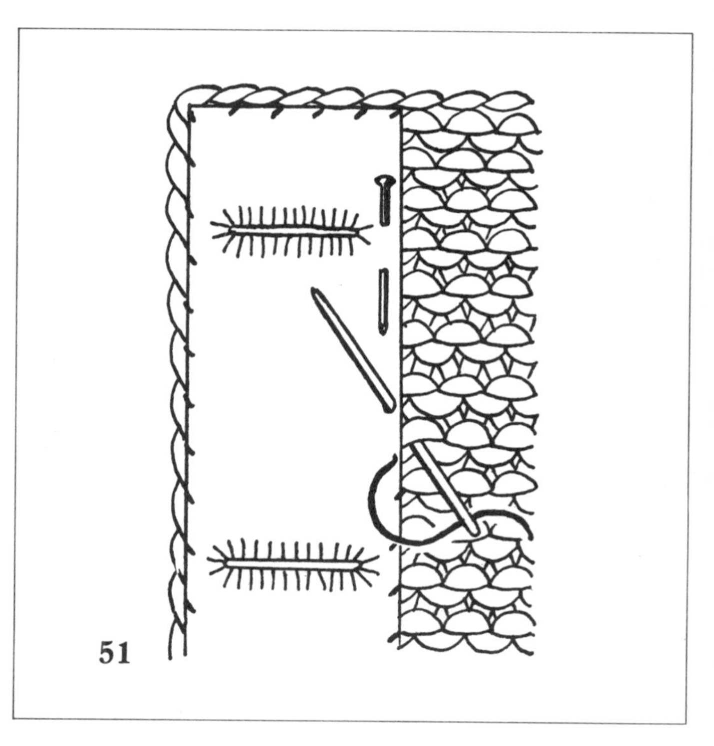

51

Making up

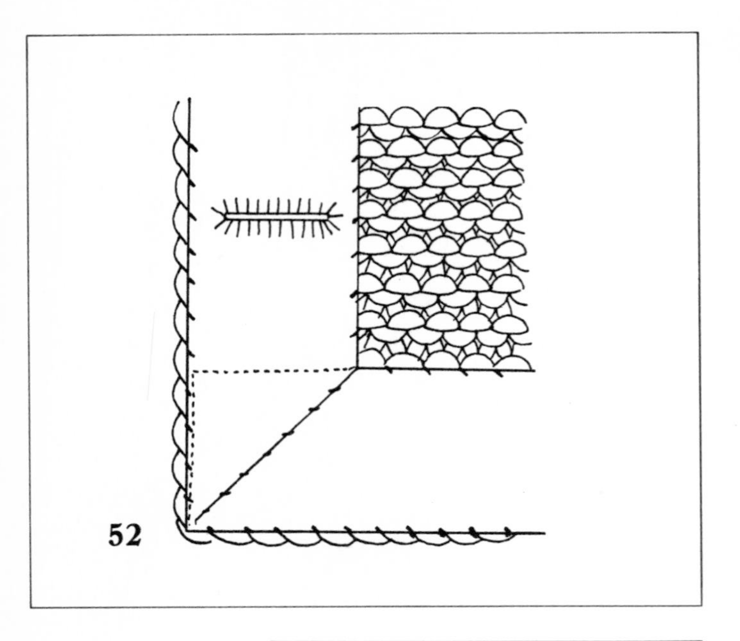

52

edge by pressing with a hot iron and gently stretching one edge until the desired curve is made.

When facing with ribbon on two edges at right angles, seam outside edge in place first, then fold ribbon into a mitred corner before seaming inside edge (fig. 52).

Decorative seam

Lapped seams can be used on yokes and square-set sleeves when a firm fabric stitch has been worked. Place the parts to be joined right sides together, with the underneath part projecting ½" beyond the upper part. Backstitch along edge, turn to the right side and backstitch ½" from the first seam through both thicknesses of fabric, taking care to keep the line of stitching straight and even.

Shrinking

Provided 100% pure wool has been used, parts of garments which have been stretched can be shrunk back into place. Place the part to be shrunk face down on to a well-padded surface, pat and pin into shape and size required. Cover with a wet cloth and hold a hot iron over the cloth to make plenty of steam. Alternatively steam then pat into shape, taking out the pins as soon as possible, until the required shape is achieved, then leave without handling until quite dry.

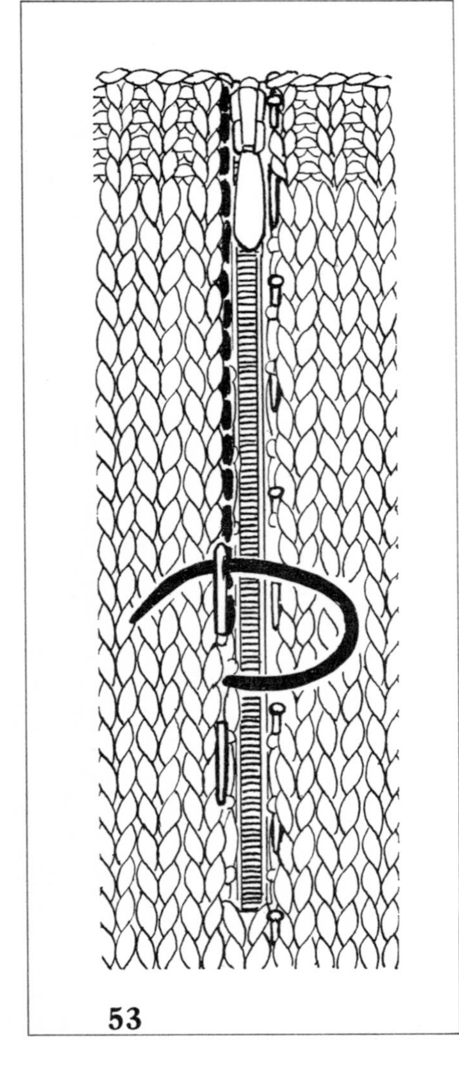

53

Sewing in zip fasteners

Pin in the zip to the opening, taking great care not to stretch the crochet. Sew in zip using backstitch, keeping the grain of the crochet straight. Except on very heavy garments, it is better to use Nylon zips because of their lightness and flexibility (fig. 53).

Skirt lining

It is generally accepted that it is better not to

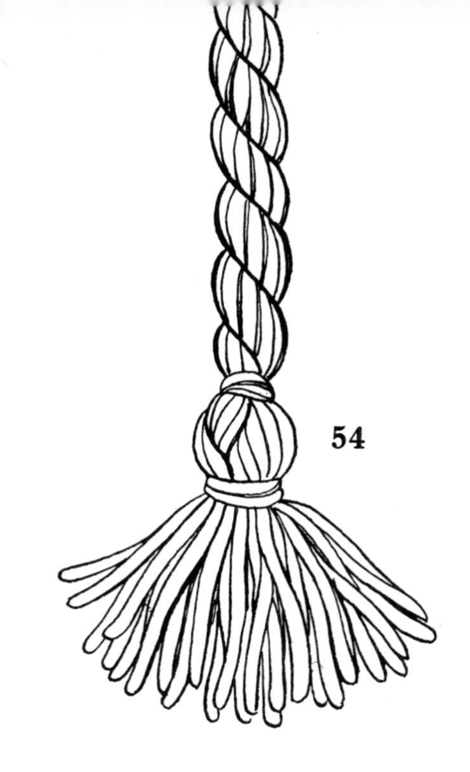

54

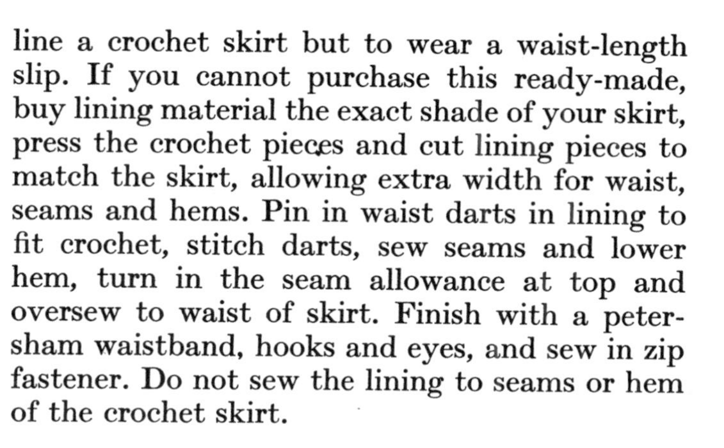

line a crochet skirt but to wear a waist-length slip. If you cannot purchase this ready-made, buy lining material the exact shade of your skirt, press the crochet pieces and cut lining pieces to match the skirt, allowing extra width for waist, seams and hems. Pin in waist darts in lining to fit crochet, stitch darts, sew seams and lower hem, turn in the seam allowance at top and oversew to waist of skirt. Finish with a petersham waistband, hooks and eyes, and sew in zip fastener. Do not sew the lining to seams or hem of the crochet skirt.

Twisted cords

The number of strands of yarn used to make a twisted cord depends on the thickness required. For a baby garment in 3 or 4-ply, 4 strands of yarn are used. Two people are required for this, and the length of each strand should be three times as long as the required cord. Each person takes one end of the strands, stand facing each other and holding the yarn taut. Twist the strands towards the *right* until a firm twist has been obtained along the whole length of the strands. Still holding the strands taut, fold the cord in half lengthwise, knot together the two loose ends and the cord will form when it is smoothed downwards from the knot between the fingers. Trim with a tassel or pom-pom (fig. 54).

Tassels

Length and thickness of tassels can be varied as required. Cut a piece of cardboard 2″ wide, wind yarn several times round cardboard and cut through yarn at one edge of cardboard only. Thread the pieces of yarn through the cord in half, finishing by winding the yarn several times round the top folded ends about ½″ down from the end of the cord. Sew in loose end of yarn and trim loose ends of tassel (fig. 55).

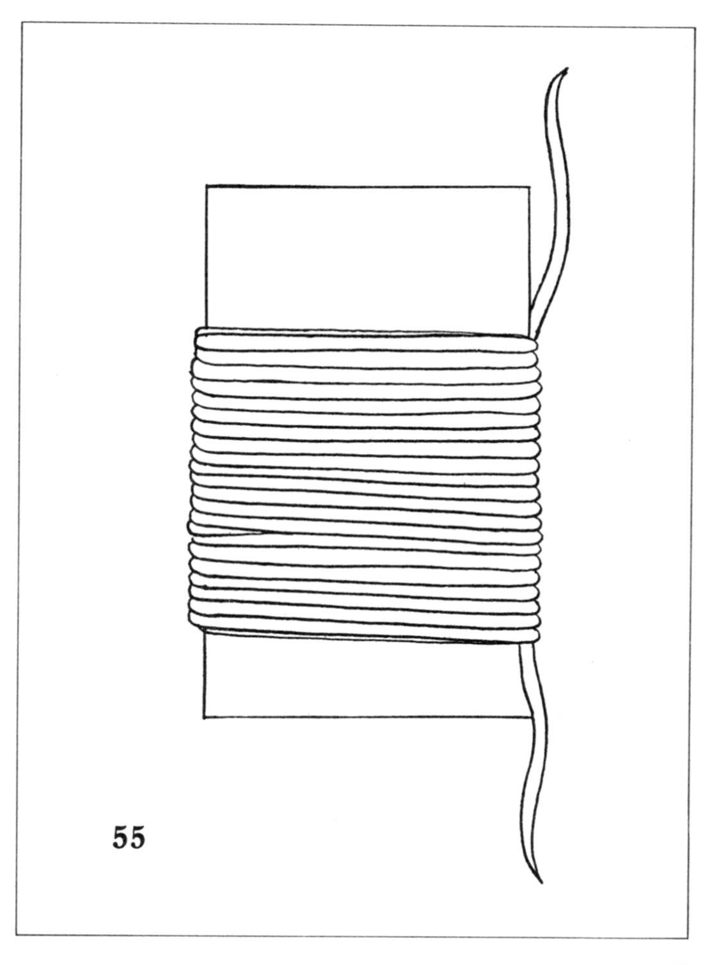

55

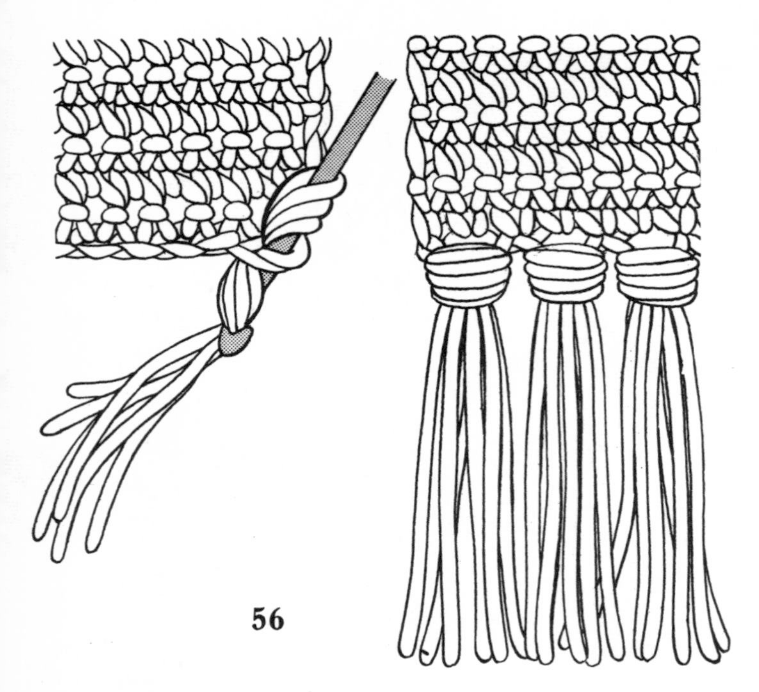

56

Making up

Fringing

Unless precise length is given in the instructions, cut strands of yarn approximately 8″ long and place in groups of 3 or 4 strands according to the thickness required. With the wrong side of the edge to be fringed facing you, insert a crochet hook as near the edge as possible, fold strands in half to form a loop, put loop on hook, pull through edge of work, place hook behind all strands of yarn and draw through loop. Continue along edge in this way at regular intervals until completed. Trim ends of fringing to neaten (fig. 56).

Pom-poms

Cut two circles of cardboard the size you require the finished pom-pom to be and cut out a circular hole in the centre of each – the larger the hole the thicker the pom-pom. Wind the yarn evenly round the two pieces of cardboard and through the centre hole until the hole is filled, and you have to put the last strand through with a threaded needle. Break off the yarn. Cut through the yarn at the outer edge of the cardboard only, firmly tie a piece of yarn round the cut pieces between the two circles of cardboard, and when strands are secured cut away the cardboard and leave end of yarn for sewing on. Shake well and trim ends into shape (fig. 57).

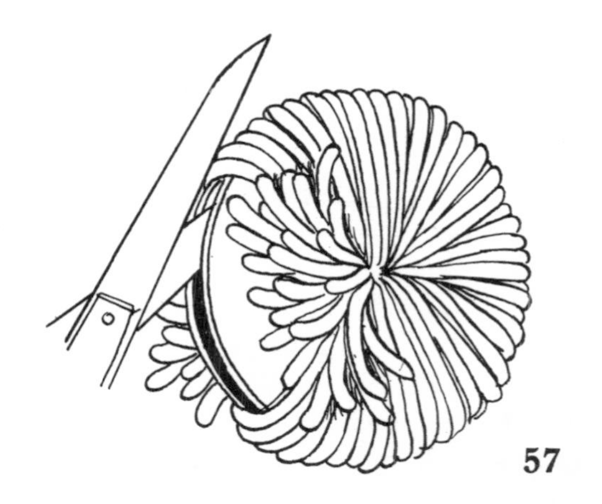

57

If you are left-handed

If you are left-handed and would like to learn to crochet, all the same basic principles will apply. The right-handed worker holds the hook in her right hand and controls the yarn with her left hand, working across the work from the right-hand edge to the left-hand corner. For the left-handed worker, the reverse of this will apply.

The hook is held in the left hand between the thumb and first finger, with the middle finger resting lightly against the tip of the hook and the shank held in the crook of the hand between the thumb and palm. The yarn is held and controlled by the right hand, exactly as given for the left hand, and the row is begun at the left-hand corner and worked across until the right-hand edge is reached.

If the illustrations given in this book confuse you, a mirror may be placed in front of the illustration to reflect it. This will then give the correct position for the left-handed worker.

Hints on care and washing

Pure wool

Although many hand-knitting wools are now given shrink-resist finishes, the structure of hand-knitted fabrics makes elementary care in washing essential if the best results are to be obtained. If hand-knitted garments are never allowed to become badly soiled they will be easily washable, and it is important to remember that pure wool stays clean longest.

Washing should be done in warm, *not* hot, water. Detergents and soap powders should always be dissolved completely and never brought into direct contact with the garments. Rubbing should be avoided and the lather gently squeezed through the fibres. All traces of soap or detergent should be rinsed out in tepid water. A loose wringer or a spin dryer may be used to remove surplus water. Wringing by hand should be avoided. The garment should then be arranged on a clean smooth surface and gently eased into its original shape. If it is finally dried on a clothes horse the sleeves should not be allowed to hang down. When dry the garment should be lightly pressed on the wrong side with a warm iron over a damp cloth.

Courtelle

Warm wash (40°C) as soon as the garment gets soiled. Use soapless detergent or, if your water is soft, soap flakes or powder dissolved in water pleasantly hot to the hand. Rinse thoroughly. Remove excess moisture by squeezing lightly, or rolling in a towel, or give a short spin dry. Finally, smooth garment and dry flat away from direct heat. Courtelle garments can be machine-washed, following instructions for delicate fabrics. When garment is completely dry, fold neatly and store in a drawer, not on a hanger.

Bri-Nylon

Wash often – wash soon. Bri-Nylon garments can be washed by hand or by machine. Use hot water (60°C, 140°F) for 'whites', and hand-hot (48°C, 118°F) for 'coloureds'. Use a synthetic detergent in hard water districts and dissolve thoroughly. Rinse until the water is clear. Do not wring knitwear but squeeze and dry flat. If spin drying is required, stop after the first rush of water from the outlet ceases.

If absolutely necessary synthetics may be pressed with a cool iron and a dry cloth.

Evening suit

Instructions are for a 34″ bust. Changes for 36″ and 38″ sizes are given in brackets.
MATERIALS: Jacket. 15(16–17) ozs Twilleys Goldfingering. **Skirt.** 17(18–20) ozs of same. No. 9 crochet hook or New International size No. 3.50. Waist length of elastic.
MEASUREMENTS: Jacket. To fit a 34″(36″–38″) bust. Length to shoulder: 21″(21″–21½″), adjustable. Sleeve seam: 18″, adjustable. **Skirt.** To fit 36″(38″–40″) hips. Length: 24″(24″–25″), adjustable.
NOTE: For extra length add 1 oz of yarn per 1″.
TENSION: 6½ sts and 3 rows to 1″ over patt.

SKIRT

FRONT: Beg at waist. With No. 9 hook make 106 (112–118) ch. **Base row:** Work 2 tr 1 ch 2 tr into 3rd ch from hook – called 1 shell – * 1 ch, miss 2 ch, 1 dc into next ch, 1 ch, miss 2 ch, 1 shell into next ch; rep from * to last ch, 1 tr into last ch, 2 ch, turn. 18(19–20) shells. **1st row:** [Wrong side.] Work 1 shell into first shell, * 1 ch, 1 d tr into dc, 1 ch, 1 shell into next shell; rep from * to end, 1 tr into t ch, 2 ch, turn. **2nd row:** Work 1 shell into first shell, * 1 ch, 1 dc into d tr, 1 ch, 1 shell into next shell; rep from * to end, 1 tr in t ch, 2 ch, turn. These 2 rows form patt. Work 2 more rows. **5th row:** [inc row.] Work 1 d tr between first tr and shell, 1 ch, work in patt ending 1 ch, 1 d tr into t ch, 1 ch, turn. **6th row:** Work 1 dc into d tr, 1 ch, work in patt ending 1 ch, 1 dc into d tr, 2 ch, turn. **7th row:** Work 1 d tr into dc, 1 ch, work in patt ending 1 ch, 1 d tr into dc, 1 ch, turn. Rep 6th and 7th rows twice more, then 6th row once ending 3 ch, turn. **13th row:** [inc row.] Work 1 shell into 3rd ch from hook, 1 ch, 1 d tr into dc, 1 ch, work in patt ending 1 ch, 1 d tr into dc, 1 ch, 1 shell into t ch, 2 ch, turn. **14th to 20th rows:** Work in patt. Rep 5th to 20th rows twice more. 24(25–26) shells. Cont without shaping until work measures 24″(24″–25″) from beg, or required length from waist ending with a 2nd row. Cut yarn and fasten off.
BACK: Work as given for Front.
TO MAKE UP: Press each piece lightly under a damp cloth with a warm iron. Join side seams. Press seams. Sew waist length of elastic to inside of waist using casing st.

JACKET

BACK: Beg at back neck. With No. 9 hook make 40 ch. Work base row as given for Skirt. **Shape shoulders.** Cont in patt as given for Skirt working 14 ch at beg of next 2 rows and 14(17–17) t ch at beg of foll 2 rows. Work 18 rows without shaping ending with a 2nd row. **Shape armholes.** Inc as given for Skirt at each end of next and every alt row 4(4–5) times in all. Cont without shaping until work measures 21″(21″–21½″) from beg, or required length from back neck, ending with a 2nd row. Cut yarn and fasten off.
LEFT FRONT: Beg at shoulder. With No. 9 hook make 16 ch. Work Base row as given for Skirt. **Shape shoulder.** Cont in patt as given for Skirt working 14 (17–17) t ch at beg of next row. Work 4 rows without shaping. **Shape neck.** Cont in patt working 20 t ch at beg of next row. Work 14 rows without shaping. **Shape armhole.** Inc as given for Skirt at armhole edge on next and every alt row 4(4–5) times in all. Cont without shaping until work measures same as Back from beg ending with a 2nd row. Cut yarn and fasten off.
RIGHT FRONT: With No. 9 hook make 16 ch. Work Base row and 1st patt row as given for Skirt. Cont in patt as given for Skirt working 14(17–17) t ch at beg of next row. Complete to match Left Front reversing shaping.
SLEEVES: Beg at top. With No. 9 hook make 28 ch. Work Base row as given for Skirt. Cont in patt, inc at each end of next and every alt rows as given for Skirt 8(8–9) times in all. Cont without shaping until sleeve measures 18″ from end of shaping or required underarm length, ending with a 2nd row. Cut yarn and fasten off.
TO MAKE UP: Press as given for Skirt. Join shoulder, side and sleeve seams. Set in sleeves. With right side of work facing and No. 9 hook beg at bottom Right Front edge and work a row of dc up right front, round neck and down left front, 1 ch, turn. **Next row:** Work 1 dc into first dc, * miss 1 dc, 2 tr 1 ch 2 tr into next dc, miss 1 dc, 1 dc into next dc; rep from * to end. Cut yarn and fasten off. Press seams.

Mohair dress

Instructions are for a 32″/36″ bust.
MATERIALS: 19 ozs Jaeger Mohair-spun. No. 2 crochet hook or New International size No. 7.00. For International hook size check tension as this is an approximate equivalent.
MEASUREMENTS: To fit a 32″/36″ bust. 34″/38″ hips. Length to shoulder: 57″ when pressed, adjustable. Sleeve seam: 19″ when pressed, adjustable.
TENSION: 1 d tr group measures approximately 2″ at base and 1¼″ in depth.
NOTE: 1 d tr group worked by making 1 d tr, 1 ch, 1 d tr, 1 ch, 1 d tr.
BODICE AND SKIRT: Beg at neck. With No. 2 hook make 128 ch and join into a circle with a sl st. **1st round:** 4 ch, * [miss 1 ch, 1 d tr group into next ch] 3 times, miss 1 ch, 2 d tr into next ch; rep from * to end, ending with 1 d tr into last ch, sl st to 4th of 4 ch [16 panels each with 3 groups of 2 d tr]. **2nd round:** 4 ch, * 1 d tr group into centre of next 3 d tr groups, 1 d tr on each of next 2 d tr; rep from * to end, ending with 1 d tr on d tr, sl st to 4th of 4 ch. **3rd round:** As 2nd. **Divide for sleeves and bodice. Next round:** 4 ch, * [1 d tr group into centre of next 3 d tr groups, 1 d tr on each of next 2 d tr] 5 times working only 1 d tr on last rep, miss [next d tr (3 d tr groups and 2 d tr) twice, 3 d tr and 1 d tr] * work 1 d tr into next d tr; rep from * to *, sl st to 4th of 4 ch.
This section [10 panels] forms bodice and skirt. Cont in patt until dress measures 53″ or required length, allowing 4″ for pressing. **Next round:** Work 1 dc into every st and 1 dc 3 ch 1 dc into centre d tr of each d tr group. Fasten off.
SLEEVES: Rejoin yarn to underarm into first d tr, 4 ch, * 1 d tr group into each of next 3 d tr groups, 1 d tr into each of next 2 d tr; rep from * twice more ending last rep with 1 d tr, sl st to 4th of 4 ch. [3 panels.] Cont in patt until sleeve seam is required length, allowing 3″ for pressing out. Finish as given for hem of dress. Work 2nd sleeve in same way.
NECK EDGING: With right side of work facing, rejoin yarn at centre back and work 1 dc into each ch, sl st to first dc. **Next round:** 1 ch, * work 2 dc tog [as follows: hook into first dc, draw through a loop, hook into 2nd dc draw through a loop, yarn over and draw through all three loops], 2 dc; rep from * to end, sl st to first ch. 96 sts. **Next round:** 1 ch, 1 dc into each dc, sl st to first ch. **Next round:** 1 ch, * work 2 dc tog as before, 1 dc; rep from * to end, 1 sl st into first ch. **Next round:** 1 ch, * 1 dc 3 ch 1 dc into next dc, dc into next dc; rep from * to end, sl st to first ch. Fasten off.
TO MAKE UP: Pin out to size and using a very wet cloth and a warm iron steam press. Allow to dry completely flat.

Cardigan coat

nstructions are for a 34"/36" bust.
MATERIALS: 24 ½-oz balls Patons Fuzzy-Wuzzy. No. 8 and No. 9 wool crochet hook or New International size Nos. 4.00 and 3.50.
MEASUREMENTS: To fit a 34"/36" bust; 36"/38" hips. Length to centre back: 35", adjustable. Sleeve seam: 18½", adjustable.
TENSION: 12 sts, 1 patt, to 2½" and approximately rows to 3" on No. 8 hook.
BACK: With No. 8 hook make 112 ch. **1st row:** 1 tr into 3rd ch from hook, * 1 tr into next 6 ch, 3 ch, 1 tr into next 6 ch; rep from * to last ch, 1 tr into last ch, ch, turn. **2nd row:** Miss first tr, * yarn over hook, insert hook into next tr and pull yarn through, insert hook into next tr and pull yarn through, yarn over hook and draw through 3 loops, yarn over hook and draw through rem 2 loops – called DT2 – 1 tr into each of next 4 tr, 1 tr 3 ch 1 tr into 3 ch loop, 1 tr into each of next 4 tr, DT2; rep from * to end, 1 tr in t ch ch, turn. 9 complete patts plus t ch at end. This row forms patt and is rep throughout. Cont in patt, dec one st at each end of 7th and every foll 4th row until 2 sts have been dec at each end and 7 patts rem. Cont without shaping until work measures 28" from beg, or required length to underarm. **Shape armholes.** Dec one st at each end of next 6 rows. Cont without shaping until armholes measure 6½" from beg, omitting t ch at end of last row. **Shape shoulders. Next row:** Sl st over first 8 sts, patt to last 8 sts, turn. Rep this row twice more. Fasten off, leaving 2 patts in centre for back neck.
LEFT FRONT: With No. 8 hook make 64 ch. Work in patt as given for Back, dec one st at beg of 7th and every foll 4th row until 12 sts have been dec and 4 patts rem. Cont without shaping until work measures same as Back to underarm, ending at armhole edge, omitting t ch at end of last row. **Shape armhole and front edge. Next row:** Sl st over first 6 sts, patt to end. Dec one st at each end of next 6 rows, then cont to dec at front edge only on every row until 2 patts rem. Cont without shaping until armhole measures same as Back to shoulder, ending at armhole edge. **Shape shoulder. Next row:** Sl st over first 8 sts, patt to end. **Next row:** Patt to last 8 sts, turn. **Next row:** Sl st over 8 sts, fasten off. **Right Front:** Work as given for Left Front, reversing all shaping.
SLEEVES: With No. 8 hook make 40 ch. Work in patt as given for Back. 3 patts. Inc one at each end of 5th and every foll 3rd row, working inc into patt when possible until 12 sts have been inc at each side. 5 patts. Cont without shaping until sleeve measures 18½" from beg, or required length to underarm, omitting t ch at end of last row. **Shape top. Next row:** Sl st over first 3 sts, patt to last 3 sts, turn. Dec one st at each end of next 6 rows. **Next row:** Sl st over first 3 sts, patt to last 3 sts, turn. Rep this row 4 times more. Fasten off, leaving 1 patt in centre.
BORDER: Join shoulder seams. With No. 9 hook work 1 row dc up Right Front, round neck and down Left Front, taking care that work lies flat. Turn and work 3 more rows. Fasten off.
TO MAKE UP: Press work very lightly with a warm iron over a damp cloth. Join side and sleeve seams. Set in sleeves, noting that sleeve seam should come in centre of 6 sts cast off on front armholes. Press seams.

Patchwork waistcoats

Instructions are for a 34″/36″ bust/chest. Changes for 38″/40″ size are given in brackets.

MATERIALS: 6(7) ozs Lister Double Knitting Bri-Nylon in main shade D; 3(3) ozs each of same in contrast colours A, B and C. No. 8(7) wool crochet hook or New International size No. 4.00(4.50).

NOTE: For International hook size check tension as this is an approximate equivalent.

MEASUREMENTS: To fit a 34″/36″(38″/40″) bust/chest. Length at centre back: 21″(24″). Underarm length: 14″(16″).

TENSION: Each motif measures approximately $3\frac{1}{2}'' \times 3\frac{1}{2}''$ on No. 8 hook; $4'' \times 4''$ on No. 7 hook.

NOTE: Quantities are based on following colour variations of A, B and C on first 3 rounds of motifs, and D is used throughout for rounds 4 and 5. Make 52 motifs in all; 9 using A, B, C and D; 9 using B, C, A and D; 9 using C, B, A and D; 9 using B, A, C and D; 8 using A, C, B and D; and 8 using C, A, B and D. Make 2 Half Motifs, 1 using D, B, C and A, and 1 using D, B, A and C.

FULL MOTIF: With No. 8(7) hook and A, make 7 ch and join into a circle with a sl st to first ch. **1st round:** With A work * 1 dc, 2 tr, 1 dc into circle, 3 ch; rep from * 3 times more, join with a sl st to first dc. **2nd round:** Break off A, join in B to first 3 ch loop, 2 ch, work 2 tr, 1 ch, 3 tr into this loop, * work 3 tr, 1 ch, 3 tr into next 3 ch loop, 2 ch; rep from * twice more, join with a sl st to 2nd of 2 ch. **3rd round:** Break off B, join in C into first 2 ch loop, 1 ch, work 1 tr, 1 dc into this loop, * 1 ch, work 1 dc, 2 tr, 1 ch, 2 tr, 1 dc into 1 ch loop between trs, 1 ch, work 1 dc, 1 tr, 1 dc into 2 ch loop; rep from * twice more, 1 ch, work 1 dc, 2 tr, 1 ch, 2 tr, 1 dc into 1 ch loop between trs, 1 ch, join with a sl st to first ch. **4th round:** Break off C and join in D into 1st 1 ch loop, 2 ch, 1 tr, * 1 ch, 2 tr into next 1 ch loop, 1 ch, work 3 dc, 1 ch, 3 dc into 1 ch loop at corner, 1 ch, 2 tr into next 1 ch loop; rep from * twice more, 1 ch, 2 tr into next 1 ch loop, 1 ch, 3 dc, 1 ch, 3 dc into 1 ch loop at corner, 1 ch, sl st into 2nd of 2 ch. **5th round:** With D work 1 ch, 1 dc into back loop of next tr, 1 dc into back loop of ch, 1 dc into back loop of each of next 2 tr, 1 dc into back loop of next ch, 1 dc into back loop of next 3 dc, 2 dc into back loop of next ch, 1 dc into back loop of next 3 dc, continue thus, working 1 dc into back of each st and inc one st at each corner as before all round. Fasten off.

HALF MOTIF: With No. 8(7) hook and D make 31 ch. **1st row:** With D work 1 dc into 3rd ch from hook, work 1 dc into each of next 12 ch, hook through next ch and pull up loop, hook through next ch and pull up loop, yarn round hook and draw through 3 loops on hook, 1 dc into each of next 14 ch, 1 ch, turn. **2nd row:** With D miss 2 dc, work 1 dc into back loop only of next 2 dc, * 1 ch, miss 1 dc, work 1 tr into back loop only of next 2 dc, 1 ch, miss 1 dc, work 1 tr into back loop only of next 2 dc, 1 ch, miss 1 dc [hook through back of loop of next dc and pull up loop] 3 times, 1 ch, miss 1 dc [hook through back loop of next dc and pull up loop] 3 times, yarn round hook and draw through 7 loops on hook; rep from * ending last rep [hook through back loop of next dc and pull up loop] 3 times, yarn round hook and draw through 4 loops on hook, 1 dc into back loop only of last dc, turn. **3rd row:** Break off D and join in B, work 1 tr 1 dc into 1 ch loop, 1 ch, 1 dc 1 tr 1 dc into 1 ch loop between trs, 1 ch, into next ch loop work 1 dc 2 tr, 1 ch, into next ch loop work 2 tr 1 dc, 1 ch, 1 dc 1 tr 1 dc into next 1 ch loop between trs, 1 ch, 1 dc 1 tr 1 dc into next 1 ch loop, 1 sl st into end loop, turn. **4th row:** Break off B and join in C, work 3 tr into first 1 ch loop, 2 ch, miss next ch loop, 3 tr 1 ch 3 tr into corner 1 ch loop, 2 ch, miss next ch loop, 3 tr into last 1 ch loop, turn. **5th row:** Break off C and join in A, work 2 tr 1 dc into first ch loop, 1 dc 2 tr 1 dc into next ch loop, 1 dc 2 tr into next ch loop, fasten off. Work 1 more Half motif in same way using colour sequence as given under Note. Sew in all ends.

TO MAKE UP: Join each motif with woven flat stitch to top loop only of last round. Join 10 motifs 4 rows deep in this way. [40 motifs.] On 5th row join 1 Half motif above first motif to form neck shaping, 1 Full motif to next motif, miss 1 motif for underarm, join 1 motif to each of next 4 motifs, miss 1 motif for underarm, join 1 Full motif to next motif and 2nd Half motif above last motif to form neck shaping. On 6th row miss Half motif and join 1 Full motif to next motif, miss underarm motif, join 1 Full motif to each of next 4 motifs, miss underarm motif, join 1 Full motif to next motif. Join top of first and last motifs of this row to 1st and 4th motifs of back for shoulders. With right side of work facing No. 8(7) hook and D join yarn at lower edge of right underarm and work 1 row dc all round working into back loop of each stitch only, join with a sl st and fasten off. Work round armholes in same way. Press lightly on wrong side under a dry cloth with a cool iron.

Crunchy cardigan

Instructions are for a 32″ bust. Changes for 34″, 36″, 38″, 40″ and 42″ sizes are given in brackets.
MATERIALS: 19(20–21–21–22–22) ozs Emu Super Crepe 4-ply in main shade A; 1 oz in contrasts B and C. I each Nos. 9, 10 and 13 crochet hooks or New International sizes Nos. 3.50, 3.00 and 2.50. 1 buckle for optional belt, not shown.
NOTE: For International hook size check tension as this is an approximate equivalent.
MEASUREMENTS: To fit a 32″(34″–36″–38″–40″–42″) bust. Length at centre back: $24\frac{3}{4}$″(25″–$25\frac{1}{4}$″–$25\frac{1}{2}$″–$25\frac{3}{4}$″–26″), adjustable. Sleeve seam: $18\frac{1}{2}$″, adjustable.
TENSION: 12 sts and 5 rows to 2″ over patt on No. 9 hook.
BACK: With No. 10 hook and A make 110(116–122–128–134–140) ch. **Next row:** 1 dc into 2nd ch from hook and into every foll ch, 2 ch, turn. Work 3 more rows dc, turning with 2 ch. 109(115–121–127–133–139) sts, including t ch. Change to No. 9 hook and commence patt. **1st row:** Miss first st, * 1 d tr in next st, 1 dc in front loop only of next st; rep from * to end, 4 ch, turn. **2nd row:** * 1 dc into front loop only of d tr, 1 d tr into dc; rep from * to last st, 1 dc into front loop only of last d tr, 1 d tr into t ch, 2 ch, turn. **3rd row:** * 1 d tr into dc, 1 dc into front loop only of d tr; rep from * to last st, 1 d tr into dc, 1 dc into t ch, 4 ch, turn. The 2nd and 3rd rows form patt and are rep throughout. Work 1 row. ** Cont in patt dec one st at each end of next and every foll 4th row until 99 (105–111–117–123–129) sts rem. Cont without shaping until work measures 18″ from beg, or required length to underarm, ending with a wrong side row and omitting t ch at end of last row. **Shape armholes. Next row:** Sl st over first 6 sts, patt to last 6 sts, turn. Dec one st at each end of next 4(5–6–7–8–9) rows. 79(83–87–91–95–99) sts. Cont without shaping until armholes measure $6\frac{1}{2}$″($6\frac{3}{4}$″–7″–$7\frac{1}{4}$″–$7\frac{1}{2}$″–$7\frac{3}{4}$″), ending with a wrong side row and omitting t ch at end of last row. **Shape shoulders. Next row:** Sl st over first 6(6–6–7–7–8) sts, patt to last 6(6–6–7–7–8) sts, turn. Rep this row twice more. **Next row:** Sl st over first 5(6–8–6–8–6) sts, patt to last 5(6–8–6–8–6) sts, turn. Fasten off, leaving 33(35–35–37–37–39) sts for centre neck.
LEFT FRONT: With No. 10 hook and A make 52 (54–58–60–64–66) ch. Work as given for Back to **. 51(53–57–59–63–65) sts. Cont in patt dec one st at beg of next and every foll 4th row until 46(48–52–54–58–60) sts rem, then cont without shaping until work measures $2\frac{1}{2}$″ less than Back to underarm, ending at front edge. **Shape front edge.** Dec one st at beg of next and every alt row until work measures same as Back to underarm, ending at armhole edge. **Shape armhole.** Cont to dec at front edge on every alt row, sl st over first 6 sts, patt to end, then dec one st at armhole edge on next 4(5–6–7–8–9) rows. Keeping armhole edge straight, cont to dec at front edge as before until 23(24–26–27–29–30) sts rem, then cont without shaping until armhole measures same as Back to shoulder, ending at armhole edge and omitting t ch at end of last row. **Shape shoulder. 1st row:** Sl st over first 6(6–6–7–7–8) sts, patt to end. **2nd row:** Patt to last 6(6–6–7–7–8) sts, turn. **3rd row:** As 1st. 5(6–8–6–8–6) sts rem. Fasten off.
RIGHT FRONT: Work as for Left Front, reversing all shaping.
SLEEVES: With No. 9 hook and A make a ch of 44 (46–48–50–52–54). Beg with 1st patt row as given for Back – 43(45–47–49–51–53) sts – inc one st at each end of 3rd and every foll 3rd row until there are 73 (75–77–79–81–83) sts, cont without shaping until sleeve measures $17\frac{1}{2}$″ from beg, or required length to underarm less 1″, ending with a wrong side row and omitting t ch at end of last row. **Shape top. Next row:** Sl st over first 6 sts, patt to last 6 sts, turn. Dec one st at each end of next 6(6–7–7–8–8) rows. 49(51–51–53–53–55) sts. **Next row:** Sl st over first 2 sts, patt to last 2 sts, turn. Rep last row twice more. **Next row:** Sl st over first 3 sts, patt to last 3 sts, turn

Rep last row once more. **Next row:** Sl st over first 4 sts, patt to last 4 sts, turn. Rep last row once more. 9(11–11–13–13–15) sts. Fasten off. **Work sleeve edges.** With right side of sleeve facing, No. 10 hook and C, work one row dc round cast on edge. Cont in dc, work one more row in C, 2 rows in A and 2 rows in B. Fasten off.

BELT: With No. 10 hook and B make a ch 34″(36″–38″–40″–42″–44″) long, or required length. Work in dc. Work 2 rows B, 2 rows A and 2 rows B. Fasten off.

CROCHET BUTTONS: [Make 6 buttons – 2 each in A, B and C.] With No. 13 hook make 3 ch and join into a ring, leaving thread about 8″ long. **1st round:** Work 6 dc into circle, joining with a sl st to first dc. **2nd round:** Work 2 dc into each dc of previous round, joining with a sl st to first dc. **3rd round:** Work 1 dc into each dc, joining with a sl st to first dc. Rep 3rd round until mould is covered. **Last round:** * Miss 1 dc, 1 dc into next dc; rep from * to end, joining with a sl st to first dc. Use thread which was left at beg for sewing on buttons, first pulling it through to other side of button.

TO MAKE UP: Press work *lightly* on wrong side under a damp cloth with a warm iron. Join shoulder, side and sleeve seams. Set in sleeves. **Work Front Border.** With right side of work facing, No. 10 hook and A work one row dc up right front, across back neck and down left front, working 3 sts into every 2 rows. Break off A. With right side of work again facing, cont in dc and work 2 rows C and one A. Mark position of buttonholes on right front edge as follows: 1st to come ½″ from lower edge and last ½″ down from beg of front shaping, and 4 more at equal distances between. **Next row:** [Wrong side facing.] With A work in dc to 1st marked position [3 ch, miss 3 dc, dc to next marked position] 5 times, 3 ch, miss 3 dc, dc to end. Work 2 rows dc in B. Fasten off. Press all seams. Sew on buttons. Sew buckle to belt.

Bikini

Instructions are for a 34″ bust. Changes for 36″ size are given in brackets.
MATERIALS: 6(7) oz balls of Twilleys Crysette. No. 13 crochet hook or New International size No. 2.50. 1 yd of round elastic.
NOTE: For International hook size check tension as this is an approximate equivalent.
MEASUREMENTS: To fit a 34″(36″) bust; 36″(38″) hips.
TENSION: 6 sts to 1″.
TRUNKS: ** Make 6 ch and join into a circle with a sl st. **1st round:** 2 ch, * into circle work 3 tr but keep last loop of each tr on hook, then draw a loop through all loops on hook – called 1 cluster – 5 ch; rep from * twice more. **2nd round:** * 1 dc into cluster, 3 ch, work 3 tr 3 ch 3 tr 3 ch into ch loop of previous round; rep from * twice more. **3rd round:** 1 dc into ch loop, 3 ch, * into ch loop between 3 tr groups work 3 tr 3 ch 3 tr 3 ch, into next ch loop work 1 dc 3 ch 1 dc 3 ch; rep from * twice more. **4th round:** * 1 tr into each tr, work 2 tr 3 ch 2 tr into ch loop, 1 tr into each tr, 3 ch, 1 tr into next ch loop, 1 cluster into next ch loop, 1 tr into next ch loop, 3 ch; rep from * twice more. **5th round:** * 1 tr into each tr, work 2 tr 3 ch 2 tr into ch loop, 1 tr into each tr, 3 ch, 1 dc into next ch loop, 3 ch, 1 dc into next ch loop, 3 ch; rep from * twice more. ** Rep 4th and 5th rounds twice more, then 4th round once. Work 1 dc into next tr, turn with 2 ch. **Next row:** 2 tr into ch loop, 1 tr into tr, 1 tr into cluster, 1 tr into tr, 1 tr into ch loop, 1 tr into each tr, 2 tr into ch loop, turn with 2 ch. 25 sts. **1st row:** 1 tr into each st to end, turn with 2 ch. **2nd row:** Miss first st, 1 tr into each st to end, turn with 2 ch. Rep 1st and 2nd rows 5 times more, turn with 2 ch. On **36″ size only** work 2 rows straight, turn with 2 ch. **Next row:** 1 tr into each st to last st, work 2 tr into last st, turn with 2 ch. **Next row:** 2 tr into first st, 1 tr into each st to last st, 2 tr into last st, turn with 2 ch. Rep last 2 rows 6 times more. 40 sts. Keeping waist edge straight, continue to inc 1 tr on every row at leg edge until there are 51(53) sts, ending at leg edge, turn with 26 ch. **1st row:** 1 tr into 3rd ch from hook, 1 tr into each st to end, turn with 2 ch. **2nd row:** 1 tr into each st to last 6 sts, 1 dc into next st, 1 sl st into next st, turn with 1 ch. **3rd row:** 1 sl st into each of first 4 sts, 1 dc into next st, 1 tr into each st to end, turn with 2 ch. **4th row:** 1 tr into each st to last 3 trs, turn with 2 ch. **5th row:** 1 tr into each st to end, turn with 2 ch. **6th row:** 1 tr into each st to end, turn with 9 ch. **7th row:** 1 dc into 2nd ch from hook, 1 dc into each of next 4 sts, 1 tr into each st to end, turn with 2 ch. **8th row:** 1 tr into each st to last st, 1 dc into last st, turn with 5 ch. **9th row:** 1 dc into 2nd ch from hook, 1 tr into each st to end, turn with 2 ch. **10th row:** 1 tr into each st to last 24 sts, turn with 2 ch. **11th row:** Miss first st, 1 tr into each st to end, turn with 2 ch. **12th row:** 1 tr into each st to last 2 sts, miss one st, 1 tr into last st, turn with 2 ch. Rep 11th and 12th rows 4(5) times more, then 11th row once. Turn with 2 ch. 40 sts. **Next row:** Miss first st, 1 tr into each st to last 2 sts, miss 1 st, 1 tr into last st, turn with 2 ch. **Next row:** Miss first st, 1 tr into each st to end, turn with 2 ch. Rep last 2 rows 6 times more, turn with 2 ch. On **36″ size only.** Work 2 rows straight, turn with 2 ch. **Next row:** 1 tr into each st to last st, 2 tr into last st, turn with 2 ch. **Next row:** 1 tr into each st to end, turn with 2 ch. Rep last 2 rows 5 times more. 25 sts. Cut yarn and fasten off.
TO MAKE UP: Oversew the last 25 sts to the opposite edge of the centre motif. Oversew the shaped edges of the crotch piece to the two remaining edges of the centre motif. Work a row of firm dc round leg, ending with 1 ch. Do not turn but work another row of dc right round, working from left to right instead of from right to left. Cut yarn and fasten off. Work round other leg in same way. Work a row of dc round waist, working over the elastic at the same time. Secure elastic firmly. Press lightly.
TOP: Work motif as given for Trunks from ** to **. On **34″ size only** rep 4th and 5th rounds twice more; on **36″ size only** rep 4th and 5th rounds twice more then 4th round once. **Next round:** * 1 dc into each tr, 3 dc into corner ch loop, 1 dc into each tr, 1 dc into ch loop, 1 dc into cluster, 1 dc into ch loop; rep from * twice more. Join with a sl st, work 1 ch then work another row of dc right round, but working from left to right instead of from right to left. Cut yarn and fasten off. Work another motif in same way.
TIES: Work 2 ch. Insert hook into 2nd ch from hook and draw up a loop, then draw another loop through both sts on hook. **Next row:** Insert hook into 2nd st from hook and draw up loop, then draw a loop through both sts on hook. Rep last row for 50″. Cut yarn and fasten off. Work another tie in same way.
TO MAKE UP: Sew one corner of each motif together. Press lightly. Attach a tie to each motif at top corner. Thread tie through remaining corners in opposite motifs.

Bedjacket

Instructions are for a 34" bust. Changes for 37", 40" and 43" sizes are given in brackets.
MATERIALS: 12(13–14–15) ozs of Emu Calypso Crepe 3-ply. No. 11 wool crochet hook or New International size No. 3.00. 1 yd 3" wide ribbon. 1½ yds 45" wide chiffon for optional lining. 2 yds of swansdown for optional trimming.
MEASUREMENTS: To fit a 34"(37"–40"–43") bust. Length to shoulder: 18½"(19"–19½"–20"), adjustable. Sleeve seam: 18½", adjustable.
TENSION: 4 patts and 14 rows to 3".
BACK: With No. 11 hook make 124(134–144–154) ch. **1st row:** 1 tr in 3rd ch from hook, 1 tr in each ch to end, 1 ch, turn. 122(132–142–152) sts. **2nd row:** 1 dc between 1st and 2nd tr, * 5 ch, miss 5 tr, 1 dc between next 2 tr; rep from * to end, 1 dc in t ch, 3 ch, turn. 147(159–171–183) sts. **3rd row:** * 5 tr in 5 ch loop, 1 ch; rep from * to end, 1 tr in t ch, 1 ch, turn. **4th row:** 1 dc in 1st 1 ch space, * 5 ch, 1 dc in next 1 ch space; rep from * to end, 1 dc in t ch, 3 ch, turn. 3rd and 4th rows form patt and are rep throughout. Cont in patt until work measures 11" from beg, or required length to underarm, ending with a 3rd row. **Shape armholes. Next row:** Sl st over first 10(11–12–13) sts, patt to last 10(11–12–13) sts, turn. Cont in patt, dec one st at each end of next 8(10–10–12) rows. 111(117–127–133) sts. Cont without shaping until armholes measure 7½" (8"–8½"–9"), ending with a right side row. **Shape shoulders. Next row:** Sl st over first 5(5–6–6) sts, patt to last 5(5–6–6) sts, turn. Rep this row 4 times more. **Next row:** Sl st over first 5(8–5–8) sts, patt to last 5(8–5–8) sts, fasten off.
LEFT FRONT: With No. 11 hook make 64(69–74–79) ch. Work in patt as given for Back until work measures same as Back to underarm, ending with a right side row. 75(81–87–93) sts. **Shape armhole. Next row:** Patt to last 10(11–12–13) sts, turn. Dec one st at armhole edge on next 8(10–10–12) rows. 57 (60–65–68) sts. Cont without shaping until armhole measures 6"(6½"–7"–7½"), ending with a right side row. **Shape neck. 1st row:** Sl st over first 14(14–17–17) sts, patt to end. **2nd row:** Patt to last 3 sts, turn. **3rd row:** Sl st over first 3 sts, patt to end. **4th row:** Patt to last 2 sts, turn. **5th row:** Sl st over first 2 sts, patt to end. Dec one st at neck edge on next 3 rows, ending at armhole edge. 30(33–35–38) sts. **Shape shoulder. Next row:** Sl st over first 5(5–6–6) sts, patt to end. **Next row:** Patt to last 5(5–6–6) sts, turn. Rep last 2 rows once more, then 1st row once. Fasten off.
RIGHT FRONT: Work as given for Left Front, reversing all shaping.
SLEEVES: With No. 11 hook make 52(52–57–57) ch. Work first 4 rows as given for Back. 63(63–69–69) sts. Cont in patt as given for Back, inc one st at each end of next and every foll 4th row until there are 105(105–111–111) sts. Cont without shaping until sleeve measures 18½" from beg, or required length to underarm, ending with a right side row. Mark each end of last row with coloured threads. Work further 6(6–8–8) rows without shaping. **Shape top.** Dec one st at each end of next 8(8–10–10) rows. **Next row:** Sl st over first 2 sts, patt to last 2 sts, turn. Rep this row 5(5–6–6) times more. **Next row:** Sl st over first 3 sts, patt to last 3 sts, turn. Rep this row 5 times more. **Next row:** Sl st over first 4 sts, patt to last 4 sts, turn. Rep last row once more. Fasten off.
BORDERS: Join shoulder seams. With right side of Right Front facing and No. 11 hook, beg at bottom, * 3 tr into end of 1st row, 1 tr into dc, 1 tr 1 ch 1 tr into end of next row, 1 tr into dc, 3 tr into end of next row, miss next dc, 1 ch; rep from * up Right Front, across Back neck and down Left Front. Turn and work 4 rows in patt as given for Back. Fasten off.
TO MAKE UP: Press work under a damp cloth with a hot iron. If lining required, cut chiffon to match crocheted pieces. Join side and sleeve seams. Set in sleeves. Make up lining and attach to Bedjacket. Sew on swansdown trimming all round fronts, neck and cuffs. Sew on ribbon to fasten front.

Instructions are for a 33″/35″ bust, when pressed.
MATERIALS: 20 ¾-oz balls of Lister Bel Air Starspun. No. 4 and No. 5 crochet hooks or New International sizes No. 6.00 and No. 5.50. One 7″ Lightning zip fastener. Optional lining takes 1½ yds of 45″ wide chiffon.
MEASUREMENTS: To fit a 33″/35″ bust; 35″/37″ hips. Length from shoulder to hem when pressed: approximately 56″.
TENSION: Approximately 4 dc to 1″ on No. 5 hook; it is crocheted very loosely. The circular motifs measure 3½″ in diameter when pressed.
SKIRT: Motif. 1st round: With No. 4 hook make 4 ch and join with a sl st to form circle. **2nd round:** Work 8 dc into circle, sl st to first dc. **3rd round:** 4 ch, 1 tr into next dc, * 1 ch, 1 tr into next dc; rep from * ending 1 ch, sl st into 3rd of 4 ch. 8 ch spaces. **4th round:** 3 ch, 3 tr into 1 ch space, * 1 tr into 1 tr, 3 tr into 1 ch space; rep from * ending sl st into 3rd of 3 ch. 31 tr. **5th round:** 9 ch, d tr into same place as sl st, * miss 3 tr, 3 d tr 5 ch 3 d tr into next tr, miss 3 tr, d tr 5 ch d tr into next tr; rep from * ending sl st into 4th st of 9 ch. **6th round:** Sl st to centre of 5 ch, 1 dc into space, 7 ch, ** 3 d tr 5 ch 3 d tr into 5 ch space, 7 ch, dc into 5 ch space, 7 ch; rep from ** ending sl st into first dc. Cut yarn and darn in end. Work 2nd motif in same way until 5th round has been completed. **6th round:** Sl st to centre of 5 ch, 1 dc into space, 7 ch, 3 d tr 2 ch into 5 ch space, sl st into 3rd st of 5 ch on first motif, 2 ch 3 d tr into 5 ch space, 3 ch, sl st into 4th st of 7 ch on first motif, 3 ch, 1 dc into 5 ch space, 3 ch, sl st into 4th st of 7 ch on first motif, 3 ch, 3 d tr 2 ch into 5 ch space, sl st into 3rd st of 5 ch on first motif, 2 ch 3 d tr into same 5 ch space, 7 ch, dc into 5 ch space, 7 ch; rep from ** on first motif. Cut yarn and darn in end. Cont in this way until there are 8 motifs in all for the width of the skirt and 4 rows in all in depth.
SLEEVES: Work motifs as given for Skirt, having [illegible] motifs in all for the width of the Sleeve and 3 rows in all in depth, but leave the last row of sleeve unjoined so that although the motifs are joined at the base, the Sleeve does not form a joined circle.
BODICE: 1st row: With No. 5 hook join yarn in sl st made by [3 d tr 2 ch sl st 2 ch 3 d tr] and make 1 dc

Wedding dress

designed by Carmini

* 4 ch, 1 dc into 4th st of 7 ch, 4 ch, 1 dc into 4th st of next 7 ch, 4 ch, 1 dc into sl st made by [3 d tr 2 ch sl st 2 ch 3 d tr]; rep from * ending sl st into first dc. [This is now centre back edge of Bodice.] **2nd row:** 1 ch, 1 dc into same place as sl st, * 4 dc into 4 ch space, 1 dc into next dc; rep from * ending sl st into first dc. 15 dc for each motif. 120 dc. **3rd row:** 3 ch, * miss 2 dc, dc into next dc, 2 ch. Rep from * to end, sl to 1st ch. **4th row:** 1 dc, dc into each ch and dc to end. Cont in dc until underarm measures 4″ from beg, or required length measured from under bustline.

Shape armholes and divide for Front and Right and Left Back. Front Bodice. Break off yarn and rejoin on 30th st from edge. **1st row:** Work 2 dc tog, work 56 dc, work next 2 dc tog, making 58 dc in all, turn. **2nd row:** 1 ch, 1 dc into each dc to end, turn. **3rd row:** 1 ch, work 2 dc tog, dc into each dc to last 2 dc, work last 2 dc tog, turn. **4th row:** 1 ch, dc into each dc to end, turn. Rep last row 13 times more. **Shape neck. 1st row:** 1 ch, work 13 dc, turn. **2nd row:** 1 ch, work 2 dc tog, dc into each dc to end, turn. **3rd row:** 1 ch, dc into each dc to end, turn. **4th row:** 1 ch, work 2 dc tog, dc into each dc to end, turn. **5th row:** 1 ch, dc into each dc to end. Cut yarn and darn in end. With wrong side of work facing rejoin yarn to 14th dc counting from armhole edge, work 1 ch, work 13 dc, turn. **Next row:** 1 ch, work in dc to last 2 dc, work 2 dc tog, turn. **Next row:** 1 ch, dc into each dc to end, turn. **Next row:** 1 ch, work in dc to last 2 dc, work 2 dc tog, turn. **Next row:** 1 ch, dc into each dc to end. Cut yarn and darn in end. With right side of Back facing, rejoin yarn to underarm edge of Right Back. **1st row:** Work next 2 dc tog, work 28 dc, making 29 dc in all, turn. **2nd row:** 1 ch, dc into each dc to end, turn. **3rd row:** 1 ch, work 2 dc tog, dc into each dc to end, turn. **4th row:** 1 ch, dc into each dc to end, turn. Rep 4th row 16 times more, ending at armhole edge. **Shape neck. 1st row:** 1 ch, work 12 dc, turn. **2nd row:** 1 ch, work 2 dc tog, dc into each dc to end, turn. **3rd row:** 1 ch, dc into each dc to end. Cut yarn and leave end long enough to join shoulder seam. Rejoin yarn to centre edge of Left Back and work to match first side, reversing shaping. Join shoulder seam.

Complete armholes. 1st round: Join yarn to underarm edge and work 1 dc into every row around armhole, making 44 dc in all; sl st to first dc. **2nd round:** 1 ch, dc into sl st, dc into each dc to end. Cut yarn and leave long enough end to sew in sleeve. Work round other arm in same way.

COLLAR: Join yarn at centre back opening and work 1 dc into each dc all round neck. Cont in dc until collar is required depth. **Next row:** Work a row of picot all round collar by working 1 dc into 1st dc, 2 ch, then work 1 dc in same place as first dc, work 1 dc in next dc; rep to end of collar then cont working in dc only down centre back opening and up other side. Fasten off and darn in end.

TO MAKE UP: Sleeves. Rejoin yarn to sl st made by [3 d tr 2 ch sl st 2 ch 3 d tr] and work up unfinished motif side and across top as follows: **1st round:** Dc into sl st, 3 ch, 1 dc into 4th st of 7 ch, 3 ch, 1 dc into 4th st of 7 ch, 3 ch, 1 dc into 3rd st of 5 ch space, * 1 dc into 4th st of 7 ch, 1 dc into 4th st of next 7 ch, 2 dc into sl st made by [3 d tr 2 ch sl st 2 ch 3 d tr]. Rep from * 3 times more. 1 dc into 4th st of 7 ch, dc into 4th st of 7 ch, dc into 3rd st of 5 ch space. Work unjoined motif side the same as first side, dc into same place as first dc and join with a sl st. **2nd round:** 1 ch, 1 dc into same place as sl st, dc into each dc to end, join with a sl st to first dc. 44 in all. Cut yarn and darn in end. Using end left from armhole sew in sleeve. Work other sleeve top in same way. **Trim hem and cuffs.** Join yarn in sl st as given for Sleeves. 1 ch, dc into same place, work 1 dc into each of next 12 sts, work picot as given for Collar in next st, work 1 dc into each of next 12 sts, picot in next sl st; rep all way round, join with a sl st to 1 ch. Cut yarn and darn in end. **Tie Belt.** With No. 5 hook make a ch approximately 112″ long, or required length to tie under bust, and work 2 rows dc. Fasten off. Steam press Dress with a very wet cloth and very hot iron. Allow to dry completely flat, taking care to spread out Skirt and Sleeves without creasing. Sew in zip to back neck to come to top of collar. Thread Tie Belt through row joining Skirt to Bodice and tie at centre front. Make a lining slip if required, lightly catching shoulder seams to shoulder seams of bodice only.

Flying motif shawl

MEASUREMENTS: Length: 120″. Depth: 60″, excluding fringe.
MATERIALS: 18 ozs Jaeger Celtic Spun in main shade A; 2 ozs each of same in contrasts B, C and D; 4 ozs of same in contrast E for fringe, and 1 oz each in 6 more contrasting colours for motifs. No. 9 crochet hook or New International size No. 3.50.
NOTE: Dc 2 tog = work 1 dc into each of next 2 sts, leave loops of each st on hook, wool round hook and draw through all loops on hook. [1 st dec.] Tr 2 tog = work 1 tr into each of next 2 sts, leaving last loop of each st on hook, wool round hook and draw through all loops on hook. [1 st dec.]
MAIN SECTION: With No. 9 hook and A make 3 ch. **1st row:** 1 tr 1 ch 1 tr, into 3rd ch from hook, 3 ch, turn. **2nd row:** 1 tr 1 ch 1 tr, into first tr, 1 ch, 1 tr 1 ch 1 tr, into last tr, 3 ch, turn. **3rd row:** 1 tr 1 ch 1 tr into first tr, 1 ch 1 tr, into each tr to last tr, 1 ch, 1 tr 1 ch 1 tr into last tr, 3 ch, turn. Rep 3rd row until work measures 54″ from beg, or required length. Break off A. Join in B by drawing a ch through loop on hook, work 2 more ch, turn.
BORDER: 1st row: 1 tr into first tr, 1 ch 1 tr, into each tr to last tr, 1 ch, 1 tr 1 ch 1 tr 1 ch 1 tr, into last tr. Cont in patt along side edge working 1 ch 1 tr, into each row and ending 1 ch, 1 tr 1 ch 1 tr 1 ch 1 tr, into corner tr. Work along 2nd side in same way but ending 1 ch, 1 sl st into 2nd of 3 ch, 3 ch, turn. **2nd row:** 1 tr into joining sl st, 1 ch 1 tr, into each tr to first corner, 1 ch, 1 tr 1 ch 1 tr 1 ch 1 tr, into corner tr, 1 ch 1 tr, into each tr to 2nd corner, 1 ch, 1 tr 1 ch 1 tr 1 ch 1 tr, into corner tr, 1 ch 1 tr, into each tr to end, 1 ch, 1 tr into sl st, 1 ch, sl st into 2nd of 3 ch. Break off B. Join in C as for B. Turn. **3rd row:** As 2nd, 3 ch, turn. **4th row:** As 2nd. Break off C and join in D as before. **5th row:** As 2nd. 3 ch, turn. **6th row:** As 2nd. 2 ch, turn. **7th row:** 1 tr into joining sl st, 1 tr into each st to first corner, 3 tr into corner tr, 1 tr into each st to 2nd corner, 3 tr into corner tr, 1 tr into each st to end, 1 tr into sl st, sl st into 2nd of 2 ch. Break off D. Fasten off. Sew in ends. Pin out to shape and press.
FRINGE: Using 6 strands of E, 16″ long for each tassel, work a fringe along the 2 short edges, with 6 tr, between each tassel. Knot 6 strands of one tassel tog with 6 strands of next tassel, working right along fringe approximately 1″ from first knot. Trim ends.
MOTIFS: [Make 8 of each motif, using different colour for each motif.]
1st MOTIF: With No. 9 hook and first colour make 12 ch. **1st row:** 1 tr into 3rd ch from hook, 1 tr into each ch to end, 2 ch, turn. **2nd row:** Tr 2 tog, 1 tr into each tr to last 2 tr, tr 2 tog, 2 ch, turn. **3rd row:** As 2nd. **4th row:** As 2nd. **5th row:** 2 tr into first tr, 1 tr into each tr to last tr, 2 tr into last tr, 2 ch, turn. **6th row:** As 5th. **7th row:** As 5th. **8th row:** 1 tr into each tr to end. Fasten off. Using 2nd colour make 10 ch. Work 1st to 3rd rows of first piece, then 5th, 6th and 8th rows. Fasten off. Place smaller piece on top of larger piece. Using 2 strands of 3rd colour work 2 dc firmly round centre to hold 2 pieces tog. Cont with double wool, making a ch of 25 sts. Fasten off, leaving ends long enough to tie to shawl.
2nd MOTIF: With No. 9 hook and first colour, wind wool 10 times round forefinger and work 28 dc into ring thus formed. **1st round:** Work 1 dc into each dc to end, working into back of st only. Break off first colour and fasten off. **2nd round:** With 2nd colour work as 1st round. **3rd round:** Working into back of st only, * work 1 dc into each of next 3 dc, 2 dc into following dc; rep from * to end. Break off 2nd colour and fasten off. **4th round:** With 3rd colour and working into back of st only * work 1 dc into next dc, 2 dc into following dc; rep from * ending 1 dc into last dc. **5th round:** With 3rd colour work as 1st round. Join in another strand of 3rd colour and with double wool make a ch of 20 sts. Fasten off, leaving ends long enough to tie to shawl.
3rd MOTIF: With No. 9 hook and first colour make 5 ch and join with a sl st to form a ring. **1st round:** Work 15 dc into ring. **2nd round:** 1 dc into first dc, * 5 ch, miss 2 dc, 1 dc into next dc; rep from * ending 5 ch, miss 2 dc. **3rd round:** Into each 5 ch loop work 1 dc, 1 h tr, 5 tr, 1 h tr and 1 dc [5 petals]. Break wool and fasten off. **4th round:** Using 2nd colour, * 1 dc round next dc of 2nd round inserting hook from back, 6 ch; rep from * to end. **5th round:** Into each 6 ch loop work 1 dc, 1 h tr, 7 tr, 1 h tr and 1 dc. Break wool and fasten off. Using 2 strands of 3rd colour join wool between 2 petals and make a ch of 22 sts. Fasten off, leaving ends long enough to tie to shawl.
4th MOTIF: With No. 9 hook and first colour * make 13 ch. 1 dc into 4th ch from hook [3 ch, 1 dc into same ch as last dc] twice, 9 ch, 1 dc into first of 13 ch [first tassel completed]; rep from * twice more but ending each tassel by working 1 dc into same ch as first tassel. Break wool and fasten off. Join in 2nd colour into first

of 13 ch with a dc and work 3 more tassels, always ending each tassel by working 1 dc into same ch as first tassel. Break yarn and fasten off. Join in 3rd colour and work 3 more tassels in same way. Join in another strand of 3rd colour and with double wool make a ch of 24 sts. Fasten off, leaving ends long enough to tie to shawl.

5th MOTIF: With No. 9 hook and first colour make 16 ch. **1st row:** 1 dc into 2nd ch from hook, 1 dc into each ch to end. 1 ch turn. **2nd row:** Dc 2 tog, 1 dc into each st to end. Rep 2nd row 5 times more. Break wool and fasten off. Using 2nd colour rep 2nd row until all sts are eliminated. Break wool and fasten off. Join in 3rd colour and work a row of dc along all edges, working 1 dc for each st or row and 2 dc into corners. Join with a sl st to first dc. Join in another strand of 3rd colour and with double wool make a ch of 27 sts. Fasten off, leaving ends long enough to tie to shawl.

6th MOTIF: With No. 9 hook and first colour make 20 ch. * Into 3rd ch from hook work 3 tr, but leaving last loop of each st on hook, wool round hook, draw through all loops on hook, 3 ch, 1 dc into same ch as 3 tr; rep from * twice more, working into same ch as before. Break wool and fasten off. Make 1 more flower in first colour but starting with 25 ch. Make 2 more flowers each in same way in 2nd and 3rd colours. Knot stems tog to form a bunch, leaving ends long enough to tie to shawl.

7th MOTIF: With No. 9 hook and first colour make 6 ch, join into a circle with a sl st. **1st round:** Work 10 dc into circle. **2nd round:** 2 ch, now work a cluster into each dc as follows: [wool round hook, insert hook into st and draw loop through] 3 times, wool round hook and draw through all loops on hook, 1 ch. Join with a sl st into 2nd of 2 ch, and work 15 ch. Break wool and fasten off. Make 1 more flower in first colour and 2 flowers each in 2nd and 3rd colours. Knot stems tog to form a bunch and complete as for 6th Motif.

TO MAKE UP: Sew in ends on all motifs and press lightly. Tie motifs to shawl as required.

1				
5	2			
3	4	3		
4	5	4	2	
2	4	3	5	1

Chart

Giant motif shawl

Shown on the cover

MATERIALS: 13 ozs of Patons Totem Double Crepe in main shade A; 1 oz of same in contrast B; 2 ozs of same in contrast C; 7 ozs each of same in contrasts D and E; 3 ozs each of same in contrasts F and G. No. 5 crochet hook or New International size No. 5.50.

MEASUREMENTS: Shawl measures 70″ along long edge and 35″ at centre, excluding fringes.

TENSION: 1 square measures approximately 8″ along each side.

NOTE: 1 cl = 1 cluster made by working 3 tr but keeping last loop of each st on hook, now draw a loop through all sts on hook.

SQUARE No. 1: [Make 2.] Using 2 strands of wool in B, make a ch of 6 sts, join with a sl st to form a circle. Cont with double wool. **1st round:** 2 ch, 23 tr into ring. Join with a sl st to 2nd of 2 ch. **2nd round:** 4 ch, 1 tr into same ch as sl st, 1 ch, * miss 2 sts [1 tr, 2 ch, 1 tr] into next st, 1 ch; rep from * 6 times more. Join with a sl st to 2nd of 4 ch. **3rd round:** 2 ch [1 tr, 2 ch, 2 tr] into first ch sp, * 1 dc into 1 ch sp [2 tr, 2 ch, 2 tr] into 2 ch sp; rep from * 6 times more, 1 dc into last ch sp. Break wool and fasten off. **4th round:** Join 2 strands of A into next 2 ch sp with a dc, * 7 ch, 1 dc into next 2 ch sp, 5 ch, 1 dc into next 2 ch sp; rep from * 3 times more, ending with a sl st into joining dc instead of dc. **5th round:** 2 ch, * 7 tr into 7 ch loop [2 ch, 1 cl, 3 ch, 1 cl, 2 ch] into 5 ch loop; rep from * 3 times more. Join with a sl st into 2nd of 2 ch. **6th round:** 2 ch, * 1 tr into each tr, 2 tr into 2 ch loop [2 ch, 1 cl, 3 ch, 1 cl, 2 ch] into 3 ch loop, 2 tr into 2 ch loop; rep from * 3 times more. Join with a sl st into 2nd of 2 ch. **7th round:** As 6th but ending

1 tr into each of last 2 tr. Join with a sl st to 2nd of 2 ch. Break wool and fasten off.

SQUARE No. 2: [Make 3.] Using 2 strands of wool in C make a ch of 6 sts, 1 tr into 6th ch from hook, 2 ch, 1 tr 2 ch, 4 times into same ch as tr, join with a sl st into 3rd of 6 ch. Cont with double wool. **1st round:** 2 ch, 1 tr into same ch as sl st, * 4 tr into ch sp, 1 tr into tr; rep from * 4 times more, 4 tr into last ch sp. Join with a sl st to 2nd of 2 ch. **2nd round:** 2 ch, * 1 tr into each of next 2 tr, inserting hook through back of st only, 2 tr into next st, inserting hook through back of st; rep from * 9 times more. Join with a sl st into 2nd of 2 ch. Break wool and fasten off. **3rd round:** Join 2 strands of D into first tr with a dc, * [4 ch, miss 3 sts, 1 dc into next st] twice, 4 ch, miss 1 st, 1 dc into next st; rep from * 3 times more, ending with sl st into joining dc instead of a dc. **4th round:** 2 ch, * 3 tr into ch loop, 1 tr into dc, 3 tr into next ch loop [2 ch, 1 cl, 3 ch, 1 cl, 2 ch] into next ch loop; rep from * 3 times more. Join with a sl st into 2nd of 2 ch. **5th round:** As 6th round of Square No. 1. **6th round:** As 7th round of Square No. 1. Break wool and fasten off.

SQUARE No. 3: [Make 3.] Using 2 strands of wool in D make a ch of 6 sts. 1 tr into 6th ch from hook, 2 ch [1 tr, 2 ch] twice into same ch as tr. Join with a sl st into 3rd of 6th ch. Cont with double wool. **1st round:** Into each ch sp work [1 dc, 1 tr, 5 d tr, 1 tr, 1 dc], making 4 leaves. **2nd round:** * 1 dc into dc, 1 tr into tr, 2 tr into each d tr, 1 tr into tr, 1 dc into dc; rep from * 3 times more. Break wool and fasten off. **3rd round:** Join 2 strands of A into 10th tr of 1st leaf with a dc, * 5 ch, miss 6 sts, 1 dc into next st, 7 ch, miss 6 sts, 1 dc into next st; rep from * 3 times more but ending with a sl st into joining dc instead of a dc. 8 ch loops. **4th round:** 2 ch, * 7 tr into ch loop [2 ch, 1 cl, 3 ch, 1 cl, 2 ch] into following ch loop; rep from * 3 times more. Join with a sl st into 2nd of 2 ch. **5th round:** As 6th round of Square No. 1. **6th round:** As 7th round of Square No. 1. Break wool and fasten off.

SQUARE No. 4: [Make 4.] Using 2 strands of wool in A make a ch of 8 sts and join with a sl st to form a ring. Cont with double wool. **1st round:** 2 ch, into ring work [1 cl, 2 ch, 1 cl, 5 ch] 4 times. Join with a sl st into 2nd of 2 ch. **2nd round:** 2 ch, * 3 tr into 2 ch loop [2 ch, 1 cl, 3 ch, 1 cl, 2 ch] into 5 ch loop; rep from * 3 times more. Join with a sl st into 2nd of 2 ch. Break wool and fasten off. **3rd round:** Join 2 strands of E into joining sl st with a sl st and 2 ch, * 1 tr into each tr, 2 tr into 2 ch loop [2 ch, 1 cl, 3 ch, 1 cl, 2 ch] into 3 ch loop, 2 tr into 2 ch loop; rep from * 3 times more. Join with a sl st into 2nd of 2 ch. **4th round:** 2 ch, work as 3rd round from * 4 times, ending 1 tr into each of last 2 tr. Join as before. **5th round:** As 4th round, ending 1 tr into each of last 4 tr. Join as before. Break wool and fasten off.

SQUARE No. 5: [Make 3.] Using 2 strands of wool in D make a ch of 4 sts and join with a sl st to form a ring. Cont with double wool. **1st round:** Work 11 dc into ring. **2nd round:** 3 ch, * [1 tr, 1 ch] into each st to end. Join with a sl st into 2nd of 2 ch. [12 ch loops.] **3rd round:** 2 ch, 2 tr into 1st ch loop, 3 tr into each ch loop to end. Join with a sl st into 2nd of 2 ch. **4th round:** 1 dc into 1st st, * 4 ch, 1 dc into 2nd ch from hook, 1 h tr into 3rd ch, 1 tr into 4th ch, miss 2 sts, 1 dc into next st; rep from * to end. [12 points.] Break wool and fasten off. **5th round:** Join 2 strands of F into dc of first point with a dc, * 4 ch, 1 dc into dc of next point, 4 ch, 1 dc into dc of following point, 5 ch, 1 dc into dc of next point; rep from * 3 times more, ending with a sl st into joining dc instead of a dc. **6th round:** 2 ch, * 3 tr into 4 ch loop, 1 tr into dc, 3 tr into next 4 ch loop [2 ch, 1 cl, 3 ch, 1 cl, 2 ch] into 5 ch loop; rep from * 3 times more. Join with a sl st into 2nd of 2 ch. **7th round:** As 6th round of Square No. 1. **8th round:** As 7th round of Square No. 1. Break wool and fasten off.

THE TRIANGLES: [Make 6.] Using 2 strands of wool in A make a ch of 6 sts and join with a sl st to form a ring. Cont with double wool. **1st row:** 2 ch, now into ring work, 1 cl, 2 ch, 1 cl, 5 ch, 1 cl, 2 ch, 1 cl. Turn with 2 ch. **2nd row:** 1 cl into first st, 2 ch, 3 tr into 2 ch loop [2 ch, 1 cl, 3 ch, 1 cl, 2 ch] into 5 ch loop, 3 tr into 2 ch loop, 2 ch, 1 cl into last st. Turn with 2 ch. **3rd row:** * 1 cl into first st, 2 ch, 2 tr into 2 ch loop, 1 tr into each tr, 2 tr into 2 ch loop [2 ch, 1 cl, 3 ch, 1 cl, 2 ch] into 3 ch loop, 2 tr into 2 ch loop, 1 tr into each tr, 2 tr into 2 ch loop, 2 ch, 1 cl into last st. * Break wool, join in 2 strands of E and turn with 2 ch. **4th, 5th and 6th rows:** Work as 3rd row from * to * turning with 2 ch at end of 4th and 5th rows. Break wool and fasten off.

TO MAKE UP: Pin out pieces to correct shape and press with warm iron and damp cloth. Using 2 strands of G and working from chart, join motifs together as follows: with right side of motifs facing each other join wool into corner ch loop of 1st motif with 1 dc. Work 1 ch, 1 dc into corner ch loop of 2nd motif, 1 ch, * miss 1 st on 1st motif and work 1 dc into next st, 1 ch miss 1 st on 2nd motif and work 1 dc into next st, 1 ch; rep from *. Now with wrong side of work facing join 2 strands of G into one corner with a dc, * 1 ch, miss 1 st, 1 dc into next st; rep from * along all edges.

FRINGE: Using 8 strands of A 18″ long for each tassel, make a fringe along the 2 short edges, working into each alt ch loop. Now knot 8 strands of one tassel together with 8 strands of next tassel, working right along fringe approximately $1\frac{1}{2}$″ from first knot. Trim ends. Pin out and press lightly.

Boleros and skirts

Instructions are for a 25″ chest. Changes for 28″, 31″, 34″, 37″ and 40″ sizes are given in brackets.

MATERIALS: 12(15–18–21–23–25) ozs Patons Cameo Crepe. No. 9 crochet hook or New International size No. 3.50. Oddments of same in contrast colours or Twilleys Goldfingering for optional embroidery.

MEASUREMENTS: Bolero. To fit a 25″(28″–31″–34″–37″–40″) bust/chest. Length: 13½″(15″–16½″–18″–18″–18″), adjustable. **Skirt.** To fit 27″(30″–33″–36″–39″–42″) hips. Length: 27″(31½″–33″–40″–40″–40″), adjustable.

TENSION: 6 tr to 1″ on No. 9 hook.

SKIRT

BACK: With No. 9 hook make 93(103–113–123–133–143) ch. **1st row:** Work 1 tr into 3rd ch from hook, 1 tr into every ch to end, 3 ch, turn. 91(101–111–121–131–141) tr. **2nd row:** Miss first tr, work 1 tr into each tr to end, 1 tr in t ch, 3 ch, turn. **3rd row:** Miss first tr, work 1 tr into each of next 4 tr, * 1 ch miss next tr – called sp – work 1 tr into each of next 4 tr [wool over hook, insert hook into next tr and draw loop through] 4 times into same tr, wool over hook and draw through all loops on hook – called B 1 – work 1 tr into each of next 4 tr; rep from * to last 5 sts, sp, work 1 tr into each of next 4 tr, 1 tr in t ch, 3 ch, turn. **4th row:** Miss first tr, work 1 tr into each of next 3 tr, * sp, work 1 tr into sp of previous row, sp, work 1 tr into each of next 7 tr; rep from * to last 6 sts, sp, work 1 tr into sp of previous row, sp, work 1 tr into each of next 3 tr, 1 tr into t ch, 3 ch, turn. **5th row:** Miss first tr, work 1 tr into each of next 2 tr, * sp, 1 tr into sp, 1 tr, 1 tr into sp, sp, work 1 tr into each of next 5 tr; rep from * to last 7 sts, sp, 1 tr into sp, 1 tr, 1 tr into sp, sp, 1 tr into each of next 2 tr, 1 tr in t ch, 3 ch, turn. **6th row:** Miss first tr, work 1 tr into next tr, * sp, 1 tr into sp, 1 tr into each of next 3 tr, 1 tr into sp, sp, 1 tr into each of next 3 tr; rep from * to last 8 sts, sp, 1 tr into sp, 1 tr into each of next 3 tr, 1 tr in sp, sp, 1 tr into last tr, 1 tr into t ch, 3 ch, turn. **7th row:** Miss first tr, * sp, 1 tr into sp, 1 tr into each of next 5 tr, 1 tr into sp, sp, 1 tr into next tr; rep from * to end, 3 ch turn. **8th row:** * 1 tr into sp, 1 tr into each of next 3 tr, B 1, 1 tr into each of next 3 tr, 1 tr into sp, sp; rep from * to end but omit last sp and work 1 tr into t ch, 3 ch, turn. **9th row:** Miss first tr, * sp, 1 tr into each of next 7 tr, sp, 1 tr into sp; rep from * to end, 3 ch, turn. **10th row:** Miss first tr, * 1 tr into sp, sp, 1 tr into each of next 5 tr, sp, 1 tr into sp, 1 tr into tr; rep from * to end, ending 1 tr in t ch, 3 ch, turn. **11th row:** Miss first tr, 1 tr into next tr, * 1 tr into sp, sp, 1 tr into each of next 3 tr, sp, 1 tr into sp, 1 tr into each of next 3 tr; rep from * to last 8 sts, 1 tr into sp, sp, 1 tr into each of next 3 tr, sp, 1 tr into sp, 1 tr into last tr, 1 tr in t ch, 3 ch, turn. **12th row:** Miss first tr, 1 tr into each of next 2 tr, * 1 tr into sp, sp, 1 tr into tr, sp, 1 tr into sp, 1 tr into each of next 5 tr; rep from * to last 7 sts, 1 tr into sp, sp, 1 tr into next tr, sp, 1 tr into sp, 1 tr into each of next 2 tr, 1 tr in t ch, 3 ch, turn. **13th row:** Miss first tr, 1 tr into each of next 3 tr, * 1 tr into sp, sp, 1 tr into sp, 1 tr into each of next 3 tr, B 1, 1 tr into each of next 3 tr; rep from * to last 6 sts, 1 tr into sp, sp, 1 tr into sp, 1 tr into each of next 3 tr, 1 tr in t ch, 3 ch, turn. Rows 4 to 13 form patt and are rep throughout. Cont in patt until work measures 24″(28½″–30″–36″–36″–36″) from beg, or required length less 3″(3″–3″–4″–4″–4″), ending with a 4th or 9th row. Fasten off.

FRONT: Work as given for Back.

WAISTBAND: With No. 9 hook make 123(123–133–133–143–143) ch. Work 1st row as given for Skirt. Beg with 4th(4th–4th–3rd–3rd–3rd) patt row, work

9(9–9–11–11–11) rows patt. Work 1 row tr. Fasten off. **TO MAKE UP:** Press pieces on wrong side under a damp cloth with a warm iron. Join side seams, leaving 4″ open on left seam. Sew on waistband, gathering skirt to fit and allowing 1″ overlap. Fasten with hooks and eyes. Press seams. If required embroider with lazy daisy st round centre bobble, scattering round hem and waist.

BOLERO

BACK: With No. 9 hook make 73(83–93–103–113–123) ch. Beg with 3rd patt row work in patt as given for Skirt until work measures 8½″(9½″–10½″–11½″–11″–10½″) from beg, or required length to underarm, omitting t ch at end of last row. **Shape armholes.** Sl st over first 5(7–8–10–11–12) sts, patt to last 5 (7–8–10–11–12) sts, turn. Cont without shaping until armhole measures 5″(5½″–6″–6½″–7″–7½″) from beg, omitting t ch at end of last row. **Shape shoulders. Next row:** Sl st over first 6(6–6–6–7–8) sts, patt to last 6(6–6–6–7–8) sts, turn. Rep this row 1(1–2–2–2–2) times more. **Next row:** Sl st over first 6(8–5–7–7–7) sts, patt to last 6(8–5–7–7–7) sts. Fasten off.

LEFT FRONT: With No. 9 hook make 43(48–53–58–63–68) ch. Work in patt as given for Back, noting that on 28″, 34″ and 40″ sizes the 3rd patt row will beg as 3rd row of Skirt and end as 8th row, 4th row will beg as 9th row of Skirt and end as 4th, and so on. Cont in patt until work measures same as Back to underarm, ending with a wrong side row and omitting t ch at end of last row. **Shape armhole. Next row:** Sl st over first 10 sts, patt to end. Cont without shaping until work measures 1½″(1½″–1¾″–1¾″–2″–2″) less than Back to shoulder, ending at front edge and omitting t ch at end of last row. **Shape neck.** Sl st over first 13(16–18–21–23–25) sts, patt to end. Cont on rem 18 (20–23–25–28–31) sts until work measures same as Back to shoulder, ending at armhole edge and omitting t ch at end of last row. **Shape shoulder. 1st row:** Sl st over first 6(6–6–6–7–8) sts, patt to end. **2nd row:** Patt to last 6(6–6–6–7–8) sts, turn. Rep 1st row 0(0–1–1–1–1) time more. Fasten off.

RIGHT FRONT: Work as given for Left Front, reversing all shaping and noting that on 28″, 34″ and 40″ sizes the 3rd patt row will beg as 8th row of Skirt and end as 3rd row, and so on.

TO MAKE UP: Press as given for Skirt. Join shoulder and side seams. Work 2 rows dc round all edges, working 3 dc into each st at end of front edge. Press seams. Embroider round edges as given for Skirt.

Baby's dress

Instructions are for a 20″ size. Changes for 21½″ size are given in brackets.

MATERIALS: 5(6) ozs Twilleys Cortina. No. 12 crochet hook or New International size No. 2.50. 2 yds narrow ribbon. 2 small buttons.

MEASUREMENTS: To fit a 20″(21½″) chest. Length: 12½″(15″).

TENSION: One patt rep measures 1⅛″ in width.

FRONT: With No. 12 hook make 122(131) ch. **Next row:** 1 dc into 8th ch from hook, * 3 ch, miss 2 ch, 1 dc into next ch, 2 ch, miss 2 ch, 1 tr into next ch, 2 ch, miss 2 ch, 1 dc into next ch; rep from * 12(13) times in all, 3 ch, miss 2 ch, 1 dc into next ch, 2 ch, miss 2 ch, 1 tr into end ch, 1 ch to turn. **Commence patt. 1st row:** Miss 2 ch sp at beg of row, * [2 tr, 1 ch, 2 tr, 1 ch, 2 tr] into next 3 ch sp, 1 ch, 1 dc in tr, 1 ch; rep from * 12(13) times in all [2 tr, 1 ch, 2 tr, 1 ch, 2 tr] into next 3 ch sp, 1 dc into 3rd t ch, turn with 5 ch. **2nd row:** * 1 dc into 1 ch sp between first 2 pairs of tr, 3 ch, 1 dc into next 1 ch sp between trs, 2 ch, 1 tr into dc, 2 ch; rep from * ending with 1 tr into t ch and omitting the last 2 ch, turn with 1 ch. Rep 1st and 2nd rows 17(19) times. Fasten off. [More or less rows may be worked here if longer or shorter skirt is required.] Return to right side of foundation row. Work 76(80) dc into foundation ch, turn with 2 ch. Work 66(70) tr into dc, turn with 1 ch. ** Work 60(64) dc into tr, turn with 1 ch. Work 4 rows dc into dc. **Shape armholes. 1st row:** Sl st over 4 dc, work 52(56) dc, turn. **2nd row:** Miss 1 dc, work 1 dc into each dc until 1 dc remains, turn. **3rd row:** As 2nd.

4th row: As 2nd. 46(50) dc. Work 15(17) more rows dc. **Divide for neck. Next row:** Work 18(19) dc, turn with 1 ch. **Left Front Shoulder. Shape neck. 1st row:** Sl st into 2nd dc, work to end. **2nd row:** Work in dc until 1 dc remains, turn. Rep these 2 rows once more. **Shape shoulder. Next row:** Work 7(8) dc, sl st into next st, fasten off. With wrong side of work facing, rejoin wool to armhole edge and work 18(19) dc, turn. **Right Front Shoulder:** Work as for Left Front Shoulder.

BACK: Work as given for Front to ** and mark centre of last row. **Right Back.** Work 30(32) dc to marker, turn with 5 ch. **Next row:** 1 dc into 3rd ch, 1 dc into each of next 2 ch for underflap, 1 dc into each dc to end. 33(35) dc. Work 4 rows dc. **Shape armhole. 1st row:** Sl st over 4 dc, work to end. **2nd row:** Work in dc until 1 dc remains, turn. **3rd row:** Miss 1 dc, work to end. **4th row:** As 2nd. 26(28) dc. Work 17(19) rows dc. **Shape neck. Next row:** Sl st over 10(11) dc, work to end. Dec 1 dc at neck edge on next 2 rows. **Shape shoulder.** Sl st over 7 dc, work to end and fasten off. **Left Back.** With right side of work facing, rejoin wool at marker and work 33(35) dc into tr. Work 4 rows dc. Shape armhole and work to end as given for Right Back.

ARMHOLE EDGINGS: Join shoulder and side seams. With right side of work facing, sl st into seam, * work 2 tr 1 ch 2 tr 1 ch 2 tr into next dc, miss 1 dc – or row end – 1 dc into next dc – or row end – miss 2 dc – or row end; rep from * around armhole, sl st into first tr. Fasten off.

NECK EDGING: Work as given for Armhole Edging.

TO MAKE UP: Press work lightly on wrong side with a warm iron and damp cloth. Catch underflap in position. Beg at centre back and ending at centre front thread 2 lengths of ribbon through tr at waist and tie in bow at back and front. Thread ribbon through shell all round armholes and tie in a bow at shoulders. Thread ribbon through neck edging and secure ends at back. Sew on two small buttons at back opening using dc for buttonholes.

Baby's catsuit

Instructions are to fit a baby from birth to 6 months. Changes to fit a baby from 6 months to 1 year are given in brackets.
MATERIALS: 9(10) ozs Peter Pan Baby Courtelle 4-ply. No. 12 crochet hook or New International size No. 2.50. 11 press studs.
TENSION: 1 shell of 5 tr measures 1" in width.
NOTE: Dec worked as follows: * insert hook in next dc, yarn over hook and draw loop through; rep from * once, yarn over hook and draw through 2 loops.

LEGS: Beg at ankle. With No. 12 hook make 32(44) ch. **1st row:** 1 dc into 2nd ch from hook, * miss 2 ch, 5 tr in next ch, miss 2 ch, 1 dc in next ch; rep from * to end, 3 ch, turn. **2nd row:** 2 tr in first dc, * miss 2 tr, 1 dc in next tr [centre of shell], miss 2 tr, 5 tr in next dc; rep from * to end, ending with 3 tr in last dc, instead of 5, 1 ch, turn. **3rd row:** 1 dc into first tr, * 5 tr in next dc, miss 2 tr, 1 dc in next tr [centre of shell]; rep from * to end, 3 ch, turn. 2nd and 3rd rows form patt. Rep patt rows twice more. **Shape leg.** [inc.] 4 tr in first dc, patt to last dc, 5 tr in last dc, 3 ch, turn. **Next row:** 2 tr in first tr, miss 1 tr, 1 dc in next tr, patt to end, ending with 3 tr in last tr [i.e. t ch], 1 ch, turn. **Next row:** As 3rd patt row. Rep last 3 rows 4 times more. 10(12) shells in row. Cut yarn

nd fasten off. Make another leg in same way but do
ıot fasten off. **Join legs.** Work 2nd patt row to end
n leg just completed, working last shell into last dc of
his leg and first dc of first leg worked, working through
he 2 dcs at once. Cont in patt to end. 20(24) shells
ı all. Cont without shaping on these sts until work
ıeasures 16½″(17½″) from beginning, ending with a
nd patt row. **Shape armholes.** Work as 3rd patt
ɔw until 3(4) shells have been worked, 1 dc into
entre of next shell, 3 tr in next dc, 1 ch, turn. Cont
ithout shaping on these sts for 8(10) more rows,
nding at armhole edge. **Shape neck. 1st row:** Work
ı patt until 3(4) shells have been worked, turn. **2nd
ow:** Sl st over 2 tr, 1 dc in next tr, patt to end, 1 ch,
ırn. **3rd row:** Work 2(3) shells, 3 tr in next dc, 1 ch,
ırn. **Shape shoulder. 1st row:** Work 2(3) shells,
ırn. **2nd row:** Sl st to centre of shell, 3 tr in next dc,
1 dc in centre of shell, 3 tr in next dc. **2nd size only.**
ep from * once more. Cut yarn and fasten off.
eturn to main work. Miss 2 shells, join with a sl st
to next dc, 3 ch, 2 tr in same dc, cont in patt until
10) complete shells have been worked, 3 tr in next
:, 1 ch, turn. Cont in patt on these sts until 11(13)
ore rows have been worked. **Shape shoulders.** Sl
to centre of shell, 3 tr in next dc, 1 dc in centre of
ext shell, work 6(8) shells, 3 tr in next dc, 1 dc in
ntre of last shell. Cut yarn and fasten off. Return to
ain work. Miss 2 shells and join as for Back, and
ork to end. 3(4) complete shells, 3 ch, turn. Cont in
tt until 8(10) more rows have been worked, ending
neck edge. **Shape neck. 1st row:** Sl st to centre
shell, patt to end, 3 ch, turn. **2nd row:** Work in
tt until 2nd(3rd) complete shell has been completed,
h, turn. Work 1 row straight. **Shape shoulder.** Sl st to
ntre of shell, 3 tr in next dc, * 1 dc in centre of next
ell, 3 tr in next dc [rep from * once more for 2nd size
ly], miss 2 tr. 1 tr in t ch. Cut yarn and fasten off.
EEVES: With No. 12 hook make 37 ch. **1st row:**
iss 1 ch, work 1 dc into each ch to end, 1 ch, turn.
dc. Work 6 more rows dc. **Next row:** [inc.] * 2 dc
first dc, work 5 dc; rep from * to end, working 1
ɔre dc in last dc, 1 ch, turn. 43 dc. Work in patt as
Leg from 1st row, working 1 dc in first dc and
ssing dc, instead of ch as given in 1st row. **1st size
ly.** Cont without shaping in patt until sleeve
asures 6½″ from beg, or required length to under-
n, ending with a 3rd patt row. **2nd size only.** Work
given for Leg [7 rows without shaping, then 3 inc
ws – 3 shells in row]. Cont without shaping until
eve measures 6½″ or required length to underarm,
ding with a 3rd patt row. **Shape top. 1st row:** Sl
to centre of shell, patt to end, ending with 1 dc into
t shell, turn. Rep last row 2(3) times more.

Cut yarn and fasten off securely.

FOOT: [Both alike] With No. 12 hook make 31(39) dc along foundation ch of leg, 1 ch, turn. **2nd row:** Work 20(25) dc, 1 ch, turn. **3rd row:** Work 9(11) dc, 1 ch, turn. Work 7(9) more rows on these 9(11) sts, then dec 1 st at each end of next 2 rows. 5(7) sts. Cut yarn and fasten off. Join yarn at turn of 2nd row and work 11(14) dc to end, 1 ch, turn. **Next row:** Work 11(14) dc, then 11(13) dc up row ends of foot, then 5(7) dc across toe, 11(13) dc down row ends of other side of foot, 11(14) dc to end. Work 3(4) rows without shaping. **1st dec row:** Work 20(25) dc, dec as given in Note, work 5(7) dc, dec as before, work 20(25) dc to end, 1 ch, turn. ** **Next row:** Dec as before, work in dc to last 2 dc, dec as before. ** **Next row:** Work 19(24) dc, dec as before, 3(5) dc, dec as before, 19(24)dc. Rep from ** to ** once more. **Next row:** Work 18(23) dc, dec as before, 1(3) dc, dec as before, 18(23) dc. **1st size only.** Cut yarn and fasten off. **2nd size only.** Rep last 2 rows once more, working 1 less st between decs. Cut yarn and fasten off.

COLLAR: With No. 12 hook make 27(31) ch. **Next row:** Miss 1 ch, work 1 dc in each ch to end, 26(30) dc, 5 ch, turn. **Next row:** Miss 1 ch, 1 dc in each of next 4 ch, 1 dc in each dc to end, 5 ch, turn. Rep last row once more, turning with 10 ch instead of 5. **Next row:** Miss 1 ch, 1 dc in each of next 9 ch, work in dc to end. 10 ch. turn. Rep last row once more, turning with 1 ch instead of 10. 52(56) dc. Work 14(15) rows dc. Cut yarn and fasten off.

TO MAKE UP: *Do not press.* Join shoulder and sleeve seams. Join foot seams up to 6th row of patt on legs. **Edging:** With right side of work facing, begin at neck edge of left front and work 70(76) dc down front of crotch, then down leg, up other side of leg, down right leg, up left leg and 70(76) dc to neck edge, 1 ch, turn. **2nd row:** Work 70(76) dc, 1 ch, turn. Work 3 more rows over this row. Cut yarn and fasten off. With wrong side of work facing, rejoin yarn with a dc to 70th(76th) dc from neck edge of Left Front and work 70(76) dc to neck edge, 1 ch, turn. Work 3 more rows dc over these 70(76) sts. Cut yarn and fasten off. With wrong side of work facing join yarn with a dc at leg seam and work in dc up leg and down to seam of left leg, 1 ch, turn. Work 1 more row dc over this row. Cut yarn and fasten off. Sew 5 press stud fasteners evenly to front borders, lapping right over left for girl and left over right for boy, placing 1 fastener at neck edge and one at lower edge. Sew 3 fasteners to each leg, top one near front borders and other two evenly spaced to seam. Sew on shaped edge of collar to neck edge with ends coming in centre of front borders. Sew sleeves into armholes.

Angel set

Instructions are for an 18″ chest. Changes for 20″ and 22″ sizes are given in brackets.

MATERIALS: 5(6–8) ozs Patons Beehive Baby Wool 4-ply. No. 11(10–9) crochet hook or New International size No. 3.00(3.50–3.50). Waist length narrow elastic. 4(5–6) small buttons.

MEASUREMENTS: To fit an 18″(20″–22″) chest. Length of Top: 9″(11″–14″). Length of sleeve: 4″(6″–8″). Width of pants at widest part: 23″. Length of pants: 11″.

TENSION: 12(11–10) tr measure 2″.

NOTE: Increase by working twice into same st; decrease by taking 2 sts tog thus: insert hook into next st and pull through a loop, insert hook into foll sts and pull through another loop, wool over hook and pull through all 3 loops.

TOP: [Main part worked in one piece.] Beg at neck edge. With No. 11(10–9) hook make 61 ch. **1st row:** [Right side.] Work 1 tr into 3rd ch from hook and every foll ch to end. [59 tr] 1 ch, turn. **2nd row:** Work 1 dc in each of first 3 tr, * 2 dc in next tr, 1 dc in each of 3 foll tr; rep from * to end [73 dc], 2 ch, turn. **3rd row and every alt row:** Work 1 tr in each dc to end, 1 ch, turn. **4th row:** 1 dc in each of first 4 tr, * 2 dc in next tr, 1 dc in each of next 3 tr; rep from * to last tr, 1 dc in last tr [90 dc], 2 ch, turn. **6th row:** As 4th to last 2 tr, 1 dc in each of last 2 tr [111 dc], 2 ch, turn. **8th row:** 1 dc in each of first 5 tr, * 2 dc in next tr, 1 dc in each of next 3 tr; rep from * to last 2 tr, 1 dc in each of last 2 tr [137 dc], 2 ch, turn. **10th row:** As 8th row to last 4 tr, 1 dc in each of 4 tr [169 dc], 2 ch, turn. **12th row:** Working in dc inc in 9th tr and every foll 4th tr to last 9 sts, 1 dc in each of last 9 tr [207 dc], 5 ch, turn. **Commence lace patt.** ** **Next row:** 5 tr into 3rd dc, * miss 2 dc, 1 tr 2 ch 1 tr in next dc, miss 2 dc, 5 tr in next dc; rep from * to last 6 dc, miss 2 dc, 1 tr 2 ch 1 tr into next dc, miss 2 dc, 1 tr in last dc. ** [34 patt each one consisting of one 5 tr group and one tr 2 ch 1 tr sp], 5 ch, turn. **Next row:** * 5 tr in first sp, 1 tr 2 ch 1 tr into 3rd tr of 5 tr group; rep from * to end, 1 tr in top of t ch. This row forms main patt. Work 1 more row. **Divide for armholes. Next row:** Work 6 patt [consisting of 42 tr], miss next 38 tr [5 patts], beg with 5 tr in next sp, work 12 patt [84 tr], miss 38 tr, 5 tr in next sp, work remaining 5 patts, 5 ch, turn. [24 patts.] Rep patt row until 9″ (11″–14″) have been worked from neck edge. Fasten off.

SLEEVES: With wrong side of work facing, rejoin wool to 3rd tr of 6th group in yoke, 5 ch, 5 tr in next sp, patt to last group left free, 1 tr 2 ch 1 tr in centre tr, 5 tr in hole after next group in previous row, 1 tr 2 ch, 1 tr in next hole, 1 tr in same tr as beg, where wool is rejoined. [6 patts.] 5 ch, turn. Cont working in main patt for 3″(5″–7″), turning last row with 1 ch. **Next row:** 2 dc in each sp and 1 dc in each tr in group to end [42 dc] 1 ch, turn. **Next row:** * Working in dc work 1, dec 1; rep from * to end [28 dc] 1 ch, turn. Work 8 more rows dc. 5 ch turn. *** **Next row:** 4 tr into first dc, * miss 1 dc, 1 tr 2 ch 1 tr in next dc, miss 1 dc, 5 tr in next dc; rep from * to last 3 dc, miss 1 dc, 1 tr 2 ch 1 tr in next dc, 1 tr in last dc, 5 ch, turn. *** Work 1 more row of main patt. Fasten off. With wrong side of work facing, rejoin wool to centre of 12th group from end and complete to match first sleeve.

BUTTON BAND: With right side of work facing, work 53(65–83) dc along Left Back edge, 1 ch, turn. Work 4 more rows dc. Fasten off.

BUTTONHOLE BAND: Work as for Button Band, making 4(5–6) buttonholes in 3rd and 4th rows as folls: Beg at neck edge work 2 dc, * 3 ch, miss 3 dc, work 8(10–10) dc; rep from * 2(3–4) times more, 3 ch, miss 3, work to end. **Next row:** Work 3 dc into each 3 ch sp.

NECK EDGING: With right side of work facing, work 48 dc along neck edge, working together every 4th and 5th tr of 1st row. Work 1 more row dc, then rep from *** to *** of Sleeve cuff. Fasten off.

PANTS: [Back and Front alike.] **Beg at top.** With No. 11(10–9) hook make 58 ch. Work 1 dc in 2nd ch from hook and every foll ch to end. [57 dc.] 1 ch, turn. Work 2 more rows dc, 2 ch turn. Work 1 row tr, 2 rows dc, 5 ch, turn. Rep from ** to ** of Angel Top. 9 patts. Work 15 more rows main patt. **Next row:** 2 dc in each sp and 1 dc in each tr in group to end. [63 dc], 2 ch turn. Work 1 tr in each dc to end, 1 ch, turn. **Next row:** Working in dc * work 1, dec 1; rep from * to end. [42 dc], 2 ch, turn. Work 1 row tr, 1 row dc twice, then 1 more row tr turning each row as before. **Next row:** In dc dec all along row. 21 dc. Work 15 more rows dc, dec each end of 4th and 8th rows. Fasten off. Join both pieces at lower edge. With right side of work facing beg at last 2 rows of main patt and work 64 dc along each leg edge. Work 1 more row dc then rep from *** to *** as for Sleeve edge. Work 1 more row patt. Fasten off.

TO MAKE UP: Press lightly with a warm iron over a damp cloth. Join sleeve seams. Press seams. Sew on buttons. Join side seams of pants. Press seams. Thread elastic through the row of trs at top.

Matinee jacket and a Shawl

Instructions are for a 16″ chest. Changes for 18″ and 20″ sizes are given in brackets.

MATERIALS: 3(4–4) ozs of Marriner Bri-Nylon 3-ply. No. 12 wool crochet hook or New International size No. 2.50. 1¼ yds narrow ribbon. 6 small buttons.

MEASUREMENTS: To fit a 16″(18″–20″) chest. Length at centre back: 7¾″(8¼″–8¾″). Sleeve seam: 5½″ (6″–6½″).

TENSION: 2 shells and 4 rows to 1″ over pattern.

BACK: Beg at left shoulder and sleeve. Make a loose ch of 48(54–60) sts. **1st row:** Work 2 h tr 1 ch 2 h tr into 3rd ch from hook – called 1 shell – * miss 2 ch, 1 shell into next ch; rep from * to end, 1 ch, turn. 16(18–20) shells. **2nd row:** Work 1 shell into each ch space in centre of shells in 1st row. ** Work 24 ch. Break off yarn. **Work right shoulder and sleeve.** Work as given for left shoulder to **, 1 ch, turn. **Next row:** Work 1 shell into each ch space as before, work 8 shells along 24 ch sts of left side and 1 shell into each ch space to end, 1 ch, turn. 40(44–48) shells. Work 12 rows in patt across all sts. Break off yarn. Rejoin yarn to 12th(13th–14th) shell from sleeve edge, work 1 shell into this space and 1 shell into next 17(19–21) shells. Work 5″(5½″–6″) on these centre 18(20–22) shells. Fasten off.

LEFT FRONT: Join yarn to neck edge of starting ch for Back. Work 1 shell into bottom centre of each shell. 16(18–20) shells. Work 7 rows in patt, ending at centre front. Work 15 ch, turn. **9th row:** Work 1 shell into 3rd ch from hook, * miss 2 ch, 1 shell into next ch; rep from * 3 times more, making 5 shells worked over ch, work in patt across rem 16(18–20) shells. 21(23–25) shells. Work 6 rows, ending at sleeve edge. Break off yarn. Rejoin yarn to 12th(13th–14th) shell from sleeve edge. Work 1 shell into this space and 9(10–11) shells to front edge. 10(11–12) shells. Work until Front measures same as Back. Fasten off.

RIGHT FRONT: Work as given for Left Front reversing all shaping.

TO MAKE UP: Join side and sleeve seams matching patts, with a woven flat seam. **Work buttonholes and neck edging.** With right side of work facing rejoin yarn to centre front at 7th scallop from neck edge on Right Front. **Next row:** * 3 ch, 1 sl st into centre edge of next scallop; rep from * to neck edge [6 buttonholes made], work shells round neck edge working 1 shell into each shell and 1 sl st into each corner. Fasten off at left edge. Press lightly under a dry cloth with a warm iron. Sew on buttons and slot ribbon through sleeve edges 1 shell from edge. Slot ribbon round neck.

MEASUREMENTS: Approximately $34\frac{1}{2}'' \times 34\frac{1}{2}''$, vith edging.
MATERIALS: 9 ozs of Patons 3-ply Baby Wool. No. 9 wool crochet hook or New International size No. 3.50.
TENSION: 1 motif measures approximately $3\frac{1}{4}'' \times 3\frac{1}{4}''$.
1st MOTIF: Make 8 ch and join into a circle with a l st into first ch. **1st round:** Work 16 dc into circle, oining with a sl st into first dc. **2nd round:** 5 ch, * niss 1 dc, 1 h tr into next st, 3 ch; rep from * 6 times nore, join with a sl st into second of 5 ch. 8 spaces nade. **3rd round:** Work 1 dc, 1 h tr, 3 tr, 1 h tr, 1 dc nto each space, join with a sl st into first dc. 8 petals nade. **4th round:** 2 ch, * 3 ch, 1 dc into top of next etal, 6 ch, 1 dc into top of next petal, 3 ch, 1 h tr into pace before dc at beg of next petal, 3 ch, 1 h tr into ame space as last h tr; rep from * twice more, 3 ch, dc into top of next petal, 6 ch, 1 dc into top of next etal, 3 ch, 1 h tr into space before dc at beg of next etal, 3 ch, join with a sl st to first of 3 ch. **5th round:** 4 ch, 3 tr 3 ch 3 tr into 6 ch space, 4 ch, 1 dc into tr, 1 dc into next 3 ch space, 1 dc into top of next tr; rep from * to end of round, join with a sl st into rst of 4 ch. **6th round:** * 5 ch, 1 tr into each of next tr, 5 ch, insert hook into 3rd ch from hook and work dc to form picot. 2 ch, 1 tr into each of next 3 tr, ch, 1 sl st into next dc, 4 ch, insert hook into 3rd ch rom hook and work 1 dc to form picot, 1 ch, miss 1 c, 1 sl st into next dc; rep from * to end of round, in with a sl st into first of 5 ch. Fasten off.
nd MOTIF: Work as given for 1st motif until 5th ound has been completed. **6th round:** 5 ch, 1 tr into ach of next 3 tr, 2 ch, 1 dc into corner picot of 1st otif, 2 ch, 1 tr into each of next 3 tr of 2nd motif, 1 sl st into first of 5 ch after tr of 1st motif, 4 ch, 1 sl st into next dc of 2nd Motif, 1 ch, 1 dc into centre side picot of 1st motif, 1 ch, miss 1 dc on 2nd motif, 1 sl st into next dc, 4 ch, 1 sl st into ch before next 3 tr on 1st motif, 1 tr into each of next 3 tr on 2nd motif, 2 ch, 1 sl st into picot at end of 1st motif, 2 ch, now complete this round as given for 1st motif. Work 98 more motifs, joining one side to previous motif in same way until there are 10 motifs in a row, then join other motifs to this row in same way until there are 10 rows. 100 motifs in all.
EDGING: Join wool to right-hand corner of 1st motif with a sl st. **1st round:** * 6 ch, 1 dc into third of 3 tr on previous round, 6 ch, 1 dc into centre picot, 6 ch, 1 dc into first of 3 tr, 6 ch, 1 dc into joining picot; rep from * all round sides, joining with a sl st to first of 6 ch. **2nd round:** * 4 ch, 1 dc into next space, 6 ch, 1 dc into next dc, 8 ch, 1 dc into next space, 12 ch, 1 dc into next space, 8 ch, 1 dc into next dc, 6 ch, 1 dc into next space, 4 ch, 1 dc into next dc; rep from * all round, joining with a sl st into first of 4 ch. **3rd round:** * 2 ch, 1 dc into next space, 2 ch, 1 sl st into next dc, 3 ch, 1 dc into next space, 3 ch, 1 sl st into next dc, into next space work [1 dc, 1 h tr, 2 tr, work 1 picot by forming 3 ch and working 1 dc into first ch, 2 tr, 1 h tr, 1 dc], 1 sl st into next dc, into next space work [1 dc, 1 h tr, 4 tr, 1 picot, 4 tr, 1 h tr, 1 dc], 1 sl st into next dc, into next space work [1 dc, 1 h tr, 2 tr, 1 picot, 2 tr, 1 h tr, 1 dc], 1 sl st into next dc, 3 ch, 1 dc into next space, 3 ch, 1 sl st into next dc, 2 ch, 1 dc into next space, 2 ch, 1 sl st into next dc; rep from * all round, join with a sl st into first of 2 ch. Fasten off.
TO MAKE UP: Sew in all ends. Press lightly under a damp cloth with a warm iron.

Crochet in the house is becoming as popular nowadays as crocheted clothes. On the following pages we give you some designs. The cushions can be adapted to make rugs or bedspreads simply by making more squares.

Double bedspread

MATERIALS: 7 lbs 13 ozs of Sirdar Double Crepe. No. 6 wool crochet hook or New International size No. 5.00.
MEASUREMENTS: Each square measures 6″ × 6″. The flounce is 16″ deep.
TENSION: 7 tr to 2″ across.
EACH SQUARE: Make 4 ch and join into a ring with a sl st into first ch. **1st round:** 3 ch [to stand as 1 tr] 2 tr into ring [3 ch, 3 tr] into ring 3 times, 3 ch, sl st into top of 3 ch at beg of round, 5 ch, turn. **2nd round:** * 3 tr into corner sp, 3 ch, 3 tr in same corner sp, * 2 ch; rep from * to * once, 2 ch, rep from * to * once, 2 ch, rep from * to * once, 2 ch, sl st into 3rd of 5 ch at beg of round. **3rd round:** 3 ch, 2 tr in next sp [3 ch stands as first tr of this block], * 2 ch, 3 tr, 3 ch, 3 tr in corner sp, 2 ch, 3 tr in next sp; rep from * to end of round, ending with 2 ch, sl st into 3rd of 3 ch at beg of round. **4th round:** 5 ch, 3 tr in next sp, work corner sp as for previous round and continue in this manner working 3 tr in each 2 ch sp and 2 blocks of 3 tr in each corner sp with 3 ch between the blocks, ending with a sl st. Continue to work in this manner, enlarging the square on each row alternately beg rounds with 3 ch and 5 ch and continuing until 7 rounds in all have been worked. Fasten off. Work 125 more squares in same way, making 14 rows of 9 squares each.
TO MAKE UP: Lightly press each square with a warm iron over a damp cloth. Join squares neatly, 9 in a row, and press lightly again.
FLOUNCE: Each edge is worked separately. Join wool at corner of one of the shorter edges. **1st row:** 3 ch [to stand as first tr], 2 tr in first sp, 2 ch, 3 tr i same sp, * 2 ch, 1 tr in next sp, 2 ch, 3 tr 2 ch 3 tr i next sp; rep from * to end. 3 ch, turn. **2nd row:** 3 t 2 ch 3 tr in 2 ch sp between 2 blocks of tr, * 2 ch, 1 t on 1 tr, 2 ch, 3 tr 2 ch 3 tr in sp between blocks of tr rep from * to end. Rep 2nd row 4 times more, turnin last row with 3 ch. **Next row:** 4 tr 2 ch 4 tr in first s between blocks of tr, * 2 ch, 1 tr on tr, 2 ch, 4 tr 2 c 4 tr between the 2 blocks of tr; rep from * to end. Re last row 8 times more, turning last row with 3 ch **Next row:** 5 tr 2 ch 5 tr between blocks of tr, * 2 ch 1 tr on 1 tr, 2 ch, 5 tr 2 ch 5 tr between blocks of t rep from * to end. Rep last row 8 times more. Faste off.
LONG FLOUNCES: Neaten other short edge wit 1 row tr. Make 19 ch, miss 3 ch [3 tr 2 ch 3 tr] in nex ch, 2 ch, miss 3 ch, 1 tr in next ch, 2 ch, miss 3 ch [tr 2 ch 3 tr] in next ch, 2 ch, miss 3 ch, 1 tr in nex ch, 2 ch. Now work across one long side beg at corne of shorter flounce and noting that the extra piece jus worked is sewn on over the shorter flounce. Continu as given for shorter flounce. Fasten off. Work 2nd lon side to match but ending the 1st row by workin across 19 ch made separately.
TO MAKE UP: Sew on the extra pieces over th short flounce at lower corners. Press out each flounc to measure 16″ in depth.
SMALL ROSETTES: Make 4 ch and join into ring with a sl st. Into ring work 1 ch [3 tr 1 dc] times, ending with a sl st into 1 ch. Fasten off, leavin a long end for sewing. Make 125 more rosettes in sam way. Sew a rosette to centre of each square.

JEAN CAILAC

Single bedspread & Cushions

MEASUREMENTS: 8′ × 5′ without fringe.
MATERIALS: 6 lbs 12 ozs Sirdar Double Crepe. No. 5 wool crochet hook or New International size No. 5.50.
TENSION: 4 tr to 1″ across.
CENTRE PIECE: Make 146 ch loosely. **1st row:** Miss 3 ch, make 1 tr in each ch to end. [144 tr including 3 ch at beg which stands as first tr.] Turn with 3 ch. **2nd row:** 1 tr in 2nd tr [3 ch at beg of rows stands as first tr throughout], 1 tr in next tr, * wool over hook, hook through next tr, wool over hook and through same tr 5 times, wool over hook and pull through all loops on hook – called B1 – 1 tr in next 3 tr; rep from * to end. Turn with 3 ch. **3rd row:** 1 tr in each tr. Turn with 3 ch. **4th row:** B1 on 2nd tr from hook, * 1 tr in next 3 tr, B1 on next tr; rep from * to end. Turn with 3 ch. These 4 rows form patt. Continue in patt until work measures 8′ from beg. Fasten off.
RIGHT SIDE STRIP: Make 50 ch loosely. **1st row:** Miss 3 ch, 1 tr in each ch to end. [48 tr including 3 ch at beg.] **2nd row:** Work 4th row of patt as given fc Centre Piece. **3rd row:** 1 tr in each tr. **4th row:** Wor 2nd row of patt as given for Centre Piece. Cont unt side strip measures same as Centre Piece. Fasten of
LEFT SIDE STRIP: Work as given for Right Sid Strip.
TO MAKE UP: Press lightly on wrong side with warm iron over a damp cloth. Join seams. Press sean lightly.
FRINGING: Cut pieces of wool 21″ in length. Tak 4 strands of wool, fold in half, and with right side work facing loop these strands through the first spa on one short side of bedspread, i.e. the spaces a between the tr. Rep all round bedspread, spacin strands between every 3rd and 4th tr along short sid and missing one row along long sides. **2nd roun** Take 4 strands from one tassel and 4 strands from tl next tassel and knot them together 1″ down, rep a round. **3rd round:** Take the 2 ends from the origin tassel and knot them together 1″ down, rep all roun

MATERIALS: Cushion takes 4 ozs Lee Target Motoravia Double Knitting in assorted colours if only one side of the cover is to be crocheted, or double this quantity if both sides are to be crocheted. No. 6 crochet hook or New International size No. 5.00.
MEASUREMENTS: Cover measures approximately 16″ × 16″.
TENSION: 9 sts to 2″ over dc on No. 6 hook.
COVER: With No. 6 hook and 1st colour make 6 ch and join into a circle with a sl st. **1st round:** 3 ch, 3 tr into ring [3 ch, 4 tr into ring] 3 times, 3 ch, sl st to 3rd of 3 ch at beg of round. Break off 1st colour. **2nd round:** Join in 2nd colour to 3 ch sp, into same sp work 4 ch, 1 tr, 1 ch, 1 tr, 3 ch [1 tr, 1 ch] 3 times, into each of next 3 spaces work [1 tr, 1 ch] twice, 1 tr, 3 ch [1 tr, 1 ch] 3 times, ending with sl st into 3rd of 4 ch. Break off 2nd colour. **3rd round:** Join in 3rd colour to 1 ch sp in centre of 2 groups of tr, 1 dc in same sp, 1 ch, * 1 dc in next sp, 1 ch; rep from * to corner, 1 dc 3 ch 1 dc 1 ch into 3 ch sp at corner, rep from first * 3 times more, ** 1 dc in sp, 1 ch; rep from ** to end of round, sl st to dc. Varying colours as required rep 3rd round throughout, remembering to work 1 dc, 3 ch, 1 dc, 1 ch at each corner on every round, until work measures 16″ across. Break wool and fasten off.
TO MAKE UP: Make another piece in same way if required or cut piece of felt 16″ × 16″ and sew to crochet piece for back.
NOTE: This cover can be made larger or smaller by adding or subtracting the number of rounds worked. If a larger cover is required remember to allow for extra wool. A number of these squares can also be joined together to make a bedspread.

MATERIALS: 2 ozs Lee Target Motoravia Double Knitting in main shade A; 3 ozs each in contrasts B, C and D. For 1 side only. No. 8 crochet hook or New International size No. 4.00.
MEASUREMENTS: Cover measures 16″ × 16″.
TENSION: Each motif measures 4″ × 4″.
COVER: With No. 8 hook and B make 6 ch and join into a circle with a sl st. **1st round:** 3 ch, 3 tr into ring, * 3 ch, 4 tr into ring; rep from * twice more, 3 ch, sl st to 3rd of first 3 ch. Break off B. **2nd round:** Join in C to first 3 ch sp, 3 ch, 3 tr 3 ch 4 tr into the same sp, * [1 ch, 4 tr, 3 ch, 4 tr] into next sp. Rep from * twice more, 1 ch, sl st to 3rd of 3 ch. Break off C. **3rd round:** Join in D to first 3 ch sp, 3 ch, 3 tr 3 ch 4 tr into the same sp, * 1 ch, 4 tr into 1 ch sp, 1 ch, 4 tr 3 ch 4 tr into 3 ch sp; rep from * twice more, 1 ch, 4 tr into 1 ch sp, 1 ch, sl st to 3rd of 3 ch. Break off D. **4th round:** Join in A to first 3 ch sp, 4 ch, 1 tr 1 ch 1 tr into same sp, * 1 ch, 1 tr between 2nd and 3rd of 4 tr, 1 ch, 1 tr into 1 ch sp; rep from * once more, 1 ch, 1 tr between 2nd and 3rd of 4 tr, 1 ch 1 tr 3 times into 3 ch sp; rep from first * twice more [1 ch, 1 tr between 2nd and 3rd of 4 tr, 1 ch, 1 tr in 1 ch sp] twice, 1 ch, 1 tr between 2nd and 3rd of 4 tr, 1 ch, sl st to 3rd of 4 ch. Break off A. Fasten off. Sew in all ends. Make 15 more motifs in same way, changing 3 centre colours as required but keeping A for 4th round.
TO MAKE UP: With A join motifs into 4 strips of 4 using a woven flat seam and working into top loop only of last round. For Back make another square in same way and sew to first piece or cut a piece of felt to same size and sew to crochet piece. Larger or smaller covers can be made by working fewer or more squares, but remember to allow for extra wool.

The old-fashioned beauty of delicately fine crochet

Lace table mat

MATERIALS: 1 ball Coats Chain-Mercer Crochet No. 20. No. 3 crochet hook or New International size No. 1.25.
MEASUREMENTS: Mat measures 12″ in diameter.
TENSION: First 3 rows measure 2″ in diameter.
Commence with 12 ch, join with a sl st to form a ring.
1st row: 4 ch, 29 d tr into ring, 1 sl st into 4th of 4 ch.
2nd row: 1 dc into same place as sl st, * 3 ch, miss 1 d tr, 1 dc into next d tr; rep from * ending with 3 ch, 1 sl st into first dc. [15 loops.]
3rd row: 1 sl st into first loop, 4 ch, leaving last loop of each on hook work 2 d tr into same loop, thread over and draw through all loops on hook [a 2 d tr cluster made], * 5 ch a 3 d tr cluster into next loop; rep from * ending with 5 ch, 1 sl st into first cluster.
4th row: 1 sl st into each of next 3 ch, 1 dc into same loop, * 6 ch, 1 dc into next loop; rep from * ending with 6 ch, 1 sl st into first dc.
5th row: 1 sl st into first loop, 3 ch, 5 tr into same loop, 6 tr into each loop, 1 sl st into 3rd of 3 ch.
6th row: 1 dc into same place as sl st, * 3 ch, miss 2 tr, 1 dc into next tr; rep from * ending with 3 ch, 1 sl st into first dc. [30 loops.]
7th row: 1 sl st into last loop made, 3 ch, * 1 tr into next loop, 3 ch, 1 tr into top of last tr [a picot made], 1 tr into same loop; rep from * ending with 1 tr into same loop as first sl st, a picot, 1 sl st into 3rd of 3 ch.
8th row: 6 ch, 1 tr into 4th ch from hook [another picot made], 1 tr into next tr, * 1 ch, 1 tr into next tr, a picot, 1 tr into next tr; rep from * ending with 1 ch, 1 sl st into same ch as first picot.
9th row: 1 sl st into last loop made, 6 ch, 1 tr into 4th ch from hook, 1 tr into same sp as sl st, * 3 ch, into next 1 ch sp work 1 tr, a picot and 1 tr; rep from * ending with 1 ch, 1 tr into same ch as first picot.
10th row: 6 ch, 1 tr into 4th ch from hook, 1 tr into top of tr of previous row, * 5 ch, miss next picot, in centre ch of next 3 ch work 1 tr a picot and 1 tr; rep from * ending with 2 ch, 1 tr into same ch as first picot.
11th row: As 10th, working into centre ch of 5 ch instead of 3 ch.
12th row: 6 ch, 1 tr into 4th ch from hook, 1 tr into top of tr of previous row, * 7 ch, miss next picot, in centre ch of next 5 ch work 1 tr a picot and 1 tr; rep from * ending with 3 ch, 1 d tr into same ch as first picot.
13th row: As 12th, working into d tr instead of tr and into centre ch of 7 ch instead of 5 ch.
14th row: 6 ch, 1 tr into 4th ch from hook, 1 tr into top of d tr of previous row, * 9 ch, miss next picot, into centre ch of next 7 ch work 1 tr a picot and 1 tr; rep from * ending with 4 ch, 1 d tr into same ch as first picot.
15th row: 3 ch, into top of d tr of previous row work 1 tr 2 ch and 2 tr, * 7 ch, into centre ch of next 9 ch work 2 tr 6 ch and 2 tr [7 ch, into centre ch of next 9 ch work 2 tr 2 ch and 2 tr] twice; rep from * 8 times more, 7 ch, into centre ch of next 9 ch work 2 tr 6 ch and 2 tr, 7 ch, into centre ch of next 9 ch work 2 tr 2 ch and 2 tr, 7 ch, 1 sl st into 3rd of 3 ch.
16th row: 1 sl st into next tr and into sp, 3 ch, into same sp work 1 tr 2 ch and 2 tr [a shell made over a shell], * 5 ch, 10 d tr into next 6 ch sp, 5 ch, into next shell work 2 tr 2 ch and 2 tr [another shell made over a shell], 7 ch, a shell over next shell; rep from * omitting a shell at end of last rep, 1 sl st into 3rd of 3 ch.
17th row: 1 sl st into next tr and into sp, 3 ch, into same sp work 1 tr 2 ch and 2 tr, * 3 ch [1 d tr into next d tr, 1 ch] 9 times, 1 d tr into next d tr, 3 ch, a shell over next shell, 5 ch, a shell over next shell; rep from * omitting a shell at end of last rep, 1 sl st into 3rd of 3 ch.
Complete Pineapples individually as follows:
1st row: 1 sl st into next tr and into sp, 3 ch, into same sp work 1 tr 2 ch and 2 tr, 3 ch, miss 3 ch, 1 dc into next ch sp [3 ch, 1 dc into next 1 ch sp] 8 times, 3 ch, a shell over next shell, 5 ch, turn.
2nd row: A shell over shell, 3 ch, miss 3 ch, 1 dc into next 3 ch loop [3 ch, 1 dc into next 3 ch loop] 7 times, 3 ch, a shell over next shell, 5 ch, turn. Continue this way until one 3 ch loop remains, 5 ch, turn.
Next row: A shell over shell, 4 ch, miss 3 ch, 1 dc into next 3 ch loop, 4 ch, a shell over next shell, 5 ch, turn.
Next row: [A shell over shell] twice. Fasten off. Attach thread to sp of next free shell on 17th row and complete pineapple as before. Work all in this way.
Edging. 1st row: Attach thread to 5 ch sp at base of 2 pineapples, 1 dc into same sp, 5 ch, into turning 5 ch loop at side of pineapple work 1 tr a picot and 1 tr, * 3 ch, into next turning 5 ch loop work 1 tr a

icot and 1 tr; rep from * twice more, 3 ch, into next hell at tip of pineapple work 1 tr a picot and 1 tr, ch, into next shell work 1 tr a picot and 1 tr, ** 3 h, in next turning 5 ch loop work 1 tr a picot and 1 r; rep from ** 4 times more, 5 ch, 1 dc into next 5 ch p at base of pineapple, 5 ch, into turning 5 ch loop f next pineapple work 1 tr a picot and 1 tr; rep from rst * omitting 1 dc 5 ch 1 tr a picot and 1 tr at end f last rep, 1 sl st into first dc. Fasten off.

2nd row: Attach thread to first 3 ch sp between picots at side of pineapple, 6 ch, 1 tr into 4th ch from hook, 1 tr into same sp, * 5 ch, into next 3 ch sp between picots work 1 tr a picot and 1 tr; rep from * 8 times more, miss first picot on next pineapple, into next 3 ch sp between picots work 1 tr a picot and 1 tr; rep from first * omitting 1 tr a picot and 1 tr at end of last rep, 1 sl st into 3rd of 6 ch. Fasten off. Damp and pin out to measurements.

Spinning wheel and Star

MATERIALS: Coats Chain Mercer-Crochet No. 60 and crochet hook No. 5 or New International size No. 0.75.

MEASUREMENTS: Motif measures 2½″ in diameter.

1st MOTIF: Commence with 10 ch and join into a circle with a sl st.

1st row: 4 ch, leaving the last loop of each on hook work 2 d tr into ring, thread over and draw through all loops on hook [a 2 d tr cluster made], * 6 ch, a 3 d tr cluster into ring; rep from * 8 times more, 6 ch, 1 sl st into first cluster.

2nd row: 1 sl st into each of first 3 ch, 1 dc into same loop, * 7 ch, into next loop work [a 3 d tr cluster, 5 ch] twice, and a 3 d tr cluster, 7 ch, 1 dc into next loop; rep from * omitting 1 dc at end of last rep, 1 sl st into first dc.

3rd row: 1 sl st into each of first 4 ch, 1 dc into same loop, * 7 ch, 1 dc into next loop; rep from * ending with 7 ch, 1 sl st into first dc.

4th row: 1 sl st into each of first 3 ch, 1 dc into next ch, * 5 ch, 1 dc into centre ch of next loop; rep from * ending with 5 ch, 1 sl st into first dc.

5th row: 1 sl st into each of first 3 ch, 3 ch, into same place as last sl st work 1 tr 2 ch and 2 tr, * 2 ch, in centre ch of next loop work 2 tr 2 ch and 2 tr; rep from * ending with 2 ch, 1 sl st into 3rd of 3 ch.

6th row: 1 sl st into next tr, 1 sl st into next sp, 3 ch, into same sp work 2 tr 3 ch and 3 tr, * 1 dc into next sp, into next sp work 3 tr 3 ch and 3 tr; rep from * ending with 1 dc into next sp, 1 sl st into 3rd of 3 ch. Fasten off.

2nd MOTIF: Work as for 1st motif for 5 rows.

6th row: 1 sl st into next tr, 1 sl st into next sp, 3 ch, 2 tr into same sp, 1 ch, 1 sl st into any sp on 1st motif, 1 ch, 3 tr into same sp on 2nd motif [1 dc into next sp, 3 tr into next sp, 1 ch, 1 sl st into next sp on 1st motif, 1 ch, 3 tr into same sp on 2nd motif] twice. Complete as 1st motif.

Make 2 more motifs, joining to make a square, having 2 sps free between joinings.

FILLING: Attach thread to first free sp to left of any join on inside edge, 6 ch, * 1 d tr into next free sp, 2 ch; rep from * 6 times more, 1 sl st into 4th of 6 ch. Fasten off. This motif can be made larger if required by making more motifs and joining in same way.

MATERIALS: Coats Chain Mercer-Crochet No. 40. No. 4 crochet hook or New International size No. 1.00.
TENSION: Motif measures 2¾″.
1st MOTIF: Commence with 6 ch and join with a sl st to form a circle.
1st row: * 1 dc into circle, 5 ch; rep from * 3 times more, 1 sl st into first dc.
2nd row: 1 sl st into each of first 2 ch, 3 dc into same loop, * 5 ch, 3 dc into next loop; rep from * omitting 3 dc at end of last rep.
3rd row: 1 dc into each of next 3 dc, * 5 ch, 2 dc into next loop, 1 dc into each of next 3 dc; rep from * omitting 3 dc at end of last rep.
4th row: 1 dc into each of next 3 dc, * 5 ch, 2 dc into next loop, 1 dc into each of next 5 dc; rep from * omitting 3 dc at end of last rep.
5th row: 1 dc into each of next 3 dc, * 5 ch, 2 dc into next loop, 1 dc into each of next 7 dc; rep from * omitting 3 dc at end of last rep.
6th row: 1 dc into each of next 3 dc, * 5 ch, 1 dc into next loop, 1 dc into each of next 9 dc; rep from * omitting 3 dc at end of last rep.
7th row: 1 dc into each of next 3 dc, * 5 ch, 1 dc into next loop, 1 dc into each of next 10 dc; rep from * omitting 3 dc at end of last rep.
8th row: 1 dc into each of next 3 dc, * 8 ch, miss 1 dc, 1 dc into each of next 10 dc; rep from * omitting 3 dc at end of last rep.
9th row: 1 dc into each of next 3 dc, * 5 ch, 1 dc into next loop, 5 ch, miss 1 dc, 1 dc into each of next 9 dc; rep from * omitting 3 dc at end of last rep.
10th row: 1 dc into each of next 3 dc, * [5 ch, 1 dc into next loop] twice, 5 ch, miss 1 dc, 1 dc into each of next 8 dc; rep from * omitting 3 dc at end of last rep.
11th row: 1 dc into each of next 2 dc, * 5 ch, 1 dc in next loop, 5 ch, 4 tr into next loop, 5 ch, 1 dc into next loop, 5 ch, miss 1 dc, 1 dc into each of next 6 dc; rep from * omitting 2 dc at end of last rep.
12th row: 1 dc into next dc, * [5 ch, 1 dc into next loop] twice, 10 ch [1 dc into next loop, 5 ch] twice, miss 1 dc, 1 dc into each of next 4 dc; rep from * omitting 1 dc at end of last rep, 1 sl st into next dc.
13th row: 1 sl st into each of next 3 ch, 1 dc into same loop, * 5 ch, 1 dc into next loop, 5 ch, into next loop work 4 tr 3 ch and 4 tr [5 ch, 1 dc into next loop] twice, 2 ch, miss 1 dc, leaving the last loop of each on hook work 1 tr into each of next 2 dc, thread over and draw through all loops on hook [a 2 tr cluster made], 2 ch, 1 dc into next loop; rep from * omitting 1 dc at end of last rep, 1 sl st into first dc.
14th row: 1 sl st into each of next 3 ch, 1 dc into same loop, * 5 ch, 1 dc into next loop, 5 ch, 5 tr into next sp [5 ch, 1 dc into next loop] twice, 10 ch, miss 2 sps, 1 dc into next loop; rep from * omitting 1 dc at end of last rep, 1 sl st into first dc.

15th row: * [4 dc into next loop, 3 ch, 1 sl st into last dc – a picot made, 3 dc into same loop] twice, 1 dc into each of next 3 tr, 7 ch, 1 sl st into last dc [a corner picot made], 1 dc into each of next 2 tr [into next loop work 4 dc a picot and 3 dc] twice, into next loop work 6 dc a picot and 5 dc; rep from * ending with 1 sl st into first dc. Fasten off.
2nd MOTIF: Work as for 1st motif for 14 rows.
15th row: [Into next loop work 4 dc a picot and 3 dc] twice, 1 dc into each of next 3 tr, 3 ch, 1 dc into any corner picot on 1st motif, 3 ch, 1 sl st into last dc on 2nd motif [a joining corner picot made], 1 dc into each of next 2 tr [4 dc into next loop, 1 ch, 1 dc into next picot on 1st motif, 1 ch, 1 sl st into last dc on 2nd motif – a joining picot made, 3 dc into same loop] twice, into next loop work 6 dc a joining picot and 5 dc [into next loop work 4 dc a joining picot and 3 dc] twice, 1 dc into each of next 3 tr, a joining corner picot, 1 dc into each of next 2 tr, complete as 1st motif.
Make required number of motifs, joining adjacent sides as 2nd motif was joined to 1st. Where 4 corners meet join 3rd and 4th corners to joining of previous 2 corners.

Lace tablecloth

MATERIALS: 10 balls Coats Chain Mercer-Crochet No. 40. No. 4 crochet hook or New International size No. 1.00.
MEASUREMENTS: Cloth measures 35″ × 35″.
TENSION: Motif measures $3\frac{1}{2}$″ in diameter.
1st MOTIF: Commence with 6 ch and join into a ircle with a sl st.
1st row: 3 ch, 11 tr into ring, 1 sl st into 3rd of 3 ch.
2nd row: 1 dc into same place as last sl st, * 3 ch, 1 lc into next tr; rep from * 10 times more, 1 ch, 1 h tr nto first dc.
3rd row: * 4 ch, 1 dc into next loop; rep from * nding with 4 ch, 1 sl st into h tr of previous row. [12 oops.]
4th row: 1 sl st into first loop, 4 ch, leaving last loop f each on hook work 2 d tr into same loop, thread ver and draw through all loops on hook [a 2 d tr luster made], * 5 ch, a 3 d tr cluster into next loop; ep from * ending with 5 ch, 1 sl st into top of first luster.
5th row: 1 sl st into each of next 2 ch, 4 ch, a 2 d tr luster into sp, * 7 ch, a 3 d tr cluster into next sp; ep from * ending with 7 ch, 1 sl st into top of first luster.
6th row: 1 dc into same place as last sl st, * 5 ch, in ext sp work a 3 d tr cluster, 5 ch and a 3 d tr cluster, ch, 1 dc into top of next cluster; rep from * omitting dc at end of last rep, 1 sl st into first dc.
7th row: 1 sl st into each of next 2 ch, 1 dc into loop, 3 ch, into next 5 ch sp work 6 d tr with 1 ch between ach, 3 ch, 1 dc into each of next 2 loops; rep from * mitting 1 dc at end of last rep, 1 sl st into first c. **8th row:** * 3 dc into next sp [1 dc into next tr, 3 ch, 1 dc into top of last dc – picot made], times, 1 dc into next d tr, 3 dc into next sp; rep from * ending with 1 sl st into first dc. Fasten off.
2nd MOTIF: Work as for 1st motif for 7 rows.
8th row: * 3 dc into next sp [1 dc into next d tr, picot] twice, 1 dc into next d tr, 1 ch, 1 sl st into centre picot of corresponding point on 1st motif, 1 ch, 1 dc into top of last dc on 2nd motif [1 dc in next d tr, picot] twice, 1 dc into next d tr, 3 dc in next sp; rep from * once more, complete as for 1st motif.
Make 10 rows of 10 motifs, joining adjacent sides as 2nd was joined to 1st, leaving one point free on each motif between joinings.
FILLING: 1st row: Attach thread to centre picot of free point between motifs, 6 ch, 4 d tr with 2 ch between each into same picot, * 4 ch, miss 3 picots, leaving the last loop of each on hook work 1 tr tr into next picot, 1 tr tr into first free picot after joining of motifs, thread over and draw through all loops on hook [a joint tr tr made], 4 ch, 5 d tr with 2 ch between each into centre picot of next point; rep from * twice more, 4 ch, a joint tr tr over picots on each side of joining motifs, 4 ch, 1 sl st into 4th of 6 ch.
2nd row: 1 dc into same place as last sl st [2 dc in next sp, 1 dc into next d tr] twice, 8 ch, 1 dc into 3rd ch from hook, 1 dc into each of next 5 ch, 1 sl st into dc on top of d tr, * [2 dc into next sp, 1 dc into next d tr] twice, 4 dc into next sp, 1 dc into joint tr tr, 4 dc into next sp, 1 dc into next d tr [2 dc into next sp, 1 dc into next d tr] twice, 7 ch, remove hook, insert it into t ch of bar and draw loop through, 1 ch, miss 1 ch, 1 dc into each of next 6 ch, 1 sl st into dc on top of d tr; rep from * twice more [2 dc into next sp, 1 dc into next d tr] twice, 4 dc into next sp, 1 dc into joint tr tr, 4 dc into next sp, 1 sl st into first dc. Fasten off.
Fill in all spaces between motifs in same manner.
Damp and pin out to measurement.

Edgings

Edging for small cloth

MEASUREMENTS: Depth of edging = 1″.
MATERIALS: 1 ball Coats Chain Mercer-Crochet No. 20. No. 3 crochet hook or New International size No. 1.25. These quantities sufficient for 2 cloths measuring $12\frac{1}{4}'' \times 16\frac{1}{4}''$.
NOTE: Before beginning cut material to required size and withdraw a thread $\frac{1}{4}''$ from edge all round. Turn back a narrow hem.
EDGING: 1st row: Attach thread to any corner, 3 dc into same place at corner, work a row of dc [14 dc to 1″] over hem and into space of drawn thread, having a multiple of 10 dc plus 7 along each side and 3 dc into same place at each corner, 1 sl st into first dc.
2nd row: 1 sl st into centre dc at corner, 4 ch, miss 4 dc, 1 d tr into next dc, * 5 ch, leaving last loop of each on hook work 1 d tr into same place as last d tr, miss 4 dc, 1 d tr into next dc, thread over and draw through all loops on hook [a joint d tr made]; rep from * to next corner, 5 ch, 1 d tr 5 ch and 1 d tr into same corner dc, 5 ch, leaving last loop of each on hook work 1 d tr into same corner dc, miss 4 dc, 1 d tr into next dc, thread over and draw through all loops on hook [a joint d tr made]; rep from first * omitting joint d tr at end of last rep, 1 sl st into first d tr.
3rd row: 1 sl st into each of next 2 ch, 4 ch, leaving last loop of each on hook work 1 d tr into each of next 2 ch, thread over and draw through all loops on hook [a 2 d tr cluster made], * 5 ch, 1 d tr into centre ch of next loop, 5 ch, miss 1 ch of next loop, a 3 d tr cluster over next 3 ch; rep from * to next corner, 5 ch, 1 d tr into centre ch of next loop, 5 ch, a 3 d tr cluster over first 3 ch of next loop, 5 ch, a 3 d tr cluster in same ch as last d tr and over next 2 ch, 5 ch, 1 d tr in centre ch of next loop, 5 ch, miss 1 ch of next loop, a 3 d tr cluster over next 3 ch; rep from first * omitting 5 ch and a 3 d tr cluster at end of last rep, 2 ch, 1 tr into first cluster.
4th row: 1 dc into loop just formed, * 7 ch, 1 dc into centre ch of next loop; rep from * to next corner, 7 ch, into centre ch of corner loop work 1 d tr 7 ch and 1 d tr; rep from first * ending with 7 ch, 1 dc into centre ch of next loop, 7 ch, 1 sl st into first dc.
5th row: Into each loop work 3 dc, 3 ch and 3 dc, sl st into first dc. Fasten off.
Damp and pin out to measurements.

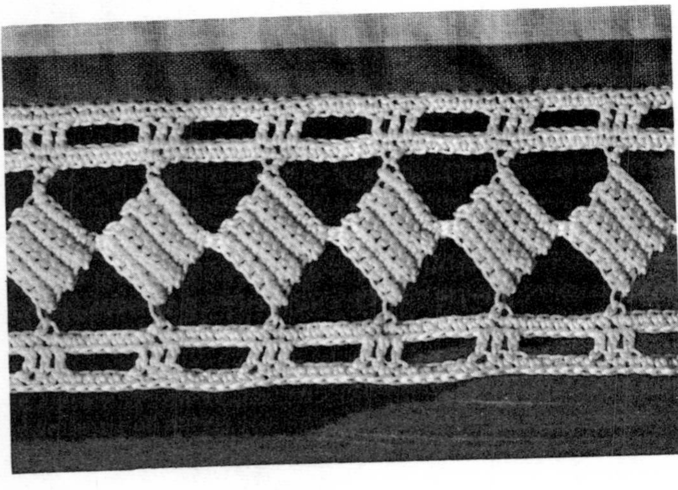

Ribbon threaded edging

MEASUREMENTS: Depth of edging: $3\frac{1}{2}''$.
MATERIALS: 5 balls Coats Chain Mercer-Crochet No. 20. No. 3 crochet hook or New International size No. 1.25. These quantities are suitable to trim 1 single sheet and 1 pillowcase. 6 yds $\frac{1}{4}''$ wide ribbon.
NOTE: Quad tr—quadruple treble; quin tr—quintuple treble. Quad tr worked as follows: work as for tr tr, see page 105, but working 1 more loop over hook. Quin tr worked as follows: work as for tr tr, see page 11, but working 2 more loops over hook.
EDGING: With No. 3 hook make ch required length, having a multiple of 12 ch plus 5.
1st row: 1 tr into 8th ch from hook, * 2 ch, miss 2 ch, 1 tr into next ch; rep from * to end, 5 ch, turn.
2nd row: Miss first tr, 1 tr into next tr, * 2 ch, 1 tr into next tr; rep from * ending with miss 2 ch, 1 tr into next ch, turn.
3rd row: 1 dc into first tr, 3 ch, miss next tr, * leaving last loop of each on hook, work 2 tr tr into next tr, thread over and draw through all loops on hook [cluster made], [4 ch, cluster into same tr] 3 times [4-cluster group made], 3 ch, miss next tr, 1 dc into next tr, 3 ch, miss next tr; rep from * omitting 3 ch at end of last rep and working last dc into 3rd of 5 ch, 8 ch, turn.
4th row: A 4-cluster group into centre loop of next 4-cluster group, 8 ch, 1 dc into next dc, 8 ch; rep from * omitting 8 ch 1 dc and 8 ch at end of last rep, 1 quin tr into last dc, turn.
5th row: 1 dc into first cluster, * [4 dc into next loop, 1 dc into next cluster] 3 times, 1 dc into next cluster; rep from * omitting 1 dc at end of last rep, 1 ch, turn.
6th row: Lifting front half of st only work 1 dc into each dc, 8 ch, turn.
7th row: Miss first 6 dc, * [1 cluster into next dc, 4 ch] 3 times, 1 cl into next dc, 8 ch, miss 5 dc, 1 dc into each of next 2 dc, 8 ch, miss 5 dc; rep from * omitting 8 ch 2 dc and 8 ch at end of last rep, 1 quin tr into last dc, turn.
8th row: 1 dc into first cluster, * 6 ch, a 4-cluster group into centre loop of next 4 tr group, 6 ch, 1 dc into last cluster of same group, 1 dc into first cluster of next group; rep from * omitting 6 ch and 2 dc at end of last rep, 1 quad tr into last cluster of group, turn.
9th row: * [1 dc into next cluster, 4 dc into next loop] 3 times, 1 dc into next cluster; rep from * to end, 1 ch, turn.
10th row: As 6th row, turning with 1 ch instead of 8 ch.
11th row: Lifting back half of st only work 1 dc into each dc. Fasten off.
HEADING: Attach thread to first of foundation ch, 3 ch.
1st row: Rep from * to * of 3rd row of Edging, working clusters into base of tr on foundation ch and omitting 3 ch 1 dc and 3 ch at end of last rep, 1 tr into 3rd of 5 ch, turn.
2nd row: As 5th row of Edging.
3rd row: As 11th row of Edging. Fasten off.
Damp and pin out to measurements. Weave ribbon through first 2 rows of edging, sew in ends. Sew foundation ch to edge of material being trimmed.

Edging for mats

MEASUREMENTS: Depth of edging: $1\frac{1}{2}''$.
MATERIALS: 2 balls Coats Chain Mercer-Crochet No. 20. No. 3 crochet hook or New International size No. 1.25. These quantities are sufficient for 4 place mats $11'' \times 16''$.
DIAMOND EDGE: With No. 3 hook make 8 ch.
1st row: 1 dc into 2nd ch from hook, 1 dc into each ch, 1 ch, turn.
2nd to 5th rows: Working only into back half of each st, work 1 dc into each dc, 1 ch, turn.
6th row: As 2nd row, ending with 8 ch, turn. [Diamond made.] Rep 1st to 6th row 17 times more, or required length, omitting turning ch at end of last rep, 9 ch, do not turn.
SIDE EDGE: 1st row: 1 dc into free point of last diamond worked, * 7 ch, 1 dc into free point of next diamond; rep from * ending with 5 ch, 1 d tr into first of foundation ch, 1 ch, turn.
2nd row: [Right side.] 1 dc into first d tr, 1 dc into each of next 5 ch, * 1 dc into next dc, 1 dc into each of next 7 ch; rep from * ending with 1 dc into next dc, 1 dc into each of next 6 ch, 3 ch, turn.
3rd row: Miss first dc, 1 tr into next dc, 3 ch, miss 3 dc, * 1 tr into each of next 3 dc, 5 ch, miss 5 dc; rep from * ending with 1 tr into each of next 3 dc, 3 ch, miss 3 dc, 1 tr into each of next 2 dc, 1 ch, turn.
4th row: 1 dc into each st. Fasten off. With wrong side facing, attach thread to first of foundation ch, 9 ch, and work along opposite side to correspond. Make 3 more edgings in same way.
Damp and pin out to measurements.
Sew crochet edgings across short ends of mats or as required.

Trimmings

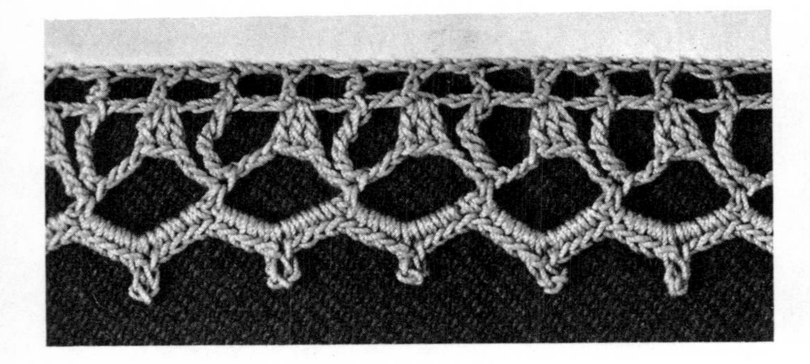

Picot lace trimming

MEASUREMENTS: 1″ in depth.
MATERIALS: Coats Chain Mercer-Crochet No. 20.
Foundation row: With No. 3 crochet hook or New International size No. 1.25 make 8 ch. 1 tr into 8th ch from hook, * 5 ch, turn, miss 2 ch, 1 tr into next ch; rep from * for length required, having a multiple of 2 spaces, 8 ch, turn and continue along side.
1st row: 3 tr into same place as last tr, * 3 ch, 1 tr tr into top of next tr, 3 ch, 3 tr into base of same tr; rep from * ending with 3 ch, miss 2 ch, 1 tr tr into next ch, 1 ch, turn.
2nd row: 1 dc into first tr tr, * 7 ch, 1 dc into next tr tr; rep from * ending with 7 ch, 1 dc into 5th of 8 ch, 1 ch, turn.
3rd row: Into each loop work 5 dc 4 ch, 1 sl st into 4th ch from hook [picot made] and 5 dc, 1 sl st into first dc of previous row. Fasten off.
Damp and pin out to measurements.

Trimming for cloth and napkins

MEASUREMENTS: Depth of edging: 1″.
MATERIALS: 4 balls Coats Chain Mercer-Crochet No. 20. No. 3 crochet hook or New International size No. 1.25. These quantities are sufficient for a cloth 36″ square and 3 napkins 12″ square.
MAIN SECTION: With No. 3 hook make * 4 ch, leaving last loop of each on hook work 2 d tr into 4th ch from hook, thread over and draw through all loops on hook [a 2 d tr cl made]; rep from * for length required to go round cloth having 2 cls extra for each, corner and taking care to have the same number of cls for opposite side, 1 sl st into base of first cl, do not fasten off.
HEADING: 1st row: [right side] 3 ch, a 2 d tr cl into same place as sl st, miss base of next cl, a 3 d tr cl into base of next cl [corner made], * 3 ch, a 3 d tr cl into base of next cl; rep from * for measurement required to next corner, miss base of next cl, a 3 d tr cl into base of next cl [another corner made] complete other sides and corners to correspond, ending with 1 sl st into first cl.
2nd row: 5 dc into each sp, 1 sl st into first dc. Fasten off.
EDGING: 1st row: With right side facing attach thread to join of Main Section, 3 ch, a 2 d tr cl into same place as join, * 3 ch, a 3 d tr cl into base of next cl of Heading; rep from * along side, 3 ch, into base of next cl of Main Section work a 3 d tr cl, 3 ch and a 3 d tr cl [corner made], 3 ch, complete other sides and corners to correspond, ending with 1 sl st into first cl
2nd row: Into each sp work 3 dc, 3 ch, 1 sl st into last dc and 2 dc, 1 sl st into first dc. Fasten off.
Damp and pin out to measurements. Sew edging round cloth and napkins.

Pointed-lace trimming

MEASUREMENTS: Approximately 2¼″ in depth.
MATERIALS: Coats Chain Mercer-Crochet No. 20.
1st row: With No. 3 crochet hook or New International size No. 1.25 make 6 ch, 1 quad tr into 6th ch from hook, * 6 ch, 1 quad tr into last quad tr; rep from * for length required.
2nd row: * Into next loop work 5 dc 4 ch 5 dc; rep from * to end of row, 1 sl st into base of first quad tr, now working along other side of 1st row, into each loop work 5 dc 4 ch 5 dc, 1 sl st into last quad tr.
3rd row: 6 ch, 1 d tr into first 4 ch loop, * into same loop work 2 d tr 6 ch [1 tr into last d tr] and 2 d tr, leaving last loop of each on hook work 1 d tr into same loop as last d tr and 1 d tr into next loop, thread over and draw through all loops on hook; rep from * to end of row, into same loop as last d tr work 2 d tr 6 ch [1 tr into last d tr] and 3 d tr, 6 ch, 1 sl st into next sl st [at end of row], ** 6 ch, now working along other side, 1 d tr into first loop; rep from * to **.
4th row: 7 dc into first loop, 1 dc into each of next 3 d tr, * into next loop work 4 dc 4 ch [1 sl st into last dc] and 3 dc, ** 1 dc into each of next 2 d tr, miss next st, 1 dc into each of next 2 d tr; rep from * to end of row, ending last rep at **, 1 dc into each of next 3 d tr, 7 dc into each of next 2 loops, 1 dc into each of next 3 d tr; rep from * to end of row, ending last rep at **, 1 dc into each of next 3 d tr, 7 dc into next loop, 1 sl st into first dc. Fasten off.
Damp and pin out to measurements.

Shell trimming

MEASUREMENTS: 1¼″ in depth.
MATERIALS: Coats Chain Mercer-Crochet No. 20.
1st row: With No. 3 crochet hook or New International size No. 1.25 make 10 ch.
2nd row: 1 tr into 7th ch from hook, 2 tr into each of next 3 ch, 4 ch, turn.
3rd row: Miss first 2 tr, 1 tr into next tr [1 ch, miss next tr, 1 tr into next tr] twice, 3 ch, 7 tr into next loop, 4 ch, turn.
Rep 3rd row for length required, omitting 6 tr and 4 ch turn at end of last rep.
Heading: 2 dc over bar of last tr worked, * 5 ch, 3 tr into next turning sp; rep from * ending with 4 ch, 1 d tr into foundation loop. Fasten off.
Edging: Attach thread to last sp worked on opposite side 3 ch, into same sp work 1 tr 2 ch 2 tr, * 4 ch, 1 dc into 3rd ch from hook, 1 ch, into next turning sp work 2 tr 2 ch and 2 tr; rep from * to end. Fasten off.
Damp and pin out to measurements.

Braids

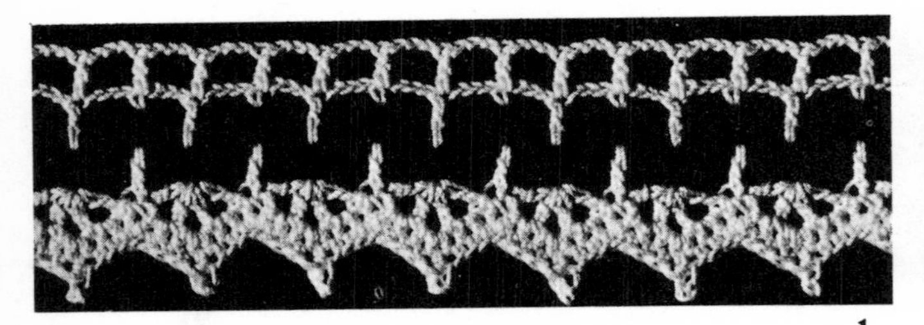

1

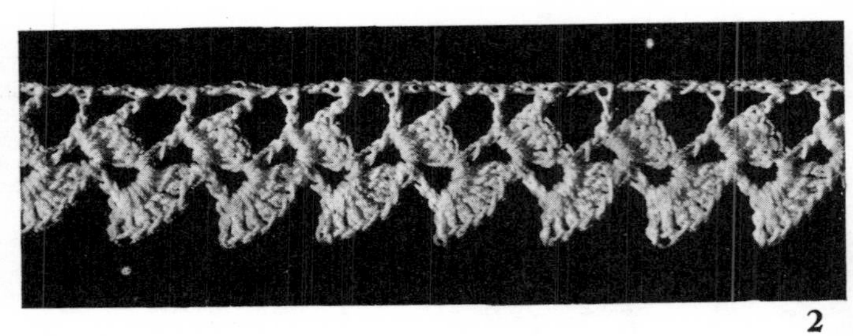

2

No. 1
MATERIALS: Coats Chain-Mercer No. 20. No. 3 crochet hook or New International size No. 1.25.
TENSION: Width of braid: 1⅛″.
1st row: Take a piece of braid of required length. Attach thread to first peak, 1 dc into same place as join, * 3 ch, 1 tr into centre of curve, 3 ch, 1 dc into next peak; rep from * to end, 6 ch, turn.
2nd row: * 1 tr into next tr, 3 ch, 1 tr into next dc, 3 ch; rep from * omitting 3 ch at end of last rep. Fasten off.
EDGING: 1st row: With right side facing, attach thread to centre of first curve on opposite side of braid, 3 ch, * into next peak work [1 tr, 2 ch] 3 times and 1 tr, 1 tr into centre of next curve; rep from * ending with 1 ch, turn.
2nd row: 1 dc into first tr, * 2 dc into next sp, 3 dc into next sp, 2 dc into next sp, miss 1 tr, 1 dc into next tr; rep from * working last dc into 3rd of 3 ch, 1 ch, turn.
3rd row: 1 dc into each of next 5 dc, * 3 ch, 1 dc into last dc – a picot made – 1 dc into each of next 8 dc; rep from * omitting 4 dc at end of last rep. Fasten off.

No. 2
MATERIALS: Coats Chain-Mercer No. 20. No. 3 crochet hook or New International size No. 1.25.
TENSION: Width of braid: ¾″.
7 ch, 6 tr into 4th ch from hook, 2 ch, 1 tr into same ch, 2 ch, miss 2 ch, 1 tr into next ch, 6 ch, turn, * miss 1 sp, into next sp work 4 tr 2 ch and 1 tr, 3 ch, turn, into next sp work 6 tr 2 ch and 1 tr, 2 ch, 1 tr into 3rd of 6 ch, 6 ch, turn; rep from * for length required. Fasten off.

No. 3
MATERIALS: Coats Chain-Mercer No. 20. No. 3 crochet hook or New International size No. 1.25.
TENSION: Width of braid: ⅝″.
Commence with a length of ch having a multiple of 10 ch plus 2.
1st row: 1 dc into 2nd ch from hook, * 5 ch, miss 4 ch 1 dc into next ch; rep from * ending with 5 ch, turn.
2nd row: 1 dc into first loop, * 6 ch, 1 dc into next loop; rep from * ending with 2 ch, 1 tr into next dc, 1 ch, turn.
3rd row: 1 dc into first tr, * 2 ch, into next loop work [2 tr, 3 ch] twice and 2 tr, 2 ch, 1 dc into next loop; rep from * working last dc into 3rd of 5 ch. Fasten off.

No. 4
MATERIALS: Coats Chain-Mercer No. 20. No. 3 crochet hook or New International size No. 1.25.
TENSION: Width of braid: ⅝″.
Commence with a length of ch having a multiple of 8 ch plus 2.
1st row: 1 dc into 2nd ch from hook, 1 dc into next ch, * 3 ch, miss 2 ch, 1 tr into next ch, 3 ch, miss 2 ch, 1 dc into each of next 3 ch; rep from * omitting 1 dc at end of last rep, 6 ch, turn.
2nd row: * 1 dc into next loop, 1 dc into next tr, 1 dc into next loop, 3 ch, miss 1 dc, 1 tr into next dc, 3 ch; rep from * omitting 3 ch at end of last rep, 1 ch, turn.
3rd row: 1 dc into first tr, * 1 dc into next loop, 3 ch, miss 1 dc, 1 tr into next dc, 4 ch, 1 dc into last tr, 3 ch, 1 dc into next loop, 1 dc into next tr; rep from * working last dc into 3rd of 6 ch. Fasten off.

3

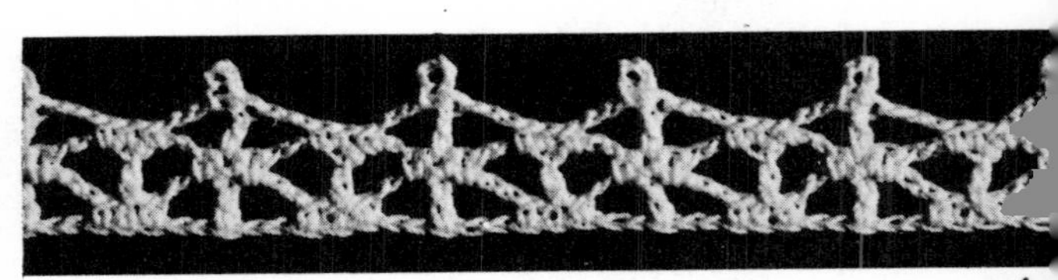

4

Editor:
Judy Brittain
Technical Editor:
Joan Fisher
Editor Condé Nast Books:
Alex Kroll

Acknowledgements:
Drawings: Barbara Firth.
Photographers: Norman Eales – front cover, pages 176, 208, 212, 215, 218, 223, 224, 226, 229, 233. Richard Imrey – page 230. Jo Swannell – pages 238, 240. John Wingrove – pages 175, 246, 247, 248, 249, 251.
Still life photography: Maurice Dunphy.
Hair on page 230 by Graham at Vidal Sassoon.

Macrame Contents

Introduction

Macramé is the art of decorative knotting, and is immensely simple and easy to do, for no hooks, needles or other tools are involved, just your hands. Knots are tied in pre-cut lengths of string, cord, wool or other yarn; by arranging the knots in different sequences, an almost limitless number of attractive patterns can be created. Knots can be worked close together to give a dense fabric, or spaced out for an open-work lacy effect.

The craft dates back to the days of prehistory, for cavemen tied knots in long grasses and in plant and animal fibres, not only to hold things together but as a form of decoration. Through the centuries knotting as a decoration was developed until, in Renaissance Italy, it came into its own as a form of beautiful lace known as *punto a gropo* (knotted lace).

Mary, the London-born wife of William of Orange, is believed to have introduced the craft to England in the seventeenth century, and its popularity quickly spread. It was an ideal drawing-room pastime for candlelit evenings when the light was too poor for needlework.

During the Victorian era, the work—now known as macramé from an Arabic word *migramah,* meaning an embroidered veil—was used extensively to embellish the already ornate homes. Heavy knotted fringes and borders were made to edge mantelpieces and shelves, and even four-poster beds.

In time macramé faded from the scene along with all the other elaborate Victorian crafts, but now it is coming into favour again. Worked in the many exciting synthetic and natural yarns which are currently available, the craft has taken on an entirely new dimension and is being widely used to make fashion accessories and decorations for the home; it is also an art form in its own right.

The decorative aspects of macramé are shown in the wall-hanging and deckchair designed by Bo Ridley for architect Ian Goss

What you will need

Unlike most other handicrafts, macramé does not necessarily require special tools, equipment or accessories. In fact, perfectly acceptable work can be done with just a ball of ordinary string and your two hands. Because no hooks, needles or other gadgets are involved in the technique, there is no correct, or for that matter incorrect, method of holding your hands: all you are doing is to tie knots in a length of string or yarn, an action which you have probably been doing for most of your life, ever since you first learned to tie your own shoelaces in early childhood. Therefore you work in the manner which suits you best, and in which you are most comfortable.

Although the requirements of macramé in material terms are minimal (being yarn, and scissors for trimming), there are a number of dressmaking aids which will help to make your work easier. Pins can be used to anchor your work to a working base, and to control and regularise the shape, size and position of knots; they are virtually essential to good, neat macramé. A separate tape measure will be required for measuring yarn, and a large-eyed darning needle is useful if you intend to darn in loose ends at the back of your work.

You will sometimes find it difficult to work without a base on which to rest your knotting. In the Victorian era, when macramé was particularly popular, heavily weighted cushions were often used as working bases, and elaborate boards were manufactured with complicated screws, pegs and ridges to support the cords. Such complex devices however are quite unnecessary; all that is needed is a firm, fairly rigid surface of adequate size for the piece of knotting you are working on.

Any oddment of wood will do for this, but if the wood is too hard to take pins easily it should be padded with a sheet of foam rubber, or a layer of thick towelling, felt or candlewick. Alternatively, several sheets of cardboard or foam rubber bound together can be used. Fibreboard and cork can also make very good working surfaces.

It is helpful to have the surface of your board marked out in inch squares, and to glue a length of tape measure along the top edge, and down one side edge. This gives you a permanent, at-a-glance guide to measurements and proportions.

This board is an ideal base for smaller items especially if you want to carry your knotting around, to do on trains or buses, in the garden or on the beach, or while watching television. Bigger items however are not so portable, and you will probably prefer a more permanent working base. You can pin your work directly to an expanse of wall, or even to the back of an unpanelled door.

If you would rather not work on such a surface the knotting may be strung between two chairs, or any other upright supports; an artist's easel or music stand can provide good support, or a child's pegboard with the pegs arranged at suitable distances.

When you come to working in the round and on three-dimensional designs, a flat base cannot be used. A block of wood, cut to the approximate size and shape of the item you are making and padded with plastic or towelling, makes the best base, but it is easy to improvise here with upturned and padded pudding basins, flower vases and other similar everyday objects, to suit your particular work.

Yarn to use
String is the best yarn of all for macramé as it knots easily, holds its shape well, and the form of the actual knot is clearly and attractively visible. As string is available in different thicknesses, and also now in colours, there is plenty of variety to suit different designs.

However, any other type of yarn, natural or synthetic, may be used successfully, although you will find each displays different characteristics; some (the bulky ones) will get used up quickly in the knots, and so prove expensive; others (usually the synthetics) tend to be slippery and trying to control this can make knotting arduous. Sometimes of course the characteristic of a particular yarn can be put to good effect, depending on the final result required.

The best knotting yarns are the smooth cottons and linens, which are robust enough to hold the knotted shape: all thicknesses of piping cord are ideal, so are marine, household and gardening twines, nylon cords, dishcloth and string vest cotton, and upholstery threads.

Rug wool is also good, as it is more substantial than ordinary knitting wools and yarns. Knitting wools however can be used successfully, where colour and all-over texture are required rather than clearly-defined, crisp knots. Many of the novelty yarns currently available, such as gold and silver metallic threads and 'jewelled' yarns, also work well. They can be effectively combined with some of the smoother and more conventional yarns.

Macramé design by Kaffe Fassett

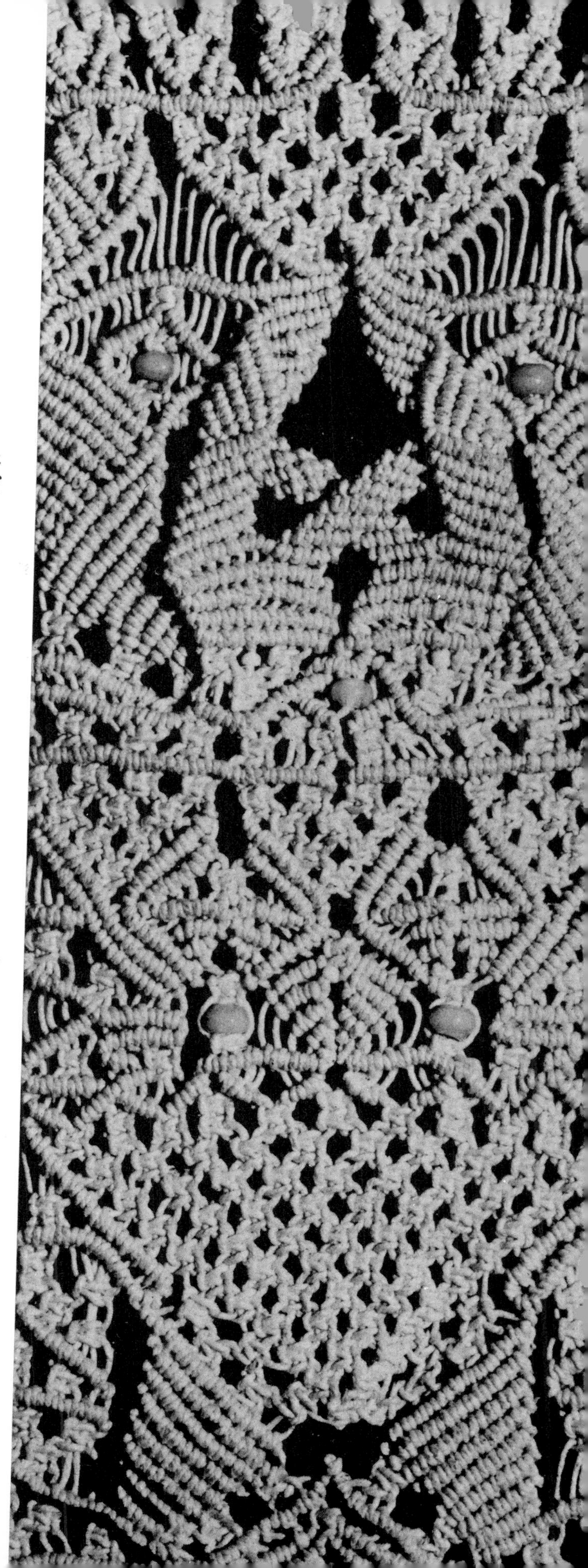

Setting on threads

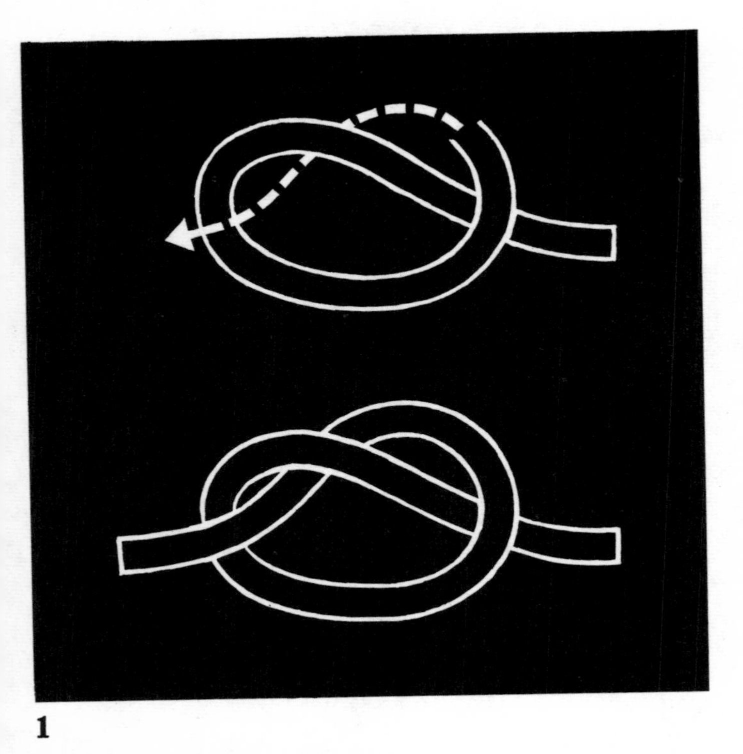

1

Before you can begin knotting, and this applies whether you are working on a simple flat sampler, a complicated design in the round, or a fringe for a fabric edge, your yarn must first be cut into suitable lengths to take them right through the proposed design, and then they must be mounted—or set on—either to another length of yarn, directly to a fabric edge (if you are making a fringe), or to a length of wooden rod or similar rigid surface.

One of the most difficult aspects of macramé is to estimate before you begin how long to cut each cord length. The tendency, especially when you first start knotting, is always to cut yarns too short—and as joining in mid-knotting can sometimes be tricky, not to say impossible, to under-estimate your requirements can be disastrous. On the other hand, it is a pity to over-estimate your needs, and thus waste valuable inches of expensive yarn.

As a very general guide, if yarn lengths are to be set on double (which is the usual method) then cut each length to eight times the required length of the finished piece. For example, if you are making a sampler to measure 6″ when complete, and you are setting on six cut cord lengths doubled, then cut each of the six cords to 48″ (6″ times 8). When they are doubled and set on, you should then have twelve working cord ends, each measuring a little under 24″.

To practise setting on threads, cut a length of string (or whatever yarn you are using for practise purposes) about 12″ long. Near one end tie

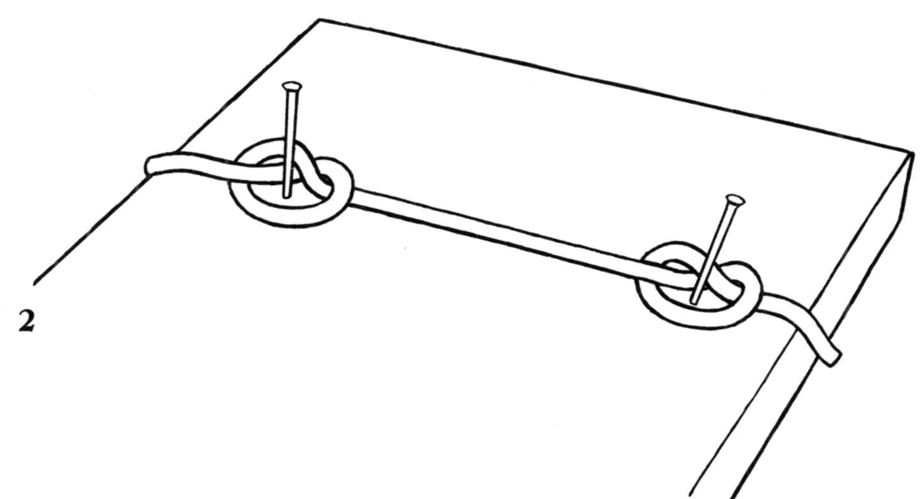

a knot by turning the yarn end back, then taking it up and round itself and through the loop formed. This is called an overhand knot (fig. 1).

Pin the cord to your working surface, taking the pin through the knot, then stretch the cord tautly across your working surface; tie a similar overhand knot at the other end and pin it in place. This cord is called a holding cord (fig. 2).

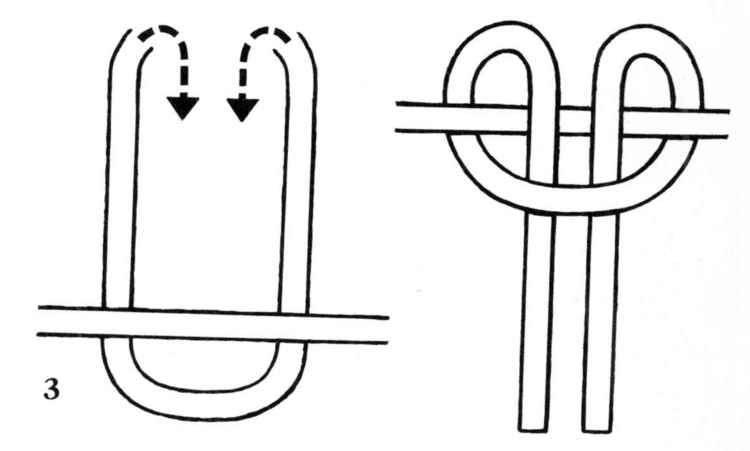

Now cut a number of lengths of yarn (as many as you wish to practise on). They should each be a minimum of 1 yard long. Take one length of yarn, double it and insert the looped end under the holding cord from top to bottom. Bring the yarn ends down over the holding cord and through the loop. Draw tight. This knot is known as the reversed double half hitch, and can be used, as you will see, decoratively as part of a pattern as well as functionally to set on threads (fig. 3).

Continue to set on the remaining cords in a similar way, pushing each set-on cord close to the previous one. There should be no spaces between cords on the holding cord. Now you are ready to begin the basic knots (fig. 4).

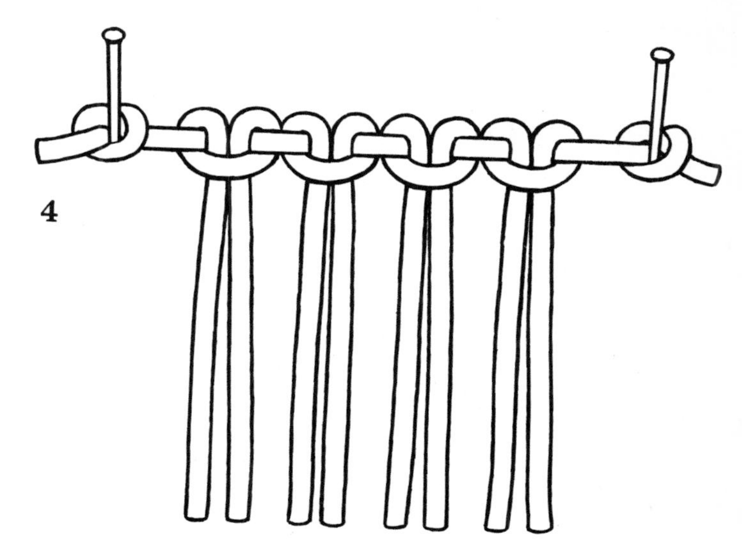

Note. *This method of setting on with reversed double half hitches also applies to setting threads directly on to fabric, or a wooden rod. In the case of setting on to fabric, however, it may be necessary to draw the yarn through the fabric with the aid of a crochet hook.*

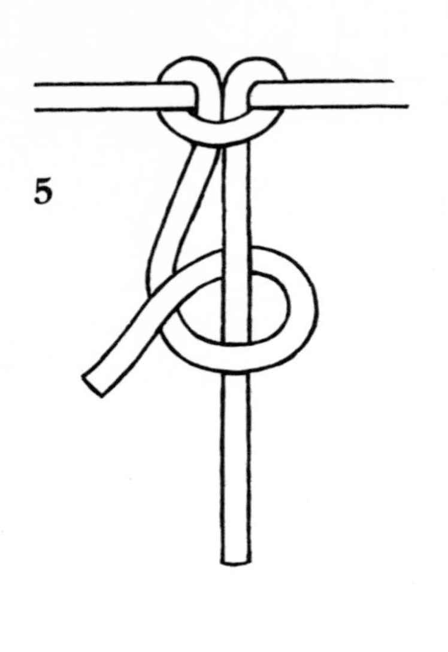

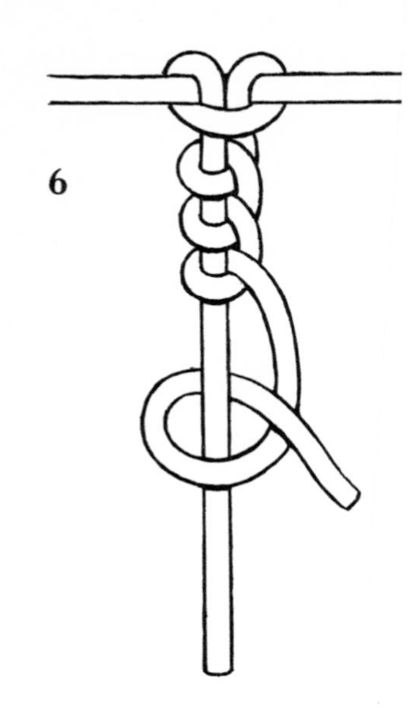

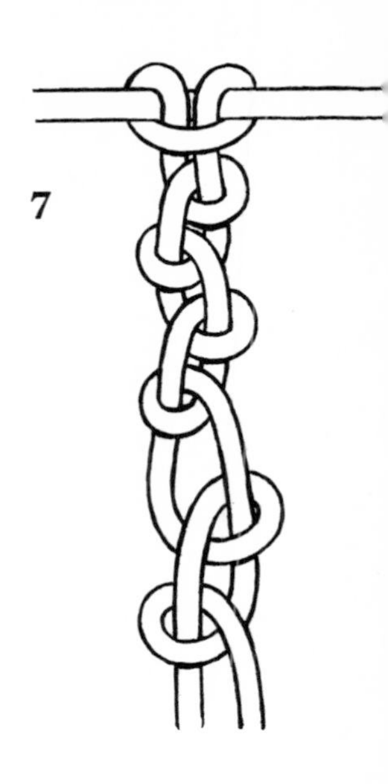

The basic knots

First basic knot: the half hitch
In almost every macramé knot you have a knotting cord (or sometimes cords) and a knotbearing cord (or cords). This means that the actual tying and forming of the knot is carried out by the knotting cord, while the knotbearing cord merely acts as a support.

In its simplest form, the half hitch is tied with two cords only, and it can be tied from the right or from the left. To tie a half hitch from the left, the right-hand cord is the knotbearing cord. It must therefore be held taut while the left-hand knotting cord forms the knot round it.

Holding the right-hand cord taut in a vertical position, bring the left-hand cord across it, then up and round behind it and through the loop formed. This is one half hitch. Continue to tie half hitches from the left in this way to form a chain. You will find the chain has a natural tendency to twist around itself but if each knot is slackened slightly and eased as you work it, the chain should lie flat (fig. 5).

To tie a flat hitch from the right, the left-han cord becomes the knotbearer, and must therefor be held taut. Bring the right-hand cord across it then up and round behind it, and down throug the loop formed. Continue in this way to tie chain of half hitches from the right; again th knots must be gently eased if the chain is to li flat (fig. 6).

An alternating half hitch chain is a pleasing an easy-to-tie chain, and used frequently in a forms of macramé designs, particularly for ba handles, belts, edgings, ties and as a form c fringing. To work this chain in its single form use two cords and tie half hitches alternatel from the left and right: i.e. for the first knot, th left-hand cord will be the knotting cord and th right-hand cord the knotbearer; in the secon knot, the right-hand cord is the knotting cor and the left-hand one the knotbearer—and s on (fig. 7).

A double alternate half hitch chain is worke

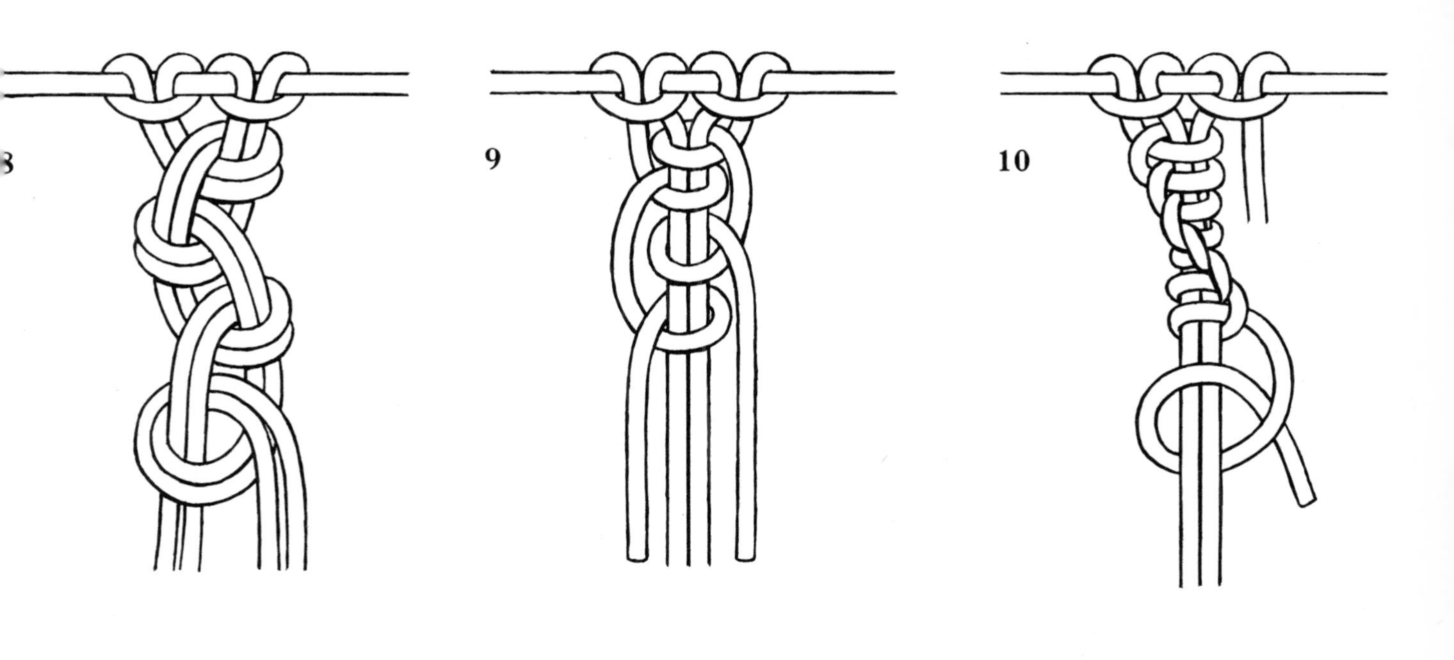

·xactly as for the single version, above, but ·louble thicknesses of cords are used throughout ·fig. 8).

·lternate half hitches may be worked over a ·entral knotbearing core of one or more cords. ·ry this simple variation, for instance, using four ·ords: tie a half hitch from the left with the first ·ord over the two central cords, then tie a half ·itch from the right over the two central cords. ·ontinue in this way, tying half hitches alter- ·ately from the left and right over the two ·entral knotbearing cords. This forms a strong ·ardwearing braid which is again useful for bag ·andles (fig. 9).
·nother simple but effective variation on the ·alf hitch makes use of three cords. Tie half ·itches continuously with the left-hand cord ·round the middle and right-hand knotbearing ·ords. This produces an attractive spiral (fig. 10).

·ther variations on the half hitch are shown in the ·not samples on pages **196** *and* **197**.

Second basic knot: the flat knot
The flat knot is used in all types of macramé, in many different forms. It is a useful and versatile knot for it can be used to create a fabric—dense or open—as well as producing attractive patterns.
In its simplest form, the flat knot is tied with four cords: the two outer cords are the knotting cords; the two central cords the knotbearers. As in the half hitch, it is important to keep the knotbearers pulled taut all the time. In long chains of flat knots you can pin the knotbearing cords to the working surface so they are kept permanently taut; at other times it is possible merely to loop the central cords around the middle two fingers of your right or left hand (whichever is easier) and hold them taut as you work (this is not so difficult as it sounds). If you are working on a very large scale, or with excessively long cords, you can tuck the knotbearing cords into your waistband or belt, or even tie them round your waist.

The flat knot may be tied from the left or right.

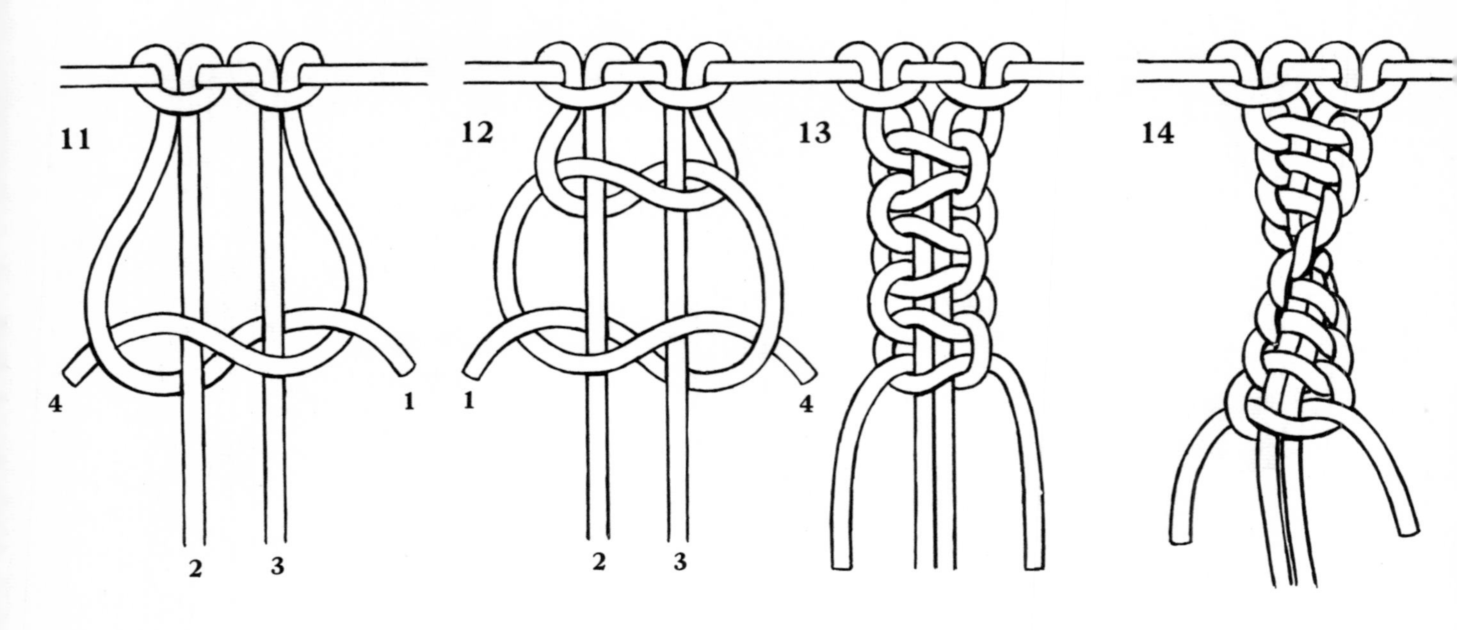

The basic knots

To tie it from the left, take cord 1 under cords 2 and 3 and over cord 4. Bring cord 4 over cords 3 and 2, and under cord 1. Pull gently into place. This is the first half of the flat knot, and is known as the half knot (fig. 11).

To complete the flat knot, bring cord 1 (which is now at the right of the knot) back under cords 3 and 2, and over 4 (at the left of the knot). Bring cord 4 over cords 2 and 3 and under cord 1. Draw knot gently into position. This is a complete flat knot, and cords are now back in their original positions (fig. 12). Continue to tie flat knots in this way to form a chain (fig. 13).

To tie a flat knot from the right, the procedure is merely reversed; cord 4 begins the knotting sequence by being taken under cords 3 and 2, and over 1. Cord 1 then is taken over 2 and 3, and under 4. The knot is completed by bringing cord 4 back under 2 and 3 and over 1, and cord 1 is taken over 3 and 2 and under 4.

If the half knot (first half of the flat knot) is tied continuously, an interesting spiral is created The spiral will twist right round on itself afte every fourth knot. Allow it to do so, and con tinue tying half knots as before with the cords i their new positions (fig. 14).

A multi-end flat knot is simply a flat knot tie with several cords at once using more than fou cords, and is useful for collecting cords togethe at the end of a design, or for creating a foca point in a motif where several cords meet. Th knot may be tied with all the extra cords be coming knotbearers and only the two outsid cords used to tie the knot; or several thicknesse of knotting cords may be used with a centra knotbearing core of only two cords; or you ca have multiple knotting cords, and multiple knot bearers, whichever suits the pattern you ar working.

Other variations on the flat knot, including th alternate flat knot pattern, one of the most importan in all macramé work, can be seen in the kno samples on pages 196, 197 *and* 198.

Cording

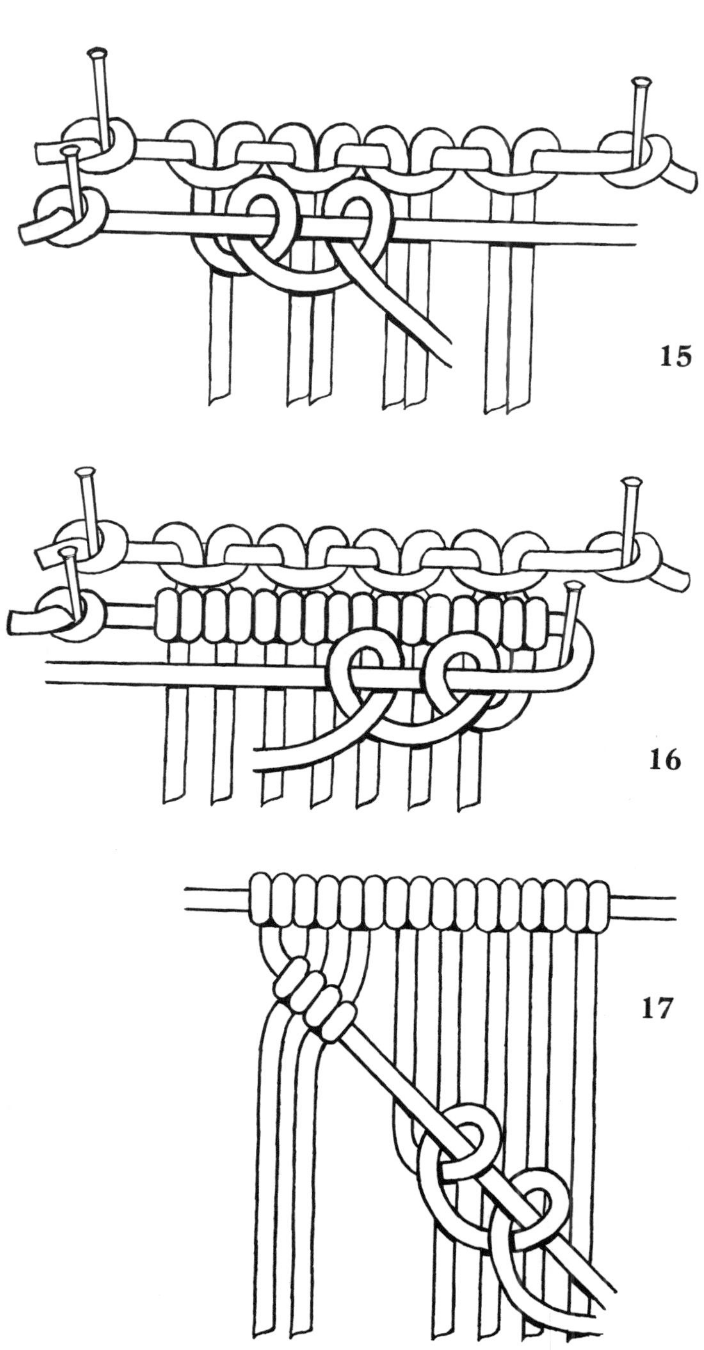

Cording is also a basic and very important knotting technique. It is based on the half hitch, and can be worked horizontally, vertically or diagonally, as wished. It is thus extremely versatile and can be used to shape edges, to control and regularise a design, and even to draw figures. It is also used in colour work to transfer colour from one part of a design to another.

In horizontal and diagonal cording the knot-bearing cord is called a leader, and its position controls the exact position in which the finished line of cording appears. The leader can be one of the set-on cords, or it can be a separate cord pinned to the side of the set-on cords. As with all knotbearing cords, it must be held taut while knots are tied round it.

To work horizontal cording from left to right, pin a separate leader to your working surface immediately to the left of the set-on cords, and stretch it tautly across them. If you wish, you can pin it to the working surface at the far side of the set-on cords to keep it taut. Now take the first set-on cord and bring it up and over the leader, then down behind it and through to the left of the loop it has just formed around the leader. Repeat this knotting sequence exactly, and you have tied one double half hitch, which is one complete cording knot. Continue in this way, tying a double half hitch with each set-on cord around the leader in turn. Push each little knot tight against the previous one (fig. 15).

To work a second row of horizontal cording (this will be from right to left), place a pin in the working surface at the end of the first row, and bring the leader around it; stretch it tautly across the set-on working cords as before, this time from right to left. Now work double half hitches over the leader with each set-on cord, beginning with the cord on the far right. In this case, each cord will be brought up and over the leader as before, but the end of the cord will be brought down and under the leader to the right of the loop formed round it (fig. 16).

The principle of diagonal cording is exactly the same as for horizontal cording, except that the leader cord is placed at an angle across the work,

Cording

according to the slant required for the finished cording. Double half hitches are worked over the leader with each set-on cord as before. You will find the areas of unworked cords above and below the diagonal cording tend to form curves. Pin these curves carefully as you work to keep them regular and evenly spaced. The leader for diagonal cording may again be either a separate cord or one of the set-on cords (fig. 17, page 185).

If you want to work diagonal cording from the centre outwards, select a set-on cord from the centre, and pin it at an appropriate angle across the work. Tie double half hitches over it as before with each of the set-on cords lying under it, working from the centre out (fig. 18).

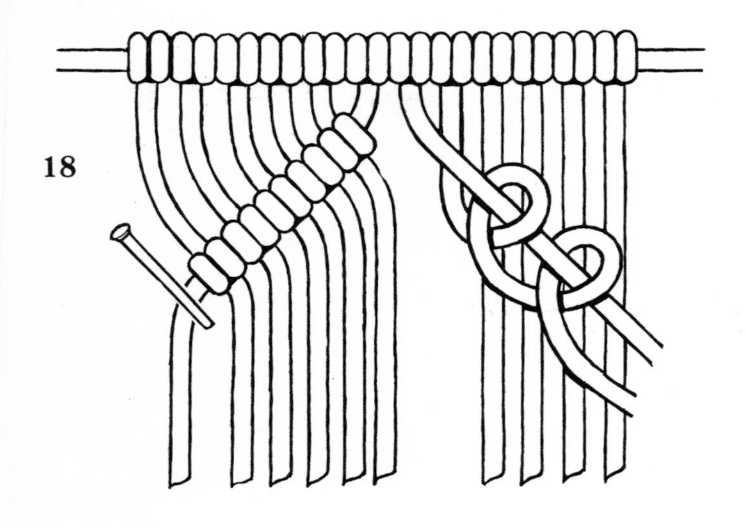

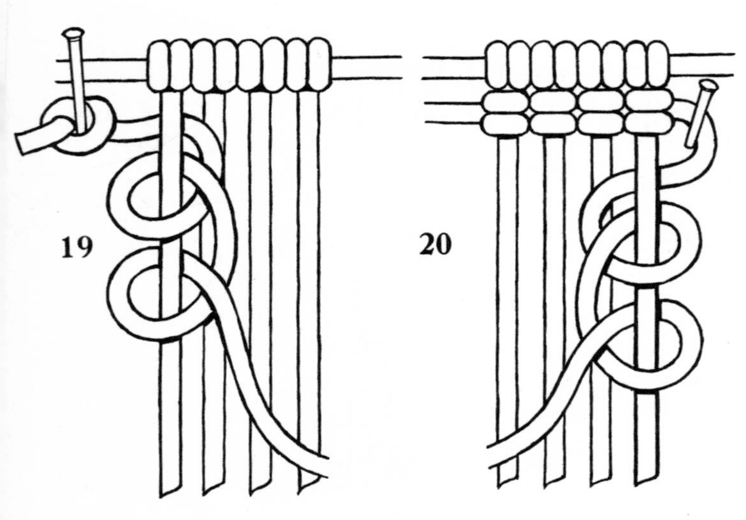

Vertical cording differs from horizontal and diagonal cording in that the knots are tied throughout with the same cord. Usually this is a separate cord, but it may be one of the set-on cords, if wished, and each of the other cords in turn become knotbearers.

Pin a separate cord immediately to the left of the set-on cords. Take it under the first set-on cord, bring it back across from right to left, then up and under it from left to right. Repeat this sequence exactly and you have tied one vertical double half hitch, or one complete vertical cording knot. Continue in this way across the row of set-on cords, so each set-on cord in turn becomes a knotbearer. Always take the knotting cord under the knotbearer before beginning to tie the knot (fig. 19).

At the end of the row, the knotting cord is brought around a pin, then vertical cording is worked across the row from right to left. The first knot will therefore be tied by taking the knotting cord under the far right cord, bringing it across the knotbearer from left to right, then up and under that cord from right to left. Complete the vertical double half hitch (fig. 20), and repeat on each knotbearing vertical cord.

Vertical cording can, if wished, be worked on a single cord only but you must still tie knots in rows if the work is not to twist and become uneven; i.e. tie the first vertical double half hitch from left to right; tie the second from right to left, and so on. However, by the nature of this technique a rather untidy series of loops is produced down either side of the cording.

If you want to work vertical cording as a 'frame' for the edge of a design, it is better to work it on the two cords nearest the side edge rather than just one. The loops are much less in evidence this way.

Other variations on the cording technique can be seen in the knot samples on page **199**.

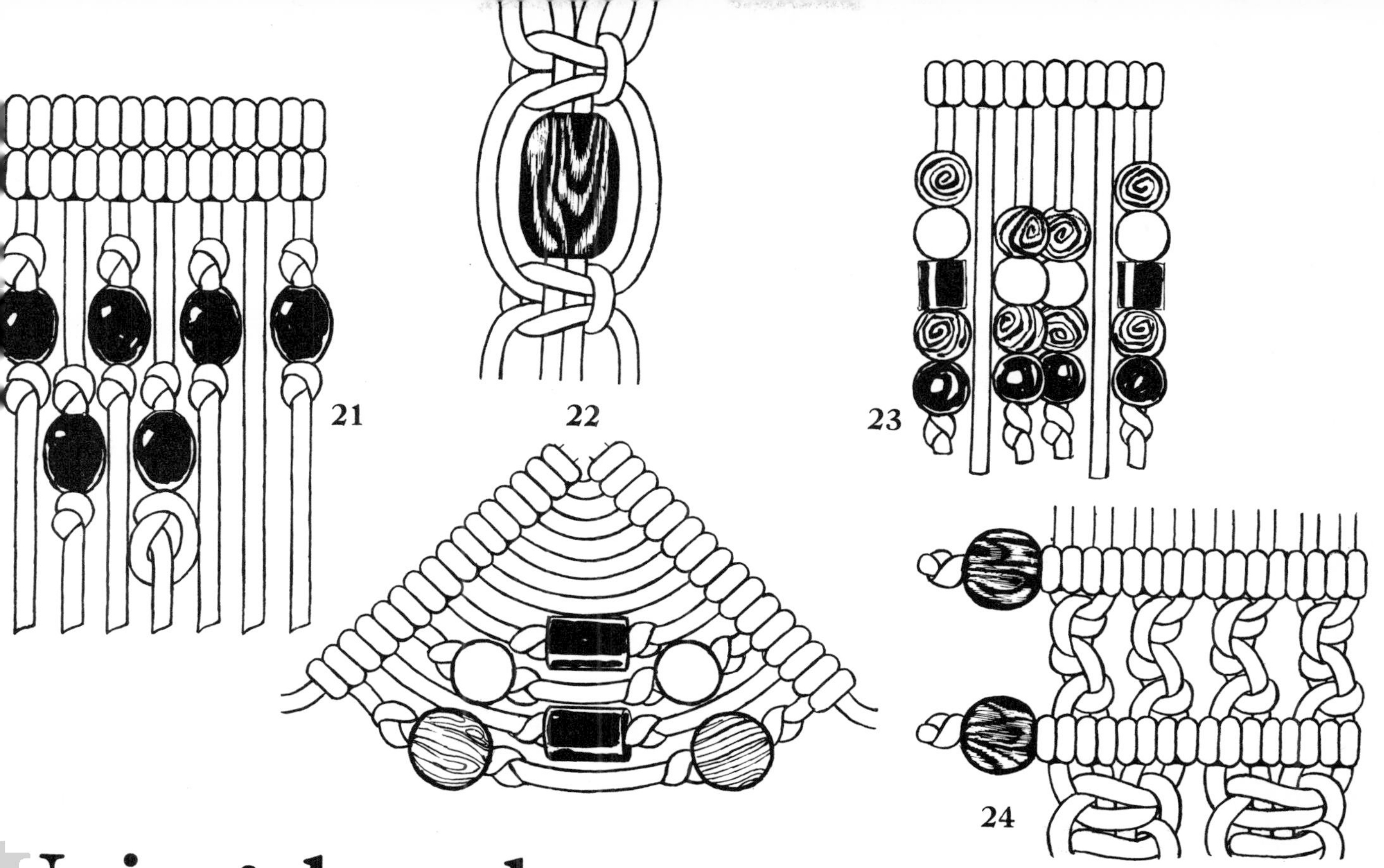

Using beads

Knotting may happily be combined with all kinds of beads, pearls, sequins, buttons and other haberdashery ornaments.

Beads can be threaded on to the cord ends after a knotting pattern is complete as a form of finishing or they may actually be incorporated into the knotting pattern itself, either haphazardly, in a free design, or regularly in a symmetrical arrangement, for example, as a focal point of a repeated diamond motif. Whichever way you may choose to use beads, it is usually best to tie simple overhand knots in the cord on which the bead is threaded, one knot above the bead, one knot below it, to hold it firmly in place (fig. 21).

The easiest way to bring beads into your knotting is merely to thread the central knotbearing cords of a flat knot sequence through the bead, after the half knot; it is held in place when the next knot is tied. However, beads may also be added to floating areas of unworked cords, perhaps in a cording pattern; or small beads may be added to the actual knotting cords (fig. 22).

Before you start work on a design using beads, it is best to plan exactly how many beads you will require and on which cords, then thread the required number on to each cord before you begin. Tie an overhand knot at the end of the cord to prevent the beads slipping off. Whenever a bead is required in the course of knotting, simply slide one up into position and secure either with an overhand knot, or by tying the next knot in the pattern (fig. 23).

If separate leader cords are used for rows of horizontal cording, an effective side decoration can be added to your work with beads. Simply slide a bead on to each end of every leader, push it gently close to the knotting, tie an overhand knot in the leader cord to secure it, and trim the ends (fig. 24).

Sometimes it is difficult, especially with thicker yarns, to thread the bead on to the yarn. The holes in wooden beads can be gently eased by working a drill through the centre; china or small wooden beads are best wired to the knotting at the place where you want the bead or pearl to appear. Take care to keep the wire hidden at the back of the work.

Multi-colour knotting

There are several ways in which macramé may be worked in two or more colours of yarn. The easiest method is merely to set on cords in different colours, arranging them in any sequence you wish, then proceed in the chosen knotting pattern. The colours will form their own pattern, depending on the knotting used.

To try this in its simplest form, set on a dozen cords, six in one colour, six in a contrasting colour, and arrange the colours alternately on a

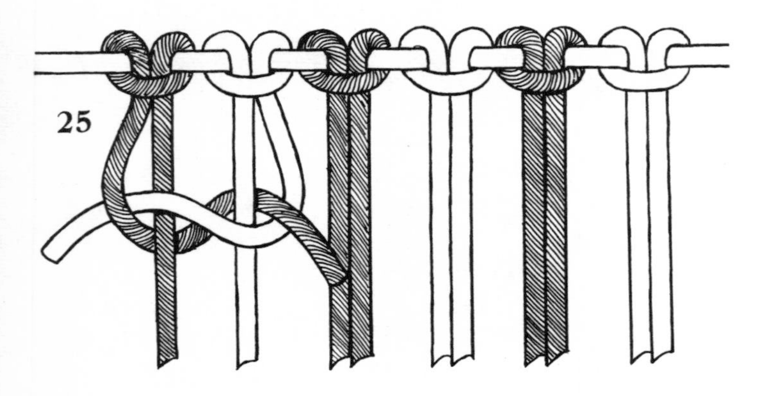

25

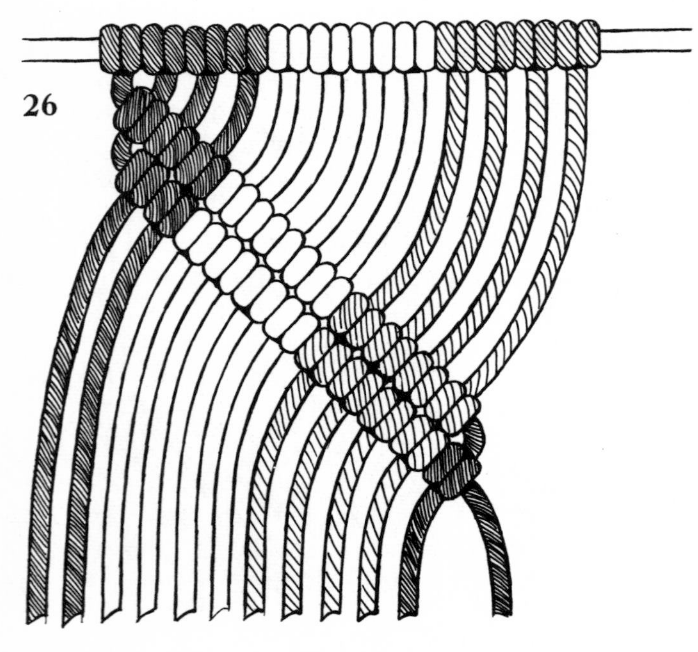

26

holding cord, so you have two working ends ir the first colour, and two working ends in the contrasting colour alternately (fig. 25). Now work any of the flat knot samples shown or page 198.

This example demonstrates the simplest use o two-colour knotting. More complex patterns car be evolved by working in any form of cording. In fact, cording is probably the most flexible tech nique of all for producing fascinating colou effects. As the leader cord in horizontal, vertica or diagonal cording is hidden in the finishec work, cording can be used to make a colou travel from one part of the work to another a though by magic. The contrast coloured cord i used as leader and when it is wished for the colour to appear, another cord is selected a leader, or else a different knotting pattern i worked.

As a simple demonstration of this, set on twelv cords, four in colour A, four in colour B, four in colour C. Now work in close rows of diagona cording from left to right, slanting rows down t the right, and using the cord on the far left a leader for every row. At the end of each row th leader will drop down to become a knotting cor in the subsequent row. An attractive multi coloured braid will be formed by working in thi way (fig. 26).

Cavandoli work

This is a particularly effective form of knottin based on the cording colour principle as describe above. In Victorian days the work was some times called wampum weaving because of it similarity in appearance to the wampum belt of the American Indians. But in the early part c the twentieth century a Madame Valentin Cavandoli, who ran an open-air school in Ital for young children, adopted the technique t amuse and occupy the children in her care, pe fected it and gave it the name by which it is no

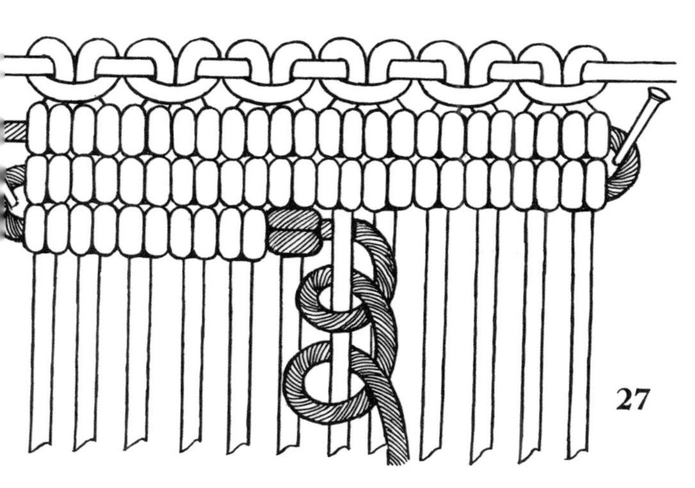

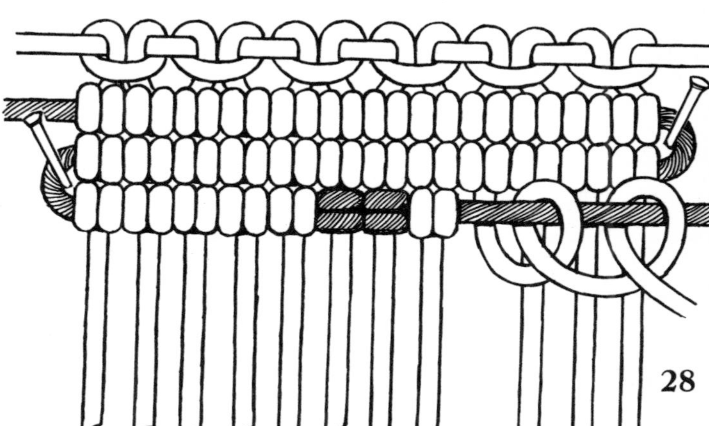

known. In fact much of her design experimenting was based on cross stitch work in embroidery.

The principle is simple: a number of cords in colour A (background colour) are set on to a holding cord. A separate leader in colour B (contrast colour) is then introduced. The knotting is worked entirely in close rows of horizontal and vertical cording: the background is worked in horizontal cording, a design is picked out in the contrast colour in vertical cording. The design is very often geometric in character, but can take the form of any sort of decorative motif. Normally a Cavandoli design is worked from a chart, each square on the chart representing one double half hitch (horizontal or vertical).

To practise the Cavandoli technique, set on six cords in colour A to a holding cord. Pin a leader cord in colour B to the left-hand side of the work.
1st row (left to right): horizontal cording.
2nd row (right to left): horizontal cording.
Note. *Only colour A will show in finished knotting so far.*
3rd row (left to right): work horizontal cording on first five cords, then work vertical cording on next two cords, so colour B is now visible (fig. 27), and work horizontal cording on final five cords (fig. 28).
4th row (right to left): horizontal cording on first five cords, vertical cording on next two cords, horizontal cording on last five cords.
5th row (left to right): horizontal cording on three cords, vertical cording on six cords, horizontal cording on last three cords.
6th row (right to left): as 5th row.
Next 2 rows: as 3rd and 4th rows.
Next 2 rows: as 1st and 2nd rows.
You should now have a piece of closely-knotted fabric (not dissimilar to a woven fabric) with a clearly defined solid cross pattern in the centre worked in the contrast coloured yarn. It is possible to work Cavandoli knotting in solid blocks of contrast colour, as in this example, or by only outlining the design in the contrast colour, and filling in the centre with background colour. Diagram A shows the example just worked set out in chart form; diagram B shows how a similar motif could be worked in outline only, using seven cords (fourteen working ends).

It is possible to work an effective chequerboard pattern by the Cavandoli principle: alternating blocks of colour are worked in colour A (horizontal cording) and in colour B (vertical cording), as set out in diagram C.

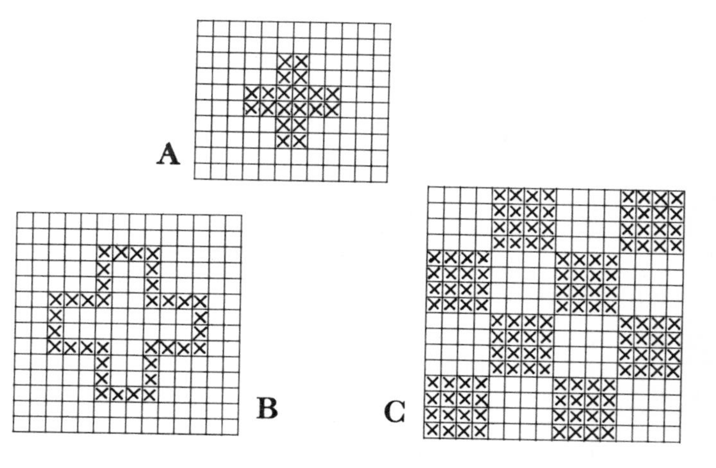

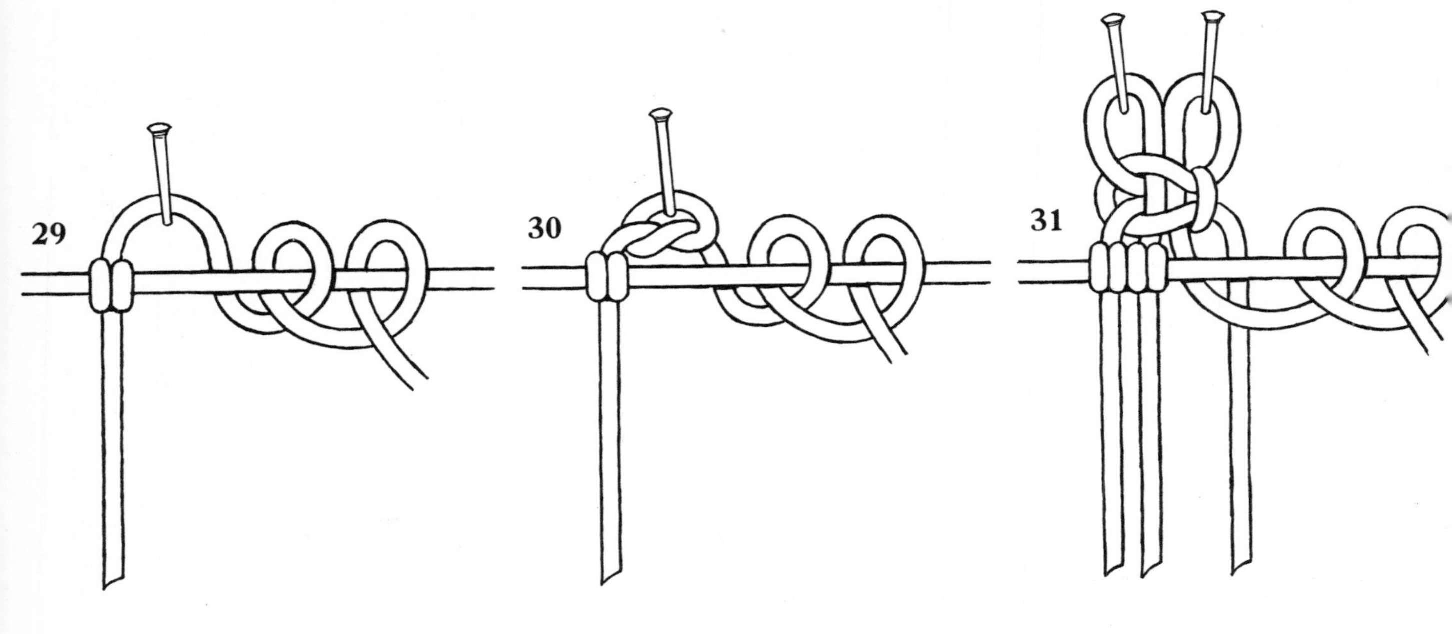

Starting and finishing

Starting

Cords set on to the holding cord with a decorative heading will add considerable attraction and interest to a particular design. The sketches and instructions below give a number of decorative beginnings, based mainly on simple picots and scallops.

Simple picot edging

Double each cord as usual for setting on, then pin it by its loop to your working surface. Lay the holding cord across the pinned cord just below the loop. Now work a double half hitch over the holding cord with each working cord in turn. The depth of the top loop will depend on the position in which you lay the holding cord. Continue to set on cords in this way so you produce a series of tiny top loops, with a row of horizontal cording below (fig. 29).

Overhand picot edging

Double each cord and tie an overhand knot at the midway point. Pin to the working surface through the overhand knot. Lay the holding cord horizontally just below the overhand knot, then work double half hitches over the holding cor with each cord in turn (fig. 30).

Flat knot picot edging

Take two lengths of yarn, double them and pi them by their loops side by side to the workin surface. Now tie a flat knot with the four cor ends, allowing the loops at the top to exten fractionally above the knot. Lay the horizonta holding cord across immediately below the fla knot, and work double half hitches over it wit each cord in turn (fig. 31).
If a greater depth of edging is required, work tw or even three flat knots before laying the holdin cord across.

Simple scalloped edging

Take two lengths of yarn, double them and pi them by the loops to the working surface, pos tioning one loop inside the other. Lay a hor zontal holding cord across and work double ha hitches over the holding cord with each cord i turn. The depth of the top loops depends en tirely on where you position the holding cor (fig. 32).

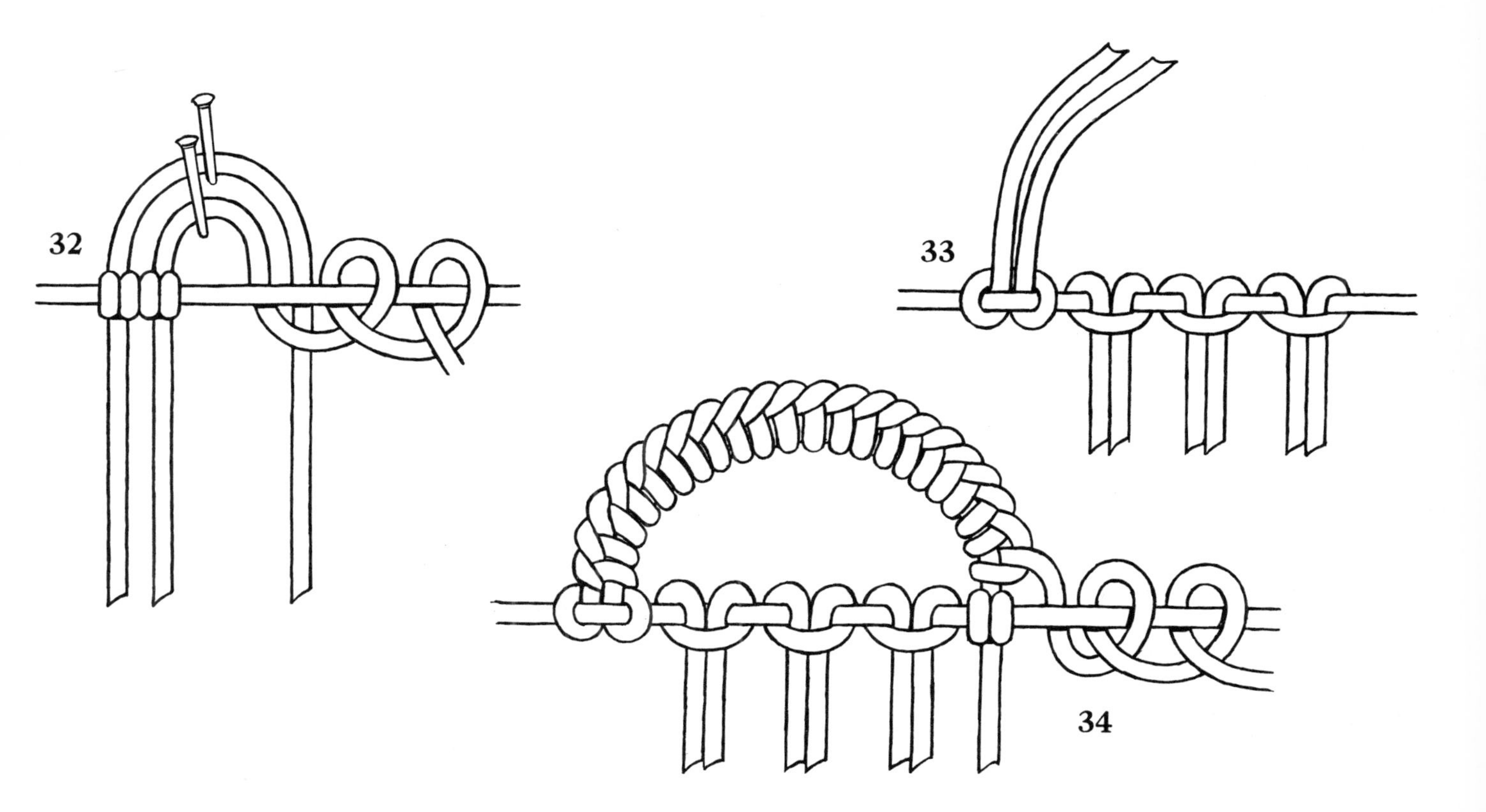

Half-hitch scalloped edging

Take four lengths of yarn. Double the first one and set it on to a horizontal holding cord by the usual setting on method, but in such a way that the working ends are hanging in the opposite direction from the work. Now set on the other three threads in the normal way (fig. 33). Work half hitches with the first two cords, knotting cord 1 over cord 2 and gradually curving the chain round as you work to form a deep arch above the other three set-on cords. When the chain reaches the holding cord with the desired arch, attach the cords to the holding cord with double half hitches (fig. 34). If preferred this scalloped edging may be worked with a scallop of alternate half hitches.

Finishing methods

Fringing. The simplest and often the most effective finish to a macramé design is a fringe. The ends are merely trimmed evenly to the depth required. The fringe may be left plain or may be threaded with beads, each held in position by overhand knots. If a knotted fringe is preferred,

36

overhand knots can be tied either in single cords, or in pairs of cords together. Or pairs of cords can be tied in alternate half hitch chains. The particular form of fringe, whether plain, knotted or beaded, depends entirely on the design being worked and of course on personal preference (fig. 35, page 191).

Weaving in ends. If a straight edge is required at the end of work rather than a fringe, it is best to work a row of horizontal cording to complete the knotting; this gives a firm, strong edge. Ends should then be trimmed to a few inches from this last row of cording. Turn work to the wrong side, thread each cord on to a large-eyed darning needle, and carefully weave the end through the reverse of the knotting (fig. 36).

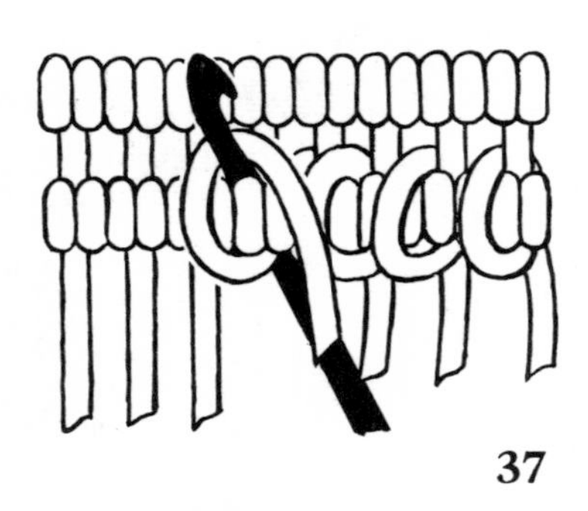

37

Alternatively, if two rows of horizontal cording are worked, ends can then be threaded from the front to the back of the work between the two rows using a crochet hook (fig. 37). Knot the ends together in pairs on the wrong side of the work in two-end flat knots (i.e. flat knots without the knotbearing central cords). Trim the ends close to the knot. If necessary, a tiny spot of glue can be put on the knot to prevent the ends coming undone (fig. 38).

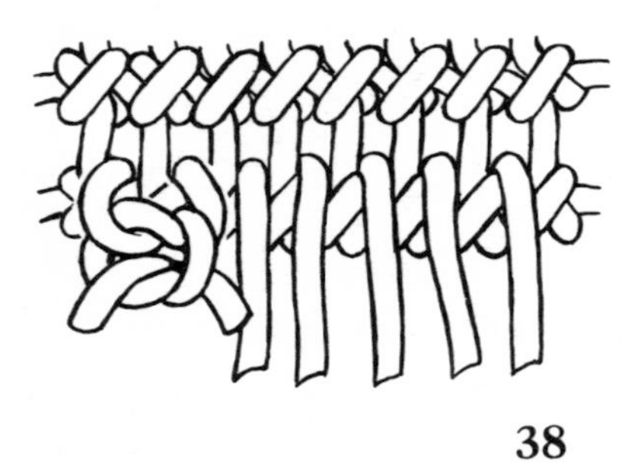

38

Garments worked in macramé are often best finished on the wrong side with a strip of seam binding sewn neatly in place to conceal the loose ends (figs. 39, 40). Better still, if the garment is completely lined, all the ends can be sandwiched between knotting and lining.

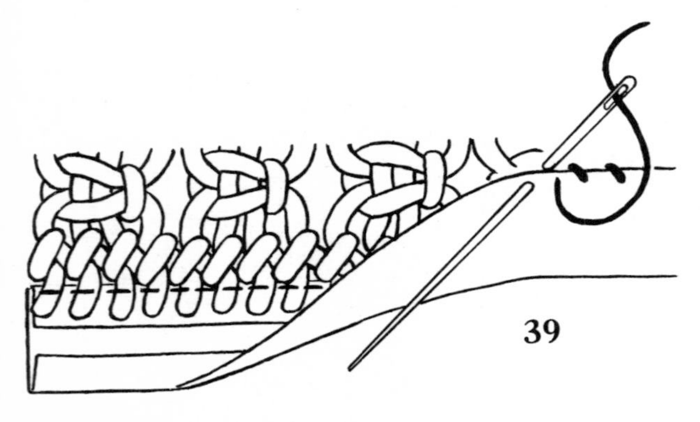

39

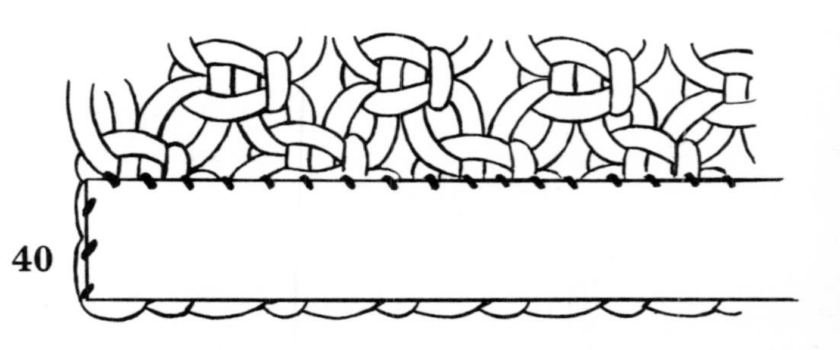

40

Working in the round

Although macramé is more usually worked flat, pinned to a working board, wall or other flat surface, knotting can also be successfully worked 'in the round'. This is useful for any item where stitched seams are not wanted, such as a skirt, bag, hat or lampshade, and for three-dimensional sculptures and hangings.

Working in the round helps to ensure regularity of knotting. Sometimes if two sections of a lesign are knotted separately and then sewn together afterwards, the knotting does not always match exactly.

The technique of working in the round can also be used for flat circular items, such as table or medallion mats, or motifs, where work commences in the centre and comes outwards from his point. It may also be used for shaped items uch as skull caps, tea cosies, and even lamphades. Alternatively, items can be worked in hree-dimensional tubular form.

Taking the tubular technique first: simply, cords are set on to a circular holding cord and work progresses downwards in the normal way. A bag, or instance, can very easily be made in the ound. A holding cord (which will form the top edge of the bag) is first cut and the required number of cords set on to this in the normal way. When all the cords are set on, unpin the holding ord from your working surface, and tie the ends f the holding cord together to form a circle. Adjust the knot until the circle is the size reuired for the top edge of bag. Now space out the et-on cords equally round the holding cord, ositioning some over the knot in the holding ord (fig. 41).

Your normal flat working surface can, of course, o longer be used as a base. Instead a three-imensional base should be used, as closely elated to the size and shape of the finished article s possible. A piece of wood cut to the right size nd shape for the item you are making is sually best, though for a hat, a wig-stand would e better. Alternatively, a pudding basin padded ith foam rubber or towelling can be used, or an pturned flower vase (fig. 42). Knotting proeeds in the normal way, and you turn the work ound as you knot. Slight shaping can be

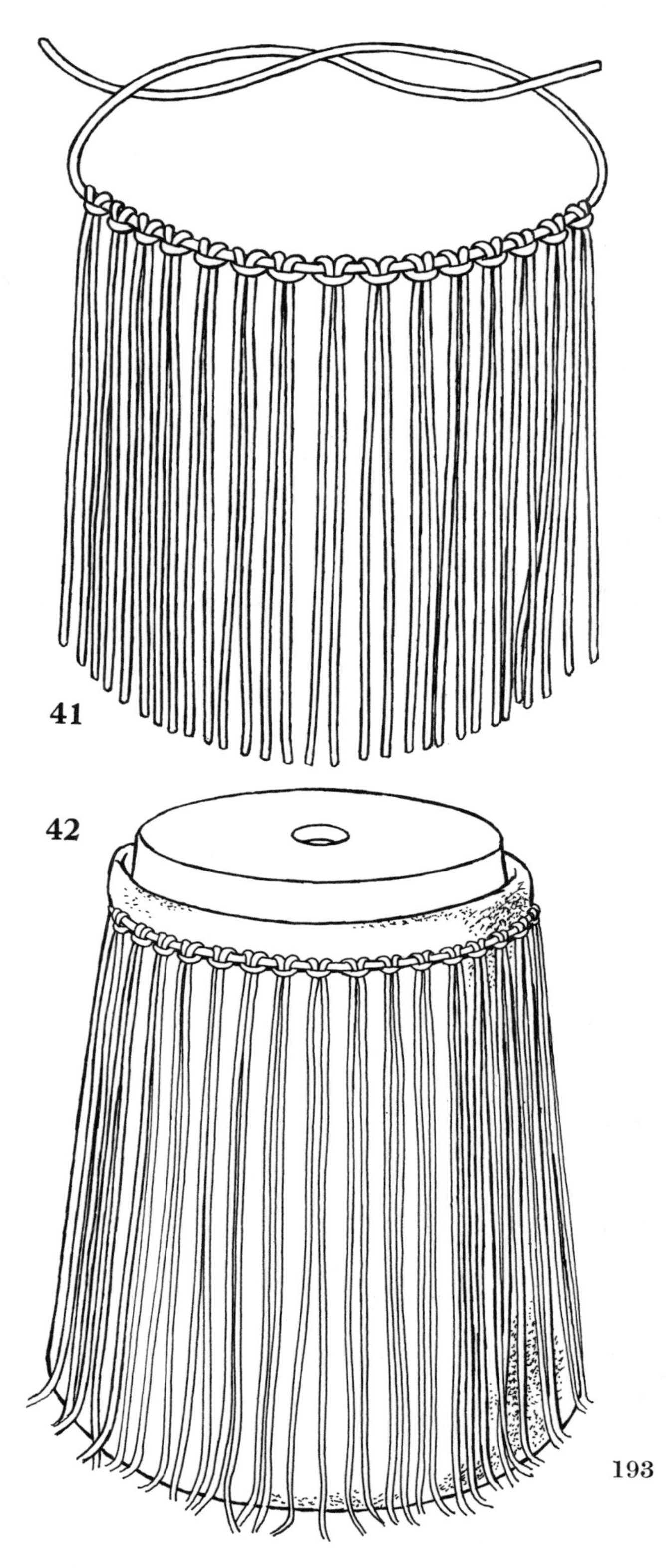

Working in the round

43

44

45

achieved by tying the knots in the first rounds
fairly tightly, and then gradually slackening
knots in subsequent rounds to increase the all-
over width of the design.

If the knotted tube is to be left open, e.g. for a
skirt, lampshade or collar, then knotting is
finished by any of the methods used for flat work
(the ends being either trimmed to a fringe, or
turned in and woven into the wrong side of the
last few rows of knotting). However, if it is
wished to close the tube, as, for instance, for a
bag, then the edges may either be sewn or
knotted together. Remove the work from the
three-dimensional base, and lay it on a flat base
so the work lies in the form of a finished bag.
Now work knots across the lower edge, combining cords from the front with cords from the back
in every knot (fig. 43). Trim the ends to a fringe
of the required depth, or add tassels.

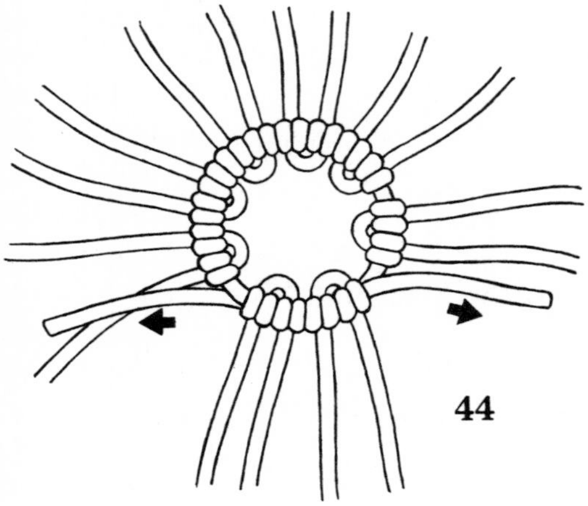

In articles to be flat in finished form, but worked
in the round (e.g. a circular table mat), start
from a central point and work outwards, using
your normal flat working surface.

The basic method of starting work is the same
for a flat or shaped item. Cords may be set on to
a holding cord or directly on to a metal, plastic
or wooden ring. If setting on to a holding cord
set on just a few cords first, then overlap the
ends of the holding cord, and set on a few more
cords over this double thickness. Pull the ends of
the holding cord to tighten to the desired size
then space out the set-on cords equally round it
adding more if required (fig. 44).

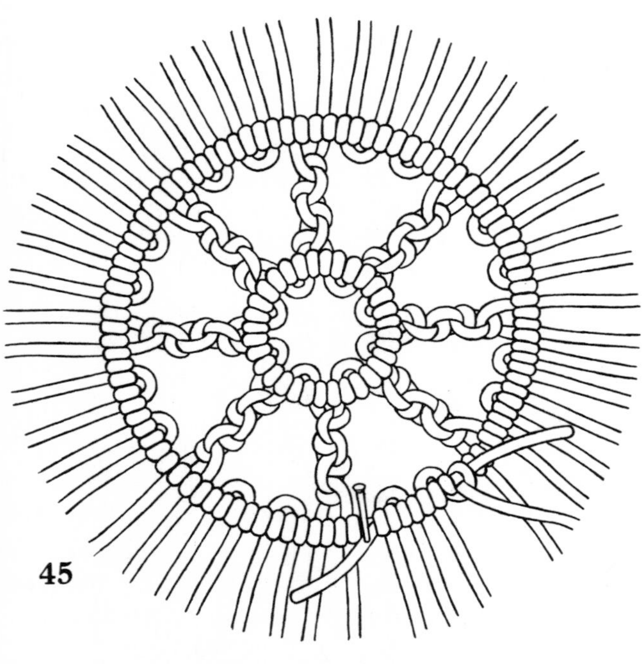

Now work knots in the chosen pattern. Unless
you are using a very open-work pattern, extra
cords will have to be added as the circle gradually
enlarges. The easiest way to do this is to work
rows of cording at intervals and introduce the
new cords into these (fig. 45).

Washing and dyeing

As with knitwear, or any other fabric, items made from macramé need careful handling and regular cleaning if they are to stay looking their best. The basic rules of laundering for different fibres, both natural and man-made, apply equally to macramé. Very heavy items, however, are best dry-cleaned, as their weight when wet could pull a design out of shape, or distort the knots. The following is a brief guide to washing different fibre types.

Cottons and linens (including ordinary string)
Add mild detergent or soap flakes to hot water. Whip up to a good lather then add cold water to reduce the temperature to hand-hot. Place macramé items in this soapy solution. Squeeze gently to remove dirt, never rub or twist. Rinse well, and leave to dry on a flat surface. A mild solution of starch dabbed over the article before you press it will give a slight stiffening.

All weights of wools
Wash very gently in lukewarm soapy water. Rinse well, at least three times. If the third rinse is still not crystal clear, then rinse again. Gently squeeze the item after the final rinse, and roll it in a clean dry white towel. Do not twist. Spread the item to dry on a flat surface, eased into its correct shape and size. Leave to dry away from direct heat or sunlight. If pressing is required, do so carefully on the wrong side of the item, with a moderate iron over a damp cloth.

Synthetics
Wash as for wool. No pressing should be required. Plastic-coated strings, polypropylene, and other similar synthetic cords need only an occasional wipe over with a soapy cloth to keep them clean.

Piping cords
Wash as for cottons. Items made in heavy piping cords should always be dry-cleaned.

Dyeing
Most macramé yarns may be successfully home dyed, thus giving a wider range of colours than would otherwise be possible. Strings dye particularly well and so do piping cords. There are many excellent proprietary brands of dyes on the market, to suit different yarns and different purposes; choose the dye to suit your material.

Yarn may either be dyed in its loose state, or after being made up into a garment or other item. If dyeing yarn in its loose state, wind it into big loose coils, then tie it together with small pieces of fine thread. Move the yarn about during the dyeing period with a wooden spoon. This will allow the dye solution to coat the surface of the yarn evenly.

Whichever type of dye you use, and whatever yarn, it is important to dye a sufficient quantity for your requirements all at once. Always overestimate your needs, as a secondary dyeing with a different dye solution rarely yields exactly the same depth of colour as the first.

The following is a basic guide to dye types:
Cold dyes: colour and light fast, many brilliant colours. Good for all natural fibres.
Wash and dye dyes: for washing-machine dyeing of large items. Suitable for natural fibres and nylons, but not polyesters, acrylics, or yarns with special finishes.
Instant liquid dyes: simple, easy and quick to use. Just add a measure of dye solution straight from the bottle to hot water. For all washable fabrics, except acrylics.
Multi-purpose dyes and tints: range of excellent colours. Suitable for all natural and most synthetic fibres.

Free service for home dyers
If you are in any doubt at all about which type of dye to use for a particular yarn, send a small sample of the yarn to Annette Stevens at the Consumer Advice Bureau, Dylon International Ltd., Lower Sydenham, London SE26 5HO.

A

Knot samples

Half hitch variations

SAMPLE A
Worked on four cords. *Work half hitches from the left with cord 1, first over cord 2, then over cords 2 and 3 together, then over cord 2; work half hitches from the right with cord 4, first over cord 3, then over cords 3 and 2 together, then over cord 3.** Repeat from * to ** for the length required.

SAMPLE B
Worked on four cords. * Work five half hitches from the left with cord 1 over cords 2 and 3, then work five half hitches from the right with cord 4 over cords 3 and 2.** Repeat from * to ** to the length required. This is a waved bar.

SAMPLE C
Worked on four cords. Work a half hitch from the left with cord 1 over cords 2 and 3. Work a second half hitch from the left with cord 1 over 2 and 3, but work the knot in reverse—i.e. take it first *under* the knotbearing cords, then bring it over them from right to left, and down through the loop formed. Draw tight. The complete knot is known as the reversed double half hitch. In a similar way, work a reversed double half hitch from the right with cord 4 over cords 3 and 2. Continue to work reversed double half hitches from the left and right alternately to the length required.

Flat knot variations

SAMPLE D
Worked on four cords. Tie a flat knot followed by the first half of a flat knot, i.e. you will have tied $1\frac{1}{2}$ flat knots (this is a triple knot). Now on the central knotbearing cords tie an overhand knot. Bring the outer (knotting) cords down on either side of the overhand knot and tie another triple knot immediately below the overhand knot, with all cords. Continue in this way alternately tying overhand knots and triple knots to the length required.

C
D

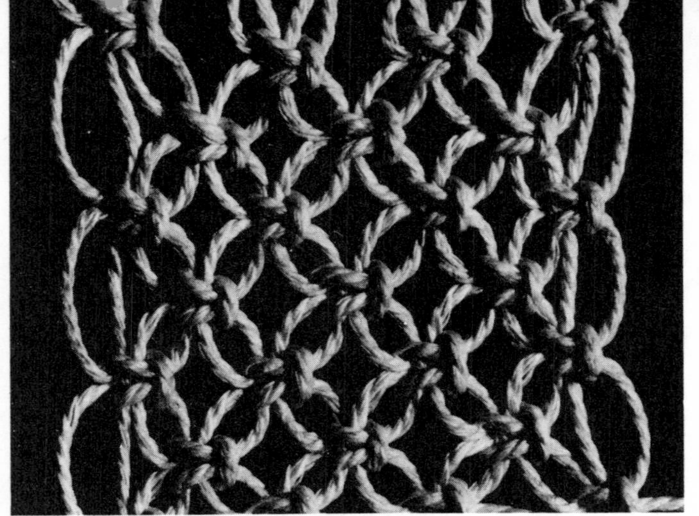

E

F

Knot samples

SAMPLE E

This is the alternate flat knot pattern which occur frequently in all types of macramé work. Set on cords i any multiple of four.

1st row: tie four-end flat knots with each group of fou cords to the end of the row.
2nd row: leave the first two cords unworked; tie fla knots with each group of four cords to the last two cords leave these last two cords unworked.
3rd row: as first row.
4th row: as second row.
Continue in this way. If the knots are pulled tightl together a dense fabric will be produced; if they ar spaced out evenly a lacy pattern will be made.

SAMPLE F

A variation on the alternate flat knot pattern. Set o cords in multiples of four. Work as for Sample **E**, bu work chains of three flat knots each time instead c single knots.

SAMPLE G

Another variation on the alternate flat knot pattern. Se on cords in multiples of four.

***1st row:** work three flat knots with each group of fou cords to the end of the row.
Next row: leave the first two cords unworked; ti single flat knots with each group of four cords to the las two cords; leave these two cords unworked.
Next row: work single flat knots with each group o four cords to the end of the row.
Next row: leave the first two cords unworked; tie thre flat knots with each group of four cords to the last tw cords; leave these last two cords unworked.
Next row: tie single flat knots with each group of fou cords to the end of the row.
Next row: leave the first two cords unworked.**
Repeat from * to ** to the length required.

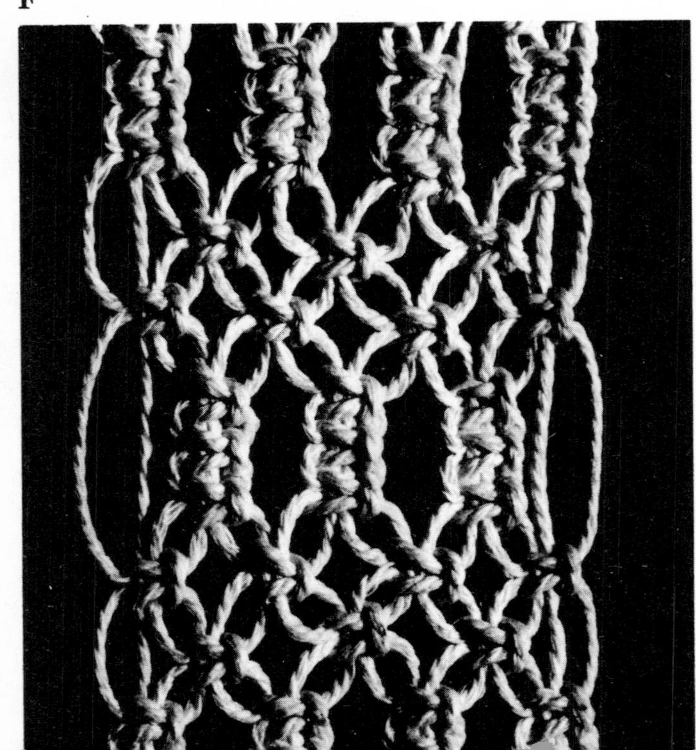

G

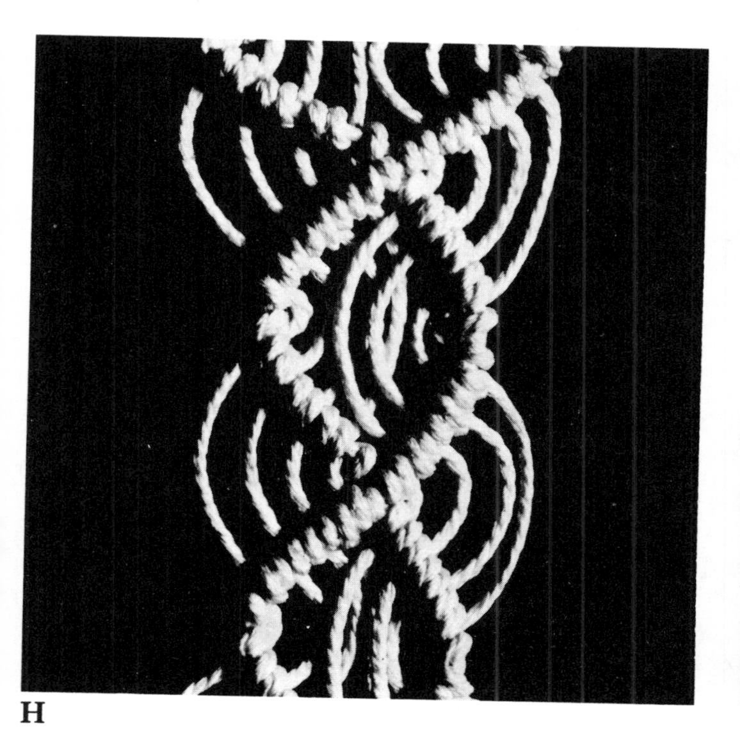
H

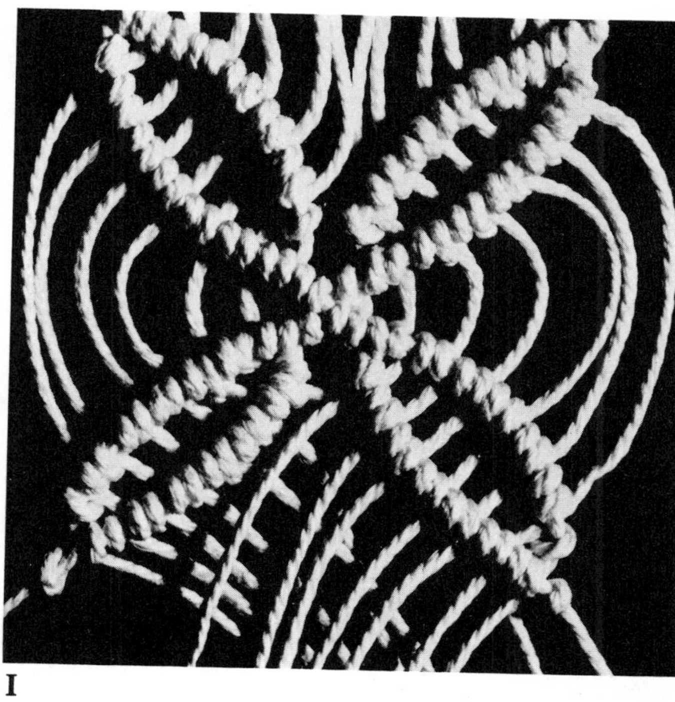
I

Cording variations

SAMPLE H

Worked on 10 cords. With cord 1 as leader, work diagonal cording slanting down to the right with cords 2, 3, 4 and 5. With cord 10 as leader, work diagonal cording slanting down to the left with cords 9, 8, 7 and 6. Link the two leaders by working cording with cord 1 over cord 10. Cord 10 now continues as leader across the work at the same slant as before. Work diagonal cording over it with cords 5, 4, 3 and 2.

Cord 1 continues as leader across the other side of the work, and diagonal cording slanting down to the right is worked over it with cords 6, 7, 8 and 9.

Reverse the direction of cord 10 round a pin and let it continue as leader slanting down to the right. Work cording over it with cords 2, 3, 4 and 5. Similarly reverse the direction of cord 1 round a pin, and work cording slanting down to the left over it with cords 9, 8, 7 and 6. Link the two leaders by knotting cord 10 over cord 1. Continue in this way to form diamonds of cording.

SAMPLE I

A four-leaf cording motif worked on 16 cords. Work the top left-hand leaf first: with cord 1 as leader, pin it in position to form the upper curve of a leaf. Work cording over it with cords 2, 3, 4, 5, 6, 7 and 8. With cord 2 as leader, pin it in position to form the lower curve of a leaf. Work cording over it with cords, 3, 4, 5, 6, 7, 8 and 1. In a similar way work the top right-hand leaf. This time cord 16 will be leader for the top curve of the leaf, and cording will be worked from right to left. Cord 15 will be the leader for the lower curve of the leaf.

Link the lower corners of the two leaves just worked by knotting cord 15 over cord 2.

Now work the lower left-hand leaf. Cord 15 continues across the work as leader for the top curve of the leaf, and cording is worked over it from right to left with cords 1, 8, 7, 6, 5, 4 and 3. Cord 1 then becomes leader for the lower curve of the leaf and cords 8, 7, 6, 5, 4, 3 and 15 are knotted over it.

Complete the motif with the lower right-hand leaf: cord 2 continues across the work as leader for the top curve of the leaf, cording worked over it from left to right. Finally cord 16 is leader for the lower curve of this leaf.

Braids

A

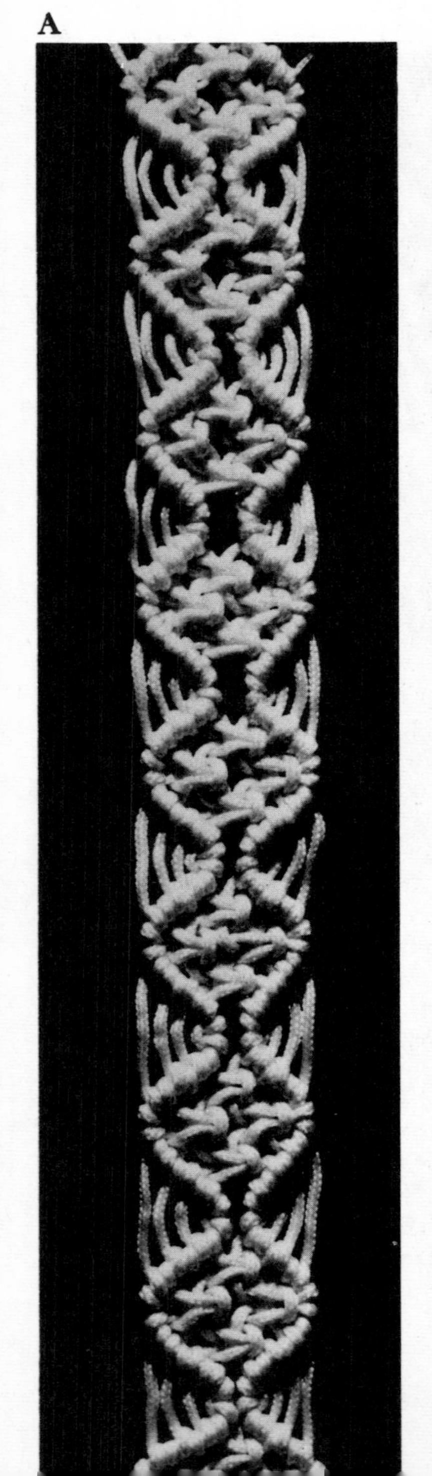

B

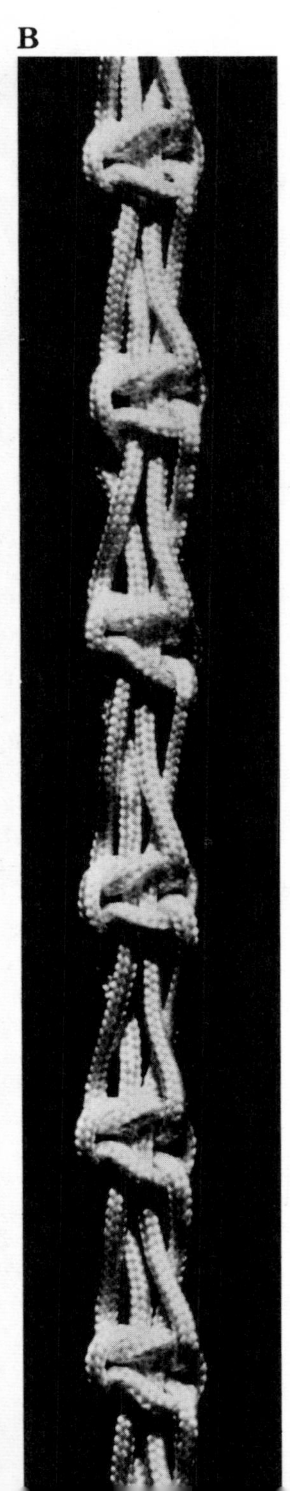

BRAID A

MATERIAL. Fine nylon cord.

NUMBER OF CORDS. Ten.

TO MAKE

With cord 5 as leader, work diagonal cording slanting down to the left with cords 4, 3, 2 and 1. In a similar way work diagonal cording slanting down to the right using cord 6 as leader, and knotting cords 7, 8, 9 and 10 over it.

Now tie a flat knot in the centre with cords 3, 4, 7 and 8.

Next row: tie a flat knot with cords 1, 2, 3 and 4, and another flat knot with cords 7, 8, 9 and 10.

Next row: tie a flat knot with cords 3, 4, 7 and 8. Continuing to use cord 5 as leader, reverse its direction round a pin and work diagonal cording slanting to the right with cords 1, 2, 3 and 4. Similarly work diagonal cording slanting to the left with cords 10, 9, 8 and 7 over cord 6. Reverse the direction of the leaders round pins and repeat the motif, allowing unworked areas of cords at the sides (between motifs) to form gentle and regular curves. Continue in this way until braid is the desired length.

BRAID B

MATERIAL. Medium nylon cord.

NUMBER OF CORDS. Four.

TO MAKE

Work flat knots at $1\frac{1}{2}''$ intervals. After each knot is tied, cross cord 2 over 1, and 3 over 4, so the knotting cords of the previous knot become the knotbearers in the following knot.

BRAID C

MATERIAL. Rug wool in two contrasting shades.
NUMBER OF CORDS. Six, arranged in the following colour sequence: three cords in colour A, two in colour B, and one in colour A.
TO MAKE
Tie flat knots at 1″ intervals, using only the two outer cords as knotting cords, i.e. the knotbearing core will consist of two cords in colour A, two in colour B. Let the knotting cords form regular loops (picots) at either side of the braid.

BRAID D

MATERIAL. Piping cord No. 1.
NUMBER OF CORDS. Eight.
TO MAKE
*Knot a reversed double half hitch from left to right with cord 1 over cords 2 and 3; take cord 5 under cord 4 and use it to tie a reversed double half hitch from right to left over cords 2 and 3. Now tie a reversed double half hitch from right to left with cord 8 over cords 6 and 7, then tie a reversed double half hitch from left to right with cord 4 over 6 and 7.
Tie a reversed double half hitch from left to right with cord 1 over cords 2 and 3, bring cord 4 under cord 5 and use it to tie a reversed double half hitch from right to left over cords 2 and 3. Tie a reversed double half hitch from right to left with cord 8 over cords 6 and 7; tie a reversed double half hitch from left to right with cord 5 over cords 6 and 7.** Repeat from * to ** until braid is the required length.

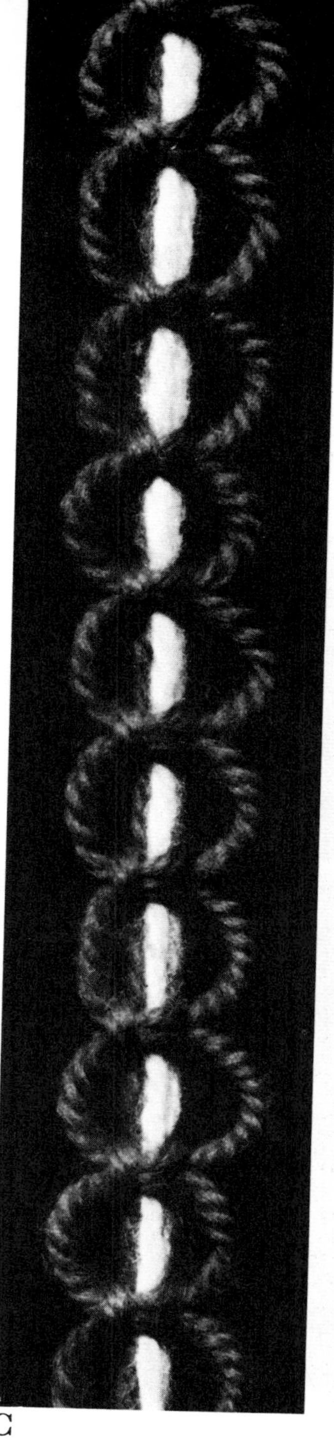
C

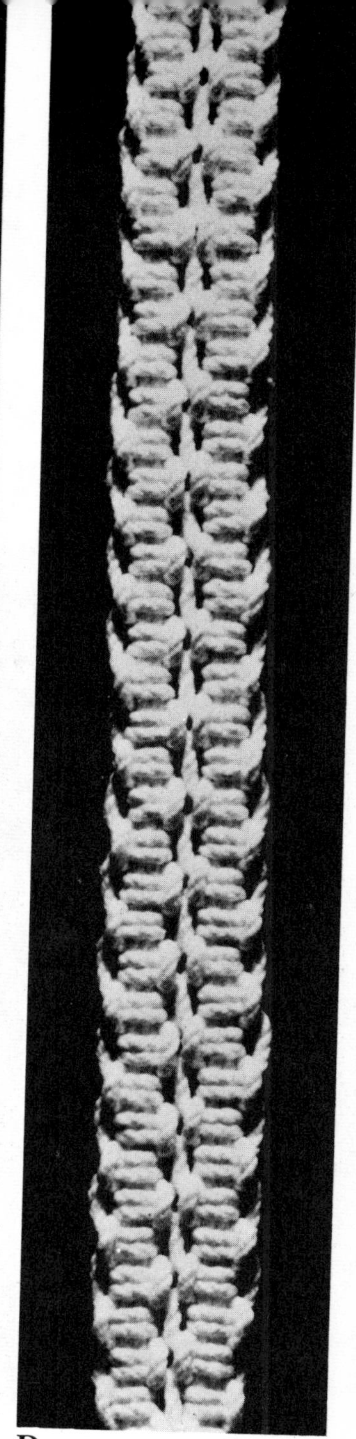
D

Braids

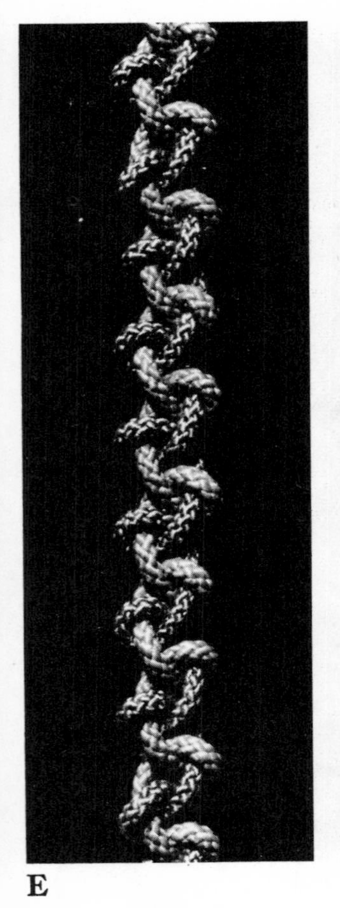

E

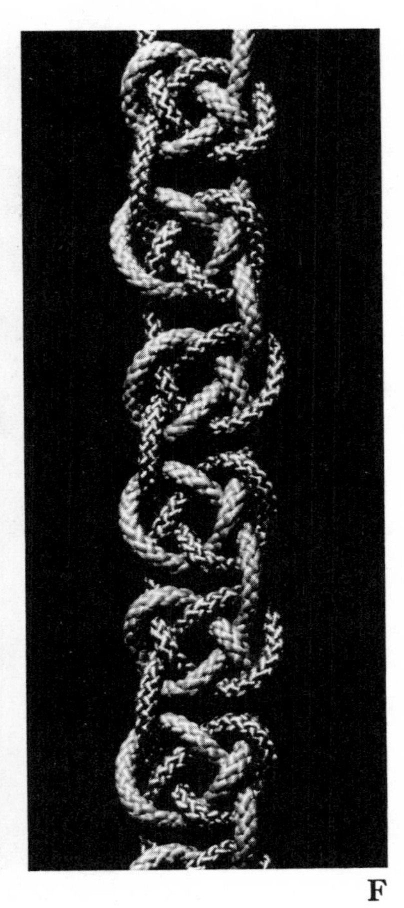

F

BRAID E

MATERIAL. Synthetic coloured rope from a marine supply store.
NUMBER OF CORDS. Two (one in each of two contrasting colours).
TO MAKE
Work a chain of alternate half hitches.

BRAID F

MATERIAL. Synthetic coloured rope from a marine supply store.
NUMBER OF CORDS. Two (one in each of two contrasting colours).
TO MAKE
The braid is worked in Josephine knots, an attractive fancy knot. Tie the first knot from the left as follows: make a loop with cord 1, as shown in Fa. Now bring cord 2 across the loop, up behind the end of cord 1, over the top part of 1, under the top strand of the loop, under cord 2 where it lies across the loop, and under the lower strand of the loop (Fb). Pull both ends gently and the knot will form itself into a pleasing symmetrical shape. Tie a second knot immediately below the first, but this time tie it from the right: i.e. form a loop with cord 2, then bring cord 1 across it and weave it in and out as before. Continue to tie Josephine knots alternately from left and right to the length required.

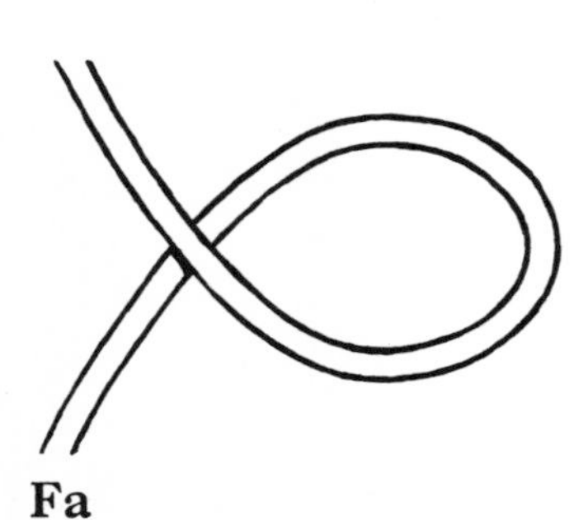

Fa

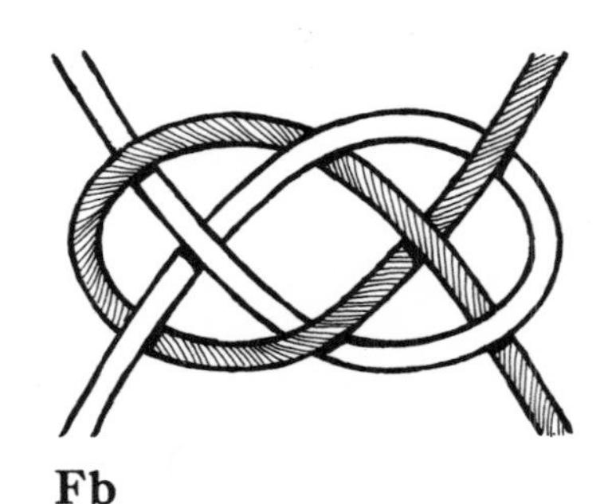

Fb

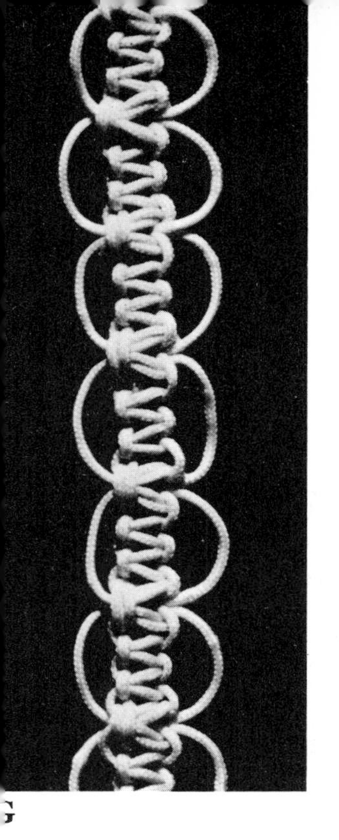

G

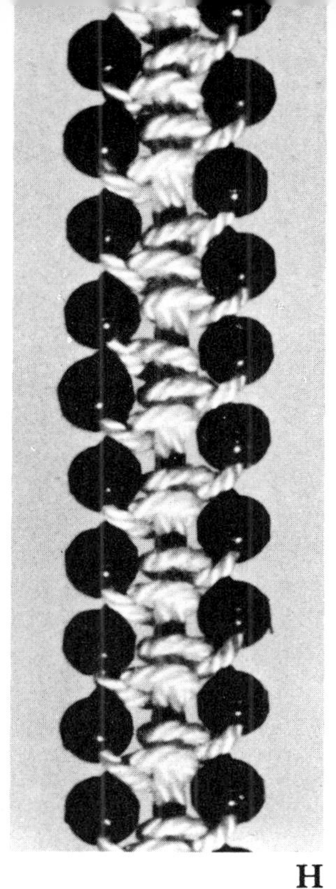

H

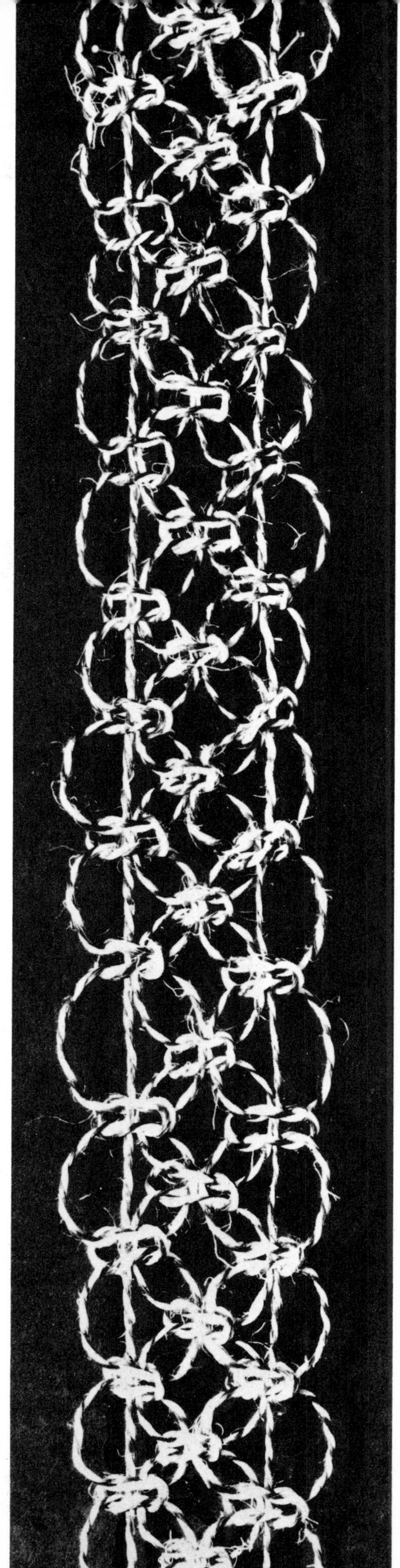

I

BRAID G

MATERIALS. Fine nylon cord; coloured plastic twine.
NUMBER OF CORDS. Six (four nylon cords arranged in pairs on either side of two plastic twine cords).
TO MAKE
*Tie a flat knot, using double strands of knotting cords (the nylon cords) and the plastic twine as knotbearing cords. Now leave the outer cords unworked and tie two flat knots, using single strands of nylon as knotting cords, and the plastic twine as knotbearing cords.** Repeat from * to ** to the length required; let the outer nylon cords form regular picot loops at each side.

BRAID H

MATERIALS. Medium silk cord. China beads.
NUMBER OF CORDS. Four.
TO MAKE
Work throughout in half hitches tied alternately with cord 1 over cords 2 and 3, and cord 4 over cords 3 and 2. Before tying each knot, slip a bead on to each knotting cord and slide it up close to the last knot.

BRAID I

MATERIAL. Two-colour sisal string.
NUMBER OF CORDS. Eight.
TO MAKE
Work in an alternate flat knot pattern throughout (i.e. one knot in one row, followed by two knots in the next row, and so on). Space the knots out evenly so a very open-work pattern is created, and let the outside cords form large loops (picots) between the rows of knots.

Fringes

FRINGE A

MATERIAL. Cash's cording No. 950.
MEASUREMENTS. Depth of finished fringe, including tassel, 10″.
PREPARATION. Cut cords each 4 ft 4″. Each repeat of the fringe motif requires 12 working ends (i.e. six cut cords), so the total number of cords cut should be a multiple of six.

TO MAKE

Set on cords with ribbed picot headings as follows:
pin cords to working surface in pairs, one cord inside the other so you have a double top loop. Using cords double, slant cords 3 and 4 to the left across cords 1 and 2 then work a diagonal double half hitch with 1 and 2 over 3 and 4. Now slant cords 1 and 2 down to the left across 3 and 4, and work a double half hitch with 3 and 4 over 1 and 2. Lay a holding cord across and work horizontal cording over it with each of the four cords in turn.
Repeat with each pair of cords until all are set on.

A

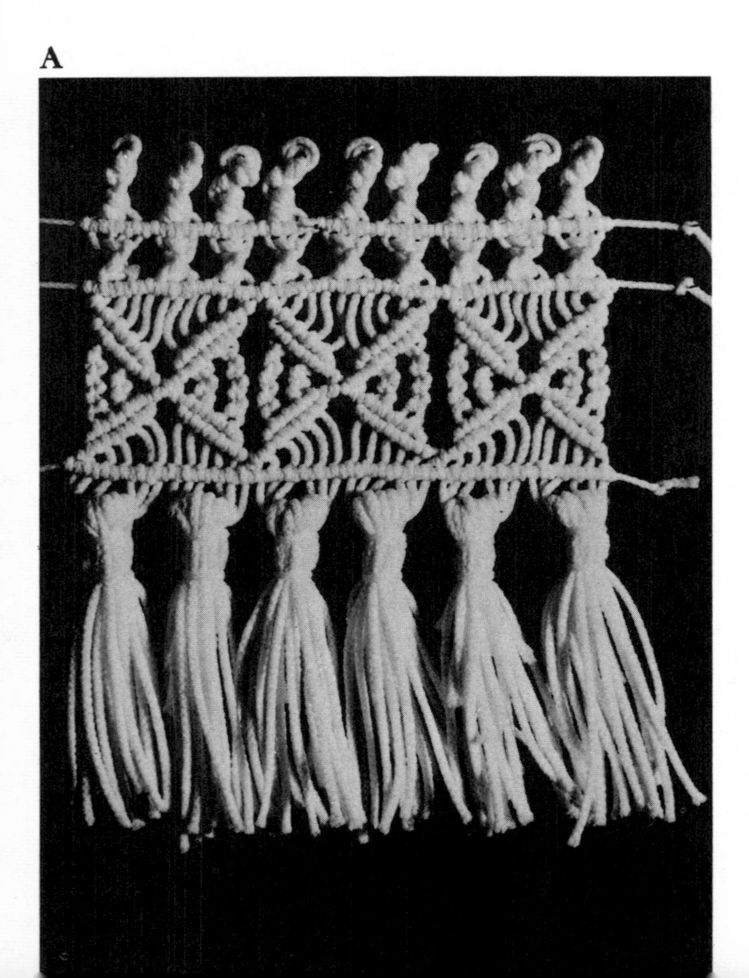

Next row: tie four half knots (first half of flat knot) with each group of four cords. Let spiral twist round on itself once.
Next row: introduce a separate leader and work one row of horizontal cording across all cords.
Pattern motif: divide cords into groups of 12. Work on the first group of 12 thus:
*with cord 1 as leader, work a row of diagonal cording slanting down to the right with cords 2, 3, 4, 5 and 6.
Work a second row immediately below, with cord 2 as leader. Knot over it cords 3, 4, 5, 6 and 1.
Similarly with cord 12 as leader, work a row of diagonal cording slanting down to the left with cords 11, 10, 9, 8 and 7. Work a second row immediately below, with cord 11 as leader. Knot over it cords 10, 9 8, 7 and 12.
Link the centre point of the motif by knotting cord 2 over 11. Work seven alternate half hitches with cords 3 and 4. Work four alternate half hitches with cords 5 and 6. Similarly work seven alternate half hitches with cords 9 and 10, and four alternate half hitches with cords 7 and 8.
Now cord 11 continues as leader; work diagonal cording slanting down to the left over it with cords 1, 6, 5, 4 and 3. With cord 1 as leader, work a second row immediately below, knotting over it cords 6, 5, 4, 3 and 11.
In a similar way work a double row of diagonal cording slanting down to the right with cord 2 as leader for the first row, and knotting over it cords 12, 7, 8, 9 and 10 and cord 12 as leader for second row, knotting over it cords 7, 8, 9, 10 and 2.**
Repeat from * to ** with each group of 12 cords.
Next row: introduce a separate leader and work one row of horizontal cording across all cords.

TO FINISH

Divide cords into groups of six. Work on the first group only:
divide cords into two groups of three and tie in the first half of a flat knot without a central knotbearing core (see page 42, F and G).
Now cut 12 lengths of yarn, each about 10″ (or more for a deeper tassel). Fold cut cords in half, and loop them over the half knot just tied. Complete the tassel as described on page 214, for the Cashmere Shawl.
Repeat with each group of six cords.
Finally trim tassels evenly.

B

FRINGE B

ıATERIAL. Aran knitting wool in two contrasting hades.

ıEASUREMENTS. Depth of fringe (excluding ringing) approximately $4\frac{3}{4}$".

PREPARATION. Cut cords each 5 ft long and set hem on to a holding cord in the following colour equence: one in colour A; two in colour B; two in olour A; two in colour B, and so on, ending with one in olour A. Each repeat of the pattern is worked on eight ord ends (two in colour A, four in colour B, two in olour A).

'O MAKE

Jsing the cord on the far left as leader, work horizontal ording from left to right across all cords. Reverse the irection of the leader round a pin and work a second ɔw of horizontal cording immediately below, from right) left.

Vork on the first group of eight cords:
with cord 2 as leader, work diagonal cording slanting own to the right with cords 3 and 4. Work a second row nmediately below, with cord 1 as leader, and knotting ver it cords 3 and 4.

'ow work diagonal cording slanting down to the left ith cord 7 as leader; knot cords 6 and 5 over it. Work a econd row of diagonal cording immediately below with ɔrd 8 as leader, and knotting cords 6 and 5 over it. Now ɔrd 7 continues across the work as a leader at the same ant as before; cording is worked over it with cords 2, 4 and 3 in turn.

imilarly cord 8 continues across the work as a leader, ıd cording is worked over it with cords 2, 1, 4 and 3.

'ow cord 2 continues as a leader slanting to the right, ıd cording is worked over it with cords 5 and 6. Cord 1 ɔntinues as leader for a second row below and cords 5 ıd 6 are knotted over it.**

epeat from * to ** with each group of eight cords.

otifs are now linked by using cord 7 from the right-ınd motif as a leader slanting down to the left, and cords and 1 of the left-hand motif are knotted over it. milarly, cord 8 of the right-hand motif becomes leader r the row of diagonal cording immediately below, and ɔrds 2 and 1 of the left-hand motif are knotted over it. ɔntinue to link the motifs together in this way.

'ork both odd cords at ends of the fringe as follows:
cords at the far left (first motif): use cord 8 as leader, and knot cord 7 over it. Reverse the direction of 8 round a pin and let it continue as the leader, slanting down to the right. Work diagonal cording over it with cord 7.

Cords at the far right (last motif): in a similar way, knot cord 2 over cord 1. Reverse the direction of cord 1 to slant down to the left and knot cord 2 over it again.***

Several cords by this time will have travelled across the work as leaders; as numbering is becoming confusing divide cords across the row into groups of eight, and re-number them for ease of identification.

Repeat from * to *** twice more (or to the depth of fringe required). At the end of the last repeat, only work the first cording knot on odd cords at either end; i.e. for left-hand cords, knot 7 over 8 once only (do not reverse direction of 8); for right-hand cords, knot 2 over 1 once only.

TO FINISH

With the cord on the far left as leader, work horizontal cording from left to right across all cords. Reverse the direction of the leader round a pin, and work a second row of horizontal cording immediately below, this time from right to left.

Trim fringe evenly.

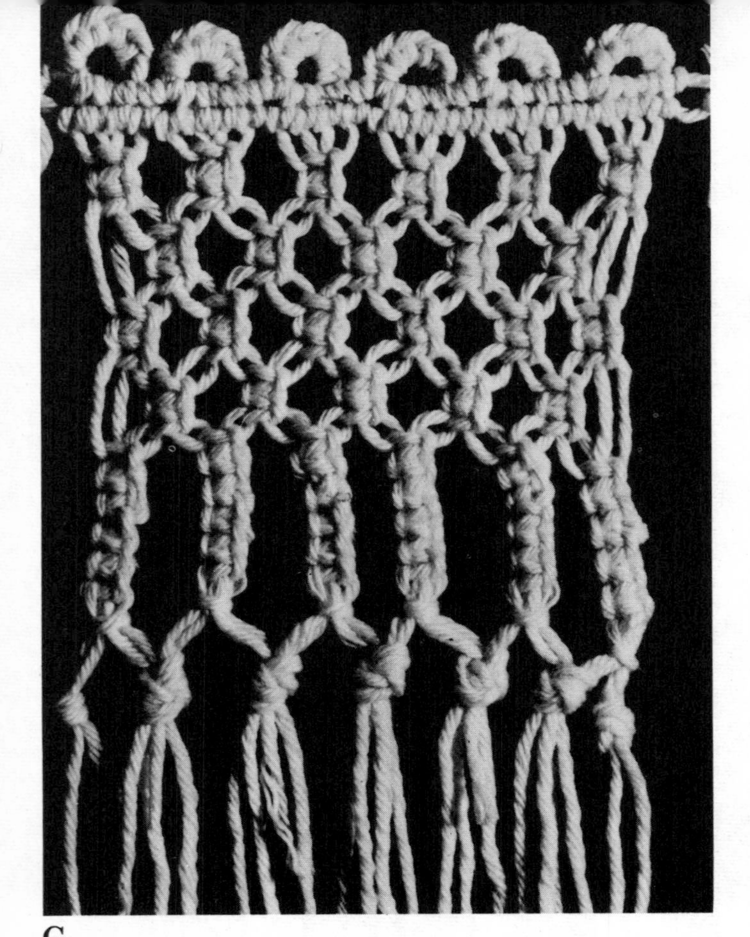

C

Fringes

FRINGE C

MATERIAL. Rug wool.
MEASUREMENTS. Depth of fringe approximately 8″, excluding fringing.
PREPARATION. Cut cords each 70″ long. Set on (in multiples of four working ends) to holding cord by the half hitch scalloped edge method (see page 191).

TO MAKE

Introduce a separate leader and work one row of horizontal cording from left to right across all cords.

*Work two flat knots with each group of four cords to the end of the row.

Next row: leave the first two cords unworked; work two flat knots with each group of four cords to the two last cords; leave these unworked.**

Repeat from * to **.

Next row: work chains of five flat knots with each group of four cords to the end of the row.

TO FINISH

Combine two right-hand cords from each flat knot chain with two left-hand cords of the chain next to it. Tie them together in an overhand knot. Tie the odd pairs of cords at the far left and far right in an overhand knot. Trim fringe evenly.

FRINGE D

MATERIAL. Dishcloth cotton in two contrasting shades.
MEASUREMENTS. Depth of fringe to the tip of the design (excluding fringing) approximately $5\frac{1}{2}$″.
PREPARATION. Cut cords each $1\frac{1}{2}$ yd long and set them in pairs on to a holding cord with overhand picot edging (see page 190) in the following colour sequence: one pair in colour A (two cut cords, giving four working ends); three pairs in colour B; two pairs in colour A; three pairs in colour B; two pairs in colour A, and so on to the end, finishing with one pair of cords in colour A. Each repeat of the pattern is worked on 20 cord ends (four in colour A, twelve in colour B, four in colour A).

TO MAKE

With a separate leader, work one row of horizontal cording across all cords. Begin pattern.

Divide cords into pairs across the work. With cord 2 as leader slanting down to the left, work a diagonal double half hitch with cord 1 over it. With cord 3 as leader slanting down to the right, work a diagonal double half hitch with cord 4 over it. Continue in this way across cords, knotting each pair of cords with a single diagonal double half hitch, and alternating the direction of each pair. Renumber the cords in groups from 1–4 in the order in which they now lie.

With cord 1 as leader, work a row of horizontal cording with cords 2, 3 and 4. Reverse the direction of cord 1 and work a row of horizontal cording from right to left with the same cords.

With cord 1 as leader slanting down to the right, work a diagonal double half hitch over it with cord 2.

With cord 4 as leader slanting down to the left, work diagonal cording over it with cords 3, 1 and 2.

Now work the centre group of colour B cords: divide cords into three groups of four cords each. Working on the first group, the cords at present lie in the order: 2, 1, 4 and 3.

Let cord 4 continue as leader slanting down to the left and work diagonal cording over it with cords 1 and 2. Let cord 1 continue as leader slanting down to the right and work a diagonal double half hitch over it with cord 3. Reverse the direction of cord 4 to slant down to the right and work a diagonal double half hitch over it with cord 2. Similarly reverse the direction of cord 1 to slant down to the left and work diagonal cording over it with cords 3, 1 and 2. Letting cord 1 continue as leader slanting down to the right, work a diagonal double half hitch over it with cord 3.

Work similar cording diamond motifs with each of the next two groups of four cords (three motifs in the band). Then work a 2nd band of cording diamonds in a similar way by linking the right-hand cords from motif 1 with the left-hand cords from motif 2, then linking right-hand cords from the 2nd motif with the left-hand cords of the 3rd motif (two motifs in band). Work a 3rd band with only a single motif in it, combining the right-hand cords and left-hand cords of the two motifs in the previous band. You should now have a triangular panel of cording diamonds in colour B, with six cords coming from each side of the triangle.

Work on the left-hand six cords first, linking them to the colour A cords on their left as follows:

with the first of the colour B cords as leader slanting down to the left, work a diagonal double half hitch over it with the first colour A cord on its left. Similarly with the 2nd of colour B cords as leader slanting to the left, work a diagonal double half hitch over it with the first colour A cord.

The 2nd of colour A cords now becomes a leader slanting down to the right, and diagonal cording is worked over it with each of the two colour B cords, the row worked tight against the previous one. The 3rd cord in colour A then becomes leader slanting down to the right, and diagonal cording is worked over it with the two colour B cords. Finally, each of the two colour B cords is used in turn as leader slanting down to the left, and a diagonal double half hitch is worked over each with the fourth colour A cord.

To complete the two-colour cording diamond, the cord on the far right (in colour A) is slanted down to the left following the line of the rest of the motif so far worked, then diagonal cording is worked over it with each of the other colour A cords in turn.

Work two more two-colour cording motifs in a similar way with the other cords in colour B coming from the left-hand side of the triangle.

Now go on to the 2nd group of colour A cords. With the cord on the far left as leader, work a row of horizontal cording across all colour A cords in the group. Reverse its direction and work a 2nd row of horizontal cording.

Divide the cords into two groups of four, and, with the first group, work a band of two-colour cording diamonds to match the first, but this time combine colour A cords with colour B cords from the right-hand side of the triangle, and slant the band down to the left.

Now work the next group of colour B cords in a triangle of cording diamonds, as in the first, and combine its left-hand cords with the remaining colour A cords on the left to form a band of two-colour cording diamonds slanting down to the right.

Continue in this way across the row.

Finally fill in the space between the bands of two-colour cording diamonds by working a complete large diamond of colour B small cording diamonds. The first row in each large diamond will have just one small diamond, then as cords from either side of the work are brought into the pattern, the 2nd row will have two motifs, and the 3rd will have three motifs.

Decrease the motifs as before, so the next row will have just two motifs, and the final row only one motif.

Work half diamonds with the odd cords at either end of the fringe.

TO FINISH

With a separate leader, work a row of cording on all cords, closely following the shaped outline of the design. Trim the ends to give a fringe of the required depth.

D

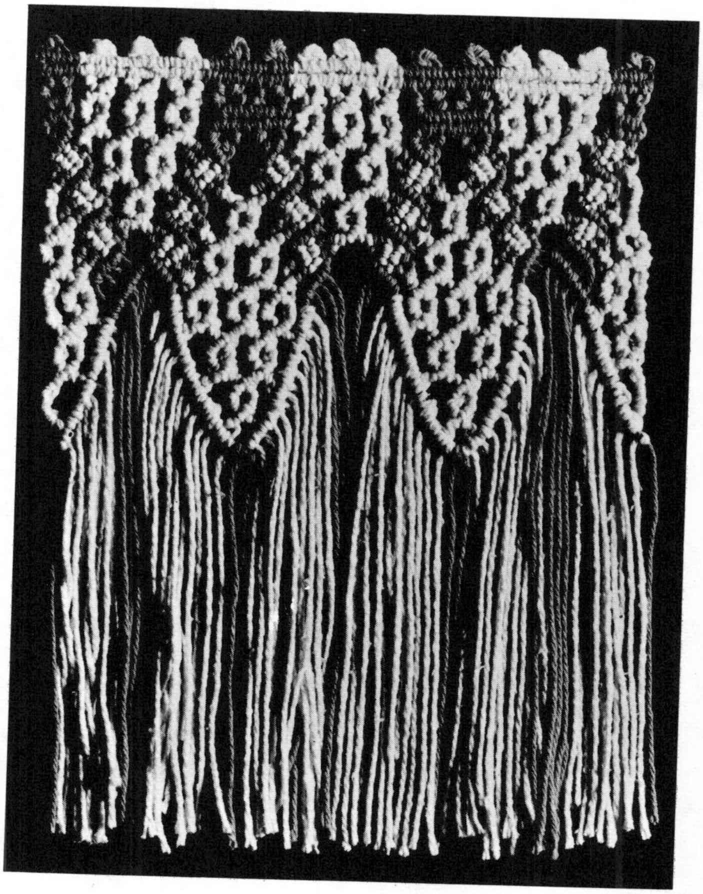

Sampler sweater

Shown on front cover

MATERIALS. 938 yards Cash's cording No. 950, from J. & J. Cash Ltd., Coventry.
MEASUREMENTS. To fit average bust size 34/36″; underarm sleeve length 20″, depth of sleeve 7″; centre back length (excluding fringe) approximately 20″.
TENSION CHECK. Over the diamond yoke pattern: approximate depth of diamond 1½″. On main pattern section: a chain of six flat knots measures 2″.
PREPARATION. The back and front of the sweater are made alike. For each piece therefore cut 168 cords (total of 336 cords for the entire sweater) in the following lengths: 112 at 5 ft, 56 at 5 yd. For each side of the sweater cut a holding cord approximately 70″ long (this will form the shoulder and neckline edge). Set cords on in the following order: 40 at 5 ft; (one at 5 yd, three at 5 ft) four times; (three at 5 yd, one at 5 ft) four times; 24 at 5 yd; (one at 5 ft, three at 5 yd) four times; (three at 5 ft, one at 5 yd) four times; 40 at 5 ft. You now have 336 working ends for each side of the sweater.

TO MAKE THE SWEATER FRONT

Work the diamond yoke pattern first.
Divide the cords into groups of eight and work thus:
*with cord 1 as leader slanting down to the right, work diagonal cording over it with cords 2, 3 and 4; with cord 8 as leader slanting down to the left, work diagonal cording over it with cords 7, 6 and 5. Link the two leaders by knotting cord 8 over cord 1.**
Repeat from * to ** with each group of eight cords to the end of the row.
***Return to the first group of eight cords. Cord 8 continues as leader slanting to the left; work cording over it with cords 4, 3 and 2. Cord 1 continues as a leader slanting down to the right; work cording over it with cords 5, 6 and 7.
Repeat this sequence with every group of cords to the end of the row.
Return to the first group of cords.
Reverse the direction of cord 8 round a pin, and with it as leader slanting down to the right, work cording over it with cords 2, 3 and 4.
Link cord 1 of the first motif to cord 8 of the second motif by knotting cord 8 over cord 1.
Cord 8 (of second motif) now continues as leader slanting down to the left and cords 7, 6 and 5 of the first motif are knotted over it.
Repeat this sequence to the end of the row.
The four odd cords at the far right will be worked thus: cord 1 of this motif will continue as leader for diagonal cording slanting to the right, and cords 5, 6 and 7 are worked over it. It is then reversed round a pin and it continues as leader slanting down to the left. Cords 7, 6 and 5 are then knotted over it.
Continue to work thus in the diamond pattern until four complete diamonds have been worked from ***, or until the depth of sleeve is 7″. (If your tension is a little tight, it may be necessary to work another half diamond to reach the required depth.)

Main pattern section. Work on the centre 112 cords only. With the cord on the far left as leader, work a row of horizontal cording from left to right. Reverse the direction of the leader at the end of the row and work a 2nd row of horizontal cording immediately below, this time from right to left.
1st pattern panel: work chains of six flat knots with each group of four cords across the row.
Divider row: with the cord on the far left as leader, work one row of horizontal cording from left to right.
2nd pattern panel: divide cords into groups of 16. Work on the first group thus:
with cord 8 as leader slanting down to the left, work diagonal cording with cords 7, 6, 5, 4, 3, 2 and 1. With cord 7 as leader work a second row of diagonal cording immediately below with cords 6, 5, 4, 3, 2, 1 and 8.
In a similar way work a double row of diagonal cording

Sampler sweater

slanting down to the right with cords 9–16 (cord 9 will be leader for the first row, cord 10 leader for the 2nd row).
Now fill in the centre of the diamond area:
using cords double, tie a half hitch from the left with cords 4 and 5 over 6 and 11; then tie a half hitch from the right with cords 12 and 13 over 6 and 11. Tie a half hitch from the left with cords 8 and 1 over cords 2 and 3; tie a half hitch from the right with cords 4 and 5 over 2 and 3.
Tie a half hitch from the left with cords 12 and 13 over cords 14 and 15; tie a half hitch from the right with cords 16 and 9 over 14 and 15.
Complete this centre pattern by tying a half hitch from the left with cords 4 and 5 over 6 and 11; tie a half hitch from the right with cords 12 and 13 over 6 and 11.
Complete the lower half of the diamond:
reverse the direction of cord 7 round a pin and, with it as leader slanting down to the right, work diagonal cording over it with cords 8, 1, 2, 3, 4, 5 and 6. With cord 8 as leader, work a second row of diagonal cording immediately below, knotting over it cords 1, 2, 3, 4, 5, 6 and 7.
Similarly work the other side of the diamond with a double row of cording slanting down to the left: cord 10 will be leader for the first row; cord 9 leader for the second.
Repeat this pattern sequence with each group of 16 cords to the end of the row.
Divider row: with the cord on the far right as leader, work a row of horizontal cording from right to left.
3rd pattern panel: work in alternate flat knot pattern for five rows, being careful not to tie the knots too tightly, but spacing them out regularly to form an attractive lacy pattern.
Divider row: with the cord on the far left as leader, work a row of horizontal cording from left to right.
4th pattern panel: divide cords into groups of 16. Work on the first group thus:
*with cord 8 as leader slanting down to the left, work a row of diagonal cording with cords 7, 6, 5, 4, 3, 2 and 1.
With cord 9 as leader slanting down to the right, work a row of diagonal cording with cords 10, 11, 12, 13, 14, 15 and 16.**
Repeat from * to ** across the row but link V motifs together each time by knotting cord 8 of the motif on the right over cord 9 of the motif on its left.
Return to the first 16 cords. With cord 7 as leader slanting down to the right, work a row of diagonal cording immediately below the previous one with cords 10, 11, 12, 13, 14, 15, 16 and cord 8 of the second motif.
With cord 10 as leader slanting down to the left, work diagonal cording immediately below the previous one with cords 6, 5, 4, 3, 2, 1 and 8.
Continue in this way across the row, but again link V motifs together each time by knotting the leader cords from right-hand motifs over the leader cords of left-hand motifs.
Continue until six rows of cording have been worked altogether in each V—you should now have a continuous six-band zigzag of cording going right across the work.
With the half motifs at either end of the row, the leader cords in every row drop down to become knotting cords in subsequent rows.
Divider row: with the cord on the far right as leader, work a row of horizontal cording from right to left.

TO MAKE THE SWEATER BACK

Work exactly as for Sweater Front.

TO FINISH

Trim the holding cords to within an inch of the work, turn to the wrong side and stitch neatly to the back of the set-on cords. Place the back to the front, wrong sides together. Oversew together along the top of the sleeves for 20″ in from each cuff edge, thus leaving 20″ free in the centre for the neck edge. Stitch underarm seam by oversewing the tips of the diamond cording motifs together along their lower edge.
Oversew the side seams together.
Finally trim the lower fringe to 8″ (or depth required).
Trim underarm fringe to 6″.

Pebble necklace

Designed by Kaffe Fassett

MATERIALS. 1 ball each of parcel string and sisal string; a metal choker ring; 5 medium-sized and 1 large beach pebble with holes in them.
MEASUREMENTS. To fit an average sized neck; depth of necklace—as wished.
TENSION CHECK. Again, variable, depending on the type of string used and the number of strands; as this is a 'free' design it is not vital to have a constant tension measurement.
PREPARATION. Cut 32 lengths of string, each 5 ft for a necklace about 6″ deep (longer if you want it deeper). Set these cords directly on to the choker ring, having the knot of setting-on at the back of the ring (so the knots will not show on the right side of the necklace). Cords can be set on in any arrangement you wish; you may only want a few sisal cords, for instance, or you may wish an equal number of each sort of string.

TO MAKE

With the cord on the far left as leader, work a row of horizontal cording. Divide cords into six unequal groups; it does not matter which have a lot of cords, and which have only a few. Between each group of cords, leave two single cords.
Now tie each multiple group in a flat knot chain for approximately 1″—in every case use single knotting cords, multiple knotbearing central cords. Slide a medium-sized pebble on to each pair of cords between the chains.
With the cord on the far left as leader, work a row of horizontal cording across all cords.
Work chains of two flat knots with each group of four cords to the end of the row.
Divide cords into eight unequal groups.
Work on two centre groups first: work a chain of flat knots with each group (again with single knotting cords) for about $1\frac{1}{2}$″.
Combine a few right-hand cords from the chain on the left with a few left-hand cords from the chain on the right and thread these through the remaining pebble.
Work a chain of flat knots with the remaining cords on the left round the outside of the pebble. Similarly work a chain of flat knots with the remaining cords on the right.
Combine both chains under the pebble and work a flat knot chain for about an inch. Tie an overhand knot. Work another inch of flat knots, and tie a second overhand knot.
Work chains of flat knots with the remaining groups of cords to depth required. In a similar way tie an overhand knot about an inch before the end of each chain. Then tie a final overhand knot to complete each chain.

TO FINISH

Trim cords to depth required.

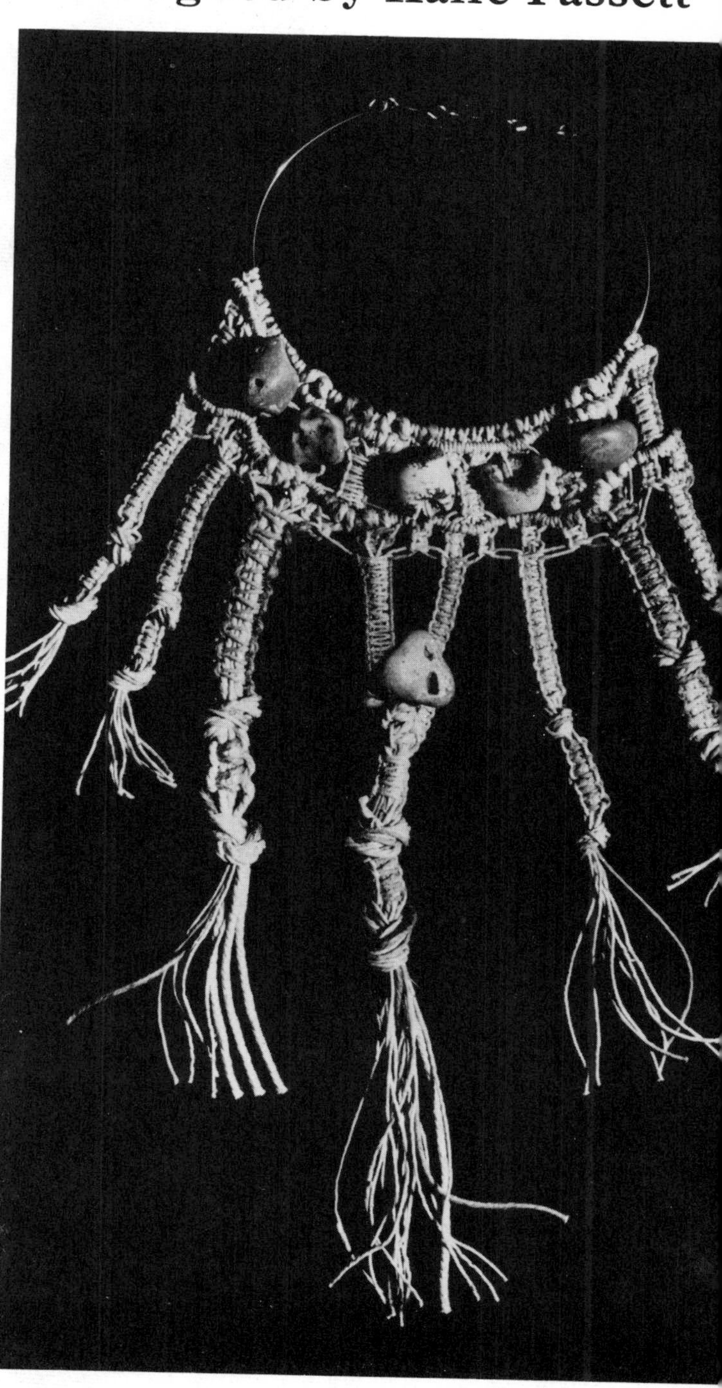

Cashmere shawl

MATERIALS. $1\frac{3}{4}$ yd cashmere fabric, 48″ wide, from George Harrison and Co (Edinburgh) Ltd, at Harrods; sixteen $\frac{1}{2}$ oz balls Lister's Cashmere yarn.
MEASUREMENTS. Finished shawl measures 42″ square (excluding fringe); depth of fringe approx. 7″, including tassels.
TENSION CHECK. Six horizontal double half hitches worked with double strands measure 1″.
Note. *Yarn is set on double, and used double throughout to give the knotting slightly more 'body' than would otherwise be obtained from single thickness cashmere yarn.*
This shawl is based on Vogue Pattern 8038.
PREPARATION. Cut 492 double lengths of yarn, each 36″ long (i.e. you will in fact cut 984 lengths altogether before arranging them in pairs). Cut a 43″ square from cashmere fabric.

TO MAKE

Turn in a $\frac{1}{2}$″ hem round all raw edges on the fabric square and stitch neatly.
Set on 119 double threads along each edge of the fabric, spacing the threads equally (there will be very approximately $\frac{1}{4}$″ between each set-on thread). The easiest way to set on the yarn is to thread each pair of threads on to a large-eyed darning needle and stitch them on to the fabric edge (see A).
Pull ends down through the loop, so the finished effect is similar to the normal setting on (see B).
Foundation round: starting around the midpoint of one edge, introduce a separate leader, approx. 180″ long, and work horizontal cording round on all cords. As each corner is reached, set two new double threads on to the leader. At the end of the round you will have 968 working ends.
Trim the end of the leader cord to about an inch from the last knot, lay the end over the beginning of the round of cording, and oversew firmly to hold together.
Next round: work on each pair of cords thus: using the left-hand cord as leader, work one diagonal double half hitch slanting down to the right with the right-hand cord.
Next round: again beginning around the midpoint of one edge, introduce a separate leader, approx. 184″ long, and work horizontal cording with every cord, as for the foundation round. At each corner, set on another two new cords to the leader.
At the end of the round you will have 984 working ends. Oversew the end of the leader to the beginning of the cording, as in the foundation round.
Now begin pattern. Divide cords into groups of 12. Work on one set of 12 only:
***1st row:** using cord 1 as leader, work diagonal cording slanting down to the right with cords 2, 3 and 4.
Next row: with cord 2 as leader, work a row of diagonal cording immediately below with cords 3, 4 and 1. With cord 2 still as leader, and continuing the same slant to the right as in the first row, work a row of diagonal cording with cords 5 and 6 (see C).
Now using cord 1 as leader, work a row of diagonal cording immediately below the previous one with cords 5, 6 and 2 (see D).
Work the other half of the V pattern: using cord 12 as leader, work diagonal cording slanting down to the left

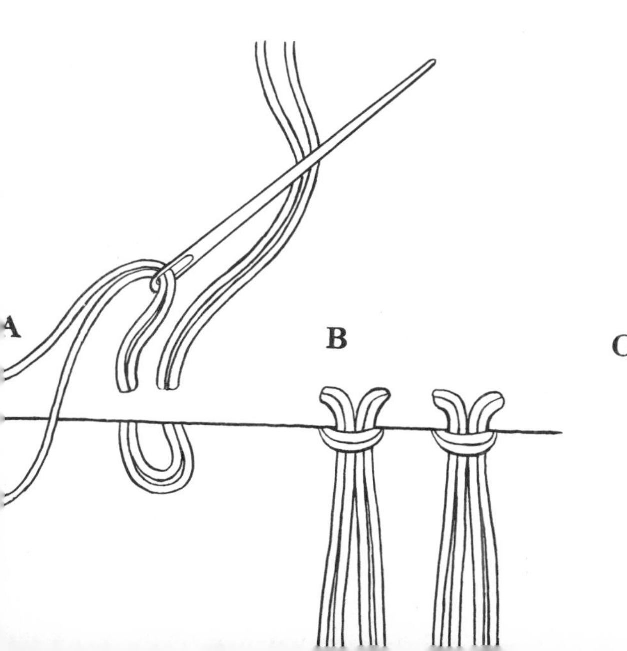

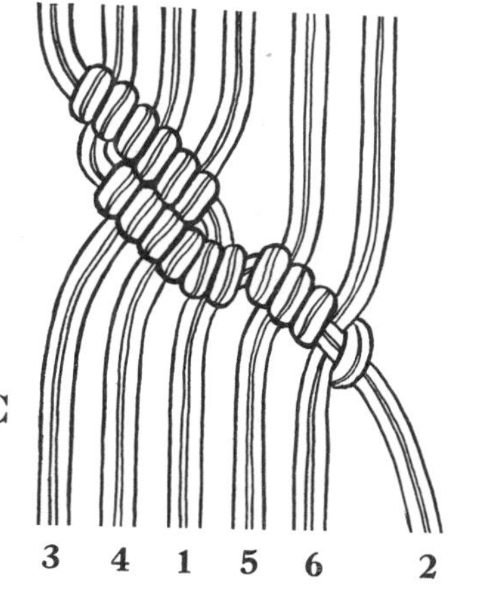

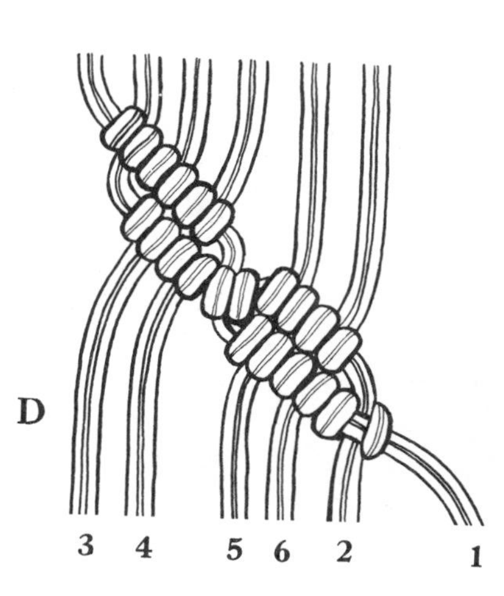

Cashmere shawl

with cords 11, 10 and 9. Work a second row immediately below with cord 11 as leader, and knotting cords 10, 9 and 12 over it.

Continue to make the second half of the diagonal cording motif with cord 11 still as leader and knotting over it cords 8 and 7. Work a second row beneath this with cord 12 as leader, and knotting over it cords 8, 7 and 11.

Now link the two double rows of diagonal cording at the tip of the V by working a double half hitch with cord 1 over cord 12 (see E).

Repeat this knotting sequence with each group of 12 cords right round.

Cords for each motif now lie in the following order: 3, 4, 5, 6, 2, 12, 1, 11, 7, 8, 9 and 10.**

2nd pattern round: *** divide cords in groups of 12 again but this time combine cords 1, 11, 7, 8, 9 and 10 from one motif with cords 3, 4, 5, 6, 2 and 12 of the motif on its right.

Loop cords 3 and 4 round cords 9 and 10 to hold the centre of the motif together. Now re-number each group of 12 cords from 1 to 12 as before.

Repeat pattern from * to **. ****

3rd pattern round: repeat from *** to ****

TO FINISH

Make a tassel between each motif on the final round for each tassel cut 12 lengths of yarn, approx. 9″ long.

Between every motif along the last round worked tak the cords on the left and the cords on the right and ti them together in the first half of a flat knot without an central core (see F).

Fold the tassel cords in half and loop them over the hal knot just tied. Use any one of the tassel cords to bin tightly round all the cords just below the loop. Secur the end by tying a collecting knot: form a loop at th front of the tassel with the binding cord, then take th cord across the front of the tassel from right to left round the back and through to the front through th loop. Draw tight (see G).

Make a second tight binding round the tassel about hal an inch below the first, finishing with a collecting knot Make tassels right round in this way. Finally trim th tassels evenly.

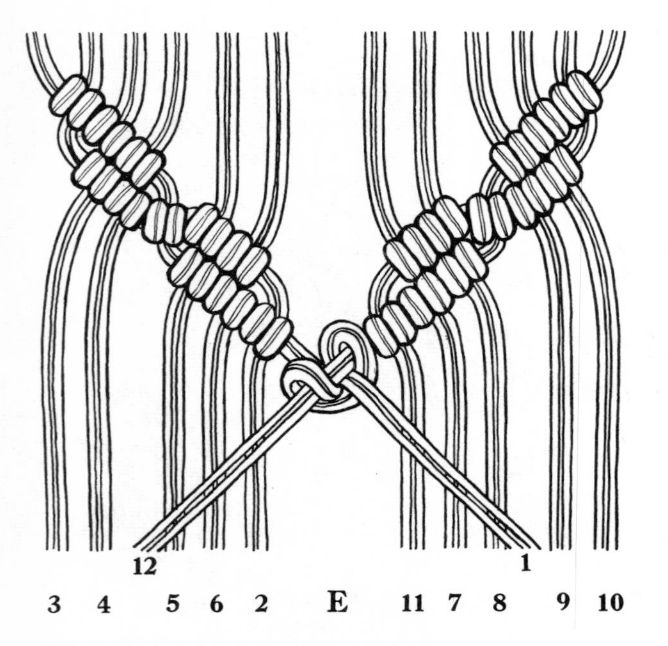

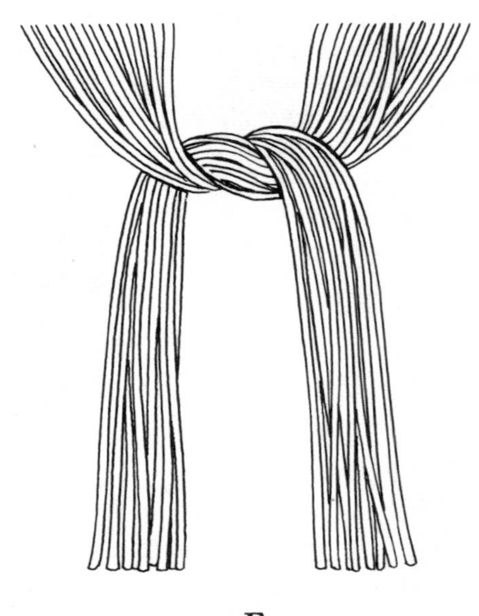

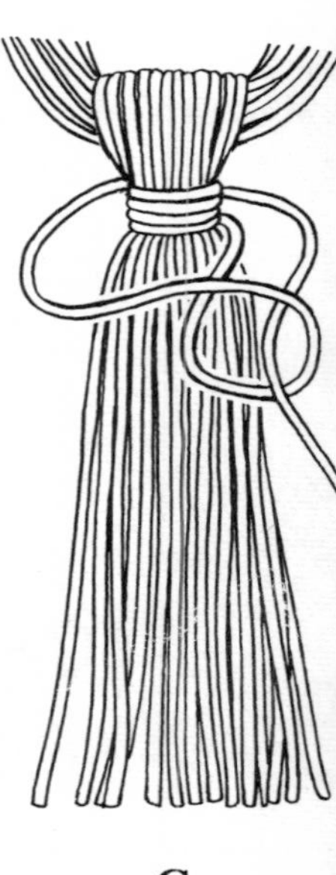

Braid braces

MATERIALS. 3 balls of heavyweight parcel string; 1 press stud.
DRESS. Vogue Pattern No. 2648, sizes 10–16, in Heather Mills Trelya pure wool crêpe, from Harrods.
MEASUREMENTS. Length of waistband 28″; length of each shoulder braid 36″.
TENSION CHECK. Three flat knots measure 1″.

Braid braces

PREPARATION. For waistband: cut 10 cords, each 6 yd long. Take one of these cords, double it and pin it to the working surface so it forms an inverted V from its midway point. On the right-hand arm of the V, working from centre point down, set on four cords, setting each on with double half hitches (cording) instead of the usual method. On the left-hand arm of the V set on the remaining five cords, also by double half hitches. The holding cords now drop down to become knotting cords, so you have a total of 20 working cords. Number them from 1 to 20 in the order they now lie. **For each shoulder braid:** cut six cords, each 8 yd long. Place four cords together, double them and pin them to the working surface by the top loop. Now cross the left-hand cords over the right-hand cords, making the cross about 2″ down from the top loop. Set on the remaining two cords over this crossed point. This forms a loop by which the braid can be slid on to the waistband.

TO MAKE WAISTBAND

With cord 11 as leader slanting down to the right, work a row of diagonal cording immediately below the set-on edge with cords 12, 13, 14, 15, 16, 17, 18 and 19.
With cord 12 as leader slanting down to the left, work diagonal cording immediately below the other set-on edge with cords 10, 9, 8, 7, 6, 5, 4, 3 and 2.
Now tie a multi-end flat knot, with cords 2, 3, 4, 5 and 6, and cords 15, 16, 17, 18 and 19 as knotting cords, and cords 7, 8, 9, 10, 13 and 14 as the knotbearing central cords.
With cord 12 as leader slanting down to the right, work diagonal cording with cords 2, 3, 4, 5, 6, 7, 8 and 9. Work a 2nd row of diagonal cording immediately below with cord 1 as leader slanting down to the right, knotting over it cords 2, 3, 4, 5, 6, 7, 8 and 9.
In a similar way work two rows of cording at the othe side of the diamond, with cord 11 as the first leade slanting down to the left, and cord 20 as the seconc leader, knotting over them cords 19, 18, 17, 16, 15, 14 13 and 10. Link the tip of the diamond by knotting cord 11 and 20 over cord 12, and then over cord 1.
Work a chain of 12 alternate half hitches with cords and 3.
Tie a chain of two flat knots with cords 4, 5, 6 and 7. O the other side of the diamond, tie two flat knots wit cords 14, 15, 16 and 17.
Work a chain of 12 alternate half hitches with cords 1 and 19.
Now repeat the diamond motif, using the same tw leaders. Continue in this way working diamond moti outlined with double rows of cording, and with alterna half hitch chains and flat knots between the diamor motifs, until work measures 28″ (or length required End after a complete diamond motif has been worked Trim ends to about 1″, turn to the wrong side and wea the ends through the back of the knotting. Secure t ends with a spot of fabric glue, if wished.
Sew the press stud to fasten the belt at the centre fro

TO MAKE EACH SHOULDER BRAID

Work two braids alike.
1st pattern section: on first four cords work a spiral half knots for approximately 6″; on the centre four co work a chain of flat knots to the same depth; work spiral of half knots on the last group of four cords.
2nd pattern section: tie single flat knots with ea

of the three groups of four cords, in the usual way.
Next row: leave the first two cords unworked; tie flat knots with each of the next two groups of four cords; leave the final two cords unworked.
Next row: tie flat knots with each group of four cords.
On the first and last groups of cords, cross cord 1 over cord 2, and cross cord 4 over cord 3. Tie a flat knot (about an inch below the previous flat knot). Repeat the crossing of cords and flat knot sequence twice more.
On the centre four cords tie flat knots, spacing them out at ½″ intervals so the last flat knot lines up with the last flat knot tied in the other two groups of cords.
Next row: leave the first two cords unworked; tie a triple knot (1½ flat knots) with each of the next two groups of four cords; leave the final two cords unworked.
3rd pattern section: tie chains of flat knots spaced out at ½″ intervals with the first and last groups of four cords, to 3½″.
With the centre group, tie a chain of continuous flat knots (i.e. not spaced out) to the same depth.
4th pattern section: work in alternate flat knot pattern for about 5½″.
5th pattern section: work chains of continuous flat knots with the first and last groups of four cords, to about 4½″. Tie a chain of flat knots, spaced out at ½″ intervals, with the centre four cords.
Work two rows in the alternate flat knot pattern.
6th pattern section: tie chains of flat knots spaced out at ½″ intervals with the first and last groups of four cords.
With the centre group, cross cord 1 over cord 2, and cross cord 4 over cord 3. Tie a flat knot. Repeat crossing of cords and flat knot sequence until the chain is the same length as the other two in the section.

Work two rows in the alternate flat knot pattern with all cords.
7th pattern section: as first pattern section.
Trim cord ends to about 8″.

TO FINISH

Lay waistband flat and decide at what point the braids should be attached at the centre. Lay the braids in position. Take the cord ends of one braid down across the front of the waistband, and up behind it; divide them into two equal groups, cross them at the back and bring them to the front; cross them over again, and finally take them to the back and knot together in a multi-end flat knot. Repeat with the cord ends of the other braid. Do not tie too tightly: the braids should be able to slide fairly easily along the waistband.
Keeping the braids in position, measure up about 11″ on one braid from the top edge of the waistband. Cut two cords each 32″ long, and set these on at right angles to the braid at this point, directly on to a loop at the edge nearest the centre front (i.e. a loop on the far right of the left-hand braid, or a loop on the far left of the right-hand braid).
Work a chain of flat knots spaced out at ½″ intervals with these four working cords for about 4″.
Attach the cords to the other braid at a corresponding point, by taking the two centre cords through a loop along the edge of the braid from front to back, then tying the four cords firmly in a flat knot on the wrong side of the work. Trim the ends neatly.
Finally cut four cords, each 8″ long. Double each length and set them on to the loops along the lower edge of the horizontal crosspiece just worked. Tie each pair of cords in an overhand knot, and fray out the ends, if wished.

Apron

IATERIALS. 2 balls of jute string (or any other type f fairly soft, fine string); 3 yd ribbon braid, 1″ wide.
RESS. Miss Vogue Pattern 8132, sizes 6–14, in Liberty 'ana lawn.
IEASUREMENTS. Length of apron (excluding inge) 16″; width of yoke 6″; width of skirt section 9½″.
ENSION CHECK. Chain of five flat knots, tied with ouble thickness cords, is 1″.
REPARATION. Cut 52 cords, each 4 yd long; cut 4 cords each 3 yd long. Set the 52 cords on to a holding ord of about 1 ft.
ote. *Unless otherwise stated, cords are to be used double roughout.*
O MAKE
ntroduce a separate leader and work a row of horizontal ording across all cords.
ivide cords into groups of four double cords.
Work on the first group of double cords:
e a chain of four flat knots.
Vork on the second group of double cords:
ith cord 4 as leader slanting down to the left, work a ow of diagonal cording with cords 3, 2 and 1. With cord as leader, work a second row of diagonal cording immediately below with cords 2, 1 and 4.
ork on the third group of four double cords:
a chain of four flat knots.
ork on the fourth group of four double cords:
ith cord 1 as leader slanting down to the right, work a w of diagonal cording with cords 2, 3 and 4. With cord as leader, work a second row of diagonal cording immediately below with cords 3, 4 and 1.**
rom * to ** is the pattern. Repeat it twice using other oups of cords across the row.
omplete the row by tying a chain of four flat knots with e last group of four double cords.
ivider row: with the cord on the far right as leader, ork a row of horizontal cording across all cords.
ivide the cords into groups of four double cords again.
ork on the first group of four double cords:
e a chain of 11 flat knots.
ow work across the row as follows:
tie chains of two flat knots with each of the next three groups of four double cords; leave the next four double cords unworked. * Repeat from *** to ****; tie chains of two flat knots with each of the next three groups of double cords.
Tie a chain of 11 flat knots with the last group of double cords.
Beneath the two-knot chains just worked, continue as follows:
leave the first two cords unworked, tie chains of two flat knots with each of the next two groups of four double cords; leave the next eight double cords unworked; tie chains of two flat knots with each of the next two groups of four double cords; leave the next eight double cords unworked; tie chains of two flat knots with each of the next two groups of four double cords; leave the last two cords unworked.
Now with the first four double cords tie a chain of four flat knots; tie a chain of two flat knots with next four double cords; leave the next 12 cords unworked; tie a chain of two flat knots with the next four double cords; leave the next 12 cords unworked; tie a chain of two flat knots with the next four double cords; tie a chain of four flat knots with the last four double cords.
Now return to the first area of unworked cords, and work a cording diamond as follows:
number cords from 1 to 14 (cords 1 and 14 will be taken from the last chains of flat knots worked either side of the area; cords 2 through to 13 are the cords left unworked).
With cord 7 as leader slanting down to the left, work diagonal cording over it with cords 6, 5, 4, 3, 2 and 1. With cord 8 as leader slanting down to the right, work diagonal cording over it with cords 9, 10, 11, 12, 13 and 14.
With cord 9 as leader slanting down to the left, work a row of diagonal cording over it with cords 6, 5 and 4. With cord 10 as leader slanting down to the left, work a second row of diagonal cording immediately below with cords 6, 5 and 4. With cord 11 as leader work a third row of diagonal cording, also with cords 6, 5 and 4.
With cord 3 as leader slanting down to the right, work

Apron

diagonal cording over it with cords 9, 10 and 11. Work two more rows of diagonal cording immediately below with these same three cords, first over cord 2 as leader, then over cord 1.
Continuing in a similar way at the right-hand side of the diamond, work three rows of diagonal cording slanting down to the right with cords 12, 13 and 14. Cord 6 will be the leader for the first row, cord 5 the leader for the second row, cord 4 the leader for the third row.
Complete the lower part of the diamond by working three rows of diagonal cording slanting to the left with cords 3, 2 and 1. Cord 12 will be leader for the first row, cord 13 the leader for the second row, cord 14 the leader for the third row.
Finally reverse the direction of cord 7 round a pin and work a row of diagonal cording over it slanting down to the right with cords 9, 10, 11, 12, 13 and 14. Reverse the direction of cord 8 round a pin, and work a row of diagonal cording over it slanting down to the left with cords 6, 5, 4, 3, 2 and 1.
Note. *As you will see, the cords from the left of the diamond have crossed to the right, and cords from the right have crossed over to the left.*
Work a second cording diamond with the other group of unworked cords.
Complete the lower part of the pattern panel to match the upper part, in alternating chains of two flat knots.
Divider row: with the cord on the far left as leader, work a row of horizontal cording across all cords. Divide cords into groups of four double cords. Work on each group as follows:
with cord 4 as leader slanting down to the left, work diagonal cording with cords 3, 2 and 1.
Divider row: with the cord on the far right as leader, work a row of horizontal cording across all cords.
*With cord 4 as leader slanting down to the left, work diagonal cording with cords 3, 2 and 1. With cord 5 as leader slanting down to the right, work diagonal cording with cords 6, 7 and 8.
Reverse the direction of cord 4 round a pin and work diagonal cording over it slanting down to the right with cords 1, 2 and 3. Similarly reverse the direction of cord 5 and work diagonal cording over it slanting down to the left with cords 8, 7 and 6.**
Repeat from * to ** twice.
With the next group of four double cords, tie a chain of five flat knots.
Repeat from * to ** three times.

Divider row: with the cord on the far left as leader, work a row of horizontal cording across all cords. Cut a separate leader, approximately 18″ long. Pin this in position across the work. Set on the remaining 24 cords to this leader, 12 on the left of the section just worked, 12 on the right, to give the increased width for the skirt section of the apron.
Now work horizontal cording over this leader, with the central (yoke) cords.
Work on the first 12 cords (left-hand side panel):
*with cord 4 as leader slanting to the left, work diagonal cording with cords 3, 2 and 1. Reverse the direction of cord 4 and work diagonal cording slanting to the right with cords 1, 2 and 3.
With the next four double cords tie a chain of four flat knots. With the next four double cords, use cord 9 as the leader, slanting down to the right, and work diagonal cording with cords 10, 11 and 12. Reverse the direction of cord 9 and work diagonal cording slanting to the left with cords 12, 11 and 10.**
Tie a multi-end flat knot with the next 12 double cords (four double cords each side as knotting cords; four double cords as the central knotbearing core).*
Repeat from *** to ****.
With the next group of four double cords tie 16 half knots. Let the spiral twist round on itself after every fourth knot.
Repeat from *** to **** twice.
Repeat from * to ** with the last 12 double cords.
On the first 12 double cords, use cord 12 as leader and work a row of horizontal cording from right to left to the end of the row.
On the last group of 12 double cords, use cord 1 as leader and work a row of horizontal cording from left to right to the end of the row.
Now with the cord on the far left as leader, work a row of horizontal cording across all cords.
The side panels of the apron are now worked separately as follows:
working on the left-hand side panel, divide cords into three groups of four double cords. With the first group work six rows of diagonal cording slanting to the right using the cord on the far left as leader for each row. After the sixth row, reverse the direction of the last leader used and then work six rows of diagonal cording slanting down to the left, this time using the cord on the far right as leader for each row.
Repeat this pattern sequence with each of the other two groups of four double cords, then work a row of horizontal cording across all 12 double cords, using the cord on the far left as leader.
With the first group of four double cords, tie a chain of three flat knots. With the second group of four double

cords tie eight half knots. With the third group of four double cords, tie a chain of three flat knots.
Work a row of horizontal cording across all cords with the cord on the far left as leader.
Now repeat the six-band cording braid pattern worked previously.
Work a row of horizontal cording across all cords with the cord on the far left as leader.
With cord 6 as leader slanting down to the left, work diagonal cording with cords 5, 4, 3, 2 and 1. With cord 7 as leader slanting down to the right, work diagonal cording with cords 8, 9, 10, 11 and 12.
Tie two multi-end flat knots with cords 2, 3, 4, 5, 8, 9, 10 and 11 (two double knotting cords from each side, four double central knotbearing core cords).
With cord 6 as leader slanting down to the right, work diagonal cording with cords 1, 2, 3, 4 and 5.
With cord 7 as leader slanting down to the left, work diagonal cording with cords 12, 11, 10, 9 and 8.
With the cord on the far left as leader, work a row of horizontal cording across all cords.
On each group of four double cords, with cord 4 as leader slanting down to the left, work three rows of diagonal cording slanting down to the left, using the cord on the far right as leader for each row.
Tie two flat knots and an overhand knot to finish.
Repeat this entire section for the right-hand side panel.
Now work on the central skirt panel as follows:
work a pattern panel as for the last pattern panel of the yoke section, followed by a row of horizontal cording.
Work a pattern panel as for the second last pattern panel of the yoke section, followed by two rows of horizontal cording.
Now work a panel of cording leaf motifs:
on the first group of four double cords, work two rows of diagonal cording slanting down to the right, with the cord on the far left as leader for each row. Work two rows of diagonal cording slanting down to the left with the next four double cords, using the cord on the far right as the leader for each row.
Link these two groups together by knotting the leader from the left-hand group over the leader from the right-hand group. Now work two rows of diagonal cording slanting to the left on the first group, using the cord on the far right as leader for each row. Work two rows of diagonal cording slanting to the right on the second group, with the cord on the far left as leader for each row.
Work two more leaf motifs across the row in a similar way; leave the next group of four double cords unworked for the moment. Work three leaf motifs with each group of eight double cords to the end of the row.
Work a second band of leaf motifs immediately below the band just worked, linking the tips of the motifs together if wished by knotting one leader over another.
Return to the cords left unworked in the centre and work 11 rows of diagonal cording slanting to the left, with the cord on the far right as leader for each row.
Work a row of horizontal cording across all cords.
Work as follows for the next pattern band:
chain of five flat knots; spiral of 12 half knots; two cords unworked; chain of five flat knots; two cords unworked; chain of five flat knots; four cords unworked; spiral of 12 half knots; four cords unworked; chain of five flat knots; two cords unworked; chain of five flat knots; two cords unworked; spiral of 12 half knots; chain of five flat knots.
Work two rows of horizontal cording.
Work a pattern panel as for the last pattern panel of the yoke section, followed by a row of horizontal cording.
With each group of four double cords, work a cording braid pattern as worked for the side panels, but only work four rows of diagonal cording each time (instead of six).
Work a row of horizontal cording.
Work crossovers of diagonal cording on each group of eight double cords, with a chain of three flat knots worked on the centre four double cords. Have half motifs at the beginning and end of the row, also at either side of the central flat knot chain.
Finally divide the cords across the row into groups of four double cords. On each group tie a flat knot followed by an overhand knot to finish.

TO FINISH

Trim the fringe to the length required. Cut ribbon braid into three equal lengths. Stitch a length to the top of each side panel to form waist ties. Stitch one end of the third length to the left-hand top corner of the yoke, the other end to the right-hand top corner of the yoke. Trim holding and leader cords, turn to the wrong side and secure with a few neat stitches.

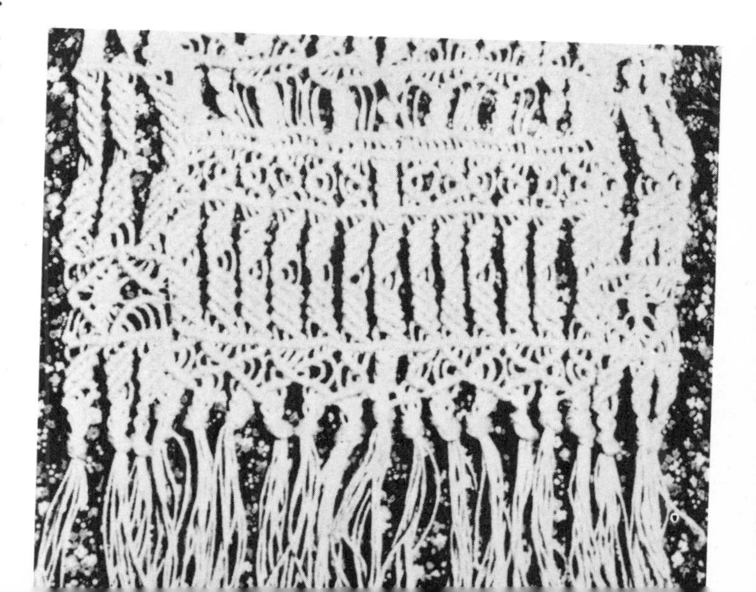

Vest top

MATERIALS. 159 yards Nylofil nylon cord size 2H.
DRESS. Miss Vogue Pattern 8132, in Liberty Tana lawn.
MEASUREMENTS. Vest should fit an average bust size 34/36″; the waistband can be made longer or shorter as required for a neat fitting. Similarly, the braids which go up either side of the bib front, over the shoulder, and down to meet the waistband at the back can be made longer or shorter as required.
TENSION CHECK. Chain of four flat knots is ¾″.
PREPARATION. For waistband: cut ten lengths of cord at 6 yd each, one at 6 yd 6″, and one at 6 yd 1 ft. Pin 6 yd 6″ length to a working surface centrally, so it can be used as a holding cord. Set on the other cords, setting on the 6 yd 1 ft length first and work it to form an alternate half hitch scalloped edging (see page 19). This will form a chain loop across the edge to be used as the centre back fastening of the waistband. When all the cords are set on, each end of the holding cord drops down to become a working cord: you should now have 24 working ends.
For bib front: cut 19 lengths at 1½ yd each, and one at 2 yd. Pin the 2 yd length centrally to the working surface so it can be used as a holding cord. Set the other cords on to it with a simple picot edging (see page 190). When all the cords are set on, each end of the holding cord drops down to become a working cord. You should now have 40 working ends.
For each shoulder braid: cut four lengths at 7 yd each. Place all four cords together, and pin to the working surface so you have a quadruple top loop.

TO MAKE THE WAISTBAND

***1st row:** work four flat knots with each group of four cords to the end of the row.
2nd row: leave the first two cords unworked; work single flat knots with each group of four cords to the last two cords; leave these two cords unworked.
3rd row: work single flat knots with each group of four cords to the end of the row.
4th row: leave the first two cords unworked; work four flat knots with each group of four cords to the last two cords; leave these two cords unworked.
5th row: work single flat knots with each group of four cords to the end of the row.
6th row: leave the first two cords unworked; work single flat knots with each group of four cords to the last two cords; leave these two cords unworked.**
Repeat from * to ** 9 times (or until the waistband is the length required).
Next row: with the cord on the far left as leader, work a row of horizontal cording across all cords.
Work on first eight cords: divide them into two groups of four and work an alternate half hitch chain, with four-strand knotting cords. When the chain is about 8″ long tie an overhand knot to finish, and trim the ends to about an inch from the overhand knot.
In a similar way, tie a double alternate half hitch chain with the next four cords; then tie another double alternate half hitch chain with the following four cords. Finally, tie a quadruple alternate half hitch chain with the last eight cords.

TO MAKE THE BIB FRONT

Work in the pattern of the waistband until five rows of four flat knot chains have been worked.
Next row: with the cord on the far left as leader, work one row of horizontal cording from left to right.
Unpin the work from the board, turn it to the wrong side and work another row of horizontal cording across the lower edge, with the cord on the far left as leader. Trim the ends to about ½″ from this last row of cording.

TO MAKE THE SHOULDER BRAIDS (make two alike)

Tie a continuous chain of Josephine knots (see page 202) using four-strand cords; tie the knots alternately from the left and right. When the chain is about 30″ long, stop knotting and trim the ends to about 8″.

TO FINISH

Stitch the lower edge of the bib front centrally to the top edge of the waistband. Stitch each shoulder braid down each side of the front bib, and to the top edge of the front waistband. Secure the other ends of each braid to the top edge of the back waistband by weaving the cord ends through the waistband to the back of the work then, working on four cords at a time, tie a two-knot flat knot chain.
Trim the ends to within an inch of the last flat knot, and secure this chain to the wrong side of the waistband with a few overcasting stitches.

Yoked smock

MATERIALS. 118½ yd Cash's striped cording 917, from J. & J. Cash Ltd., Coventry; 1 yd each of as many colours of Cash's striped cording as wished; 15 buttons, each about ½″ in diameter.

DRESS. Vogue Pattern No. 7952, sizes 8–16, in Tootal's gingham.

MEASUREMENTS. To fit bust size 34/36″. Depth of yoke approximately 10″. Depth of cuff 2″.

TENSION CHECK. Two flat knots measure ½″.

PREPARATION. For the yoke: each side is worked in a similar way over a pattern piece. Take the pattern piece for the yoke, trim away any seam allowance on the pattern, then pin the piece to your working surface. Cut a holding cord of about 18″ and pin it in place along the shoulder edge of the pattern piece. Let the left-hand end of the holding cord come down to follow the curve of the neckline edge, and pin it in place. Similarly let the right-hand end of the holding cord come down to follow the armhole curve, and pin it in place. Now cut 16 cords, each 2 yd 1 ft long, and set these on to the holding cord along the shoulder edge. Cut another six cords, each 1½ yd long and set these on to the holding cord along the neck edge, positioning them at the centre front edge. The other side of the yoke will be prepared in a similar way, but the pattern piece must be reversed.

For each cuff (both made alike): cut six cords, each 2 yd long. Cut a holding cord about 6″. Set these cords on to the holding cord with simple picot edging (see page 18), so picot loops (for buttons) are about ½″ deep.

TO MAKE THE YOKE

Make two pieces alike, but remember to reverse the pattern piece for the second section so you have a left and a right yoke.

Work in a two-knot alternate flat knot pattern throughout (i.e. alternate blocks of two flat knots). At each side edge loop the working cords round the holding cords between each row of knots. As the work becomes level with the set-on cords at the centre front neck edge, bring them into the pattern.

Tie the knots fairly tightly and close together near the top of the yoke. Gradually increase the distance between knots and rows as you work down to achieve shaping. Keep the centre front edge straight all the time.

Right-hand yoke section only: let the knotting cord nearest to the centre front edge form picot loops at nine evenly-spaced intervals (approx. ¾″) along the edge, for button loops.

Finish the yoke by working a row of horizontal cording across all cords, using the cord on the far left as leader, and following the outline of the pattern piece closely.

TO MAKE THE CUFFS (make two alike)

Work in pattern as for the yoke until the cuff is 7″ long. Work a row of horizontal cording to the end, with the cord on the far left as leader.

TO FINISH

Trim the ends of the yoke and cuff pieces to about 1″, turn to the wrong side of the work and secure with a line of machine stitching or running stitches. Make up the dress according to instructions, using a plain lining fabric for the yoke sections (remember to add seam allowances to the pattern piece if these have been trimmed away). Omit cuffs. Place the macramé yoke sections in position on the right side of the fabric yoke. Oversew together round the armhole, shoulder, neck and centre front edges. Sew buttons to the left front centre edge opposite the button loops. Sew each macramé cuff in position to each sleeve end. Sew three buttons to each cuff, opposite the picot button loops (use two loops for fastening each button).

Between every chain of flat knots along the lower edge of the yoke set on a different coloured length of striped cording, to make a long fringe.

Child's sailor top

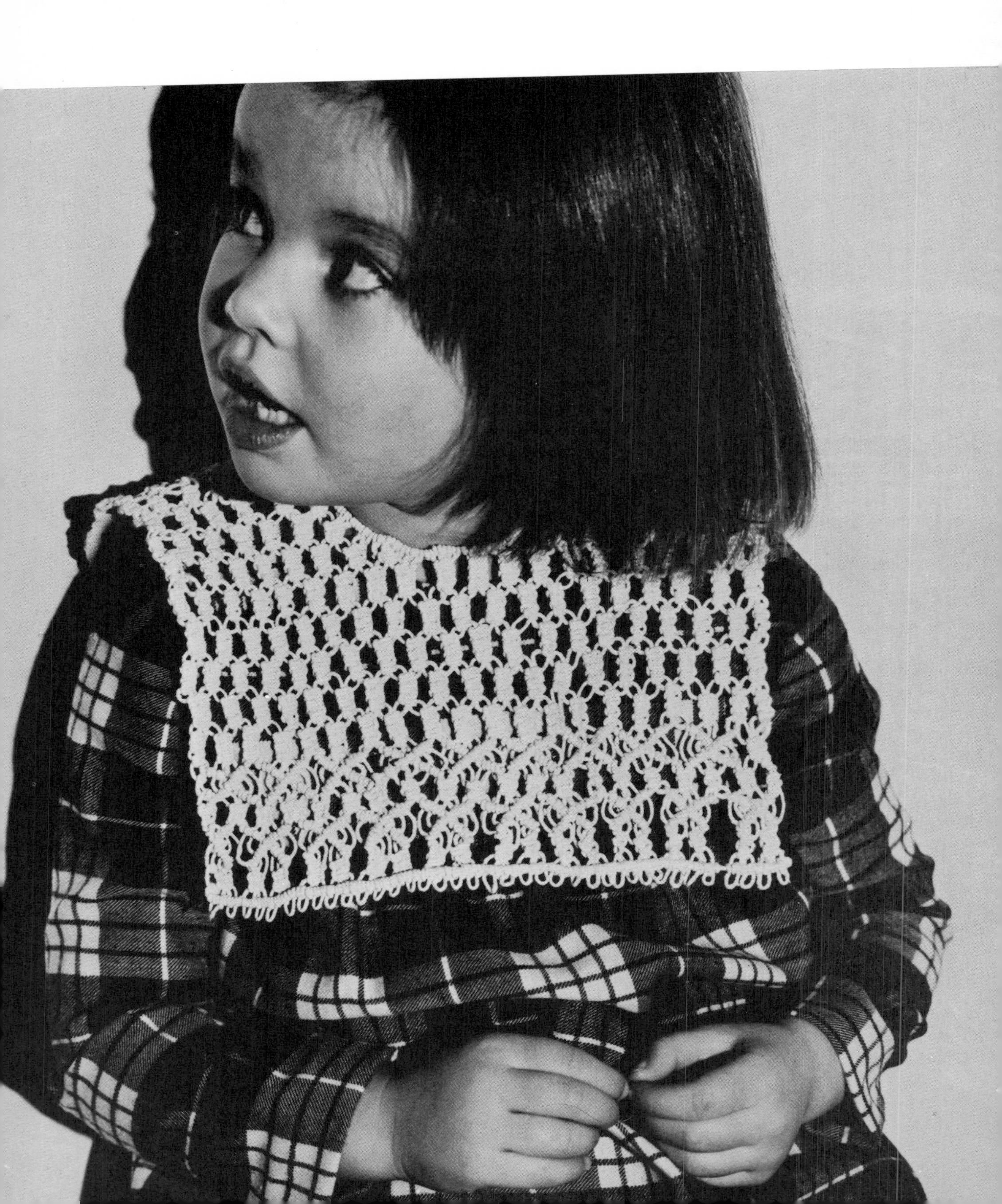

MATERIALS. 1 ball W. H. Smith C3 medium string; three press studs.

DRESS. Vogue Pattern No. 6032, sizes 2–6, in checked Viyella.

MEASUREMENTS. Finished bib measures approximately 8½″ across, 14″ in total depth (from front to back).

TENSION CHECK. Three flat knots measure ½″.

PREPARATION. Cut 24 cords at 3 yd, 14 at 1½ yd. Cut a holding cord approximately 18″, and set cords on to it with simple picot edging (see page 18) in the following order: 12 at 3 yd, 14 at 1½ yd, 12 at 3 yd.

TO MAKE

1st row: Work two flat knots with each group of four cords to the end of the row.

Divide the cords into nine groups of eight (have the odd four cords at the end).

Work on the first group of eight cords:

*work a crossover of diagonal cording with cords 1 and 8 as leaders, knotting 1 over 8 at the crossover point.**

Work from * to ** eight more times. Work a half motif with the four cords at the end of the row.

Next row: work two half hitches from the right with cord 2 over cord 1; tie two flat knots with each group of four cords to the last two cords; tie two half hitches from the right with these two last cords.

Next row: work eight-cord crossovers of diagonal cording as before, but this time have the half motif with four cords at the beginning of the row.

Now begin the main pattern.

***Next row:** work three flat knots with each group of four cords to the end of the row.

Next row: work three flat knots with the first six cords, having single knotting cords, and a central knotbearing core of four cords; tie three flat knots with each group of four cords to the last six cords; tie three flat knots with these last six cords, having single knotting cords and a centre knotbearing core of four cords.**

Repeat from * to ** once, then work the first row of the pattern again.

Divide for the neck opening. Keeping in pattern, work the first six chains of flat knots, then on the next group of four cords tie only two flat knots; on the next group of four cords tie only one flat knot.

Leave the next 12 cords unworked, then tie one flat knot with the next four cords, two flat knots with the following four cords, then complete the row in the pattern (six chains of flat knots).

Next row: still in pattern, work the first six chains of flat knots, then work two flat knots with the next group of four cords; leave the next 24 cords unworked; work two flat knots with the next four cords, then complete the row in pattern.

Next row: six chains of flat knots; leave the next 28 cords unworked; six chains of flat knots.

Now cut a separate length of string, approximately 14″ long (this will form the neck edge of the bib). Lay this cord on top of the unworked area of cords in the centre, close to the last knots tied, and following the curve of the shaped edge. Work cording over this leader with all the central cords; fill in the gaps on the leader where necessary by working half hitches with the cords nearest to hand.

This completes the front of the bib to the shoulder edge. Now pin the leader cord to form the curve of the back neck. Cut 22 cords each 1½ yd, and set on to the leader, 11 for the left back, 11 for the right back.

Work on the left back first.

Next row: leave the first two cords unworked; work chains of two flat knots with each of the next two groups of four cords, then work four chains of three flat knots (the last chain will use the first four of the new cords). Now continuing round the shaped neck edge, work five chains of two flat knots each: the first of these chains will use two cords from the last three-knot chain worked and the next two new set-on cords.

Keeping in alternate flat knot pattern, work two rows of two flat knot chains round the yoke centre area, but have three knots in the chains nearer the outside edge; this is necessary to achieve the shaping for the shoulder slope. Provided you maintain the continuity of the alternate pattern, it does not matter which chains have two knots, and which have three.

When you are satisfied shaping is complete, and all the cords line up evenly, continue in the pattern until the back measures the same as the front yoke.

Work the right back to match, reversing all shaping.

TO FINISH

Using the cord on the far left as leader, work one row of horizontal cording across all cords.

Trim every second cord close to the last row of cording, turn, and stitch to the wrong side of the work to secure. Loop the remaining cords on to the wrong side of work to simulate the picot edging at the beginning, and stitch to secure. Trim the holding and leader cords to within ½″ of the work, turn to the wrong side and secure with a few stitches.

Sew press studs to the centre back edge to fasten, placing the first press stud at the neck edge, the other two at 2″ intervals below.

Child's pinafore

MATERIALS. 2 balls of W. H. Smith C3 thin string; 2 yd of ribbon, 1″ wide; a medium crochet hook.
DRESS. Vogue Pattern No. 6088, sizes ½–4, in flower-printed Viyella.
MEASUREMENTS. To fit size 4; length of pinafore 16″.
TENSION CHECK. Approximately three rows of flat knots over the lacy pattern measure 1″.
PREPARATION. With the crochet hook and string, work two crochet chains each approximately 50″ long. The back and front of the pinafore are made alike. For each side, therefore, cut cords as follows: cut 16 cords each 3½ yd long, 10 cords each 3 yd long. Take the paper pattern piece for the pinafore section. Trim away any seam allowance on the pattern, then pin the piece to your working surface. Now take one crochet chain and very carefully pin this in position round the outside edge of the pattern; begin pinning at the lower left-hand corner. Take the chain up the left side edge to the shoulder, across the shoulder, down round the neckline, up to the other shoulder and across it, then down the right-hand side edge to the right-hand lower corner. Do not pin the chain along the hem edge. Set eight cords directly on to the crochet chain at the shoulder edges, spacing the cords evenly across the edge. Set the remaining ten cords on to the lower curve of the neckline.

TO MAKE

Work in the alternate flat knot pattern throughout. Between every row the end cords should be looped through the crochet chains at the armhole and neck edges. The two shoulder sections will be knotted first; the neck edge cords should be taken into the pattern when they are reached.
Keep knots fairly tightly tied near the top of the pinafore, and gradually increase the distance between knots and rows to achieve the slightly flared shaping of the pinafore skirt.

TO FINISH

With the cord on the far left as leader, work a row of horizontal cording across all cords, following the line of the hem edge of the paper pattern as closely as possible. Trim the ends to about 2″.
Unpin work from the board, remove the paper pattern, then turn the work on its side and pin to the board so the hem edge is running vertically. Cut a length of string about 3 yd long. Double it and pin the top loop immediately above the lower edge of the pinafore. Now using the left-hand cord as a knotting cord, tie half hitches tightly down the entire hem edge, catching in the loose ends as you work. About 2″ from the end of the hem, turn the remaining ends up so they too are caught into the half hitch chain. When the chain is complete, trim the end of the knotting cord to about 1″, turn to the wrong side and secure it with a few neat overcasting stitches.
Stitch pinafore back to the front at the shoulder edges. Cut the ribbon in half and thread each length through the side edges of the pinafore to use as ties.

Bobble sweater

[ATERIALS. 16 oz Mahony's Blarney Bainin wool.
[EASUREMENTS. Sweater will comfortably fit a ıst size 34/36″; length of sweater at centre front,)proximately 26″.
ENSION CHECK. Over open-work diamond pattern oke section) each 'leg' of the diamond measures ½″; ch cording diamond motif measures 1″ square.
REPARATION Cut 86 cords, each 6 yd long. Set ese in pairs on to a triple thickness holding cord of out 50″.
ote. *The entire sweater is worked as a flat rectangle, om the neck edge down. The shaping for the neckline, oulders and yoke section is achieved after the knotting is mplete, by drawing up the holding cord.*
ords are used double throughout; therefore you now ve 86 double thickness knotting cords.

O MAKE

egin open-work diamond pattern:
orking on the *wrong* side, divide the cords into pairs d work a diagonal double half hitch with each left-nd cord over each right-hand cord.
-divide the cords into pairs so each right-hand cord the last row is combined with each left-hand cord. aving an area of about ½″ of unworked cords from the t row, work another row of diagonal double half ches this time knotting each right-hand cord over ch left-hand cord.
ntinue in this way working an alternate pattern of gle diagonal double half hitches until 12 rows have en worked.
ow divide for armholes as follows.
ext row: keeping in pattern, work ten knots. Continue this set of cords only.
ext row: leave first cord unworked; work nine knots.
ext row: leave first two cords unworked; work eight ots.
ntinue in this way, dropping a cord from each side til the row with only a single knot in it is worked.
a similar way, work four more V patterns, first on the xt 12 cords (six knots in the first row), then on the xt 22 cords (11 knots in the first row), then on 12 ds, and finally on 20 cords.
e two V shapes worked on 12 cords will form the oulders and armholes of the sweater. Trim the cord ls from these V shapes and, if necessary, stitch the ls neatly to the last knot to conceal and strengthen.
w turn the work to the right side.
it three strands of yarn together to make a length of out 46″. Lay this across the work so it is just touching tips of the V shapes; work horizontal cording over it h all the remaining cords (i.e. those not trimmed away). As you work, between the double half hitches set on 82 new cords each 8 ft long. Set these on in pairs as before. At the end of the row you should have a total of 144 working (double) ends.
Work on groups of eight cords:
with cord 5 as leader slanting down to the left, work diagonal cording over it with cords 4, 3, 2 and 1.
Work three more rows of diagonal cording on these same four cords, one below the other, using cord 6 as leader for the 2nd row, cord 7 as leader for the 3rd row, and cord 8 as leader for the 4th row.
Work across the row in this way.
In the 2nd row, the four left-hand cords of each motif of the previous row are combined with the four right-hand cords of the motif next to it. The same cording diamond as before is then worked. Leave an area of about ¼″ of unworked cords between the motifs. Let the unworked cords at either end of the 2nd and other even-numbered rows form even curves at the ends of the rows.
Continue in this way working an alternate pattern of cording diamonds.
When the cording diamond section of the work measures 12″ (or length of sweater required) introduce a separate double thickness leader and work horizontal cording across all cords.

TO FINISH

Trim cords to about ½″, press to the wrong side and secure with a line of running stitches. Trim the leader cords in the centre of the work and at the end to about 1″, press to the wrong side and secure with a few neat overcasting stitches.
Now take hold of both ends of the neck edge holding cord and pull gently, to draw in the work. Try on the sweater (the open edges meet at centre back) and adjust the gathering round the neck edge until it fits neatly and evenly. Tie an overhand knot at either end of the holding cord to stop the gathering coming undone. Take off the sweater, and stitch each overhand knot firmly to the first set-on cords at either end to give further strength to the edge. Adjust gathers evenly. Stitch the centre back seam from the lower edge to the top of the cording diamond section.
Plait the ends of the neck edge holding cord into a three-strand plait; use them as ties for the back neck.
Make 15 pompons, each 2½″ in diameter. Stitch five at intervals round each armhole edge, one at the centre front neck edge, one at each shoulder, one to the centre back neck (on the left back), and the other one halfway down the centre back opening edge (on the left back). Set on a loop of yarn to the edge opposite this last pompon to fasten round it; this closes the opening.

Beaded poncho

MATERIALS. 9 balls W. H. Smith C3 medium string; approximately 500 wooden beads, from Ells and Farrier, 5 Princes Street, London W.1.
MEASUREMENTS. Length of poncho at the centre front 30″; width at widest point, about 30″.
TENSION CHECK. Chain of five flat knots measures $1\frac{1}{2}$″.
PREPARATION. The entire poncho is worked flat in one piece, starting at the shoulder edges and working either side for front and back. You will therefore need an extensive area of suitable working surface, and preferably one which will take pins easily. A large piece of soft wood placed on the floor is probably most convenient; alternatively a well-padded table could be used.
Cut 124 cords, each 15 ft 6″ long. Lay two groups of 48 cords singly side by side on your working surface, leaving a gap of 8″ between the two groups. Now measure the midway point of the cords and place a line of pins right across all the cords at this point. This line of pins marks the shoulder line. Tie a row of four-end flat knots across on this line, removing the pins as you work. Space out the knots so the measurement of each shoulder is about 24″. Work now proceeds on either side of this shoulder line of knots.

TO MAKE

In the alternate flat knot pattern, work four more rows of knots on either side of the shoulder line with each group of cords, spacing out the knots in a fairly open pattern. Now cut two holding cords, each about 12″ long, one for the centre front neck edge, the other for the centre back neck edge.
Lay these holding cords in position between the shoulder cords, looping each end of each holding cord round the nearest convenient knot. Set 14 new cords (the remaining 28 cut cords from Preparation) on to each holding cord. Keeping in pattern, work a row of flat knots across all the cords to link the shoulder cords to the new cords. You should now have a total of 124 working ends on the front of the poncho, and 124 ends for the back.
Continue in the alternate flat knot pattern for two more rows for both back and front.
Now work in the main pattern, and complete one side of the poncho first (it does not matter which) before r turning to work the other side.
The main pattern is an alternate pattern of chains of fi flat knots. Beads are threaded onto and between chai as required, in the following arrangements: panels beaded chains using single beads in each chain: tie tw flat knots, slide a bead on to the knotbearing cords, t another two flat knots to secure. Four panels of bead arrangement are worked on each side of the ponc (see photograph opposite for arrangement). A cent beaded panel is worked for the front only; it includes t following arrangements of beads: work one knot, sli three beads on to the knotbearing cords, work anoth knot to secure. Pairs of beads are also threaded on cords between the chains to give horizontal beadir Again refer to the photograph to see where the differe beaded arrangements occur.
Continue until the poncho is the required length. Grad ate the lower edge so it is deeper at the centre front a centre back by dropping a knot from each side on eve row until the length is as required.
Work three rows of horizontal cording to finish.

TO FINISH

Trim the cord ends, leader cords and neck edge holdi cords, and darn neatly into the back of the knotting.
Neck braid. Cut two cords, each 2 yd long, and these on to a short holding cord. Introduce a separ leader about 3 yd long and work a braid of zig-z cording long enough to fit round the neck edge of t poncho. When the braid is long enough trim the en join the two short ends of the braid together to forr circle, then stitch this in position to the neck edge of poncho.
Outside edge braid. Work a similar braid to go rig round the outside edge of the poncho; use three cor each cut 12 yd long, and a leader of 14 yd. After ea row of diagonal cording is worked, before the leade direction is reversed to work the next row, slide a b on to the leader cord. The braid should be about 1 long when finished, to fit around the edge of the ponc Join the short ends of the braid together, and then sti the entire braid in position to the poncho edge.

Layette

ATERIALS. For the jacket: 3 oz Wendy Invitation ›tton; 1 yd ribbon, $\frac{5}{8}$″ wide; 1 yd ribbon, $\frac{1}{4}$″ wide; $\frac{1}{2}$ yd am binding, $\frac{5}{8}$″ wide.

›r the shawl: quantity of yarn and ribbon depends on e finished size required, but 1 oz of Wendy Invitation ›tton will make a section about 8″ square, plus fringe. length of ribbon, 1″ wide, will be required to thread rough the outside edges.

EASUREMENTS. The jacket will comfortably fit up a 14″ chest size; length of jacket at centre back is 8″; eve seam is $5\frac{1}{2}$″.

ENSION CHECK. Chain of eight alternate half ches measures $\frac{1}{2}$″.

REPARATION FOR THE JACKET. The picot ck edging for the back and fronts of the jacket is rked first as a continuous strip. This is the only part the jacket where curved shaping is required—the nainder of the jacket is worked straight. If possible, an sting jacket of similar size and shape should be used a guide. Begin by cutting 59 cords, each 2 yd long. Set se on to a holding cord of about 15″ with overhand ot edging (see page 18). With each pair of cords work ingle alternate half hitch chain to a depth of $\frac{5}{8}$″. Cut a arate leader, about 15″, and work a row of horizontal ding across all cords. Now unpin work from the ard, and fold the strip so that the centre 4″ will form back neck edge; the remaining ends will form the ht and left front edges respectively. Gently pull the ls of the leader and holding cords to draw the front ges down into a curve—this is where a ready-made ment or paper pattern will be useful as a guide. When ı are satisfied that the curve of the front neckline is ht, trim the leader and holding cords to about an inch, ss to the back of the work and secure with a few neat ercasting stitches. Alternatively, before trimming the ls, thread each end on to a large-eyed darning needle l darn into the back of the work.

›rk now proceeds flat, working the front of the jacket t. Counting from the centre front, select the 16th ernate half hitch chain worked on the left front and the h alternate half hitch chain worked on the right front. ese double cords form each shoulder edge, and the naining cords for front and back are set on to them. each front, cut 16 cords, each 2 yd long. Pin the rked neck edge to a working surface, so the shoulder ds are in position to use as holding cords, and set ds on to them.

› MAKE THE JACKET

ft front. Working from the shoulder edge down, k three rows in alternate flat knot pattern, tying knots se together to give a dense fabric. On the 2nd row ng the next two cords from the neck edge into the tern.

Next row: with the cord on the far left (coming from the neck edge) as leader, work a row of horizontal cording. Continue in this way working three-row bands of alternate flat knots, divided by rows of horizontal cording, gradually bringing the cords from the neck edge into the pattern until a row of flat knots is worked across all cords. Work another row of horizontal cording. Leave the first 16 cords unworked for the moment, and with the remaining cords work another three-row band of alternate flat knots, followed by a row of horizontal cording. Work now continues on these cords for another $4\frac{1}{4}$″ in the alternate flat knot pattern. On the first 16 cords, three-row crossovers of diagonal cording are worked to the same depth as the alternate flat knots. If wished, the flat knots and the cording motifs may be worked separately, and the edges where the two pattern strips meet will be stitched together later. Alternatively, the two bands of pattern may be worked concurrently and the end cords from one looped round the end cords of the other at regular intervals to link them together.

Work the cording motif.

With cord 1 as leader slanting down to the right, work diagonal cording with cords 2, 3, 4, 5, 6, 7 and 8. Work a 2nd row below with cord 2 as leader, and knotting over it cords 3, 4, 5, 6, 7 and 8. Then work a 3rd row with cord 3 as leader, and knotting over it cords 4, 5, 6, 7 and 8.

With cord 16 as leader slanting down to the left, work diagonal cording with cords 15, 14, 13, 12, 11, 10 and 9. Work a 2nd row with cord 15 as leader, and knotting over it cords 14, 13, 12, 11, 10 and 9. Then work a 3rd row with cord 14 as leader, and knotting over it cords 13, 12, 11, 10 and 9.

Complete the lower half of the motif.

Reverse direction of cord 3 to form a leader slanting down to the left and work diagonal cording with cords 8, 7, 6, 5 and 4.

Reverse the direction of cord 2 to form a leader slanting down to the left and work diagonal cording over it with cords 8, 7, 6, 5, 4 and 3. Loop cord 1 round cord 16 then let cord 1 continue as leader for the 3rd row of diagonal cording and work over it with cords 8, 7, 6, 5, 4, 3 and 2.

Complete the remaining section of the motif to match.

When motifs and flat knots have been completed, work a row of horizontal cording across.

Divide cords into pairs and work an alternate half hitch chain with each for $\frac{5}{8}$″.

Work three rows of cording to finish.

Right front. Work as for left front, reversing shaping so the cording motifs lie at the end of the row (for centre front edge) instead of at the beginning.

Back. When the fronts are completed, unpin the work and turn it round so the back neck edge is facing.

Layette

Cut 32 cords, each 2 yd long and set 16 on to each shoulder edge over those set on for the jacket fronts. Work five bands of three rows of flat knots followed by a row of horizontal cording (as for the front yoke section) then continue in alternate flat knots until the back measures the same as the fronts, to the end of the flat knot section.

Complete the lower edge with chains of alternate half hitches and rows of horizontal cording, as for the fronts.

Sleeves (make 2 alike). Cut 42 cords, each 4 ft long. Set these on to a holding cord about 12″ long with overhand picot edging as for the jacket neck edge. With a separate leader (about 12″), work a row of horizontal cording.

Divide cords into pairs and work alternate half hitch chains to a depth of about $\frac{1}{4}$″. With a separate leader (about 12″), work a row of horizontal cording.

Now continue in the alternate flat knot pattern until the sleeve measures 5″ (or length required). Finish with three rows of horizontal cording.

TO FINISH JACKET

Stitch side seams. Stitch each sleeve seam, first trimming the ends of the holding and leader cords, then folding them to the inside of the work so they are sandwiched in the seam. Set each sleeve into each armhole by threading cords from the armhole edge of each sleeve individually on to a large-eyed darning needle, and sewing from the right through to the wrong side of the jacket in position along the armhole. Carefully darn ends into the back of the work, and trim ends when darning is complete.

Cut the narrow ribbon in half and thread a length through the alternate half hitch chains around each cuff edge.

Cut the wider ribbon in half, and thread one length through the neck edge half hitch chains to form a ribbon tie. Thread the other length through the half hitch chains at the hem edge. Turn each end of the ribbon at the centre front edges to the wrong side of the work. Trim cord ends at the lower edge to about an inch, then press them to the wrong side; stitch seam binding on the inside round the entire lower edge to enclose cord ends and ribbon.

PREPARATION FOR THE SHAWL. Decide the width required for the central flat knot section of the shawl and set a number of cords on to a holding cord to give this measurement; (as a rough guide, four set-on cords on the holding cord measure 1″). Cut each cord to eight times the total length required (this measurement should include one complete fringe—the other one is added afterwards).

TO MAKE THE SHAWL

Work in the alternate flat knot pattern as for the jack to the required length.

Introduce a separate leader which should be long enou to go round all four sides of the shawl and work a row horizontal cording.

Divide cords into pairs and work an alternate half hit chain with each pair of cords to a depth of about 1″.

Introduce another separate leader, again long enough go round all four sides of the shawl, and work a row horizontal cording.

Now work the fringe as follows.

Divide cords into groups of 12. On the first group, lea the first cord unworked for the moment. With the ne pair of cords tie two alternate half hitches; with the ne pair, tie four alternate half hitches; with the next pa tie six; with the next pair, four; with the next pair, tw and leave the last cord unworked. Now work a three-r V of cording: with cord 1 as leader slanting down to t right, work diagonal cording over it with cords 2, 3, 4 and 6. With cord 12 as leader slanting down to the le work diagonal cording over it with cords 11, 10, 9, 8 a 7. Link leaders at the tip of the V by knotting cord over cord 1.

Work another two rows of diagonal cording immediat below this first one, using the outside cords as lead for each row and linking the leaders in the centre ea time.

When motifs have been worked across the row, wo chains of alternate half hitches with pairs of cords b tween the motifs, graduating them as before: this mea that between each pair of motifs you will work a fo knot chain, six-knot chain, eight-knot chain, six-kn chain and a four-knot chain, in that order.

Work another band of three-row cording Vs, alternati the sequence, i.e. each unit of twelve cords will co prise cords 7 to 12 and 1 to 6 from motifs of t previous cording band.

Tie each pair of cords with an overhand knot and tr the ends to give a fringe of the required depth.

TO FINISH THE SHAWL

Cut a number of cords, each 30″ long, and set these all the way round the other three sides of the shawl.

Continuing with the leader from the first row of cordi already worked, work horizontal cording round all cor

Divide cords in pairs and work alternate half hitch cha as before.

Continuing with the leader from the second row cording already worked, work horizontal cording rou all cords.

Work the fringe to match the first section. If necessary on more cords at the corners to fill in the fringe at th areas.

Tasselled cap

MATERIALS. Two 4 oz cones of Glacé for macram
by English Sewing Ltd.
MEASUREMENTS. To fit average-sized head; dep
of cap from crown to outer edge 7".
TENSION CHECK. Two flat knots measure $\frac{1}{4}$".

PREPARATION. Cut 20 cords, each 40″ long. Place these cords together and make a tight binding round the whole bunch about 10″ from one end. Work now proceeds downwards from this point. As the cap is worked in the round, a suitable three-dimensional base will have to be used; a wig stand is ideal. Position the cords on your working base, so the tasselled top is at the highest point on your base. Spread the 20 working ends round evenly. New cords are cut and added as knotting progresses to give increased width to the cap; these will be described at the appropriate point in the design in the following instructions.

TO MAKE

The cap is worked in panels of different knotting patterns as follows.

1st panel: chains of two flat knots with each group of four cords.

Dividing row of horizontal cording (introduce a separate circular leader): 20 new cords are added here, each cut to 5 ft; four are added between each pair of flat knot chains. Total of 60 working ends.

Note. *Cords are doubled and set on the leader with double half hitches.*

2nd panel: single flat knots worked round on each group of four cords, then chains of three flat knots worked in the alternate sequence from the last row of knots. After the third knot in each chain is worked, add wo extra cords, each 5 ft long, to give four extra working ends. The extra cords can be threaded round the loop of he last knot in each chain. Total of 120 working ends.

rd panel: work in a single alternate flat knot pattern or two rows, then, maintaining the alternate pattern, vork chains of two flat knots. Work two rows more of ingle alternate flat knots.

till keeping to the alternate pattern, work single flat nots with every second group of four cords to the end of ne round (leave the other cords unworked for the noment).

th panel: work a criss-cross pattern of flat knot chains, ing each chain with two cords from the last row of flat nots and the two cords nearest to it left unworked in the revious row.

ie two flat knots in each chain, then combine the pairs chains together by tying a multi-end flat knot. At this oint loop in two more new cords to each group, each w cord cut to 3 ft long. Divide into chains after the ulti-end flat knot and complete each chain with two ore flat knots. Tie a single flat knot below the multi-end ot with the four new cords. Total of 180 working ends.

ote. *No more new cords need now be added; to achieve y further shaping, slacken or tighten knots as required. If preferred, further new cords may in fact be looped in where appropriate.*

Work single flat knots right round in an alternate sequence.

5th panel: still in the alternate pattern, work chains of two flat knots.

Work a single row of flat knots, continuing in alternate sequence.

6th panel: work double row crossovers of diagonal cording on each group of 12 cords right round. Link the crossover point on each motif by knotting the right-hand leader over the left-hand leader.

Tie a single flat knot to link the motifs together with the two outer cords from each motif.

7th panel: work in a single alternate flat knot pattern, but form 15 diamond panels of knots by stopping the knotting on each successive row (working in groups of 12 cords) two cords from each end until eventually a row is worked with only one flat knot in it.

8th panel: selecting leaders from the tip of each diamond, work cording down each side close to the last flat knots to form the top two sides of the diamonds.

Tie a multi-end flat knot with all the cords within each inverted V of cording just worked (three knotting cords from each side, four central knotbearing cords).

Link the leaders to each other all the way round, by always knotting the right-hand leader over the left-hand one.

Complete the lower two sides of each diamond by working diagonal cording over the same leaders.

Between each motif along the lower edge, divide the cords into groups of three, six and three.

Collect these groups by working several half hitches from the left with the cord on the far left in each group. Introduce a separate circular leader and work a row of horizontal cording round all cords.

Working on every second group of four cords right round, tie flat knot balls (see page 248). Leave the other cords unworked.

Finish with two rows of horizontal cording right round, immediately below the flat knot balls.

TO FINISH

Trim the ends, press to the inside of the cap and secure with a line of running stitches.

Work a coil knot at the tip of each cord on the crown tassel as follows: form a large loop near the end of the cord. At the point where the loop crosses, wind the cord round itself several times. Gently pull both ends of the cord and the 'winds' will form themselves into a coil. The more winds you work the deeper will be the coil produced.

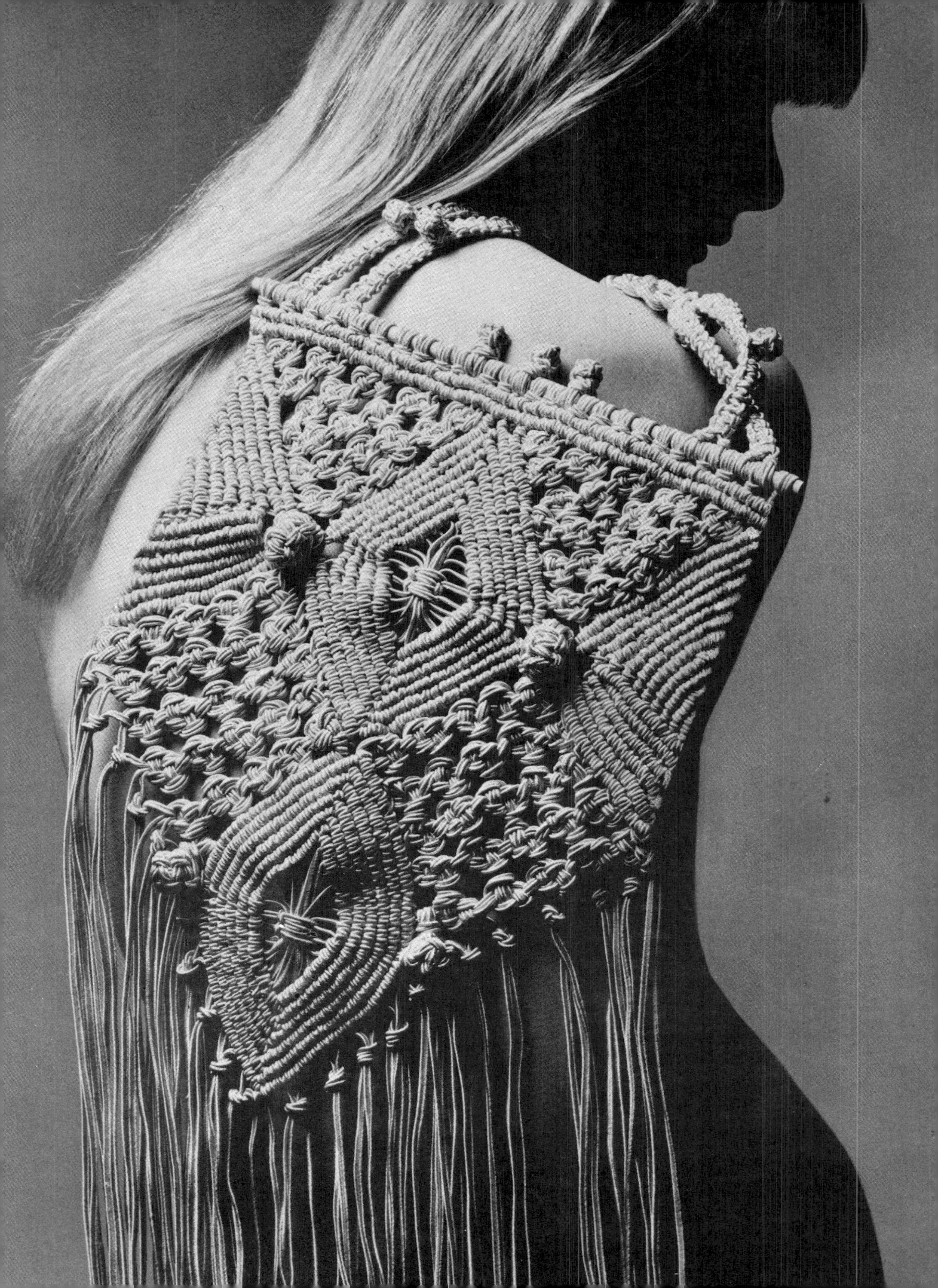

Braid bag

Designed by Christine Hanscomb

MATERIALS. 177 yd Russia braid No. 4; two 10″ lengths of wooden dowelling; lining fabric (optional).

MEASUREMENTS. Maximum depth of bag to centre tip, excluding fringe, is 12″; width at widest point is 10″.

TENSION CHECK. One Josephine knot, tied with double strands, measures $\frac{3}{4}''$ across.

PREPARATION. Both sides of the bag are made alike. For each side therefore, cut 24 cords, each 3 yd long. Set these directly on to a length of dowelling.

TO MAKE

With the cord on the far left as leader, work a row of horizontal cording across all cords.

Reverse the direction of the leader and work a second row of horizontal cording from right to left across all cords.

Leave the first two cords unworked for the moment; tie a Josephine knot with each of the next five groups of four cords (using double thickness knotting cords).

Continuing to work on these cords only, work rows of Josephine knots (see page 202) in the alternate sequence, tying one knot fewer in each row (i.e. dropping two cords from each end of every row) until you reach the row with only one Josephine knot.

Continuing across the work, leave the centre four cords unworked, then work another panel of Josephine knots like the first on the next 20 cords. Leave the final two cords unworked.

Return to the cords at the beginning.

With cord 1 as a leader slanting down to the right, work diagonal cording over it with cord 2, then with all the cords coming from the left-hand side of the Josephine knot panel.

Continuing to use the cord on the far left as leader for each row, work 10 more rows of diagonal cording beneath the first. Stop cording on the same cord for every row (i.e. do not let the leader cords drop down to become knotting cords in subsequent rows).

In a similar way, work a six-row band of cording slanting down to left on the other side of the Josephine knot panel, and a six-row band of diagonal cording slanting down to the right on the left-hand side of the second Josephine knot panel. Cords from the centre will be used as leaders for these bands, and will cross from one side of the work to the other, so the inverted V panel of cording is linked in the centre.

Work 11 rows of cording slanting down to the left on the right-hand side of the second Josephine knot panel, using the cord at the far right as leader for every row.

At the tip of each Josephine knot panel, work a flat knot ball (see page 248), with the leaders from the last two rows of cording on each side. Tie four flat knots before taking the knotbearing cords up and over the chain.

In the centre of the inverted V of cording tie two multi-end flat knots, using single thickness knotting cords, and multiple knotbearing cords.

With the cord on the far left as leader, work a row of horizontal cording immediately below the edge of the previous panel of diagonal cording, using all the cords hanging from that edge to work the cording.

Work another three rows immediately below using the same leader for each row, and reversing its direction at the end of each row.

Now work another two rows of cording immediately below these four rows, using two left-hand cords from the flat knot balls as leaders. In each row work right along every cord to the end.

Work a similar panel of six-row cording with the cords at the far right of the work.

Complete the lower half of the central diamond of cording to match the upper half.

Now work two diamond panels of Josephine knots in alternate sequence, starting immediately below each flat knot ball. Begin with a single knot, and work one more knot in each row until the full width of the diamond is reached, then reduce by one knot in each row, as before.

Work another central diamond of cording below the first, in a similar way.

At each side of the cording diamond, at a central point, work a flat knot ball.

Braid bag

TO FINISH

To make the handle, cut four cords, each eight times the required length of the finished handle. Set these directly on to one end of the dowelling on one side of the bag, over cords already set on; set the new threads on so they are hanging in the opposite direction from the main bag threads.

The handle pattern is worked in sections as follows: chains of flat knots with each group of four cords, with a flat knot ball in the centre of the chain. Then combine the cords and work a multi-end flat knot ball, followed by a strip of Josephine knots (four knotting cords from each side); then work another multi-end flat knot ball and divide the cords into two groups of four.

Continue in this way and work chains of flat knots followed by Josephine knots, ending with chains of flat knots to match the chains worked at the beginning of the handle. The length worked of each section depends on the length of handle required.

When the handle is complete, loop the cord ends round the other end of the dowelling, take the cords to the back of the work and tie in a flat knot to secure. Trim ends.

Cut six more cords, each 10″ long. Set these on to the dowelling on which the handle was worked, position two cords exactly in the centre of the dowelling; then position two cords about ¾″ away on either side. Again set cords on so that they hang in the opposite direction from the main bag cords.

With each four cords, work a chain of flat knots to about 1″. Fold the chains back on themselves so the cord ends are on the wrong side of the work. Tie another flat knot to secure in this position. Stitch ends to the inside of the work to neaten.

Now place the two bag sections together, wrong sides facing, and oversew the sides together for about 4″ from each lower corner (leave the top unstitched so the bag can open freely).

Cut three more cords, each 8″ long. Set these on to the second dowelling rod with a simple picot edging (see page 190), positioning one opposite each flat knot ball on the first dowelling. Make the picot loops large enough to fasten comfortably over a flat knot ball.

Along the lower edge of the bag, tie the cords together in groups of four with overhand knots, combining two cords from each side of the bag in every knot to close the lower edge.

If wished, make a lining to fit the bag. Insert it into the bag, wrong sides facing; oversew round the inside of the top edge.

Evening bag

MATERIALS. Five balls of Jaeger Astral Spun; a 7″ bag frame; fabric and lining material to make up bag; jewelled clasp (optional).
MEASUREMENTS. The bag itself measures 7″ wide by 7″ long, but the macramé covering measures $11\frac{1}{2}$″ long, excluding tassels.
TENSION CHECK. Each three-row cording motif measures $\frac{1}{2}$″.
PREPARATION. Each side of the bag is made alike. For each side therefore cut 35 cords, each 3 yd long. Cut a holding cord approximately 1 ft long, and set cords on to this. Before beginning work it is advisable to dip the cord ends into colourless nail varnish to prevent them from unravelling.

TO MAKE

With the cord on the far left as leader, work 1 row of horizontal cording across all cords. Now begin pattern. Divide cords into groups of five.
With the first group, work three rows of diagonal cording slanting down to the left, using the cord on the far right as leader for each row. Each leader will drop down to become a knotting cord in subsequent rows.
With the second group of five cords, work three rows of diagonal cording slanting down to the right, using the cord on the far left as leader for each row.
Continue in this way across the row, working groups of diagonal cording alternately to the left and right.
Next row: between the first and second motifs of the previous row loop two right-hand cords from the first motif round two left-hand cords of the second motif.
Between the second and third motifs link the leaders by knotting the leader from the second motif over the leader of the third.
Continue in this way across the row, alternately looping cords together to link motifs, and knotting the leaders together.
Next row: work as for first row, but begin with three rows of cording slanting down to the right. Continue in this way until you have worked three bands of cording motifs altogether.
Now work the other side of the evening bag to the same point.
Work now proceeds in the round, so unpin work from your flat working surface, and use a suitable three-dimensional working base. Place the bag sections together, wrong sides facing.
At each lower corner tie together the outside cord from each side in a loose half knot. Set on over this half knot 10 new cords, each cut to 2 yd 1 ft. This will link the sides of the bag together. Repeat at the other lower corner, setting on 10 new cords in the same way.
Now continue in pattern, bringing new cords into the pattern, until another six bands of cording motifs have been worked.
Divide the cords into two groups of 25 on each side of the bag, and a group of 30 at each corner. Work in pattern on each group of cords separately until six bands of cording motifs have been worked from the point where the work divided.

TO FINISH

Trim the holding cord to 1″ at either end, turn to the wrong side and secure at the back of the work with a few overcasting stitches. Make a flat knot chain handle with four cords to the length required.
Make up the bag with fabric, lining and frame. Stitch macramé fabric in place to the right side of the bag, stitching round the top edges and down the sides as far as the bottom of the bag frame.
Stitch the handle in place.
Finish each long macramé strip with a 4″ tassel (see page 214 for instructions).
Add a clasp to fasten, if wished.

Shoulder bag

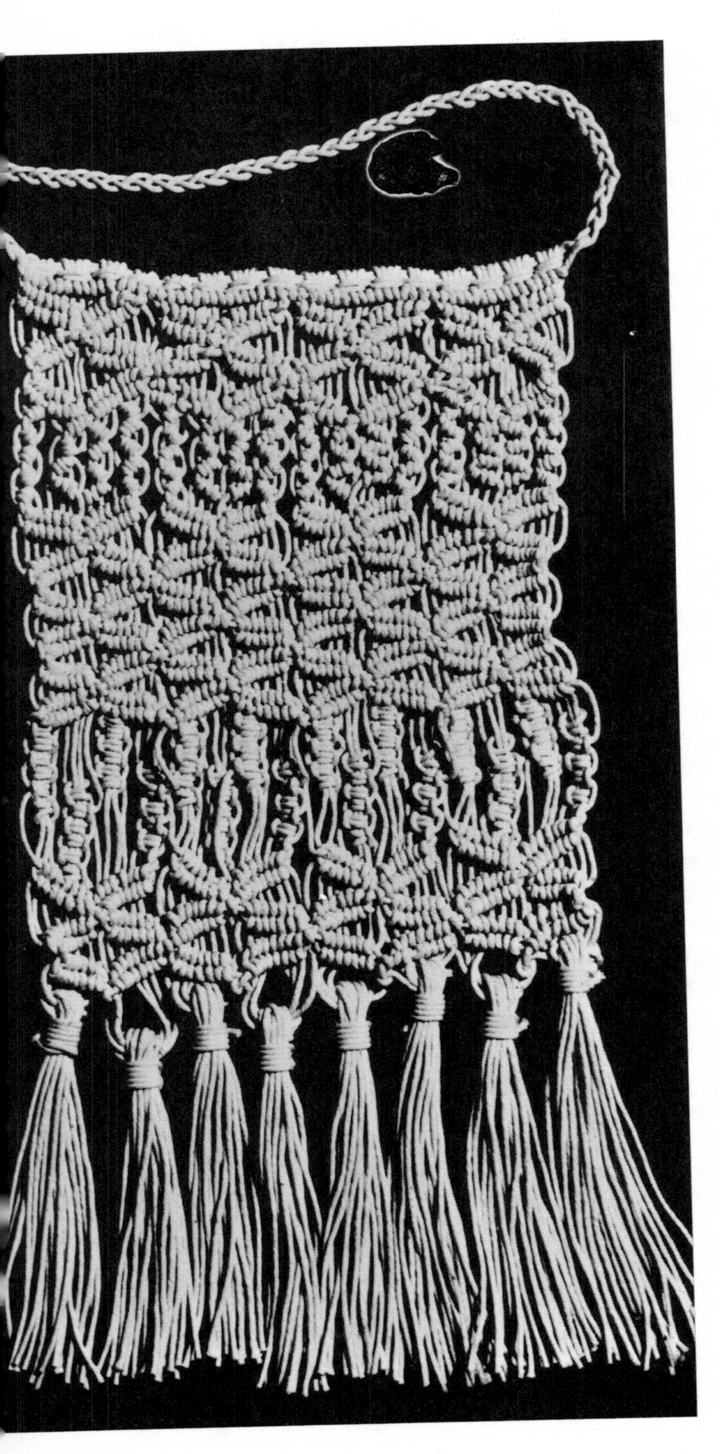

MATERIALS. 2 balls W. H. Smith C3 medium string; piece of lining fabric 15″ by 21″ (optional).
MEASUREMENTS. Bag measures 7″ wide, 10″ long, excluding tassels.
TENSION CHECK. Eight loops of cording measured on a horizontal row are 1″.
PREPARATION. For each side of the bag, cut 32 cords, each 80″ long. For the first side of the bag, cut a double thickness holding cord which should measure 10″, plus double the total measurement required for the bag handle (e.g. if you want a finished handle length of 20″, cut 50″ cord). Pin this double holding cord centrally to your working surface then set cords on in pairs. For the second side of the bag, cut a double thickness holding cord of about 16″ and set the remaining 32 cords on to this, also setting them on in pairs.
Note. *Throughout this design, cording, both horizontal and diagonal, is worked with a single loop on the leader cord, i.e. single half hitches, instead of double.*

TO MAKE

First side of bag. Cut a leader to the same measurement as the holding cord. Lay it centrally across the work, and work cording (single half hitches) over it with every cord to the end of the row.
Work double row crossovers of diagonal cording with each group of 16 cords to the end of the row. Link the central point of each crossover by knotting the left-hand leader over the right-hand leader.
Work another half band of this pattern, linking the tips of the motifs by knotting one leader over another.
Now divide the cords into groups of four, and work zig-zag chains of diagonal cording on each. The leader for every chain will be the cord on the far right. Work four zig-zags with the cords coming from the top of the previous motif, three zig-zags with cords coming from the bottom of the previous motif.
Work three more bands of double row crossovers of diagonal cording as before.
Divide cords into groups of four.
Work chains of reversed double half hitches with each group, using the outer cords as knotting cords, two central cords as knotbearers. Work six knots in each chain, but with the first and all odd-numbered chains work the six knots at the top of the cords, then leave an area of unworked cords below. With the second and a

Josephine belt

Designed by Christine Hanscomb

even-numbered cords, leave an unworked area of cords at the top, then work a chain of six knots starting around the point where the odd-numbered chains end.

Work 1½ bands of double row crossovers of diagonal cording as before.

Other side of bag. Work as for the first side, but cut the leader for the first row of horizontal cording to about 16″.

TO FINISH

On the first side of the bag, work a plaited handle at each side of the top edge, using the two strands from the holding cord and one from the leader cord to work the plait. When the plaits are the desired length tie the ends together with an overhand knot.

On the other side of the bag, trim the holding and leader cord ends to 1″, press to the wrong side of the work, and stitch neatly in place to the back of the work.

Place the bag sections together, wrong sides facing, and oversew neatly together down the side edges. Make 5″ tassels along the lower edge, as described on page 214, combining cords from the front and back of the bag in every tassel; this closes the lower edge.

If wished, make up a lining to fit the bag, insert into the bag and, with wrong sides together, sew it in place round the inside top edge.

MATERIALS. 50 ft of heavy cord.

MEASUREMENTS. To fit an average waist size 24/26″.

TENSION CHECK. One Josephine knot measures approximately 1½″ by 2½″.

PREPARATION. Cut yarn into four equal lengths, each 12 ft 6″ long.

TO MAKE

Place four cords side by side on your working surface. Starting about 27″ from one end (depending on how long you wish the ties to be) tie a chain of Josephine knots (see page 202), working them from the same direction every time, and keeping each knot close below the previous one. Tie 13 knots in all (or enough to fit the waist).

TO FINISH

Bind the ends of the cords tightly with cotton thread to prevent unravelling. If the first and last knots are inclined to slip, a tiny dab of fabric adhesive should keep them firmly in place.

Note. *Tying the Josephine knots from the same direction each time gives the belt a slight twist which makes it fit snugly to the curve of a waist. If it is preferred to have a straighter belt, alternate the direction in which each knot is worked.*

Rug

MATERIALS. Furnishing piping cord, $\frac{1}{2}$" in diameter.
MEASUREMENTS. Variable; it can be any size wished.
TENSION CHECK. One flat knot measures 1" across; two flat knots measure 1" deep; two set-on cords on the holding cord measure 1".
PREPARATION. Set a number of cords on a holding cord to measure the required width of the finished rug. Cut cords to eight times the finished measurement required, including a fringe at one end.

TO MAKE

Work two rows of alternate flat knot pattern.

Cords now divide into groups of 12 and four alternately across the row. Work groups of 12 cords in the alternate flat knot pattern. Work groups of four as chains of flat knots, but space out the knots at intervals on the knot bearing cords.

When the work is the required length, work two row straight across in the alternate flat knot pattern.

With separate leaders, work two rows of horizonta cording across all cords.

Lower border. Divide cords into groups of four an three at random. Work these groups in any knotted chai as wished: e.g. flat knot chains; half knot spirals; two fla knots, followed by a Josephine knot, followed by tw flat knots; one flat knot, cross cord 2 over 1, and 4 ove 3, another flat knot, followed by a third flat knot 1 below; three-cord groups in reversed double half hitche worked continuously from the same side with on knotting cord over two knotbearers.

Work all the chains to a depth of $3\frac{1}{2}''$ (or as wished). Work another row of horizontal cording with a separate leader.

TO FINISH

Tie each group of four cords below the horizontal cording in single flat knots, then tie each individual cord in an overhand knot close to the flat knot just worked. Trim the cords to give a fringe of the required depth, and fray out ends if wished.

Now cut a number of cords equal to the number of set-on cords used for the rug, each about 8 ft long. Set these directly on to the set-on edge of the rug, over the cords already set on, but have them hanging in the opposite direction.

With separate leaders, work two rows of horizontal cording across these new cords, then divide cords into groups of four and three; work a border to match the one at the other end. Finish with a row of horizontal cording and a fringe, as before.

Trim the holding and leader cords to about an inch, press to the wrong side of the work, and secure them at the back with a few overcasting stitches.

Hammock

MATERIALS. 375 yd Strutt's piping cord No. 6; two lengths of wooden dowelling, each $\frac{7}{8}''$ in diameter and 20″ long.

MEASUREMENTS. Finished hammock measures approximately 70″ long, excluding fringe, and 27″ wide at the widest point.

TENSION CHECK. Each flat knot measures $1\frac{1}{4}''$ across, 1″ deep.

PREPARATION. Cut 45 cords, each 25 ft long. Lay these single cords side by side (i.e. cords are not set on doubled as usual) on a working surface; as you are working on a large scale, a suitable area of floor is probably the most convenient working surface. Measure down from the cord ends the depth of fringe required, then from this point work two rows of the alternate flat knot pattern (as you have an unequal number of cords, one flat knot—preferably an end one—will use 5 cords, with three knotbearing cords).

Now lay one dowelling rod across the cords close to the last row of flat knots. Bring the central knotbearing cords of each knot over the top of the dowelling, leave the knotting cords under it. Now work a row of flat knots below the dowelling, tying each knot fairly tightly to secure the dowelling.

TO MAKE

Continue in the alternate flat knots for another four rows. Work now proceeds with areas of unworked cords and single rows of five-end flat knots (three knotbearing cords in each knot) divided by rows of horizontal cording. Areas of unworked cords can be as deep as you wish, and cording rows can be curved to give shaping to the hammock. In order to increase the width of the hammock towards the centre, in the cording rows work three half hitches with each cord, instead of the normal two.

Finish with five rows of alternate flat knots to match the beginning of the hammock.

TO FINISH

Lay the other dowelling rod across cords; bring the knotbearing cords over the top of it, and the knotting cords under it, as before. Secure on the other side of the dowelling with two rows of flat knots in the alternate pattern.

Trim the fringe to match the one at the beginning. Fray out the ends if wished.

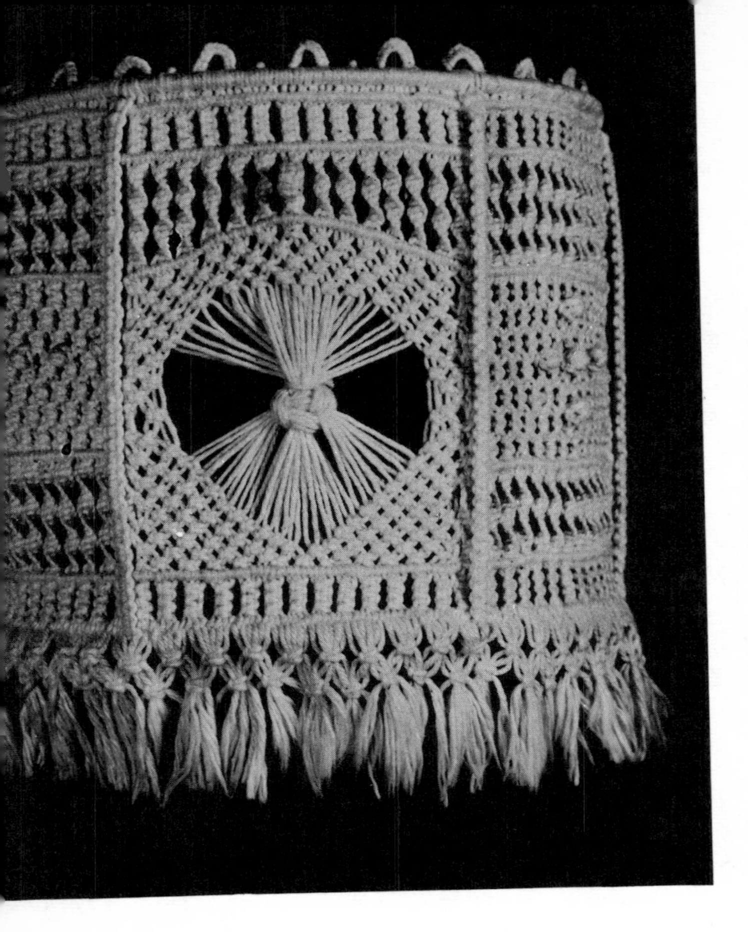

Lampshade

MATERIALS. 12 oz Twilley's dishcloth cotton; a drum lampshade, 10" in diameter, 8" deep; 4 yd binding tape.
MEASUREMENTS. To fit the lampshade frame.
TENSION CHECK. Three flat knots measure ½".
PREPARATION. Bind the lampshade frame firmly with binding tape. The shade is worked in six panels: three panels of Pattern A, three panels of Pattern B, but with a slight variation for each panel. Panels may be worked separately then stitched at the side edges to the lampshade struts, or the entire shade may be worked continuously in the round. Whichever method you choose, it is best to set on all the cords at once to give a neat continuous top edge; cords may then be divided into groups and each panel worked separately if wished. For each panel (Pattern A or B), cut 28 threads, each 8 ft long. Set them directly on to the top edge of the frame, and work alternately with half hitch scalloped edging and overhand picot edging (see page 191) to give a decorative top edge.

TO MAKE
PATTERN A (make 3 times to form panels 1, 3 and 5)
With the cord on the far left as leader, work a row of horizontal cording.
1st pattern panel: divide cords into groups of four, and work chains of three flat knots with each group.
1st divider row: with the cord on the far right as leader, work a row of horizontal cording.
2nd pattern panel: divide cords into groups of four; work chains of half knots starting with 20 half knots in the left-hand spiral. Work one half knot fewer in each chain to the seventh (leave this seventh chain unworked for the moment), then increase each chain by one half knot on each of the remaining spirals to the right-hand chain. Let the spirals twist around themselves after every fourth knot.
To work the 7th chain: work two flat knots, then make a flat knot ball as follows. Work six more flat knots, leaving a small space between the first two flat knots in the chain and the six knots now being worked. After the sixth knot, bring the central knotbearing cords up in front of the chain, through to the back via the space above the chain, then pull them firmly down on the wrong side of the work. Tie another flat knot to secure the ball and hold it firmly in place. Work another two flat knots to complete the chain.
2nd divider row: with the cord on the far left as leader, work a row of cording across all cords, following the curved shaping created by the graduated spiral chains.
3rd pattern panel: work the alternate flat knot pattern for four rows from the top of the shaped curve (i.e. start at the highest point in the centre and gradually bring in the cords from either side as you work down).
Next row: keeping in pattern, work four knots from the left-hand side, then four knots from the right-hand side. Leave all the central cords unworked. Continuing on these sets of cords only, work another four rows in pattern, keeping the outside edges straight, but decreasing by one knot on each row at the inside edges to give a shaped central area.
Now with 36 cords in the centre, work one very big multi-end flat knot—have 10 knotting cords from each side, 16 knotbearing central cords.
With the 10 cords remaining at each side of the panel continue working in the alternate flat knot pattern for seven rows (as you do not have a multiple of four in these

short rows, allow the extra cords to form loops at the ends of the rows where they occur).

Keeping in pattern, begin to increase on the inside shaped edges by bringing in two new cords to every row (at left and right) from the central cords coming from the multi-end flat knot.

Continue until the row is reached where flat knots are worked with every group of four cords right across the row.

3rd divider row: as first divider row.

4th pattern panel: as first pattern panel.

Turn work to the wrong side and work cording with every cord over the lower edge of the lampshade frame. Trim the ends to about 12″.

PATTERN B (make one each of Versions 1, 2 and 3)

Version 1. Work first row of horizontal cording, first pattern panel and first divider row as for Pattern A.

2nd pattern panel: work spiral chains of 20 half knots with each group of four cords to the end, letting the spirals twist around themselves after every fourth knot.

2nd divider row: with the cord on the far left as leader work horizontal cording.

3rd pattern panel: work seven rows of a two-knot alternate flat knot pattern.

On the 7th chain of the 2nd row, work a flat knot ball as described for the 2nd pattern panel of Pattern A, but only tie four flat knots before taking the central cords up and over the chain.

In a similar way, tie flat knot balls on the 5th, 7th and 9th chains of the 4th row, and then on the 7th chain of the 6th row.

3rd divider row: as first divider row.

4th pattern panel: as 2nd pattern panel, but only tie 16 half knots in each spiral chain.

4th divider row: as 2nd divider row.

5th pattern panel: as first pattern panel.

Finish as for Pattern A, by working cording over the lampshade on the wrong side.

Version 2. Work as for Version 1, but in the 3rd pattern panel work flat knot balls as follows: on the 4th, 7th and 10th chains of the 2nd row; on the 5th, 8th and 11th chains of the 3rd row; on the 5th, 8th and 11th chains of the 4th row; on the 6th, 9th and 12th chains of the 5th row; and on the 6th, 9th and 12th chains of the 6th row. Complete as for Version 1.

Version 3. Work as for Version 1, but in the 3rd pattern panel work flat knot balls as follows: on the 1st, 3rd, 5th, 7th, 9th, 11th and 13th chains of the 4th row. Complete as for Version 1.

TO FINISH

To cover each side strut of the frame, cut three cords, each 8 ft long. Set these on to the top row of cording immediately above a side strut. Work a continuous flat knot chain for the length of the strut; use single knotting cords, four central knotbearing cords. At the end of the strut, take the cords to the wrong side of the frame and tie a flat knot on the wrong side over the strut. Trim the ends to about an inch, fold back on to the inside of the strut and secure with a few neat overcasting stitches.

If the shade has been worked continuously in the round, it is advisable to secure the knotted fabric to the side struts with a few neat stitches at occasional points—on cording divider rows, for instance.

Work two rows of the alternate flat knot pattern around the lower edge, using six cords for each knot (single knotting cords, four central knotbearing cords). Trim a fringe to the depth required and fray out the ends, if wished.

Tablemat

MATERIALS. 59 yd 1 ft of hemp (or any coarse, heavy string).
MEASUREMENTS. Mat measures 11″ by 9″.
TENSION CHECK. Three rows of flat knots over the alternate pattern measure 1″.
PREPARATION. Cut 20 cords, each 8 ft long; cut two cords, each 9 ft long. Pin one of the 9 ft lengths centrally to your working surface so it can be used as a holding cord. Set on the 20 cords to it with double half hitches, so the set-on edge resembles a row of cording. The ends of the holding cord now drop down to become knotting cords.

TO MAKE

Using the remaining 9 ft cord as leader, lay it centrally across the work, and work horizontal cording over it with all the cords to the end of the row. The ends of the leader cord now drop down to become knotting cords: total of 44 working ends.
Work in the alternate flat knot pattern for four rows.
Now divide for the central cording diamonds.
Work flat knots with each of the first three groups of four cords. Continue on these cords only, keeping in pattern, but working one knot fewer in each row on the right-hand edge until you work a row of only one flat knot.
Work a similar triangle of flat knots with 12 cords at the end of the row, but reduce the knots along the left-hand edge.
On the centre 12 cords, work a row of three flat knots, then a row of two, finally a row of one, dropping two cords from each end of every row.
Now work cording diamonds.
Numbering four unworked cords on the left of the central flat knot triangle from 1 to 4, use cord 2 as the first leader slanting down to the right, and work diagonal cording over it with cords 3 and 4, and all the cords coming from the left-hand side of the central flat knot triangle.
Work a 2nd row of cording immediately below, with cord 1 as leader.
Now work the left-hand side of the diamond; use cord 3 as leader for the first row, slanting down to the left, and work diagonal cording over it with all the cords from the sloped flat knot edge on that side.
Work a 2nd row of cording with cord 4 as leader. In a similar way work the top two sides of the second diamond.
Link the diamonds together where the leaders cross by knotting cords 2 and 1 of the first diamond over cord 3 of the second diamond, and then over cord 4 of the second diamond.
Work a multi-end flat knot in the centre of each diamond using four knotting cords from each side, and four central knotbearing core cords.
Let cords 3 and 4 from the second diamond continue across the work to form leaders slanting down to the left for the lower right-hand side of the first diamond. Work cording over each leader in turn with the six cords along that side. In a similar way let cords 2 and 1 from the first diamond continue across the work as leaders for the left-hand lower side of the second diamond. Work cording over each in turn with the six cords along that side.
Now work the remaining side for each diamond. Leaders for the first diamond will be the last two cords used to work cording over cords 3 and 4. Leaders for the second diamond will be the two cords coming from the flat knot nearest to the point where the cording is to begin. Cords 2 and 1 (used previously as leaders) will both now become knotting cords and will begin rows of cording by knotting over the new leaders. Link lower points of the diamonds by knotting the right-hand leaders over left-hand leaders.
Now tie another multi-end flat knot in the centre of the work, then let each set of leaders continue across the work to complete a centre (third) diamond.
Return to the cords at each side and fill in a triangle of flat knots at each side of the work.
From the point where flat knots stopped before, work rows increasing by one knot on each row on the inside edge until the point of the cording diamond is reached, then work another similar number of rows, reducing by one knot each time on the same edge until you work the row with only one knot in it. Complete the remaining two diamonds to match the others.
Continue in alternate flat knot pattern, first filling in the triangular areas around the last two cording diamonds, then working straight for four rows.
Finally, with the cord on the far left as leader, work two rows of horizontal cording, reversing the direction of the leader at the end of the first row, and working the 2nd row from right to left.

TO FINISH

Trim cords to about 1″, then weave the ends into the back of the knotting.

Cavandoli castle cushion

MATERIALS. 4 oz in each of 2 constrasting colours of F.A. dishcloth cotton. (1 lb drums of cotton can be ordered from the Handicraft Centre, P.O. Box 135, 37 Lever Street, Manchester M60 1UX); fabric cushion cover approximately 12½" by 15" in a colour to match or contrast with the colours of dishcloth cotton; a cushion pad approximately 12½" by 15".
MEASUREMENTS. Finished cushion measures approximately 12½" by 15".
TENSION CHECK. Six double loops on holding cord measure 1".
PREPARATION. Cut 70 threads in colour A (background colour), each 4 yd long. Set these on in pairs to a holding cord in colour A, about 20" long.
Note. *Cords are worked double throughout, so you now have 70 working ends.*

TO MAKE

Introduce a double thickness leader in colour B, and work in solid horizontal and vertical cording from the chart below. The leader may either be kept as a ball of yarn (remember to wind the ball so you have a double thickness of yarn to use) or may be cut into more manageable lengths, so new lengths can be introduced when required. In this case it is preferable to introduce the new lengths always at the beginning of a new row.

TO FINISH

Trim cord ends, and leader and holding cord ends to about 1". Press them to the back of the work and secure with a few neat stitches.
Stitch macramé fabric to one side of the cushion cover.
Note. *This design could be used as a central motif for bedspread or a sweater.*

□ Horizontal cording, colour A.
● Vertical cording, colour B.